The
Carolina Reader

Fourth Edition

Edited by Lee Bauknight

with William W. Garland

FOUNTAINHEAD
PRESS

As a textbook publisher, we are faced with enormous environmental issues due the large amount of paper contained in our print products. Since our inception in 2002, we have worked diligently to be as eco-friendly as possible.

Our "green" initiatives include:

Electronic Products
We deliver products in non-paper form whenever possible. This includes pdf downloadables, flash drives, & CD's.

Electronic Samples
We use a new electronic sampling system, called Xample. Instructor samples are sent via a personalized web page that links to pdf downloads.

FSC Certified Printers
All of our Printers are certified by the Forest Service Council which promotes environmentally and socially responsible management of the world's forests. This program allows consumer groups, individual consumers and businesses to work together hand in hand to promote responsible use of the world's forests as a renewable and sustainable resource.

Recycled Paper
Almost all of our products are printed on a minimum of 10-30% post consumer waste recycled paper.

Support of Green Causes
When we do print, we donate a portion of our revenue to Green causes. Listed below are a few of the organizations that have received donations from Fountainhead Press. We welcome your feedback and suggestions for contributions, as we are always searching for worthy initiatives.
Rainforest 2 Reef
Environmental Working Group

Cover and text designer: Ellie Moore

For information, please call or write:
1-800-586-0330
Fountainhead Press
Southlake, TX 76092

Web site: www.fountainheadpress.com
E-mail: customerservice@fountainheadpress.com

Fourth Edition

ISBN: 978-1-59871-663-4

Printed in the United States of America

Contents

Chapter 4: Reading Green 197

Chapter 5: Reading Eating   279

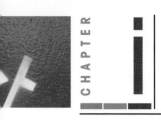

Introduction

You live in an information age. No news there, right? You've probably been hearing this in a variety of ways—as part of the wave of information that supposedly washes over you each day, every day—for several years now, and it would be hard to find someone to argue the point. You'll find far less agreement, however, about the nature of this age of information—about what exactly all of this information is and where it comes from; about how to best find information and assess its value; and about what you do with the information you encounter (or that encounters you) and what it does to you. These concerns, long at the heart of the English 102 curriculum at USC, are part of what has come to be called "information literacy."

You've probably heard the term, or something like it, before. The Association of College and Research Libraries (ACRL) defines it as the ability to find, manage, critically evaluate, and make use of information. For years in USC's English 101 and 102 classes (and probably in your high school), these have been called "research skills." And as the name has evolved along with the astronomical growth of available information, the central

1

message has become even more important. To use President Obama's words, from his proclamation below: "Rather than merely possessing data, we must also learn the skills necessary to acquire, collate, and evaluate information for any situation." Journalist and author James Gleick, in the essay "Drowning, Surfing and Surviving," puts it this way: "Choosing the genuine information requires work." And *The Carolina Reader*—as part of the English 102 curriculum—is designed to help you manage that work as you develop your writing skills.

With that in mind, we hope that you'll take another look at the cover of the *Reader* and think about the implications of the word and punctuation mark at the center of the image (which we've also reproduced above). "Next," carries with it a force, a momentum not unlike that implied by the flood metaphors Gleick writes about on the following pages: There's always something else, something more, something to come. And when it comes to information, this might seem overwhelming—this possibility that there will always be more than you can ever even look at, much less absorb. But it needn't be that way. And that's the point of information literacy. Just as writing seems daunting to many people, because it is a recursive act, until they develop some confidence and skill, the creative and effective use of information is something that can be learned through diligence and practice. To that end, we have included a variety of thinking, research, and writing prompts in the *Reader* to help you engage with the texts you'll be asked to read and—more importantly, perhaps—to help you develop your ability to efficiently and responsibly wade through the flood of information that you'll encounter and find the "genuine information" you need.

We begin with two short texts and a few writing prompts that we hope will get you thinking about reading, writing, research, and information. The first reading is a proclamation that President Obama issued in 2009, declaring October to be National Information Literacy Awareness Month. The second is an essay by James Gleick published in April 2011 in *New Scientist* and based on his latest book, *The Information: A History, a Theory, a Flood.* Together they offer a brief but pointed introduction to information literacy as a topic and a tool. A variety of writing prompts accompany these readings (setting the pattern for the rest of the book): Some will give you a few things to think and write about before you read; others will ask you to complete specific research and writing tasks after you've completed your reading. Your teacher may ask you to complete these for homework or in class, on your own or with some of your classmates. The prompts that follow the readings fall into three categories:

- **What?** These are the most straightforward of the writing exercises—they ask you to summarize and, sometimes, to synthesize what you've read.

- **What Else? What's Next?** These tasks ask you to reflect on and write about the readings—sometimes by themselves, sometimes in relation to other texts. Because no public issue is static, we ask you to embrace that momentum we mentioned above by thinking about what's to come. You might research how the 2012 elections are expected to affect a particular issue, for example, or you might offer informed (well-researched) speculation about the future of an issue. The point is to get you thinking not just about what you know or what you learned, but also about what else there is to know about the topic and where and how you might find this information.

■ **Who Cares?** We ask these questions—and we hope you will answer them—not with an indifferent shrug of the shoulders, but out of analytical and rhetorical curiosity. They are designed to focus your attention on the various stakeholders (authors, audience members, publishers, and so on) in the issues introduced by the readings.

Good luck!
—Lee Bauknight and the English 102 team

BEFORE YOU READ——
In a paragraph or two, craft a detailed definition of "information literacy," including examples of what it means to be "information literate" and "information illiterate." Then, based on your definition, explain whether you are information literate or not. Use other sources if you need to, but make sure you credit them in your response.

NATIONAL INFORMATION LITERACY AWARENESS MONTH: A PROCLAMATION
President Barack Obama

Every day, we are inundated with vast amounts of information. A 24-hour news cycle and thousands of global television and radio networks, coupled with an immense array of online resources, have challenged our long-held perceptions of information management. Rather than merely possessing data, we must also learn the skills necessary to acquire, collate, and evaluate information for any situation. This new type of literacy also requires competency with communication technologies, including computers and mobile devices that can help in our day-to-day decision-making. National Information Literacy Awareness Month highlights the need for all Americans to be adept in the skills necessary to effectively navigate the Information Age.

Though we may know how to find the information we need, we must also know how to evaluate it. Over the past decade, we have seen a crisis of authenticity emerge. We now live in a world where anyone can publish an opinion or perspective, whether true or not, and have that opinion amplified within the information marketplace. At the same time, Americans have unprecedented access to the diverse and independent sources of information, as well as institutions such as libraries and universities, that can help separate truth from fiction and signal from noise.

Our Nation's educators and institutions of learning must be aware of—and adjust to—these new realities. In addition to the basic skills of reading, writing, and arithmetic, it is equally important that our students are given the tools required to take advantage of the information available to them. The ability to seek, find, and decipher information can be applied to countless life decisions, whether financial, medical, educational, or technical.

This month, we dedicate ourselves to increasing information literacy awareness so that all citizens understand its vital importance. An informed and educated citizenry is essential to the functioning of our modern democratic society, and I encourage educational and community institutions across the country to help Americans find and evaluate the information they seek, in all its forms.

NOW, THEREFORE, I, BARACK OBAMA, President of the United States of America, by virtue of the authority vested in me by the Constitution and the laws of the United States, do hereby proclaim October 2009 as National Information Literacy Awareness Month. I call upon the people of the United States to recognize the important role information plays in our daily lives, and appreciate the need for a greater understanding of its impact.

IN WITNESS WHEREOF, I have hereunto set my hand this first day of October, in the year of our Lord two thousand nine, and of the Independence of the United States of America the two hundred and thirty-fourth.

DROWNING, SURFING AND SURVIVING
James Gleick

A half-century ago Marshall McLuhan wrote: "We are today as far into the electric age as the Elizabethans had advanced into the typographical and mechanical age. And we are experiencing the same confusions and indecisions which they had felt when living simultaneously in two contrasted forms of society and experience." His electric age had no email, no web-surfing, no cellphones, much less Facebook and Twitter. McLuhan was mainly watching television.

We don't call it the electric age any more. We know perfectly well that we are living in the information age. But McLuhan was right: we are still experiencing "confusions and indecisions," more than ever before. There is a universally recognized metaphor for our predicament: flood. There is a sensation of drowning, of information as a rising, churning deluge. Data washes over us from above and below. One may lose the ability to impose order on the chaos of sensations. Truth seems hard to find amid a multitude of plausible fictions.

Our world is built on the science of information theory, created by engineers and mathematicians in the 1940s, but hard on the heels of information theory have come "information overload," "information glut," "information anxiety," and "information fatigue." This last was recognized by the *Oxford English Dictionary* in 2009 as a syndrome for our times: "apathy, indifference, or mental exhaustion arising from exposure to too much information, especially (in later use) stress induced by the attempt to assimilate excessive amounts of information from the media, the internet, or at work."

In 2007, the writer David Foster Wallace coined a more ominous name for this modern condition: "total noise," created by "the tsunami of available fact, context, and perspective." He talked about the sensation of drowning and also of a loss of autonomy, of personal responsibility for being informed.

Another way to speak of the anxiety is in terms of the gap between information and knowledge. A barrage of data so often fails to tell us what we need to know. Knowledge, in turn, does not guarantee enlightenment or wisdom. As T. S. Eliot asked in his pageant play *The Rock*: "Where is the wisdom we have lost in knowledge? Where is the knowledge we have lost in information?" It is an ancient observation, but it seems to bear restating as information becomes ubiquitous—and we live in a world where all bits are created equal and information is divorced from meaning.

What do you do when you have everything at last? The philosopher Daniel Dennett imagined in 1990, just before the internet made this possible, that electronic networks could upend the economics of publishing poetry. Instead of slim books, elegant specialty items marketed to connoisseurs, what if poets could publish online, instantly reaching not hundreds but millions of readers, not for tens of dollars but fractions of pennies?

That same year, the publisher Charles Chadwyck-Healey conceived of The English Poetry Full-Text Database as he walked through the British Library one day. Four years later, he had produced it, and it represented not the present or future of poetry, but the past, and not, at first, online but in four compact discs: 165,000 poems by 1250 poets spanning 13 centuries, priced at $51,000.

Readers and critics had to work out what to make of this. Not read it, surely, the way they would read a book. Delve into it, perhaps. Search it, for a word, an epigraph, a half-remember fragment. His CD-ROMs are already obsolete. All English poetry is on the network now—or if not all, some approximation thereof, and if not now, then soon.

The past folds accordion-like into the present. Different media have different event horizons: for the written word, three millennia, for recorded sound, a century and a half—and within their time frames the old become as accessible as the new. Yellowed newspapers come back to life. Under headings of "50 Years Ago" and "100 Years Ago," veteran publications recycle their archives: recipes, card-playing techniques, science, gossip, once out of print and now ready for use. Record companies rummage through their attics to release, or re-release, every scrap of music, rarities, B-sides and bootlegs. For a certain time, collectors, scholars or fans possessed their books and their records. There was a line between what they had and what they did not. For some, the music they owned (or the books, or the videos) became part of who they were.

That line fades away. Most of Sophocles's plays are lost, but those that survive are available at the touch of a button. Most of Bach's music was unknown to Beethoven; we have it all—partitas, cantatas and ringtones. It comes to us instantly, or at light speed. It is a variety of omniscience. It is what the *New Yorker* music critic Alex Ross calls the Infinite Playlist, and he sees that as a mixed blessing: "anxiety in place of fulfillment, an addictive cycle of craving and malaise. No sooner has one experience begun than the thought of what else is out there intrudes." Another reminder that information is not knowledge, and knowledge is not wisdom.

Strategies emerge for coping. There are many, but they boil down to two: filter and search. The harassed consumer of information turns to filters to separate the metal from the dross. Filters include blogs and aggregators—the choice raises issues of trust and taste. The need for filters intrudes on any thought experiment about the wonders of abundant information. When Dennett imagined his Complete Poetry Network, he saw that filters would be needed in the shape of editors and critics. When information is cheap, attention becomes expensive.

A "file" was originally a wire on which slips of paper, bills, notes and letters could be strung for preservation and reference. Then came file folders, file drawers, file cabinets, and then their electronic namesakes. The irony, in all these cases, was the same: once a piece of information is filed, it is statistically unlikely ever to be seen again by human eyes. The British mathematician and logician Augustus de Morgan knew this even in 1847. For any random book, he said, a library was no better than a waste-paper warehouse. "Take the library of the British Museum ... valuable and useful and accessible as it is: what chance has a work of being known to be there, merely because it is there? If it be wanted, it can be asked for; but to be wanted it must be known. Nobody can rummage the library."

When new information technologies alter the landscape, they bring disruption: new channels and new dams rerouting the flow of irrigation and transport. The balance between creators and consumers is upset: writers and readers, speakers and listeners. Market forces are confused; information can seem too cheap and too expensive at the same time. The old ways of organizing knowledge no longer work. Who will search, who will filter?

We will learn new ways. No deus ex machina waits in the wings; no man behind the curtain. We have no Maxwell's demon to help with our sorting. "We want the Demon, you see," wrote Stanislaw Lem in *The Cyberiad*, "to extract from the dance of atoms only information that is genuine, like mathematical theorems, fashion magazines, blueprints, historical chronicles, or a recipe for ion crumpets, or how to clean and iron a suit of asbestos, and poetry too, and scientific advice, and almanacs, and calendars, and secret documents, and everything that ever appeared in any newspaper in the Universe, and telephone books of the future."

Because omniscience is a curse. The answer to any question may arrive at the fingertips—via Google or Wikipedia or IMDb or YouTube or Epicurious or the National DNA Database or any of their natural heirs and successors—and still we wonder what we know. Choosing the genuine information requires work. Then forgetting takes even more work.

■ WHAT?

1. Write two 250-word summaries of the Obama and Gleick texts. In the first, explain the readings to a friend in a composition class at another college. In the second, write your summary for a grandparent or another older relative. Be prepared to discuss the differences in the two summaries with your classmates and teacher.

■ WHAT ELSE? WHAT'S NEXT?

2. What else do you wish you knew about information literacy?

3. While President Obama's proclamation presents the "vast amounts of information" that inundate us every day as a challenge, James Gleick's essay takes a more ominous tone. Point to specific places in the text where Gleick expresses his concerns, either directly or through his choice of language. Then, find at least two sources that discuss information consumption and the effects the Internet is having on us in a more positive manner. Summarize these sources in a couple of paragraphs. Conclude your response by answering this question: Which of the positions you have read do you find most compelling? Why?

4. How do you think schools—from K-12 to college—should respond to Obama's and Gleick's calls for a more informed approach to information consumption?

5. Gleick ends his essay by writing: "Choosing the genuine information requires work. Then forgetting takes even more work." What do you think he means by that final sentence? What is Gleick asking us to do?

■ WHO CARES?

6. What is *New Scientist* (the journal that published Gleick's essay)? After studying its website, explain who you think reads *New Scientist*. Why do you think this?

Reading the World

IMAGE 1.1
"How can we see ourselves as only a new, temporary cast for a long-running show when a new batch of birds flies around singing and new clouds move?" Annie Dillard asks in "The Wreck of Time: Taking Our Century's Measure." What do you see in this image? Why do you think you interpret the image in the way you do?

What defines your relationship to the world? Do you engage with the world and those who inhabit it, or are you more of an observer? Are you driven by a desire to quantify and understand the things you encounter and experience? Or do you tilt toward the imagination, toward more creative interpretations? The readings in this chapter challenge you to think in new ways about how you perceive, experience, and respond to the world around you.

Plato, one of the monumental figures in Western thought and philosophy, lived and taught in ancient Greece from about 427–428 B.C. to 347 B.C. In "The Allegory of the Cave" from Book VII of The Republic, *Plato uses an imaginary dialogue between Socrates (the teacher) and Glaucon (the student) to expound on the nature of perception and reality; on knowledge and truth; on teaching and learning; and on the philosopher's place in society.*

BEFORE YOU READ

Find a representation of "The Allegory of the Cave" in another medium (art or video, for example, or music) and study it closely. Be prepared to share with the class what you've found.

THE ALLEGORY OF THE CAVE Plato

And now, I said, let me show in a figure how far our nature is enlightened or unenlightened:— Behold! human beings living in an underground den, which has a mouth open towards the light and reaching all along the den; here they have been from their childhood, and have their legs and necks chained so that they cannot move, and can only see before them, being prevented by the chains from turning round their heads. Above and behind them a fire is blazing at a distance, and between the fire and the prisoners there is a raised way; and you will see, if you look, a low wall built along the way, like the screen which marionette players have in front of them, over which they show the puppets.

I see.

And do you see, I said, men passing along the wall carrying all sorts of vessels, and statues and figures of animals made of wood and stone and various materials, which appear over the wall? Some of them are talking, others silent.

You have shown me a strange image, and they are strange prisoners.

Like ourselves, I replied; and they see only their own shadows, or the shadows of one another, which the fire throws on the opposite wall of the cave?

True, he said; how could they see anything but the shadows if they were never allowed to move their heads?

And of the objects which are being carried in like manner they would only see the shadows?

Yes, he said.

And if they were able to converse with one another, would they not suppose that they were naming what was actually before them?

Very true.

And suppose further that the prison had an echo which came from the other side, would they not be sure to fancy when one of the passers-by spoke that the voice which they heard came from the passing shadow?

No question, he replied.

To them, I said, the truth would be literally nothing but the shadows of the images. That is certain.

And now look again, and see what will naturally follow if the prisoners are released and disabused of their error. At first, when any of them is liberated and compelled suddenly to stand up and turn his neck round and walk and look towards the light, he will suffer sharp pains; the glare will distress him, and he will be unable to see the realities of which in his former state he had seen the shadows; and then conceive some one saying to him, that what he saw before was an illusion, but that now, when he is approaching nearer to being and his eye is turned towards more real existence, he has a clearer vision,—what will be his reply? And you may further imagine that his instructor is pointing to the objects as they pass and requiring him to name them,—will he not be perplexed? Will he not fancy that the shadows which he formerly saw are truer than the objects which are now shown to him?

Far truer.

And if he is compelled to look straight at the light, will he not have a pain in his eyes which will make him turn away and take in the objects of vision which he can see, and which he will conceive to be in reality clearer than the things which are now being shown to him?

True, he said.

And suppose once more, that he is reluctantly dragged up a steep and rugged ascent, and held fast until he's forced into the presence of the sun himself, is he not likely to be pained and irritated? When he approaches the light his eyes will be dazzled, and he will not be able to see anything at all of what are now called realities.

Not all in a moment, he said.

He will require to grow accustomed to the sight of the upper world. And first he will see the shadows best, next the reflections of men and other objects in the water, and then the objects themselves; then he will gaze upon the light of the moon and the stars and the spangled heaven; and he will see the sky and the stars by night better than the sun or the light of the sun by day?

Certainly.

Last of all he will be able to see the sun, and not mere reflections of him in the water, but he will see him in his own proper place, and not in another; and he will contemplate him as he is.

Certainly.

He will then proceed to argue that this is he who gives the seasons and the years, and is the guardian of all that is in the visible world, and in a certain way the cause of all things which he and his fellows have been accustomed to behold?

Clearly, he said, he would first see the sun and then reason about him.

And when he remembered his old habitation, and the wisdom of the den and his fellow-prisoners, do you not suppose that he would felicitate himself on the change, and pity them?

Certainly, he would.

And if they were in the habit of conferring honours among themselves on those who were quickest to observe the passing shadows and to remark which of them went before, and which followed after, and which were together; and who were therefore best able to draw conclusions as to the future, do you think that he would care for such honours and glories, or envy the possessors of them? Would he not say with Homer,

'*Better to be the poor servant of a poor master,*'

and to endure anything, rather than think as they do and live after their manner?

Yes, he said, I think that he would rather suffer anything than entertain these false notions and live in this miserable manner.

Imagine once more, I said, such a one coming suddenly out of the sun to be replaced in his old situation; would he not be certain to have his eyes full of darkness?

To be sure, he said.

And if there were a contest, and he had to compete in measuring the shadows with the prisoners who had never moved out of the den, while his sight was still weak, and before his eyes had become steady (and the time which would be needed to acquire this new habit of sight might be very considerable) would he not be ridiculous? Men would say of him that up he went and down he came without his eyes; and that it was better not even to think of ascending; and if any one tried to loose another and lead him up to the light, let them only catch the offender, and they would put him to death.

No question, he said.

This entire allegory, I said, you may now append, dear Glaucon, to the previous argument; the prison-house is the world of sight, the light of the fire is the sun, and you will not misapprehend me if you interpret the journey upwards to be the ascent of the soul into the intellectual world according to my poor belief, which, at your desire, I have expressed—whether rightly or wrongly God knows. But, whether true or false, my opinion is that in the world of knowledge the idea of good appears last of all, and is seen only with an effort; and, when seen, is also inferred to be the universal author of all things beautiful and right, parent of light and of the lord of light in this visible world, and the immediate source of reason and truth in the intellectual; and that this is the power upon which he who would act rationally, either in public or private life, must have his eye fixed.

I agree, he said, as far as I am able to understand you.

Moreover, I said, you must not wonder that those who attain to this beatific vision are unwilling to descend to human affairs; for their souls are ever hastening into the upper world where they desire to dwell; which desire of theirs is very natural, if our allegory may be trusted.

Yes, very natural.

And is there anything surprising in one who passes from divine contemplations to the evil state of man, misbehaving himself in a ridiculous manner; if, while his eyes are blinking and before he has become accustomed to the surrounding darkness, he is compelled to fight in courts of law, or in other places, about the images or the shadows of images of justice, and is endeavouring to meet the conceptions of those who have never yet seen absolute justice?

Anything but surprising, he replied.

Any one who has common sense will remember that the bewilderments of the eyes are of two kinds, and arise from two causes, either from coming out of the light or from going into the light, which is true of the mind's eye, quite as much as of the bodily eye;

and he who remembers this when he sees any one whose vision is perplexed and weak, will not be too ready to laugh; he will first ask whether that soul of man has come out of the brighter light, and is unable to see because unaccustomed to the dark, or having turned from darkness to the day is dazzled by excess of light. And he will count the one happy in his condition and state of being, and he will pity the other; or, if he have a mind to laugh at the soul which comes from below into the light, there will be more reason in this than in the laugh which greets him who returns from above out of the light into the den.

That, he said, is a very just distinction.

But then, if I am right, certain professors of education must be wrong when they say that they can put a knowledge into the soul which was not there before, like sight into blind eyes.

They undoubtedly say this, he replied.

Whereas, our argument shows that the power and capacity of learning exists in the soul already; and that just as the eye was unable to turn from darkness to light without the whole body, so too the instrument of knowledge can only by the movement of the whole soul be turned from the world of becoming into that of being, and learn by degrees to endure the sight of being, and of the brightest and best of being, or in other words, of the good.

Very true.

And must there not be some art which will effect conversion in the easiest and quickest manner; not implanting the faculty of sight, for that exists already, but has been turned in the wrong direction, and is looking away from the truth?

Yes, he said, such an art may be presumed.

And whereas the other so-called virtues of the soul seem to be akin to bodily qualities, for even when they are not originally innate they can be implanted later by habit and exercise, the virtue of wisdom more than anything else contains a divine element which always remains, and by this conversion is rendered useful and profitable; or, on the other hand, hurtful and useless. Did you never observe the narrow intelligence flashing from the keen eye of a clever rogue—how eager he is, how clearly his paltry soul sees the way to his end; he is the reverse of blind, but his keen eyesight is forced into the service of evil, and he is mischievous in proportion to his cleverness.

Very true, he said.

But what if there had been a circumcision of such natures in the days of their youth; and they had been severed from those sensual pleasures, such as eating and drinking, which, like leaden weights, were attached to them at their birth, and which drag them down and turn the vision of their souls upon the things that are below—if, I say, they had been released from these impediments and turned in the opposite direction, the very same faculty in them would have seen the truth as keenly as they see what their eyes are turned to now.

Very likely.

Yes, I said; and there is another thing which is likely, or rather a necessary inference from what has preceded, that neither the uneducated and uninformed of the truth, nor yet those who never make an end of their education, will be able ministers of State; not the former, because they have no single aim of duty which is the rule of all their actions, private as well as public; nor the latter, because they will not act at all except upon compulsion, fancying that they are already dwelling apart in the islands of the blest.

Very true, he replied.

Then, I said, the business of us who are the founders of the State will be to compel the best minds to attain that knowledge which we have already shown to be the greatest of all—they must continue to ascend until they arrive at the good; but when they have ascended and seen enough we must not allow them to do as they do now.

What do you mean?

I mean that they remain in the upper world: but this must not be allowed; they must be made to descend again among the prisoners in the den, and partake of their labours and honours, whether they are worth having or not.

But is not this unjust? he said; ought we to give them a worse life, when they might have a better?

You have again forgotten, my friend, I said, the intention of the legislator, who did not aim at making any one class in the State happy above the rest; the happiness was to be in the whole State, and he held the citizens together by persuasion and necessity, making them benefactors of the State, and therefore benefactors of one another; to this end he created them, not to please themselves, but to be his instruments in binding up the State.

True, he said, I had forgotten.

Observe, Glaucon, that there will be no injustice in compelling our philosophers to have a care and providence of others; we shall explain to them that in other States, men of their class are not obliged to share in the toils of politics: and this is reasonable, for they grow up at their own sweet will, and the government would rather not have them. Being self-taught, they cannot be expected to show any gratitude for a culture which they have never received. But we have brought you into the world to be rulers of the hive, kings of yourselves and of the other citizens, and have educated you far better and more perfectly than they have been educated, and you are better able to share in the double duty. Wherefore each of you, when his turn comes, must go down to the general underground abode, and get the habit of seeing in the dark. When you have acquired the habit, you will see ten thousand times better than the inhabitants of the den, and you will know what the several images are, and what they represent, because you have seen the beautiful and just and good in their truth. And thus our State which is also yours will be a reality, and not a dream only, and will be administered in a spirit unlike that of other States, in which men fight with one another about shadows only and are distracted in the struggle for power, which in their eyes is a great good. Whereas the truth is that the State in which the rulers are most reluctant to govern is always the best and most quietly governed, and the State in which they are most eager, the worst.

Quite true, he replied.

And will our pupils, when they hear this, refuse to take their turn at the toils of State, when they are allowed to spend the greater part of their time with one another in the heavenly light?

Impossible, he answered; for they are just men, and the commands which we impose upon them are just; there can be no doubt that every one of them will take office as a stern necessity, and not after the fashion of our present rulers of State.

Yes, my friend, I said; and there lies the point. You must contrive for your future rulers another and a better life than that of a ruler, and then you may have a well-ordered State; for only in the State which offers this, will they rule who are truly rich, not in silver and gold, but in virtue and wisdom, which are the true blessings of life. Whereas if they go to the administration of public affairs, poor and hungering after their own private advantage, thinking that hence they are to snatch the chief good, order there can never be; for they will be fighting about office, and the civil and domestic broils which thus arise will be the ruin of the rulers themselves and of the whole State.

Most true, he replied.

And the only life which looks down upon the life of political ambition is that of true philosophy. Do you know of any other?

Indeed, I do not, he said.

■ WHAT?

1. What are the central points that Plato makes about perception, knowledge, and learning in the "Allegory"?
2. The speaker in this piece is Socrates, and he argues that a liberated prisoner must return to the den after becoming enlightened. Why, according to Socrates, is this difficult? Why is it important?

■ WHAT ELSE? WHAT'S NEXT?

3. Plato seems to think that only a few individuals can ever leave the cave and become enlightened by understanding the Beautiful, Just, and Good. Has our thinking about this changed since the 4th century B.C.?
4. Pretend you are a lawyer tasked with defending Plato's argument that most of us experience life as series of shadows cast on a cave wall. How would you go about making your case? What evidence might you use to prove it?

■ WHO CARES?

5. Compare the text above with the representation of "The Allegory of the Cave" that you found before you started reading. How does the version you found reflect the different audiences for the two texts?

> *"A single death is a tragedy, a million is a statistic,"* poet, essayist, and novelist *Annie Dillard writes in "The Wreck of Time," quoting Josef Stalin. Later, she asks, "How can an individual count?" a question she uses to challenge readers on multiple levels. This essay, first published in* Harper's *in 1998, was adapted for her book* For the Time Being *(2000).*

BEFORE YOU READ
Dillard poses a number of questions throughout her essay. How would you respond to this one, from the end of the piece: "One small town's soup kitchen, St. Mary's, serves 115 men a night. Why feed 115 individuals?"

THE WRECK OF TIME: TAKING OUR CENTURY'S MEASURE   Annie Dillard

I

Ted Bundy, the serial killer, after his arrest, could not fathom the fuss. What was the big deal? David Von Drehle quotes an exasperated Bundy in *Among the Lowest of the Dead*: "I mean, there are *so* many people."

One R. Houwink, of Amsterdam, uncovered this unnerving fact: The human population of earth, arranged tidily, would just fit into Lake Windermere, in England's Lake District.

Recently in the Peruvian Amazon a man asked the writer Alex Shoumatoff, "Isn't it true that the whole population of the United States can be fitted into their cars?"

How are we doing in numbers, we who have been alive for this most recent installment of human life? How many people have lived and died?

"The dead outnumber the living, in a ratio that could be as high as 20 to 1," a demographer, Nathan Keyfitz, wrote in a 1991 letter to the historian Justin Kaplan. "Credible estimates of the number of people who have ever lived on the earth run from 70 billion to over 100 billion." Averaging those figures puts the total persons ever born at about 85 billion. We living people now number 5.8 billion. By these moderate figures, the dead outnumber us about fourteen to one. The dead will always outnumber the living.

Dead Americans, however, if all proceeds, will not outnumber living Americans until the year 2030, because the nation is young. Some of us will be among the dead then. Will we know or care, we who once owned the still bones under the quick ones, we who spin inside the planet with our heels in the air? The living might well seem foolishly self-important to us, and overexcited.

We who are here now make up about 6.8 percent of all people who have appeared to date. This is not a meaningful figure. These times are, one might say, ordinary times, a slice of time like any other. Who can bear to hear this, or who will consider it? Are we not especially significant because our century is—our century and its nuclear bombs, its unique and unprecedented Holocaust, its serial exterminations and refugee populations, our century and its warming, its silicon chips, men on the moon, and spliced genes? No, we are not and it is not.

Since about half of all the dead are babies and children, we will be among the longest-boned dead and among the dead who grew the most teeth—for what those distinctions might be worth among beings notoriously indifferent to appearance and all else.

In Juan Rolfo's novel *Pedro Páramo*, a dead woman says to her dead son, "Just think about pleasant things, because we're going to be buried for a long time."

II

On April 30, 1991—on that one day—138,000 people drowned in Bangladesh. At dinner I mentioned to my daughter, who was then seven years old, that it was hard to imagine 138,000 people drowning.

"No, it's easy," she said. "Lots and lots of dots, in blue water."

The paleontologist Pierre Teilhard de Chardin, now dead, sent a dispatch from a dig. "In the middle of the tamarisk bush you find a red-brick town, partially exposed. … More than 3,000 years before our era, people were living there who played with dice like our own, fished with hooks like ours, and wrote in characters we can't yet read."

Who were these individuals who lived under the tamarisk bush? Who were the people Ted Bundy killed? Who was the statistician who reckoned that everybody would fit into Lake Windermere? The Trojans likely thought well of themselves, one by one; their last settlement died out by 1,100 B.C.E. Who were the people Stalin killed, or any of the 79.2 billion of us now dead, and who are the 5.8 billion of us now alive?

"God speaks succinctly," said the rabbis.

Is it important if you have yet died your death, or I? Your father? Your child? It is only a matter of time, after all. Why do we find it supremely pertinent, during any moment of any century on earth, which among us is topsides? Why do we concern ourselves over which side of the membrane of topsoil our feet poke?

"A single death is a tragedy, a million deaths is a statistic," Joseph Stalin, that connoisseur, gave words to this disquieting and possibly universal sentiment.

How can an individual count? Do we individuals count only to us other suckers, who love and grieve like elephants, bless their hearts? Of Allah, the Koran says, "Not so much as the weight of an ant in earth or heaven escapes from the Lord." That is touching, that Allah, God, and their ilk care when one ant dismembers another, or note when a sparrow falls, but I strain to see the use of it.

Ten years ago we thought there were two galaxies for each of us alive. Lately, since we loosed the Hubble Space Telescope, we have revised our figures. There are nine galaxies for each of us. Each galaxy harbors an average of 100 billion suns. In our galaxy, the Milky Way, there are sixty-nine suns for each person alive. The Hubble shows, says a report, that the universe "is at least 15 billion years old." Two galaxies, nine galaxies … sixty-nine suns, 100 billions suns—

These astronomers are nickel-and-diming us to death.

III

What were you doing on April 30, 1991, when a series of waves drowned 138,000 people? Where were you when you first heard the astounding, heartbreaking news? Who told you? What, seriatim, were your sensations? Who did you tell? Did you weep? Did your anguish last days or weeks?

All my life I have loved this sight: a standing wave in a boat's wake, shaped like a thorn. I have seen it rise from many oceans, and I saw it rise from the Sea of Galilee. It was a peak about a foot high. The standing wave broke at its peak, and foam slid down its glossy hollow. I watched the foaming wave on the port side. At every instant we were bringing this boat's motor, this motion, into new water. The stir, as if of life, impelled each patch of water to pinch and inhabit this same crest. Each crest tumbled upon itself and released a slide of white foam. The foam's bubbles popped and dropped into the general sea while they were still sliding down the dark wave. They trailed away always, and always new waters peaked, broke, foamed, and replenished.

What I saw was the constant intersection of two wave systems. Lord Kelvin first described them. Transverse waves rise abaft the stern and stream away perpendicular to the boat's direction of travel. Diverging waves course out in a V shape behind the boat. Where the waves converge, two lines of standing crests persist at an unchanging angle to the direction of the boat's motion. We think of these as the boat's wake. I was studying the highest standing wave, the one nearest the boat. It rose from the trough behind the stern and spilled foam. The curled wave crested over clear water and tumbled down. All its bubbles broke, thousands a second, unendingly. I could watch the present; I could see time and how it works.

On a shore, 8,000 waves break a day. James Trefil, a professor of physics, provides these facts. At any one time, the foam from breaking waves covers between 3 and 4 percent of the earth's surface. This acreage of foam is equal to the entire continent of North America. By coincidence, the U.S. population, in other words, although it is the third largest population among nations, is as small a portion of the earth's people as breaking waves' white foam is of the sea.

"God rises up out of the sea like a treasure in the waves," wrote Thomas Merton.

We see generations of waves rise from the sea that made them, billions of individuals at a time; we see them dwindle and vanish. If this does not astound you, what will? Or what will move you to pity?

IV

One tenth of the land on earth is tundra. At any time, it is raining on only 5 percent of the planet's surface. Lightning strikes the planet about a hundred times every second. The insects outweigh us. Our chickens outnumber us four to one.One fifth of us are Muslims. One fifth of us live in China. And every seventh person is a Chinese peasant. Almost one tenth of us live within range of an active volcano. More than 2 percent of us are mentally retarded. We humans drink tea—over a billion cups a day. Among us we speak 10,000 languages.

We are civilized generation number 500 or so, counting from 10,000 years ago, when we settled down. We are *Homo sapiens* generation number 7,500, counting from 150,000 years ago, when our species presumably arose; and we are human generation number 125,000 counting from the earliest forms of *Homo.*

Every 110 hours a million more humans arrive on the planet than die into the planet. A hundred million of us are children who live on the streets. Over a hundred million of us live in countries where we hold no citizenship. Twenty-three million of us are refugees. Sixteen million of us live in Cairo. Twelve million fish for a living from small boats. Seven and a half million of us are Uygurs. One million of us crew on freezer trawlers. Nearly a thousand of us a day commit suicide.

Head-spinning numbers cause the mind to go slack, the *Hartford Courant* says. But our minds must not go slack. How can we think straight if our minds go slack? We agree that we want to think straight.

Anyone's close world of family and friends composes a group smaller than almost all sampling errors, smaller than almost all rounding errors, a group invisible, at whose loss the world will not blink. Two million children die a year from diarrhea, and 800,000 from measles. Do we blink? Stalin starved 7 million Ukrainians in one year, Pol Pot killed 1 million Cambodians, the flu epidemic of 1918 killed 21 or 22 million people … shall this go on? Or do you suffer, as Teilhard de Chardin did, the sense of being "an atom lost in the universe"? Or do you not suffer this sense? How about what journalists call "compassion fatigue"? Reality fatigue? At what limit for you do other individuals blur? Vanish? How old are you?

V

Los Angeles airport has 25,000 parking spaces. This is about one space for every person who died in 1985 in Colombia when a volcano erupted. This is one space for each of the corpses of more than two years' worth of accidental killings from leftover land mines of recent wars. At five to a car, almost all the Inuit in the world could park at LAX. Similarly, if you propped up or stacked four bodies to a car, you could fit into the airport parking lot all the corpses from the firestream bombing of Tokyo in March 1945, or the corpses of Londoners who died in the plague, or the corpses of Burundians killed in civil war since 1993. But you could not fit America's homeless there, not even at twenty to a car.

Since sand and dirt pile up on everything, why does the world look fresh for each new crowd? As natural and human debris raises the continents, vegetation grows on the piles. It is all a stage—we know this—a temporary stage on top of many layers of stages, but every year a new crop of sand, grass, and tree leaves freshens the set and perfects the illusion that ours is the new and urgent world now. When Keats was in Rome, I read once, he saw pomegranate trees overhead; they bloomed in dirt blown onto the Coliseum's broken walls. How can we doubt our own time, in which each bright instant probes the future? In every arable soil in the world we grow grain over tombs—sure, we know this. But do not the dead generations seem to us dark and still as mummies, and their times always faded like scenes painted on walls at Pompeii?

How can we see ourselves as only a new, temporary cast for a long-running show when a new batch of birds flies around singing and new clouds move? Living things from hyenas to bacteria whisk the dead away like stagehands hustling between scenes. To help a living space last while we live on it, we brush or haul away the blowing sand and hack or burn the greenery. We are mowing the grass at the cutting edge.

VI

In northeast Japan, a seismic sea wave killed 27,000 people on June 15, 1896. Do not fail to distinguish this infamous wave from the April 30, 1991, waves that drowned 138,000 Bangladeshi. You were not tempted to confuse, conflate, forget, or ignore these deaths, were you?

On the dry Laetoli plain of northern Tanzania, Mary Leakey found a trail of hominid footprints. The three barefoot people—likely a short man and woman and child *Australopithecus afarensis*—walked closely together. They walked on moist volcanic tuff and ash. We have a record of those few seconds from a day about 3.6 million years ago—before hominids even chipped stone tools. More ash covered their footprints and hardened. Ash also preserved the pockmarks of the raindrops that fell beside the three who walked; it was a rainy day. We have almost ninety feet of the three's steady footprints intact. We do not know where they were going or why. We do not know why the woman paused and turned left, briefly, before continuing. "A remote ancestor," Leakey said, "experienced a moment of doubt." Possibly they watched the Sadiman volcano erupt, or they took a last look back before they left. We do know we cannot make anything so lasting as these three barefoot ones did.

After archeologists studied this long strip of record for several years, they buried it again to save it. Along one preserved portion, however, new tree roots are already cracking the footprints, and in another place winds threaten to sand them flat; the preservers did not cover them deeply enough. Now they are burying them again.

Jeremiah, walking toward Jerusalem, saw the smoke from the Temple's blaze. He wept; he saw the blood of the slain. "He put his face close to the ground and saw the footprints of sucklings and infants who were walking into captivity: in Babylon. He kissed the footprints.

Who were these individuals? Who were the three who walked together and left footprints in the rain? Who was that eighteenth-century Ukrainian peasant the Baal Shem Tov, the founder of modern Hasidism, who taught, danced, and dug clay? He was among the generations of children of Babylonian exiles whose footprints on the bare earth Jeremiah kissed. Centuries later the Emperor Hadrian destroyed another such son of exile in Rome, Rabbi Akiba. Russian Christians and European Christians tried, and Hitler tried, to wipe all those survivors of children of exile from the ground of the earth as a man wipes a plate— survivors of exiles whose footprints on the ground I kiss, and whose feet.

Who and of what import were the men whose bones bulk the Great Wall, the 30 million Mao starved, or the 11 million children under five who die each year now? Why, they are the insignificant others, of course; living or dead, they are just some of the plentiful others. And you?

Is it not late? A late time to be living? Are not our current generations the important ones? We have changed the world. Are not our heightened times the important ones, the ones since Hiroshima? Perhaps we are the last generation—there is a comfort. Take the bomb threat away and what are we? We are ordinary beads on a never-ending string. Our time is a routine twist of an improbable yarn.

We have no chance of being here when the sun burns out. There must be something ultimately heroic about our time, something that sets it above all those other times. Hitler, Stalin, Mao, and Pol Pot made strides in obliterating whole peoples, but this has been the human effort all along, and we have only enlarged the means, as have people in every century in history. (That genocides recur does not mean that they are similar. Each instance of human evil and each victim's death possesses its unique history and form. To generalize, as Cynthia Ozick points out, is to "befog" evil's specificity.)

Dire things are happening. Plague? Funny weather? Why are we watching the news, reading the news, keeping up with the news? Only to enforce our fancy—probably a necessary lie—that these are crucial times, and we are in on them. Newly revealed, and I am in the know: crazy people, bunches of them! New diseases, sways in power, floods! Can the news from dynastic Egypt have been any different?

As I write this, I am still alive, but of course I might well have died before you read it. Most of the archeologists who reburied hominid footprints have likely not yet died their deaths; the paleontologist Teilhard is pushing up daisies.

Chinese soldiers who breathed air posing for 7,000 individual day portraits—twenty-two centuries ago—must have thought it a wonderful difference that workers buried only their simulacra then so that their sons could bury their flesh a bit later. One wonders what they did in the months or years they gained. One wonders what one is, oneself, up to these days.

VII

Was it wisdom Mao Tse-tung attained when—like Ted Bundy—he awakened to the long view?

"The atom bomb is nothing to be afraid of," Mao told Nehru. "China has many people. … The deaths of ten or twenty million people is nothing to be afraid of." A witness said Nehru showed shock. Later, speaking in Moscow, Mao displayed yet more generosity: he boasted that he was willing to lose 300 million people, half of China's population.

Does Mao's reckoning shock me really? If sanctioning the death of strangers could save my daughter's life, would I do it? Probably. How many others' lives would I be willing to sacrifice? Three? Three hundred million?

An English journalist, observing the Sisters of Charity in Calcutta, reasoned: "Either life is always and in all circumstances sacred, or intrinsically of no account; it is inconceivable that it should be in some cases the one, and in some the other."

One small town's soup kitchen, St. Mary's, serves 115 men a night. Why feed 115 individuals? Surely so few people elude most demographics and achieve statistical insignificance. After all, there are 265 million Americans, 15 million people who live in Mexico City, 16 million in greater New York, 26 million in greater Tokyo. Every day 1.5 million people walk through Times Square in New York; every day almost as many people—1.4 million—board a U.S. passenger plane. And so forth. We who breathe air now will join the already dead layers of us who breathed air once. We arise from dirt and dwindle to dirt, and the might of the universe is arrayed against us.

■ WHAT?

1. What is Dillard's main point in this essay? What is she trying to persuade her audience to think or do?
2. Explain Dillard's critique of the use of numbers and statistics to represent human beings and to quantify human suffering. What other ways can you think of to address human tragedies—and to make distant tragedies seem significant?
3. What is the effect of Dillard's quoting so many people? Do all of these voices strengthen her claims? What do these voices say about Dillard's relationship to the topic of death and the randomness of violence?

■ WHAT ELSE? WHAT'S NEXT?

4. Like many great writers, Dillard offers a new way of talking about a very old issue: What can we say about the value of life in light of the certainty, and ubiquity, of death? Many philosophers, theologians, and scientists have pondered this issue at length. Your research task is twofold: First, make a list of at least four academic disciplines, other than English or literature, that deal with this question. And, second, find one primary source from one of these disciplines and compare the source's treatment of the issue with Dillard's.
5. Throughout the essay, Dillard meditates on one central issue (the significance or sacredness of life in a world of random death) mostly by juxtaposing various quotations, anecdotes, and reported conversation. Use a similar quotation/collage method to ponder another issue (some possibilities: happiness, success, commitment, loyalty, virtue, evil, love).

■ WHO CARES?

6. Based on your reading of the essay—the content and style—who do you think Dillard saw as her readers? Why do you think this? (Be specific in your response.)

Jeanette Winterson is a widely acclaimed writer of fiction and essays whose best-known works include Oranges Are Not the Only Fruit *and* Written on the Body. *The following piece is from her 1997 collection* Art Objects: Essays on Ecstasy and Effrontery, *an impassioned defense of the arts. In this essay, Winterson argues forcefully for the primacy of the imagination.*

BEFORE YOU READ———————————————————————————————

In the introduction to The Carolina Reader, *you were asked to compose a definition of "information literacy." Now, think about the terms "cultural literacy" and "artistic literacy." What do they mean to you? Compare your definitions of these two terms with that of information literacy. Are all of these terms compatible?*

IMAGINATION AND REALITY Jeanette Winterson

The reality of art is the reality of the imagination.

What do I mean by reality of art?

What do I mean by reality of imagination?

My statement, and the questions it suggests, are worth considering now that the fashionable approach to the arts is once again through the narrow gate of subjective experience. The charge laid on the artist, and in particular on the writer, is not to bring back visions but to play the Court photographer.

Is this anathema to art? Is it anti-art? I think so. What art presents is much more than the daily life of you and me, and the original role of the artist as visionary is the correct one. "Real" is an old word, is an odd word. It used to mean a Spanish sixpence; a small silver coin, money of account in the days when the value of a coin was the value of its metal. We are used to notional money but "real" is an honest currency.

The honest currency of art is the honest currency of the imagination.

The small silver coin of art cannot be spent; that is, it cannot be exchanged or exhausted. What is lost, what is destroyed, what is tarnished, what is misappropriated, is ceaselessly renewed by the mining, shaping, forging imagination that exists beyond the conjectures of the everyday. Imagination's coin, the infinitely flexible metal of the Muse, metal of the moon, in rounded structure offers new universes, primary worlds, that substantially confront the pretences of notional life.

Notional life is the life encouraged by governments, mass education and the mass media. Each of those powerful agencies couples an assumption of its own importance with a disregard for individuality. Freedom of choice is the catch phrase but streamlined homogeneity is the objective. A people who think for themselves are hard to control and what is worse, in a money culture, they may be skeptical of product advertising. Since our economy is now a consumer economy, we must be credulous and passive. We must believe that we want to earn money to buy things we don't need. The education system is not designed to turn out thoughtful individualists, it is there to get us to work. When we come home exhausted from the inanities of our jobs we can relax in front of the inanities of the TV screen. This pattern, punctuated by birth, death and marriage and a new car, is offered to us as real life.

Children who are born into a tired world as batteries of new energy are plugged into the system as soon as possible and gradually drained away. At the time when they become adult and conscious they are already depleted and prepared to accept a world of shadows. Those who have kept their spirit find it hard to nourish it and between the ages of twenty and thirty, many are successfully emptied of all resistance. I do not think it an exaggeration to say that most of the energy of most of the people is being diverted into a system which destroys them. Money is no antidote. If the imaginative life is to be renewed it needs its own coin.

We have to admit that the arts stimulate and satisfy a part of our nature that would otherwise be left untouched and that the emotions art arouses in us are of a different order to those aroused by experience of any other kind.

We think we live in a world of sense-experience and what we can touch and feel, see and hear, is the sum of our reality. Although neither physics nor philosophy accepts this, neither physics nor philosophy has been as successful as religion used to be at persuading us of the doubtfulness of the seeming-solid world. This is a pity if only because while religion was a matter of course, the awareness of other realities was also a matter of course. To accept God was to accept Otherness, and while this did not make the life of the artist any easier (the life of the artist is never easy), a general agreement that there is more around us than the mundane allows the artist a greater license and a greater authority than he or she can expect in a society that recognizes nothing but itself.

An example of this is the development of the visual arts under Church patronage during the late medieval and Renaissance periods in Europe. This was much more than a patronage of money, it was a warrant to bring back visions. Far from being restricted by Church rhetoric, the artist knew that he and his audience were in tacit agreement; each went in search of the Sublime.

Art is visionary; it sees beyond the view from the window, even though the window is its frame. This is why the arts fare much better alongside religion than alongside either capitalism or communism. The god-instinct and the art-instinct both apprehend more than the physical biological material world. The artist need not believe in God, but the artist does consider reality as multiple and complex. If the audience accepts this premise it is then possible to think about the work itself. As things stand now, too much criticism of the arts concerns itself with attacking any suggestion of arts as Other, as a bringer of realities beyond the commonplace. Dimly, we know we need those other realities and we think we can get them by ransacking different cultures and rhapsodizing work by foreign writers simply because they are foreign writers. We are still back with art as the mirror of life, only it is a more exotic or less democratic life than our own. No doubt this has its interests but if we are honest, they are documentary. Art is not documentary. It may incidentally serve that function in its own way but its true effort is to open to us dimensions of the spirit and of the self that normally lie smothered under the weight of living.

It is in Victorian England that the artist first becomes a rather suspect type who does not bring visions but narcotics and whose relationship to different levels of reality is not authoritative but hallucinatory. In Britain, the nineteenth century recovered from the shock of Romanticism by adopting either a manly Hellenism, with an interest in all things virile and Greek, or a manly philistinism, which had done with sweet Jonney Keats and his band and demanded of the poet, if he must be a poet, that he is either declamatory or decorative. Art could be rousing or it could be entertaining. If it hinted at deeper mysteries it was effeminate and absurd. The shift in sensibility from early to late Wordsworth is the shift of the age. For Tennyson, who published his first collection in 1830, the shift was a painful one and the compromises he made to his own work are clear to anyone who flicks through the collected poems and finds a visionary poet trying to hide himself in legend in order to hint at sublimities not allowed to his own time. Like Wordsworth before him, Tennyson fails whenever he collapses into the single obsessive reality of the world about him. As a laureate we know he is lying. As a visionary we read him now and find him true.

And what are we but our fathers' sons and daughters? We are the Victorian legacy. Our materialism, our lack of spirituality, our grossness, our mockery of art, our utilitarian attitude to education, even the dull grey suits wrapped around the dull grey lives of our eminent City men, are Victorian hand-me-downs. Many of our ideas of history and society go back no further than Victorian England. We live in a money culture because they did. Control by plutocracy is a nineteenth-century phenomenon that has been sold to us as a blueprint for reality. But what is real about the values of a money culture?

Money culture recognizes no currency but its own. Whatever is not money, whatever is not making money, is useless to it. The entire efforts of our government as directed through our society are efforts towards making more and more money. This favors the survival of the dullest. This favors those who prefer to live in a notional reality where goods are worth more than time and where things are more important than ideas.

For the artist, any artist, poet, painter, musician, time in plenty and an abundance of ideas are the necessary basics of creativity. By dreaming and idleness and then by intense self-discipline does the artist live. The artist cannot perform between 9 and 6, five days a week, or if she sometimes does, she cannot guarantee to do so. Money culture hates that. It must know what it is getting, when it is getting it, and how much it will cost. The most tyrannical of patrons never demanded from their protégées what the market now demands of artists; if you can't sell your work regularly and quickly, you can either starve or do something else. The time that art needs, which may not be a long time, but which has to be its own time, is anathema to a money culture. Money confuses time with itself. That is part of its unreality.

Against this golden calf in the wilderness where all come to buy and sell, the honest currency of art offers quite a different rate of exchange. The artist does not turn time into money, the artist turns time into energy, time into intensity, time into vision. The exchange that art offers is an exchange in kind; energy for energy, intensity for intensity, vision for vision. This is seductive and threatening. Can we make the return? Do we want to? Our increasingly passive diversions do not equip us, mentally, emotionally, for the demands that art makes. We know we are dissatisfied, but the satisfactions that we seek come at a price beyond the resources of a money culture. Can we afford to live imaginatively, contemplatively? Why have we submitted to a society that tries to make imagination a privilege when to each of us it comes as a birthright?

It is not a question of the money in your pocket. Money can buy you the painting or the book or the opera seat but it cannot expose you to the vast energies you will find there.

Often it will shield you from them, just as a rich man can buy himself a woman but not her love. Love is reciprocity and so is art. Either you abandon yourself to another world that you say you seek or you find ways to resist it. Most of us are art-resisters because art is a challenge to the notional life. In a money culture, art, by its nature, objects. It fields its own realities, lives by its own currency, aloof to riches and want. Art is dangerous.

FOR SALE: MY LIFE. HIGHEST BIDDER COLLECTS

The honest currency of art is the honest currency of the imagination.

In Middle English, "real" was a variant of "royal."

Can we set aside images of our own dishonored monarchy and think instead about the ancientness and complexity of the word "royal"?

To be royal was to be distinguished in the proper sense; to be singled out, by one's fellows and by God or the gods. In both the Greek and the Hebraic traditions, the one who is royal is the one who has special access to the invisible world. Ulysses can talk to Hera, King David can talk to God. Royalty on earth is expected to take its duties on earth seriously but the King should also be a bridge between the terrestrial and the supernatural.

Perhaps it seems strange to us that in the ancient world the King was more accessible to his people than were the priests. Although King and priests worked together, priesthood, still allied to magic, even by the Hebrews, was fully mysterious. The set-apartness of the priest is one surrounded by ritual and taboo. The priest did not fight in battle, take concubines, hoard treasure, feast and riot, sin out of humanness, or if he did, there were severe penalties. The morality of the priesthood was not the morality of Kingship and whether you read *The Odyssey* or The Bible, the difference is striking. The King is not better behaved than his subjects, essentially he was (or should have been) the nobler man.

In Britain, royalty was not allied to morality until the reign of Queen Victoria. Historically, the role of the King or Queen had been to lead and inspire, this is an imaginative role, and it was most perfectly fulfilled by Elizabeth the First, Gloriana, the approachable face of Godhead. Gloriana is the Queen whose otherness is for the sake of her people, and it is important to remember that the disciplines she laid upon her own life, in particular her chastity, were not for the sake of example but for the sake of expediency. The Divine Right of Kings was not a good conduct award; it was a mark of favor. God's regent upon earth was expected to behave like God and anyone who studies Greek or Hebrew literature will find that God does not behave like a Christian schoolmistress. God is glorious, terrifying, inscrutable, often capricious to human eyes, extravagant, victorious, legislative but not law-abiding, and the supreme imagination. "In the beginning was the Word."

At its simplest and at its best, royalty is an imaginative function; it must embody in its own person, subtle and difficult concepts of Otherness. The priest does not embody these concepts, the priest serves them. The priest is a functionary, the King is a function.

Shakespeare is preoccupied with Kingship as a metaphor for the imaginative life. Leontes and Lear, Macbeth and Richard II, are studies in the failure of the imagination. In *The Winter's Tale*, the redemption of Leontes is made possible through a new capacity in him; the capacity to see outside of his own dead vision into a chance as vibrant as it is unlikely. When Paulina says to him, "It is required you do awake your faith" she does not mean religious faith. If the statue of Hermione is to come to life, Leontes must believe it *can* come to life. This is not common sense. It is imagination.

In the earliest Hebrew creation stories Yahweh makes himself a clay model of a man and breathes on it to give it life. It is this supreme confidence, this translation of forms, the capacity to recognize in one thing the potential of another, and the willingness to let that potential realize itself, that is the stamp of creativity and the birthright that Yahweh gives to humans. Leontes' failure to acknowledge any reality other than his own is a repudiation of that birthright, a neglect of humanness that outworks itself into the fixed immobility of his queen. When Hermione steps down and embraces Leontes it is an imaginative reconciliation.

I hope it is clear that as I talk about King and priest I am dealing in abstracts and not actualities. I do not wish to upset republicans anywhere. What I do want to do is to move the pieces across the chessboard to see if that gives us a different view.

By unraveling the word "real" I hope to show that it contains in itself, and without any wishful thinking on my part, those densities of imaginative experience that belong to us all and that are best communicated through art. I see no conflict between reality and imagination. They are not in fact separate. Our real lives hold within them our royal lives; the inspiration to be more than we are, to find new solutions, to live beyond the moment. Art helps us to do this because it fuses together temporal and perpetual realities.

To see outside of a dead vision is not an optical illusion.

The realist (from the Latin *res* = thing) who thinks he deals in things and not images and who is suspicious of the abstract and of art, is not the practical man but a man caught in a fantasy of his own unmaking.

The realist unmakes the coherent multiple world into a collection of random objects. He thinks of reality as that which has an objective existence, but understands no more about objective existence than that which he can touch and feel, sell and buy. A lover of objects and of objectivity, he is in fact caught in a world of symbols and symbolism, where he is unable to see the thing in itself, as it really is, he sees it only in relation to his own story of the world.

The habit of human beings is to see things subjectively or not to see them at all. The more familiar a thing becomes the less it is seen. In the home, nobody looks at the furniture, they sit on it, eat off it, sleep on it and forget it until they buy something new. When we do look at other people's things, we are usually thinking about their cachet, their value, what they say about their owner. Our minds work to continually label and absorb what we see and to fit it neatly into our own pattern. That done, we turn away. This is a sound survival skill but it makes it very difficult to let anything have an existence independent of ourselves, whether furniture or people. It makes it easier to buy symbols, things that have a particular value to us, than it does to buy objects.

My mother, who was poor, never bought objects, she bought symbols. She used to save up to buy something hideous to put in the best parlor. What she bought was factory made and beyond her purse. If she had ever been able to see it in its own right, she could never have spent money on it. She couldn't see it, and nor could any of the neighbors dragged in to admire it. They admired the effort it had taken to save for it. They admired how much it cost. Above all, they admired my mother; the purchase was a success.

I know that when my mother sat in her kitchen that had only a few pieces of handmade furniture, she felt depressed and conscious of her lowly social status. When she sat in her dreadful parlor with a china cup and a bought biscuit, she felt like a lady. The parlor, full of objects unseen but hard won, was a fantasy chamber, a reflecting mirror. Like Mrs. Joe, in *Great Expectations*, she finally took her apron off.

Money culture depends on symbolic reality. It depends on a confusion between the object and what the object represents. To keep you and my buying and upgrading an overstock of meaningless things depends on those things having an acquisitional value. It is the act of buying that is important. In our society, people who cannot buy things are the underclass.

Symbolic man surrounds himself with objects as tyrants surround themselves with subjects: "These will obey me. Through them I am worshipped. Through them I exercise control." These fraudulent kingdoms, hard-headed and practical, are really the soft-center of fantasy. They are wish fulfillment nightmares where more is piled on more to manufacture the illusion of abundance. They are hands of emptiness and want. Things do not satisfy. In part they fail to satisfy because their symbolic value changes so regularly and what brought whistles of admiration one year is next year's car boot sale bargain. In part they fail to satisfy because much of what we buy is gadgetry and fashion, which makes objects temporary and the need to be able to purchase them, permanent. In part they fail to satisfy because we do not actually want the things we buy. They are illusion, narcotic, hallucination.

To suggest that the writer, the painter, the musician, is the one out of touch with the real world is a doubtful proposition. It is the artist who must apprehend things fully, in their own right, communicating them not as symbols but as living realities with the power to move.

To see outside of a dead vision is not an optical illusion.

According to the science of optics, if an image consists of points through which light actually passes, it is called real. Otherwise it is called virtual.

The work of the artist is to see into the life of things; to discriminate between superficialities and realities; to know what is genuine and what is a make-believe. The artist through the disciplines of her work, is one of the few people who does see things as they really are, stripped of associative value. I do not mean that artists of whatever sort have perfect taste or perfect private lives. I mean that when the imaginative capacity is highly developed, it is made up of invention and discernment. Invention is the shaping spirit that re-forms fragments into new wholes, so that even what has been familiar can be seen fresh. Discernment is to know how to test the true and the false and to reveal objects, emotions, ideas in their own coherence. The artist is a translator; one who has learned how to pass into their own language the languages gathered from stones, from birds, from dreams, from the body, from the material world, from the invisible world, from sex, from death, from love. A different language is a different reality; what is the language, the world, of stones? What is the language, the world, of birds? Of atoms? Of microbes? Of colors? Of air? The material world is closed to those who think of it only as a commodity market.

How do you know but every bird that cuts the airy way
Is an immense world of delight closed by your senses five?
William Blake, *The Marriage of Heaven and Hell* (c. 1790)

To those people every object is inanimate. In fact they are the ones who remain unmoved, fixed rigidly within their own reality.

The artist is moved.

The artist is moved through multiple realities. The artist is moved by empty space and points of light. The artist tests the image. Does light pass through it? Is it illuminated? Is it sharp, clear, its own edges, its own form?

The artist is looking for real presences. I suppose what the scientist Rupert Sheldrake would call "morphic resonance;" the inner life of the thing that cannot be explained away biologically, chemically, physically. In the Catholic Church "real presence" is the bread and wine that through transubstantiation becomes the living eucharist; the body and blood of Christ. In the Protestant Church the bread and wine are symbols only, one of the few places where we recognize that we are asking one thing to substitute for another. For the average person, this substitution is happening all the time.

The real presence, the image transformed by light, is not rare but it is easily lost or mistaken under clouds of subjectivity. People who claim to like pictures and books will often only respond to those pictures and books in which they can clearly find themselves. This is ego masquerading as taste. To recognize the worth of a thing is more than recognizing its worth to you. Our responses to art are conditioned by our insistence that it present to us realities we can readily accept, however virtual those realities might be. Nevertheless art has a stubborn way of cutting through the subjective world of symbols and money and offering itself as a steady alternative to the quick change act of daily life.

We are naturally suspicious of faculties that we do not ourselves possess and we do not quite believe that the poet can read the sermons in stones or the painter know the purple that bees love. Still we are drawn to books and pictures and music, finding in ourselves an echo of their song, finding in ourselves an echo of their sensibility, an answering voice through the racket of the day.

Art is for us a reality beyond now. An imaginative reality that we need. The reality of art is the reality of the imagination.

The reality of art is not the reality of experience.

The charge laid on the artist is to bring back visions.

In Shakespeare's *Othello*, we find that the Moor wins Desdemona's heart by first winning her imagination. He tells her tales of cannibals and of the Anthropophagi whose heads grow beneath their shoulders. What he calls his "round unvarnished tale" is a subtle mixture of art and artfulness. When a Shakespearean hero apologies for his lack of wit we should be on our guard. Shakespeare always gives his heroes the best lines, even when the hero is Richard II.

Othello's untutored language is in fact powerful and wrought. He is more than a master of arms, he is a master of art. It is his words that win Desdemona. She says "I saw Othello's visage in his mind." His face, like his deeds, belongs to the world of sense-experience, but it is his wit that makes both dear to her. For Desdemona, the reality of Othello is his imaginative reality.

> OTHELLO she thank'd me,
> And bade me, if I had a friend that lov'd her,
> I should but teach him how to tell my story,
> And that would woo her.

The clue here is not the story but the telling of it. It is not Othello the action man who has taught Desdemona to love him, it is Othello the poet.

We know that Shakespeare never bothered to think of a plot. As a good dramatist and one who earned his whole living by his work, he had to take care to make his historical ransackings state-satisfactory. The engineering of the plays gives pleasure even to those who are not interested in the words. But the words are the thing. The words are what interested Shakespeare and what should closely interest us. Shakespeare is a dramatic poet. He is not a chronicler of experience.

I have to say something so obvious because of the multitude of so-called realists, many making money out of print, who want art to be as small as they are. For them, art is a copying machine busily coping themselves. They like the documentary version, the "life as it is lived." To support their opinions they will either point to Dickens or Shakespeare. I have never understood why anyone calls Dickens a realist, but I have dealt with that myth elsewhere in these essays. As for Shakespeare, they will happily disregard the pervading spirit behind the later plays, and quote *Hamlet* Act III, Scene II "The purpose of playing … is, to hold, as 'twere, the mirror up to nature."

But what is nature?

From the Latin *Natura*, it is my birth, my characteristics, my condition.

It is my nativity, my astrology, my biology, my physiognomy, my geography, my cartography, my spirituality, my sexuality, my mentality, my corporeal, intellectual, emotional, imaginative self. And not just my self, every self and the Self of the world. There is no mirror I know that can show me all of these singularities, unless it is the strange distorting looking-glass of art where I will not find my reflection not my representation but a nearer truth than I prefer. *Natura* is the whole that I am. The multiple reality of my existence.

The reality of the imagination leaves out nothing. It is the most complete reality that we can know. Imagination takes in the world of sense experience, and rather than trading it for a world of symbols, delights in it for what it is. The artist is physical and it is in the work of true artists in any medium that we find the most moving and the most poignant studies of the world that we can touch and feel. It is the writer, the painter, and not the realist, who is intimate with the material world, who knows its smells and tastes because they are fresh in her nostrils, full in her mouth. What her hand touches, she feels. R.A. Collingwood said that Cézanne painted like a blind man (critics at the time agreed though for different reasons). He meant that the two dimensional flimsy world of what is overlooked by most of us, suddenly reared out of the canvas, massy and tough. Cézanne seems to have hands in his eyes and eyes in his hands. When Cézanne paints a tree or an apple, he does not paint a copy of a tree or an apple, he paints its nature. He paints the whole that it is, the whole that is lost to us as we pass it, eat it, chop it down. It is through the painter, writer, composer, who lives more intensely than the rest of us, that we can rediscover the intensity of the physical world.

And not only the physical world. There is no limit to new territory. The gate is open. Whether or not we go through is up to us, but to stand mockingly on the threshold, claiming that nothing lies beyond, is something of a flat earth theory.

The earth is not flat and neither is reality. Reality is continuous, multiple, simultaneous, complex, abundant and partly invisible. The imagination alone can fathom this and it reveals its fathomings through art.

The reality of art is the reality of the imagination.

■ WHAT?

1. What arguments is Winterson making about art and imagination in this essay?
2. How does Winterson define "notional life"? What are her objections to this way of living? What does she propose in its place?
3. Is Winterson fair in characterizing contemporary Americans (i.e., you and me) as "credulous and passive" in the face of "notional reality"? Give three reasons why she may be partly right, and three reasons why she may be partly wrong.
4. In her essay, Winterson writes: "At the time when they [children] become adult and conscious they are already depleted and prepared to accept a world of shadows," a subtle allusion to Plato's "Allegory of the Cave." In what ways do you feel this is an accurate description of your situation as a college student? In what ways do you feel it is inaccurate or unfair?

■ WHAT ELSE? WHAT'S NEXT

5. What else do you need to know to have a better understanding of Winterson's essay? How would you go about finding this information?

■ WHO CARES?

6. Do you feel like you are among the readers Winterson had in mind when she wrote this piece? Explain your response, pointing to specific elements of the text to support your answer.

Kwame Anthony Appiah is a philosophy professor at Princeton University
and the author of several books, including 2010's The Honor Code: How
Moral Revolutions Happen. In this piece, published in September 2010 in
The Washington Post, he offers a future-oriented way of thinking about the
consequences of our actions as individuals and as a society.

BEFORE YOU READ————————————————————————

*Research the author of this piece, Kwame Anthony Appiah, and compose an
informational paragraph that summarizes his central philosophical positions. In other
words, based on your research, summarize Appiah's worldview and point to at least
one bit of information that you think others might find interesting or helpful as they
read the essay.*

WHAT WILL FUTURE GENERATIONS
CONDEMN US FOR? Kwame Anthony Appiah

Once, pretty much everywhere, beating your wife and children was regarded as a father's
duty, homosexuality was a hanging offense, and waterboarding was approved—in act,
invented—by the Catholic Church. Through the middle of the 19th century, the United
States and other nations in the Americas condoned plantation slavery. Many of our
grandparents were born in states where women were forbidden to vote. And well into the
20th century, lynch mobs in this country stripped, tortured, hanged and burned human
beings at picnics.

Looking back at such horrors, it is easy to ask: What were people thinking?

Yet, the chances are that our own descendants will ask the same question, with the
same incomprehension, about some of our practices today.

Is there a way to guess which ones? After all, not every disputed institution or practice
is destined to be discredited. And it can be hard to distinguish in real time between
movements, such as abolition, that will come to represent moral common sense and those,
such as prohibition, that will come to seem quaint or misguided. Recall the book-burners of
Boston's old Watch and Ward Society or the organizations for the suppression of vice, with
their crusades against claret, contraceptives and sexually candid novels.

Still, a look at the past suggests three signs that a particular practice is destined for
future condemnation.

First, people have already heard the arguments against the practice. The case against
slavery didn't emerge in a blinding moment of moral clarity, for instance; it had been
around for centuries.

Second, defenders of the custom tend not to offer moral counterarguments but instead invoke tradition, human nature or necessity. (As in, "We've always had slaves, and how could we grow cotton without them?")

And third, supporters engage in what one might call strategic ignorance, avoiding truths that might force them to face the evils in which they're complicit. Those who ate the sugar or wore the cotton that the slaves grew simply didn't think about what made those goods possible. That's why abolitionists sought to direct attention toward the conditions of the Middle Passage, through detailed illustrations of slave ships and horrifying stories of the suffering below decks.

With these signs in mind, here are four contenders for future moral condemnation.

■ Our Prison System

We already know that the massive waste of life in our prisons is morally troubling; those who defend the conditions of incarceration usually do so in non-moral terms (citing costs or the administrative difficulty of reforms); and we're inclined to avert our eyes from the details. Check, check and check.

Roughly 1 percent of adults in this country are incarcerated. We have 4 percent of the world's population but 25 percent of its prisoners. No other nation has as large a proportion of its population in prison; even China's rate is less than half of ours. What's more, the majority of our prisoners are non-violent offenders, many of them detained on drug charges. (Whether a country that was truly free would criminalize recreational drug use is a related question worth pondering.)

And the full extent of the punishment prisoners face isn't detailed in any judge's sentence. More than 100,000 inmates suffer sexual abuse, including rape, each year; some contract HIV as a result. Our country holds at least 25,000 prisoners in isolation in so-called supermax facilities, under conditions that many psychologists say amount to torture.

■ Industrial Meat Production

The arguments against the cruelty of factory farming have certainly been around a long time; it was Jeremy Bentham, in the 18th century, who observed that, when it comes to the treatment of animals, the key question is not whether animals can reason but whether they can suffer. People who eat factory-farmed bacon or chicken rarely offer a moral justification for what they're doing. Instead, they try not to think about it too much, shying away from stomach-turning stories about what goes on in our industrial abattoirs.

Of the more than 90 million cattle in our country, at least 10 million at any time are packed into feedlots, saved from the inevitable diseases of overcrowding only by regular doses of antibiotics, surrounded by piles of their own feces, their nostrils filled with the smell of their own urine. Picture it—and then imagine your grandchildren seeing that picture. In the European Union, many of the most inhumane conditions we allow are already illegal or—like the sow stalls into which pregnant pigs are often crammed in the United States—will be illegal soon.

The Institutionalized and Isolated Elderly

Nearly 2 million of America's elderly are warehoused in nursing homes, out of sight and, to some extent, out of mind. Some 10,000 for-profit facilities have arisen across the country in recent decades to hold them. Other elderly Americans may live independently, but often they are isolated and cut off from their families. (The United States is not alone among advanced democracies in this. Consider the heat wave that hit France in 2003: While many families were enjoying their summer vacations, some 14,000 elderly parents and grandparents were left to perish in the stifling temperatures.) Is this what Western modernity amounts to—societies that feel no filial obligations to their inconvenient elders?

Sometimes we can learn from societies much poorer than ours. My English mother spent the last 50 years of her life in Ghana, where I grew up. In her final years, it was her good fortune not only to have the resources to stay at home, but also to live in a country where doing so was customary. She had family next door who visited her every day, and she was cared for by doctors and nurses who were willing to come to her when she was too ill to come to them. In short, she had the advantages of a society in which older people are treated with respect and concern.

Keeping aging parents and their children closer is a challenge, particularly in a society where almost everybody has a job outside the home (if not across the country). Yet the three signs apply here as well: When we see old people who, despite many living relatives, suffer growing isolation, we know something is wrong. We scarcely try to defend the situation; when we can, we put it out of our minds. Self-interest, if nothing else, should make us hope that our descendants will have worked out a better way.

The Environment

Of course, most transgenerational obligations run the other way—from parents to children—and of these the most obvious candidate for opprobrium is our wasteful attitude toward the planet's natural resources and ecology. Look at a satellite picture of Russia, and you'll see a vast expanse of parched wasteland where decades earlier was a lush and verdant landscape. That's the Republic of Kalmykia, home to what was recognized in the 1990s as Europe's first man-made desert. Desertification, which is primarily the result of destructive land-management practices, threatens a third of the Earth's surface; tens of thousands of Chinese villages have been overrun by sand drifts in the past few decades.

It's not as though we're unaware of what we're doing to the planet: We know the harm done by deforestation, wetland destruction, pollution, overfishing, greenhouse gas emissions—the whole litany. Our descendants, who will inherit this devastated Earth, are unlikely to have the luxury of such recklessness. Chances are, they won't be able to avert their eyes, even if they want to.

■ WHAT?

1. Early in his essay, Appiah writes that "a look at the past suggests three signs that a particular practice is destined for future condemnation." What are these three signs? Briefly explain what each of them means, using an example other than one of those that Appiah lists.
2. Do you agree with Appiah's list of "four contenders for future moral condemnation"? Address each of the four he discusses, explaining why you agree or why you object.

■ WHAT ELSE? WHAT'S NEXT?

3. Select one of the four topics that Appiah lists—the prison system, industrial meat production, our treatment of the elderly, or the environment—and further develop his argument for including that issue on his list. You'll need to conduct some research to find different kinds of support—data, expert opinion, anecdotal evidence—for Appiah's claim.
4. Working with a group of classmates, and using Appiah's suggestions as a guideline, identify other current practices that might bring "future moral condemnation." As you talk through possible practices with your group, make sure that you apply Appiah's "three signs" (see Question 1 above) during your discussion. Your group should be prepared to share its findings with the rest of the class.

■ WHO CARES?

5. What are we—those of us who read Appiah's essay—supposed to do with the information he provides? How do you think he expects his audience to respond? What in the text makes you think this?

IMAGES 1.2 and 1.3
Are these images funny? Explain why (or why not).

Joel Warner is a staff writer for Westword, *an alternative newspaper and website based in Denver. He wrote this article for the May 2011 issue of* Wired *magazine. You can find out more about the benign violation theory of humor by going to http://blog.petermcgraw.org/.*

BEFORE YOU READ

Find a humorous text that is suitable for classroom consumption (think about your audience). This can be a joke, a video clip, an image—anything that you think is funny. Then, write a paragraph or two explaining why, exactly, the text is funny.

ONE PROFESSOR'S ATTEMPT TO EXPLAIN EVERY JOKE EVER Joel Warner

The writer E. B. White famously remarked that "analyzing humor is like dissecting a frog. Few people are interested and the frog dies." If that's true, an amphibian genocide took place in San Antonio this past January. Academics from around the world gathered there for the first-ever comedy symposium cosponsored by the Mind Science Foundation.

The goal wasn't to tell jokes but to assess exactly what a joke is, how it works, and what this thing called "funny" really is, in a neurological, sociological, and psychological sense. As Sean Guillory, a Dartmouth College neuroscience grad student who organized the event, says, "It's the first time a roomful of empirical humor researchers have ever gotten together!"

The first speaker at the podium, University of Western Ontario professor Rod Martin, began with a lament over the lack of comedy scholarship. He pointed out that you could fill a library with analyses of subjects like mental illness or aggression. Meanwhile, the 1,700-plus-page *Handbook of Social Psychology*—the preeminent reference work in its field—mentions humor once.

The crux of Martin's argument involves semantics. It takes issue with the imperfect terminology we use to describe the emotional state that humor triggers. Standardizing language would help humor studies earn the respect of related fields, like aggression research. Martin exhorted his audience to adopt his preferred word for the "pleasurable feeling, joy, gaiety of mind" that humor elicits. *Happiness, elation*, and even *hilarity* don't quite fit, to his mind. The best word, he said, is *mirth*.

For those curious about the physiology of humor, Helmut Karl Lackner of the Medical University of Graz, Austria, presented his research on the relationship between humor, stress, and respiration. By tracking breathing cycles and heart rates, he has determined that social anxiety makes things less funny. (Fittingly, he seemed nervous as he read his paper in halting English.) Nina Strohminger, a researcher at the University of Michigan, explained how she's been exposing test subjects to unpleasant odors. She extolled the virtues of a spray called Liquid Ass, which can be purchased at fine novelty stores everywhere. (Her conclusion: Farts make everything funnier.) The audience members take the subject of amusement very seriously, yet they couldn't help but chuckle at this.

Other speakers peppered their talks with multivariate ANOVAs and mesolimbic reward systems. Some presented research on whether people with Asperger's syndrome get jokes and how to determine the social consequences of put-downs. But as the sessions wound on, no one had addressed the underlying mechanism of comedy: What, exactly, makes things funny?

That question was the core of Peter McGraw's lecture. A lanky 41-year-old professor of marketing and psychology at the University of Colorado Boulder, McGraw thinks he has found the answer, and it starts with a tickle. "Who here doesn't like to be tickled?"

A good number of hands shot up. "Yet you laugh," he said, flashing a goofy grin. "You experience some pleasurable reaction even as you resist and say you don't like it."

If you really stop to think about it, McGraw continued, it's a complex and fascinating phenomenon. If someone touches you in certain places in a certain way, it prompts an involuntary but pleasurable physiological response. Except, of course, when it doesn't. "When does tickling cease to be funny?" McGraw asked. "When you try to tickle yourself … Or if some stranger in a trench coat tickles you." The audience cracked up. He was working the room like a stand-up comic.

Many would assert that this tickling conundrum is the perfect evidence that humor is utterly relative. There may be many types of humor, maybe as many kinds as there are variations in laughter, guffaws, hoots, and chortles. But McGraw doesn't think so. He has devised a simple, Grand Unified Theory of humor—in his words, "a parsimonious account of what makes things funny." McGraw calls it the benign violation theory, and he insists that it can explain the function of every imaginable type of humor. And not just what makes things funny, but why certain things *aren't* funny. "My theory also explains nervous laughter, racist or sexist jokes, and toilet humor," he told his fellow humor researchers.

Coming up with an essential description of comedy isn't just an intellectual exercise. If the BVT actually is an unerring predictor of what's funny, it could be invaluable. It could have warned Groupon that its Super Bowl ad making light of Tibetan injustices would bomb. *The Love Guru* could've been axed before production began. Podium banter at the Oscars could be less excruciating. If someone could crack the humor code, they could get very rich. Or at least tenure.

It's a wintry February afternoon in Boulder and a 53-year-old tech worker named Kyle fires up a joint he obtained from a medical marijuana dispensary. After smoking his medicine and waiting 15 minutes for it to take effect, Kyle opens a 10-page printed questionnaire. He sees a Photoshopped image of a man picking his nose so vigorously that his finger pokes out of his eye socket. "To what extent is this picture funny?" the survey asks, inviting Kyle to rate the picture on a scale of 0 to 5. He gives it a 3.

Kyle is one of 50 or so marijuana aficionados who have volunteered to take part in a study run by McGraw's laboratory at CU-Boulder—the Humor Research Lab, or HuRL for short. Founded in 2009, HuRL is unorthodox, to put it mildly, even for academia.

But McGraw is doing serious enough work at HuRL to have earned two grants from the Marketing Science Institute, a nonprofit funded by respectable organizations like Bank of America, Pfizer, and IBM. The professor and a team of seven student researchers have been asking test subjects to gauge whether *Hot Tub Time Machine* is funnier if you sit close to the screen or far away. They show subjects a YouTube video of a guy driving a motorcycle into a fence over and over again to see when it ceases to be amusing.

The medical marijuana patients will help HuRL researchers answer a momentous question: Can smoking pot make things more funny? The answer may seem forehead-smackingly obvious, but according to McGraw it's impossible to know for sure without applying scientific rigor. "Your intuition often leads you astray," he says. "It's only within the lab that you can set different theories against one another." McGraw believes that the tests will ultimately prove that marijuana does in fact make broad sight gags more funny. But he needs more data before he can be certain. He's begun soliciting input from more potheads through Amazon.com's crowdsourcing marketplace, Mechanical Turk.

McGraw didn't set out to become a humorologist. His background is in marketing and consumer decisionmaking, especially the way moral transgressions and breaches of decorum affect the perceived value of things. For instance, he studied a Florida megachurch that tarnished its reputation when it tried to reward attendees with glitzy prizes. The church's promise to raffle off a Hummer H2 to some lucky congregant was met with controversy in the community—what the hell did that have to do with eternal salvation? But when McGraw related the anecdote at presentations, it prompted laughter—a holy Hummer!— rather than repulsion. This confused him.

"It had never crossed my mind that moral violations could be amusing," McGraw says. He became increasingly preoccupied with the conundrum he saw at the heart of humor: Why do people laugh at horrible things like stereotypes, embarrassment, and pain? Basically, why is Sarah Silverman funny?

Philosophers had pondered this sort of question for millennia, long before anyone thought to examine it in a lab. Plato, Aristotle, and Thomas Hobbes posited the superiority theory of humor, which states that we find the misfortune of others amusing. Sigmund Freud espoused the relief theory, which states that comedy is a way for people to release suppressed thoughts and emotions safely. Incongruity theory, associated with Immanuel Kant, suggests that jokes happen when people notice the disconnect between their expectations and the actual payoff.But McGraw didn't find any of these explanations satisfactory. "You need to add conditions to explain particular incidents of humor, and even then they still struggle," he says. Freud is great for jokes about bodily functions. Incongruity explains Monty Python. Hobbes nails Henny Youngman. But no single theory explains all types of comedy. They also short-circuit when it comes to describing why some things *aren't* funny. McGraw points out that killing a loved one in a fit of rage would be incongruous, it would assert superiority, and it would release pent-up tension, but it would hardly be hilarious.

These glaringly incomplete descriptions of humor offended McGraw's need for order. His duty was clear. "A single theory provides a set of guiding principles that make the world a more organized place," he says.

McGraw and Caleb Warren, a doctoral student, presented their elegantly simple formulation in the August 2010 issue of the journal *Psychological Science*. Their paper,

"Benign Violations: Making Immoral Behavior Funny," cited scores of philosophers, psychologists, and neuroscientists (as well as Mel Brooks and Carol Burnett). The theory they lay out: "Laughter and amusement result from violations that are simultaneously seen as benign." That is, they perceive a violation— "of personal dignity (e.g., slapstick, physical deformities), linguistic norms (e.g., unusual accents, malapropisms), social norms (e.g., eating from a sterile bedpan, strange behaviors), and even moral norms (e.g., bestiality, disrespectful behaviors)"—while simultaneously recognizing that the violation doesn't pose a threat to them or their worldview. The theory is ludicrously, vaporously simple. But extensive field tests revealed nuances, variables that determined exactly how funny a joke was perceived to be.

McGraw had his HuRL team present scenarios to hundreds of CU-Boulder students. (Some were bribed with candy bars to participate.) Multiple versions of scenarios were formulated, a few too anodyne to be amusing and some too disgusting for words. Ultimately, McGraw determined that funniness could be predicted based on how committed a person is to the norm being violated, conflicts between two salient norms, and psychological distance from the perceived violation.

The ultimate takeaway of McGraw's paper was that the evolutionary purpose of laughter and amusement is to "signal to the world that a violation is indeed OK." Building on the work of behavioral neurologist V. S. Ramachandran, McGraw believes that laughter developed as an instinctual way to signal that a threat is actually a false alarm—say, that a rustle in the bushes is the wind, not a saber-toothed tiger. "Organisms that could separate benign violations from real threats benefited greatly," McGraw says.

The professor was able to plug the BVT into every form of humor. Dirty jokes violate social norms in a benign way because the traveling salesmen and farmers' daughters that populate them are not real. Punch lines make people laugh because they gently violate the expectations that the jokes set up. The BVT also explains Sarah Silverman, McGraw says; the appalling things that come out of her mouth register as benign because she seems so oblivious to their offensiveness, and "because she's so darn cute." Even tickling, long a stumbling block for humor theorists, appears to fit. Tickling yourself can't be a violation, because you can't take yourself by surprise. Being tickled by a stranger in a trench coat isn't benign; it's creepy. Only tickling by someone you know and trust can be a benign violation.

McGraw and the HuRL team continue to test the theory even as they begin to deploy it in the real world. They've partnered with mShopper, a mobile commerce service, to see whether BVT-tested humor can make text-message product offers more compelling. They've also launched FunnyPoliceReports.com, which aggregates law enforcement dispatches that are likely to amuse readers, such as a woman who called the cops when she was sold fake cocaine.

If the website sounds sort of like FAIL Blog, that's no accident. McGraw knows Ben Huh, CEO of the Cheezburger Network, who has been using HuRL's findings to help determine what content and features have the potential to be the next big meme. The lolcats baron points to a recent post about a priest cracking down on cell phones in church after a parishioner's "Stayin' Alive" ringtone went off during a funeral. "The benign violation theory applies to that," Huh says. "I'm a guy who makes his living off of Internet humor, and McGraw's model fits really well. He's just a lot more right than anyone else."

❖

The conference in San Antonio was the first time McGraw presented his theory to other humor researchers. His well-honed delivery gets a lot of laughs, but his theory ultimately receives the same polite applause as everything else. There are no stunned looks of amazement in the audience, no rumblings of a field torn asunder.

Maybe it's because a discipline that can't even agree on what to call the response elicited by humor isn't ready for a universal theory of humor. At this point, there's still no single way to measure it. (The International Society for Humor Studies lists 14 tests and scales for measuring humor, from the Multidimensional Sense of Humor Scale to the Humorous Behavior Q-Sort Deck.)

The BVT also has its fair share of detractors. ISHS president Elliott Oring says, "I didn't see many big differences between this theory and the various formulations of incongruity theory." Victor Raskin, founder of the academic journal *Humor: International Journal of Humor Research*, is more blunt: "What McGraw has come up with is flawed and bullshit—what kind of a theory is that?" To his mind, the BVT is a "very loose and vague metaphor," not a functional formula like $E=mc^2$. He's also quick to challenge McGraw's standing in the tight-knit community of scholarship: "He is not a humor researcher; he has no status."

McGraw's lecture did impress Robert Mankoff, cartoon editor at *The New Yorker*, who also gave a presentation in San Antonio. (Fun fact: *New Yorker* cartoons must endure the infamous rigors of the magazine's fact-checkers; just because a cartoon bluebird can talk doesn't mean it shouldn't resemble a genuine *Sialia*.) After the symposium ended, he offered to provide HuRL with thousands of caption-contest entries to examine. Mankoff says he admires McGraw's work, "and I admire him even more for having the balls to take his theory on the road as stand-up." But he also has a caveat for McGraw and other humor scientists: "All these theories are so general that they're of no use when you're trying to craft a good cartoon." He cites one that he's particularly fond of, an illustration of a Swiss Army knife featuring nothing but corkscrews. The caption reads "French Army knife." No Venn diagram, he says, has ever produced a joke like that.

It's a half hour to showtime at Denver's Paramount Theatre and McGraw is milling around in the lobby, hoping to get green-room access to the comedian Louis CK. The prof is convinced that his theory works in the lab, and he's increasingly interested in testing it in the wild. Kind words from Huh and Mankoff are fine, but the endorsement of a comedian with his own eponymous show on cable would be invaluable. CK is one of McGraw's favorites. "I am fascinated by his ability to make things funny that I wouldn't have thought could be funny," McGraw says, "how he portrays his role as a father in an unflattering way."

McGraw gets the go-ahead, and with curtain time closing in, he's soon sitting in the presence of his idol. The comedian slumps into a chair, the toll of weeks on the road apparent on his face. Knowing that he has only a few minutes, McGraw gives a nutshell version of his well-honed spiel. He lays out the BVT and describes the tickling conundrum that killed at the humor symposium. But CK cuts him off. "I don't think it's that simple," he says, directing as much attention to a preshow ham sandwich as to McGraw. "There are thousands of kinds of jokes. I just don't believe that there's one explanation."

Oof, tough room. His research dismissed, McGraw casts about for another subject of inquiry. Luckily, he'd polled fellow attendees for questions while waiting for an audience with CK. "A woman in the lobby wants to know how big your penis is," he says.

CK cracks the faintest of smiles, shakes his head. "I am not going to answer that."

"I wouldn't either," McGraw says. With a chuckle he adds, "But I've heard that if you don't answer that, it means it's small."

The silence that follows is so thick you could pound in a nail and hang a painting from it. That last remark is a violation, and it isn't benign. McGraw changes the subject again. "So, you're friends with Chris Rock?" he says. He wonders whether CK could ask Rock for seed funding, even offering to rename his facility the Chris Rock Humor Research Lab (CRoHuRL?).

"No," CK says. This time, there's no smile.

Sensing that his time is up, McGraw heads for the door. He did get one valuable takeaway: "My approach to this sort of research needs to be more professional."

When the show begins a bit later, Louis CK has shed all vestiges of his preshow reticence. It takes only a couple of jokes about slavery to get McGraw chuckling in his front-row seat. By the time the comedian describes having a bizarre dream about Gene Hackman, the professor is completely overcome. His body jerks uncontrollably as he emits a series of deep, braying laughs that end with a little nasal honk. This is full-on mirth.

The other people in the theater are also in hysterics. They don't know exactly why, and maybe it doesn't matter.

WHAT?

1. Briefly explain McGraw's benign violation theory of humor.
2. Do you see value in trying to figure out why we perceive some things in the world to be funny? Explain your response.
3. What benefits do you see in using humor to broach difficult subjects? Do you think some topics can or should never be made funny? Explain your response.

WHAT ELSE? WHAT'S NEXT?

4. McGraw and his co-researcher have encountered resistance to their work from within the field of humor studies. Using this article as a starting point, research some of the objections to the benign violation theory and explain how other theorists approach the topic of humor.

WHO CARES?

5. Explain the role that audience plays in the analysis of humorous texts. Can you think of any jokes or other humorous texts that are universally funny?

Comedian, actor, and author Patton Oswalt's (@pattonoswalt) first book,
Zombie Spaceship Wasteland came out last year. Oswalt wrote this essay,
in which he explains his plan for reviving the nerd-dom subculture ruined by
mainstream acceptance, for the January 2011 issue of Wired *magazine.*

BEFORE YOU READ
Research the term "geek culture" and explain at least three different interpretations
that you find. Then, think about why the definitions you find are different—even if
they vary only slightly.

WAKE UP, GEEK CULTURE. TIME TO DIE.
Patton Oswalt *with contributions by* **Chris Buck**

I'm not a nerd. I used to be one, back 30 years ago when *nerd* meant something. I entered the '80s immersed, variously, in science fiction, Dungeons & Dragons, and Stephen King. Except for the multiple-player aspect of D&D, these pursuits were not "passions from a common spring," to quote Poe.

I can't say that I ever abided nerd stereotypes: I was never alone or felt outcast. I had a circle of friends who were similarly drawn to the exotica of pop culture (or, at least, what was considered pop culture at the time in northern Virginia)—Monty Python, post-punk music, comic books, slasher films, and video games. We were a sizable clique. The terms *nerd* and *geek* were convenient shorthand used by other cliques to categorize us. But they were thin descriptors.

In Japan, the word *otaku* refers to people who have obsessive, minute interests—especially stuff like anime or videogames. It comes from a term for "someone else's house"—otaku live in their own, enclosed worlds. Or, at least, their lives follow patterns that are well outside the norm. Looking back, we were American otakus. (Of course, now all America is otaku—which I'm going to get into shortly. But in order to do so, we're going to hang out in the '80s.)

I was too young to drive or hold a job. I was never going to play sports, and girls were an uncrackable code. So, yeah—I had time to collect every Star Wars action figure, learn the Three Laws of Robotics, memorize Roy Batty's speech from the end of *Blade Runner*, and classify each monster's abilities and weaknesses in TSR Hobbies' *Monster Manual*. By 1987, my friends and I were waist-deep in the hot honey of adolescence. Money and cars and, hopefully, girls would follow, but not if we spent our free time learning the names of the bounty hunters' ships in *The Empire Strikes Back*. So we each built our own otakuesque thought-palace, which we crammed with facts and nonsense—only now, the thought-palace was nicely appointed, decorated neatly, the information laid out on deep mahogany shelves or framed in gilt. What once set us apart, we hoped, would become a lovable quirk.

Our respective nerdery took on various forms: One friend was the first to get his hands on early bootlegs of Asian action flicks by Tsui Hark and John Woo, and he never looked back. Another started reading William Gibson and peppered his conversations with cryptic (and alluring) references to "cyberspace." I was ground zero for the "new wave" of mainstream superhero comics—which meant being right there for Alan Moore, Frank Miller, and Neil Gaiman. And like my music-obsessed pals, who passed around the cassette of Guns n' Roses' *Live ?!*@ Like a Suicide* and were thus prepared for the shock wave of *Appetite for Destruction*, I'd devoured Moore's run on *Swamp Thing* and thus eased nicely into his *Watchmen*. I'd also read the individual issues of Miller's *Daredevil: Born Again* run, so when *The Dark Knight Returns* was reviewed by *The New York Times*, I could say I saw it coming. And I'd consumed so many single-issue guest-writing stints of Gaiman's that when he was finally given *The Sandman* title all to himself, I was first in line and knew the language.

Admittedly, there's a chilly thrill in moving with the herd while quietly being tuned in to something dark, complicated, and unknown just beneath the topsoil of popularity. Something about which, while we moved *with* the herd, we could share a wink and a nod with two or three other similarly connected herdlings.

When our coworkers nodded along to Springsteen and Madonna songs at the local Bennigan's, my select friends and I would quietly trade out-of-context lines from Monty Python sketches—a thieves' cant, a code language used for identification. We needed it, too, because the essence of our culture—our "escape hatch" culture—would begin to change in 1987.

That was the year the final issue of *Watchmen* came out, in October. After that, it seemed like everything that was part of my otaku world was out in the open and up for grabs, if only out of context. I wasn't seeing the hard line between "nerds" and "normals" anymore. It was the last year that a T-shirt or music preference or pastime (Dungeons & Dragons had long since lost its dangerous, Satanic, suicide-inducing street cred) could set you apart from the surface dwellers. Pretty soon, being the only person who was into something didn't make you outcast; it made you ahead of the curve and someone people were quicker to befriend than shun. Ironically, surface dwellers began repurposing the symbols and phrases and tokens of the erstwhile outcast underground.

Fast-forward to now: Boba Fett's helmet emblazoned on sleeveless T-shirts worn by gym douches hefting dumbbells. The *Glee* kids performing the songs from *The Rocky Horror Picture Show*. And Toad the Wet Sprocket, a band that took its name from a Monty Python riff, joining the permanent soundtrack of a night out at Bennigan's. Our below-the-topsoil passions have been rudely dug up and displayed in the noonday sun. *The Lord of the Rings* used to be ours and *only* ours simply because of the sheer goddamn thickness of the books. Twenty years later, the entire cast and crew would be trooping onstage at the Oscars to collect their statuettes, and replicas of the One Ring would be sold as bling.

The topsoil has been scraped away, forever, in 2010. In fact, it's been dug up, thrown into the air, and allowed to rain down and coat everyone in a thin gray-brown mist called the Internet. Everyone considers themselves otaku about something—whether it's the mythology of *Lost* or the minor intrigues of *Top Chef*. *American Idol* inspires—if not in depth, at least in length and passion—the same number of conversations as does *The Wire*. There are no more hidden thought-palaces—they're easily accessed websites, or Facebook pages with thousands of fans. And I'm not going to bore you with the step-by-step specifics of how it happened. In the timeline of the upheaval, part of the graph should be interrupted by the words *the Internet*. And now here we are.

The problem with the Internet, however, is that it lets anyone become otaku about anything *instantly*. In the '80s, you couldn't get up to speed on an entire genre in a weekend. You had to wait, month to month, for the issues of *Watchmen* to come out. We couldn't BitTorrent the latest John Woo film or digitally download an entire decade's worth of grunge or hip hop. Hell, there were a few weeks during the spring of 1991 when we couldn't tell whether Nirvana or Tad would be the next band to break big. Imagine the terror!

But then reflect on the advantages. Waiting for the next issue, movie, or album gave you time to reread, rewatch, reabsorb whatever you loved, so you brought your own idiosyncratic love of that thing to your thought-palace. People who were obsessed with *Star Trek* or the *Ender's Game* books were all obsessed with the same object, but its light shone differently on each person. Everyone had to create in their mind unanswered questions or what-ifs. What if Leia, not Luke, had become a Jedi? What happens *after* Rorschach's journal is found at the end of *Watchmen*? What the hell was *The Prisoner* about?

None of that's necessary anymore. When everyone has easy access to their favorite diversions and every diversion comes with a rabbit hole's worth of extra features and deleted scenes and hidden hacks to tumble down and never emerge from, then we're all just adding to an ever-swelling, soon-to-erupt volcano of trivia, re-contextualized and forever rebooted. We're on the brink of Etewaf: Everything That Ever Was—Available Forever.

I know it sounds great, but there's a danger: Everything we have today that's cool comes from someone wanting more of something they loved in the past. Action figures, videogames, superhero movies, iPods: All are continuations of a love that wanted more. Ever see action figures from the '70s, each with that same generic Anson Williams body and one-piece costume with the big clumsy snap on the back? Or played Atari's *Adventure*, found the secret room, and thought, that's it? Can we all admit the final battle in *Superman II* looks like a local commercial for a personal-injury attorney? And how many people had their cassette of the *Repo Man* soundtrack eaten by a Walkman?

Now, with everyone more or less otaku and everything *immediately* awesome (or, if not, just as immediately rebooted or recut as a hilarious YouTube or Funny or Die spoof), the old inner longing for more or better that made our present pop culture so amazing is dwindling. *The Onion*'s A.V. Club—essential and transcendent in so many ways—has a weekly feature called Gateways to Geekery, in which an entire artistic subculture—say, anime, H. P. Lovecraft, or the Marx Brothers—is mapped out so you can become otaku on it but avoid its more tedious aspects.

Here's the danger: That creates weak otakus. Etewaf doesn't produce a new generation of artists—just an army of sated consumers. Why create anything new when there's a mountain of freshly excavated pop culture to recut, repurpose, and manipulate on your iMovie? *The Shining* can be remade into a comedy trailer. Both movie versions of the Joker can be sent to battle each another. The Dude is in *The Matrix*The coming decades—the 21st-century's '20s, '30s, and '40s—have the potential to be one long, unbroken, recut spoof in which everything in *Avatar* farts while Keyboard Cat plays eerily in the background.

But I prefer to be optimistic. I choose hope. I see Etewaf as the Balrog, the helter-skelter, the A-pop-alypse that rains cleansing fire down onto the otaku landscape, burns away the chaff, and forces us to start over with only a few thin, near-meatless scraps on which to build.

In order to save pop culture future, we've got to make the present pop culture suck, at least for a little while. Why create anything new when there's a mountain of pop culture to recut, repurpose, and manipulate on iMovie?

How do we do this? How do we bring back that sweet longing for more that spawned *Gears of War*, the *Crank* films, and the entire Joss Whedon oeuvre? Simple: We've got to speed up the process. We've got to stoke the volcano. We've got to catalog, collate, and cross-pollinate. We must bring about **Etewaf**, and soon.

It has already started. It's all around us. VH1 list shows. *Freddy vs. Jason*. Websites that list the 10 biggest sports meltdowns, the 50 weirdest plastic surgeries, the 200 harshest nut shots. *Alien vs. Predator*. Lists of fails, lists of boobs, lists of deleted movie scenes. Entire TV seasons on iTunes. An entire studio's film vault, downloadable with a click. Easter egg scenes of wild sex in *Grand Theft Auto*. Hell, *Grand Theft Auto*, period. And yes, I know that a lot of what I'm listing here seems like it's outside of the "nerd world" and part of the wider pop culture. Well, I've got news for you—pop culture *is* nerd culture. The fans of *Real Housewives of Hoboken* watch, discuss, and absorb their show the same way a geek watched *Dark Shadows* or obsessed over his eighth-level half-elf ranger character in Dungeons & Dragons. It's the method of consumption, not what's on the plate.

Since there's no going back—no reverse on the out-of-control locomotive we've created—we've got to dump nitro into the engines. We need to get serious, and I'm here to outline my own personal fantasy: We start with lists of the best lists of boobs. Every Beatles song, along with every alternate take, along with every cover version of every one of their songs and every alternate take of every cover version, all on your chewing-gum-sized iPod nano. *Goonies vs. Saw*. Every book on your Kindle. Every book *on* Kindle on every Kindle. *The Human Centipede* done with the cast of *The Hills* and directed by the Coen brothers.

That's when we'll reach Etewaf singularity. Pop culture will become self-aware. It will happen in the A.V. Club first: A brilliant Nathan Rabin column about the worst Turkish rip-offs of American comic book characters will suddenly begin writing its own comments, each a single sentence from the sequel to *A Confederacy of Dunces*. Then a fourth and fifth season of *Arrested Development*, directed by David Milch of *Deadwood*, will appear suddenly in the TV Shows section of iTunes. Someone BitTorrenting a Crass bootleg will suddenly find their hard drive crammed with Elvis Presley's "lost" grunge album from 1994. And everyone's TiVo will record *Ghostbusters III*, starring Peter Sellers, Lee Marvin, and John Candy.

This will last only a moment. We'll have one minute before pop culture swells and blackens like a rotten peach and then explodes, sending every movie, album, book, and TV show flying away into space. Maybe tendrils and fragments of them will attach to asteroids or plop down on ice planets light-years away. A billion years after our sun burns out, a race of intelligent ice crystals will build a culture based on dialog from *The Princess Bride*. On another planet, intelligent gas clouds will wait for the yearly passing of the "Lebowski" comet. One of the rings of Saturn will be made from blurbs for the softcover release of *Infinite Jest*, twirled forever into a ribbon of effusive praise.

But back here on Earth, we'll enter year zero for pop culture. All that we'll have left to work with will be a VHS copy of *Zapped!*, the soundtrack to *The Road Warrior*, and Steve Ditko's eight-issue run on *Shade: The Changing Man*. For a while—maybe a generation— pop culture pastimes will revolve around politics and farming.

But the same way a farmer has to endure a few fallow seasons after he's overplanted, a new, richer loam will begin to appear in the wake of our tilling. From *Zapped!* will arise a telekinesis epic from James Cameron. Paul Thomas Anderson will do a smaller, single- character study of a man who can move matchbooks with his mind and how he uses this skill to pursue a casino waitress. Then the Coen brothers will veer off, doing a movie about pyrokenesis set in 1980s Cleveland, while out of Japan will come a subgenre of telekinetic horror featuring pale, whispering children. And we'll build from there—precognition, telepathy, and, most radically, normal people falling in love and dealing with jobs and life. Maybe also car crashes.

The Road Warrior soundtrack, all Wagnerian strings and military snare drums, will germinate into a driving, gut-bucket subgenre called waste-rock. And, as a counterpoint, flute-driven folk. Then there'll be the inevitable remixes, mashups, and pirated-only releases. A new Beatles will arise, only they'll be Iranian.

Shade: The Changing Man will become the new *Catcher in the Rye*. Ditko's thin- fingered art will appear on lunch boxes, T-shirts, and magazine covers. Someone will write an even thinner, sparser, simpler version called *Shade*. Someone else will write a 1,000- page meditation about Shade's home planet. Eventually, someone will try to kill the Iranian John Lennon with a hat, based on one panel from issue 3. A whole generation of authors under 20 will have their love—or disgust—of these comics to thank for their careers.

So the topsoil we're coated in needs to wash away for a while. I want my daughter to have a 1987 the way I did and experience the otaku thrill. While everyone else is grooving on the latest Jay-Z, *5 Gallons of Diesel*, I'd like her to share a secret look with a friend, both of them hip to the fact that, from Germany, there's a bootleg MP3 of a group called Dr. Cali-gory, pioneers of superviolent line-dancing music. And I want to her to enjoy that secret look for a little while before Dr. Cali-gory's songs get used in commercials for cruise lines.

Etewaf now!

■ WHAT?

1. Based on Oswalt's essay, define the following terms and explain how they are important to the argument: nerd, geek, otaku, etewaf.
2. Compare Oswalt's essay with Jeanette Winterson's "Imagination and Reality." How does each explain the role of imagination and creativity in developing and sustaining a culture? What part does passion play, according to the two essays? Do you think Winterson would be persuaded by Oswalt's argument? Why or why not?
3. What, according to Oswalt, is the problem with "weak otakus" and the "army of sated consumers" that they might spawn?

■ WHAT ELSE? WHAT'S NEXT?

4. Working with a group of classmates, develop definitions of "culture" and "subculture" that apply to your lives. Make sure you include in your response examples of each and an explanation of the relationship between the two.
5. Look online to find responses to Oswalt's essay (you might start by visiting the page where it was originally published). Look through these and summarize what others have said about the essay. Do you see any patterns?

■ WHO CARES?

6. Visit the website for the magazine that published Oswalt's essay. What, based on the content of the site—including advertisements and links— can you deduce about the magazine's and the website's readership? Based on this analysis and on your reading of the essay, explain who you think Oswalt is trying to reach and whether (and how) he is successful.

Mark Slouka, a novelist and a contributing editor of Harper's Magazine, *has taught creative writing at several universities, among them the University of Chicago and Columbia University. In this essay, which appeared in* Harper's *in 2009, Slouka argues that a humanities-based education is vital to understanding the world so that we might "shape how it shapes us" and "make our condition more human, not less." After reading Slouka's essay, turn your attention to David Leonhardt's piece that follows for a different accounting of the value of education.*

BEFORE YOU READ———————————————————————————

Near the beginning of his essay, Slouka quotes then-District of Columbia Schools Chancellor Michelle Rhee as saying: "This is exactly what life is about. You get a paycheck every two weeks. We're preparing children for life." Slouka makes his position on this concept of education clear. But what is yours? Write a paragraph or two in which you explain why you have decided to continue your education beyond high school.

DEHUMANIZED: WHEN MATH AND SCIENCE RULE THE SCHOOL Mark Slouka

Many years ago, my fiancée attempted to lend me a bit of respectability by introducing me to my would-be mother-in-law as a future Ph.D. in literature. From Columbia, I added, polishing the apple of my prospects. She wasn't buying it. "A doctor of philosophy," she said. "What're you going to do, open a philosophy store?"

A spear is a spear—it doesn't have to be original. Unable to come up with a quick response and unwilling to petition for a change of venue, I ducked into low-grade irony. More like a stand, I said. I was thinking of stocking Kafka quotes for the holidays, lines from Yeats for a buck-fifty.

And that was that. I married the girl anyway. It's only now, recalling our exchange, that I can appreciate the significance—the poetry, really—of our little *pas de deux*. What we unconsciously acted out, in compressed, almost haiku-like form (*A philosophy store? / I will have a stand / sell pieces of Auden at two bits a beat*), was the essential drama of American education today.

It's a play I've been following for some time now. It's about the increasing dominance—scratch that, the unqualified triumph—of a certain way of seeing, of reckoning value. It's about the victory of whatever can be quantified over everything that can't. It's about the quiet retooling of American education into an adjunct of business, an instrument of production.

The play's almost over. I don't think it's a comedy.

■ State of the Union

Then there's amortization,
the deadliest of all;
amortization
of the heart and soul.
        —Vladimir Mayakovsky

Despite the determinisms of the day, despite the code-breakers, the wetware specialists, the patient unwinders of the barbed wire of our being, this I feel is true: That we are more nurture than nature; that what we are taught, generally speaking, is what we become; that torturers are made slowly, not minted in the womb. As are those who resist them. I believe that what rules us is less the material world of goods and services than the immaterial one of whims, assumptions, delusions, and lies; that only by studying this world can we hope to shape how it shapes us; that only by attempting to understand what used to be called, in a less embarrassed age, "the human condition" can we hope to make our condition more human, not less.

All of which puts me, and those in the humanities generally, at something of a disadvantage these days. In a visible world, the invisible does not compute; in a corporate culture, hypnotized by quarterly results and profit margins, the gradual sifting of political sentiment is of no value; in a horizontal world of "information" readily convertible to product, the verticality of wisdom has no place. Show me the spreadsheet on skepticism.

You have to admire the skill with which we've been outmaneuvered; there's something almost chess-like in the way the other side has narrowed the field, neutralized lines of attack, co-opted the terms of battle. It's all about them now; every move we make plays into their hands, confirms their values. Like the narrator in Mayakovsky's "Conversation with a Tax Collector About Poetry," we're being forced to account for ourselves in the other's idiom, to argue for "the place of the poet / in the workers' ranks." It's not working.

What is taught, at any given time, in any culture, is an expression of what that culture considers important. That much seems undebatable. How "the culture" decides, precisely, on what matters, how openly the debate unfolds—who frames the terms, declares a winner, and signs the check—well, that's a different matter. Real debate can be short-circuited by orthodoxy, and whether that orthodoxy is enforced through the barrel of a gun or backed by the power of unexamined assumption, the effect is the same.

In our time, orthodoxy is economic. Popular culture fetishizes it, our entertainments salaam to it (how many millions for sinking that putt, accepting that trade?), our artists are ranked by and revered for it. There is no institution wholly apart. Everything submits; everything must, sooner or later, pay fealty to the market; thus cost-benefit analyses on raising children, on cancer medications, on clean water, on the survival of species, including—in the last, last analysis—our own. If humanity has suffered under a more impoverishing delusion, I'm not aware of it.

That education policy reflects the zeitgeist shouldn't surprise us; capitalism has a wonderful knack for marginalizing (or co-opting) systems of value that might pose an alternative to its own. Still, capitalism's success in this case is particularly elegant: by bringing education to heel, by forcing it to meet its criteria for "success," the market is well on the way to controlling a majority share of the one business that might offer a competing product, that might question its assumptions. It's a neat trick. The problem, of course, is that by its success we are made vulnerable. By downsizing what is most dangerous (and most essential) about our education, namely the deep civic function of the arts and the humanities, we're well on the way to producing a nation of employees, not citizens. Thus is the world made safe for commerce, but not safe.

We're pounding swords into cogs. They work in Pyongyang too.

■ Capital Investment

This is exactly what life is about. You get a paycheck every two weeks. We're preparing children for life.
—District of Columbia Schools Chancellor Michelle Rhee

The questions are straightforward enough: What do we teach, and why? One might assume that in an aspiring democracy like ours the answers would be equally straightforward: We teach whatever contributes to the development of autonomous human beings; we teach, that is, in order to expand the census of knowledgeable, reasoning, independent-minded individuals both sufficiently familiar with the world outside themselves to lend their judgments compassion and breadth (and thereby contribute to the political life of the nation), and sufficiently skilled to find productive employment. In that order. Our primary function, in other words, is to teach people, not tasks; to participate in the complex and infinitely worthwhile labor of forming citizens, men and women capable of furthering what's best about us and forestalling what's worst. It is only secondarily—one might say incidentally—about producing workers.

I'm joking, of course. Education in America today is almost exclusively about the GDP. It's about investing in our human capital, and please note what's modifying what. It's about ensuring that the United States does not fall from its privileged perch in the global economy. And what of our political perch, you ask, whether legitimate or no? Thank you for your question. Management has decided that the new business plan has no room for frivolity. Those who can justify their presence in accordance with its terms may remain; the rest will be downsized or discontinued. Alternatively, since studies have suggested that humanizing the workspace may increase efficiency, a few may be kept on, the curricular equivalent of potted plants.

If facetiousness is an expression of frustration, it does not necessarily follow that the picture it paints is false. The force of the new dispensation is stunning. Its language is the language of banking—literal, technocratic, wincingly bourgeois; its effects are visible, quite literally, everywhere you look.

Start with the newspaper of record. In an article by *New York Times* editorialist Brent Staples, we learn that the American education system is failing "to produce the fluent writers required by the new economy." No doubt it is, but the sin of omission here is both telling and representative. Might there be another reason for seeking to develop fluent writers? Could clear writing have some relation to clear thinking and thereby have, perhaps, some political efficacy? If so, neither Staples nor his readers, writing in to the *Times,* think to mention it. Writing is "a critical strategy that we can offer students to prepare them to succeed in the workplace." Writing skills are vital because they promote "clear, concise communications, which all business people want to read." "The return on a modest investment in writing is manifold," because "it strengthens competitiveness, increases efficiency and empowers employees." And so on, without exception. The chairman of the country's largest association of college writing professors agrees. The real problem, he explains, is the SAT writing exam, which "hardly resembles the kinds of writing people encounter in business or academic settings." An accountant, he argues, needs to write "about content related to the company and the work in which she's steeped." It's unlikely that she'll "need to drop everything and give the boss 25 minutes on the Peloponnesian War or her most meaningful quotation."

What's depressing here is that this is precisely the argument heard at parent-teacher meetings across the land. When is the boss ever going to ask my Johnny about the Peloponnesian War? As if Johnny had agreed to have no existence outside his cubicle of choice. As if he wasn't going to inherit the holy right of gun ownership and the power of the vote.

At times, the failure of decent, intelligent, reliably humane voices like Staples's to see the political forest for the economic trees is breathtaking. In a generally well-intentioned editorial, Staples's colleague at the *Times,* Nicholas Kristof, argues that we can't "address poverty or grow the economy" unless we do something about the failure of our schools. So far, so good, though one might quibble that addressing poverty and growing the economy are not the same thing.

But never mind, because the real significance of the failure of our schools is soon made manifest. "Where will the workers come from," Kristof worries, "unless students reliably learn science and math?" If our students "only did as well as those in several Asian countries in math and science, our economy would grow 20 percent faster." The problem, though, is that although our school system was once the envy of all (a "first-rate education," we understand by this point, is one that grows the economy), now only our white suburban schools are "comparable to those in Singapore, which may have the best education system in the world."

Ah, Singapore. You'll hear a good deal about Singapore if you listen to the chorus of concern over American education. If only we could be more like Singapore. If only our education system could be as efficient as Singapore's. You say that Singapore might not be the best model to aspire to, that in certain respects it more closely resembles Winston Smith's world than Thomas Jefferson's? What does that have to do with education?

And the beat goes on. Still another *Times* editorialist, Thomas Friedman, begins a column on the desperate state of American education by quoting Bill Gates. Gates, Friedman informs us, gave a "remarkable speech" in which he declared that "American high schools are obsolete." This is bad, Friedman says. Bill Gates is telling us that our high schools, "even when they are working exactly as designed—cannot teach our kids what they need to know today."

What *do* our kids need to know today? As far as Friedman is concerned, whatever will get them hired by Bill Gates. "Let me translate Mr. Gates's words," he writes. What Mr. Gates is saying is: "If we don't fix American education, I will not be able to hire your kids." Really worried now, Friedman goes to talk to Lawrence Summers, who explains that "for the first time in our history," we're facing "competition from low-wage, high-human-capital communities, embedded within India, China and Asia." The race is on. In order to thrive, Summers says, we will "have to make sure that many more Americans can get as far ahead as their potential will take them," and quickly, because India and China are coming up on the inside. It's "not just about current capabilities," Friedman concludes, by this point quoting the authors of *The Only Sustainable Edge,* "it's about the relative pace and trajectories of capability-building."

Sustainable edges. Returns on capital investment. Trajectories of capability-building. What's interesting here is that everyone speaks the same language, everyone agrees on the meaning of the terms. There's a certain country-club quality to it. We're all members. We understand one another. We understand that the capabilities we should be developing are the capabilities that will "get us ahead." We understand that Bill Gates is a logical person to talk to about education because billionaire capitalists generally know something about running a successful business, and American education is a business whose products (like General Motors', say), are substandard, while Singapore's are kicking ass. We understand that getting ahead of low-wage, high-human-capital communities will allow us "to thrive."

Unlike most country clubs, alas, this one is anything but exclusive; getting far enough beyond its gates to ask whether that last verb might have another meaning can be difficult. Success means success. To thrive means to thrive. The definitions of "investment," "accountability," "value," "utility" are fixed and immutable; they are what they are. Once you've got that down, everything is easy: According to David Brooks (bringing up the back of my *Times* parade), all we need to do is make a modest investment in "delayed gratification skills." Young people who can delay gratification can "master the sort of self-control that leads to success"; they "can sit through sometimes boring classes" and "perform rote tasks." As a result, they tend to "get higher SAT scores," gain acceptance to better colleges, and have, "on average, better adult outcomes."[1]

A little of this can go a long way, and there's a lot of it to be had. When it comes to education in America, with very few exceptions, this is the conversation and these are its terms. From the local PTA meeting to the latest Presidential Commission on Education, the only subject under discussion, the only real criterion for investment—in short, the alpha and omega of educational policy—is jobs. Is it any wonder, then, that our educational priorities should be determined by business leaders, or that the relationship between industry and education should increasingly resemble the relationship between a company and its suppliers, or that the "suppliers" across the land, in order to make payroll, should seek to please management in any way possible, to demonstrate the viability of their product?

Consider the ritual of addressing our periodic "crises in education." Typically, the call to arms comes from the business community. We're losing our competitive edge, sounds the cry. Singapore is pulling ahead. The president swings into action. He orders up a blue-chip commission of high-ranking business executives (the 2006 Commission on the Future of Higher Education, led by business executive Charles Miller, for example) to study the problem and come up with "real world" solutions.

Thus empowered, the commission crunches the numbers, notes the depths to which we've sunk, and emerges into the light to underscore the need for more accountability. To whom? Well, to business, naturally. To whom else would you account? And that's it, more or less. Cue the curtain. The commission's president answers all reasonable questions. Eventually, everyone goes home and gets with the program.

It can be touching to watch supporters of the arts contorting themselves to fit. In a brochure produced by The Education Commission of the States, titled "The Arts, Education and the Creative Economy," we learn that supporting the arts in our schools is a good idea because "state and local leaders are realizing that the arts and culture are vital to economic development." In fact, everyone is realizing it. Several states "have developed initiatives that address the connections between economic growth and the arts and culture." The New England states have formed "the Creative Economy Council . . . a partnership among business, government and cultural leaders." It seems that "a new economy has emerged . . . driven by ideas, information technology and globalization" (by this point, the role of painting, say, is getting a bit murky), and that "for companies and organizations to remain competitive and cutting edge, they must attract and retain individuals who can think creatively."

You can almost see the air creeping back into the balloon: We can do this! We can make the case to management! We can explain, as Mike Huckabee does, that trimming back funding for the arts would be shortsighted because "experts and futurists warn that the future economy will be driven by the 'creative class.'" We can cite "numerous studies" affirming that "a student schooled in music improves his or her SAT and ACT scores in math," and that "creative students are better problem solvers . . . a trait the business world begs for in its workforce." They'll see we have some value after all. They'll let us stay.

To show that they, too, get it, that like Cool Hand Luke they've "got their mind right," our colleges and universities smile and sway with the rest. In "A Statement by Public Higher Education Leaders Convened by Carnegie Corporation of New York"—to pick just one grain from a sandbox of evidence—we learn that our institutions of higher learning are valuable because they can "help revitalize our nation's economy and educate and train the next generations of Americans to meet the challenges of global competition." Both the tune and the lyrics should be familiar by now. "The present economic crisis requires an investment in human capital." And where better to invest than in our colleges and universities, whose innovative researchers "invented the technologies that have fueled economic progress and enhanced America's economic competitiveness." The statement's undersigned, representing colleges and universities from California to New Hampshire, conclude with a declaration of faith: "Leaders of the country's public higher education sector are committed to create a long-term plan *to serve the nation by enhancing public universities' critical role in creating jobs,* increasing graduates, enhancing the quality and skills of the workforce, and assisting in national technology and energy initiatives through research."

Think of my italics above as a hand going up in the back of the audience. Could there exist, buried under our assumptions, another system of value? Could our colleges and universities have another, truly "critical role," which they ignore at our peril? A role that might "serve the nation" as well?

■ The Case for the Humanities

Only the educated are free.
—Epictetus

Rain does not follow the plow. Political freedom, whatever the market evangelists may tell us, is not an automatic by-product of a growing economy; democratic institutions do not spring up, like flowers at the feet of the magi, in the tire tracks of commerce. They just don't. They're a different species. They require a different kind of tending.

The case for the humanities is not hard to make, though it can be difficult—to such an extent have we been marginalized, so long have we acceded to that marginalization—not to sound either defensive or naive. The humanities, done right, are the crucible within which our evolving notions of what it means to be fully human are put to the test; they teach us, incrementally, endlessly, not what to do but how to be. Their method is confrontational, their domain unlimited, their "product" not truth but the reasoned search for truth, their "success" something very much like Frost's momentary stay against confusion.

They are thus, inescapably, political. Why? Because they complicate our vision, pull our most cherished notions out by the roots, flay our pieties. Because they grow uncertainty. Because they expand the reach of our understanding (and therefore our compassion), even as they force us to draw and redraw the borders of tolerance. Because out of all this work of self-building might emerge an individual capable of humility in the face of complexity; an individual formed through questioning and therefore unlikely to cede that right; an individual resistant to coercion, to manipulation and demagoguery in all their forms. The humanities, in short, are a superb delivery mechanism for what we might call democratic values. There is no better that I am aware of.

This, I would submit, is value—and cheap at the price. This is utility of a higher order. Considering where the rising arcs of our ignorance and our deference lead, what could represent a better investment? Given our fondness for slogans, our childlike susceptibility to bullying and rant, our impatience with both evidence and ambiguity, what could earn us, over time, a better rate of return?

Like a single species taking over an ecosystem, like an elephant on a see-saw, the problem today is disequilibrium. Why is every Crisis in American Education cast as an economic threat and never a civic one? In part, because we don't have the language for it. Our focus is on the usual economic indicators. There are no corresponding "civic indicators," no generally agreed-upon warning signs of political vulnerability, even though the inability of more than two thirds of our college graduates to read a text and draw rational inferences could be seen as the political equivalent of runaway inflation or soaring unemployment.

If we lack the language, and therefore the awareness, to right the imbalance between the vocational and the civic, if education in America—despite the heroic efforts of individual teachers—is no longer in the business of producing the kinds of citizens necessary to the survival of a democratic society, it's in large part because the time-honored civic function of our educational system has been ground up by the ideological mills of both the right and the left into a radioactive paste called values education and declared off-limits. Consider the irony. Worried about indoctrination, we've short-circuited argument. Fearful of propaganda, we've taken away the only tools that could detect and counter it. "Values" are now the province of the home. And the church. How convenient for the man.

How does one "do" the humanities value-free? How does one teach history, say, without grappling with what that long parade of genius and folly suggests to us? How does one teach literature other than as an invitation, a challenge, a gauntlet—a force fully capable of altering not only what we believe but how we see? The answer is, of course, that one doesn't. One teaches some toothless, formalized version of these things, careful not to upset anyone, despite the fact that upsetting people is arguably the very purpose of the arts and perhaps of the humanities in general.

Even a desiccated, values-free version of the humanities has the potential to be dangerous, though, because it is impossible to say where the individual mind might wander off to while reading, what unsettling associations might suggest themselves, what unscripted, unapproved questions might float to the surface. It's been said before: in the margins of the page, over the course of time, for the simple reason that we shape every book we read and are slightly shaped by it in turn, we become who we are. Which is to say individuals just distinct enough from one another in our orientation toward "the truth" or "the good" to be difficult to control.

This "deep" civic function of the humanities, not easily reducible to the politics of left or right but politically combustible nonetheless, is something understood very well by totalitarian societies, which tend to keep close tabs on them, and to circumscribe them in direct proportion to how stringently the population is controlled. This should neither surprise nor comfort us. Why would a repressive regime support a force superbly designed to resist it? Rein in the humanities effectively enough—whether through active repression, fiscal starvation, or linguistic marginalization—and you create a space, an opportunity. Dogma adores a vacuum.

■ MATHANDSCIENCE

Nobody was ever sent to prison for espousing the wrong value for the Hubble constant.

—Dennis Overbye

Nothing speaks more clearly to the relentlessly vocational bent in American education than its long-running affair with math and science. I say "affair" because I am kind; in truth, the relationship is obsessive, exclusionary, altogether unhealthy. Whatever the question, math and science (so often are they spoken of in the same breath, they've begun to feel singular) are, or is, the answer. They make sense; they compute. They're everything we want: a solid return on capital investment, a proven route to "success." Everything else can go fish.

Do we detect a note of bitterness, a hint of jealousy? No doubt. There's something indecent about the way math and science gobble up market share. Not content with being heavily subsidized by both government and private industry and with serving as a revenue-generating gold mine for higher education (which pockets the profits from any patents and passes on research expenses to students through tuition increases—effectively a kind of hidden "science tax"), math and science are now well on the way to becoming the default choice for anyone having trouble deciding where to park his (or the taxpayers') money, anyone trying to burnish his no-nonsense educational bona fides, or, most galling, anyone looking for a way to demonstrate his or her civic pride.

But let me be clear: I write this not to provide tinder to our latter-day inquisitors, ever eager to sacrifice the spirit of scientific inquiry in the name of some new misapprehension. That said, I see no contradiction between my respect for science and my humanist's discomfort with its ever-greater role in American culture, its ever-burgeoning coffers, its often dramatically anti-democratic ways, its symbiotic relationship with government, with industry, with our increasingly corporate institutions of higher learning. Triply protected from criticism by the firewall of their jargon (which immediately excludes the non-specialist and assures a jury of motivated and sympathetic peers), their economic efficacy, and the immunity conferred by conveniently associated terms like "progress" and "advancement," the sciences march, largely untouched, under the banner of the inherently good. And this troubles me.

It troubles me because there are many things "math and science" do well, and some they don't. And one of the things they don't do well is democracy. They have no aptitude for it, no connection to it, really. Which hasn't prevented some in the sciences from arguing precisely the opposite, from assuming even this last, most ill-fitting mantle, by suggesting that science's spirit of questioning will automatically infect the rest of society.

In fact, it's not so. Science, by and large, keeps to its reservation, which explains why scientists tend to get in trouble only when they step outside the lab. That no one has ever been sent to prison for espousing the wrong value for the Hubble constant is precisely to the point. The work of democracy involves espousing those values that in a less democratic society *would* get one sent to prison. To maintain its "sustainable edge," a democracy requires its citizens to actually risk something, to test the limits of the acceptable; the "trajectory of capability-building" they must devote themselves to, above all others, is the one that advances the capability for making trouble. If the value you're espousing is one that could never get anyone, anywhere, sent to prison, then strictly democratically speaking you're useless.

All of this helps explain why, in today's repressive societies, the sciences do not come in for the same treatment as the humanities. Not only are the sciences, with a few notable exceptions, politically neutral; their specialized languages tend to segregate them from the wider population, making ideological contagion difficult. More importantly, their work, quite often, is translatable into "product," which any aspiring dictatorship recognizes as an unambiguous good, whereas the work of the humanities almost never is.

To put it simply, science addresses the outer world; the humanities, the inner one. Science explains how the material world is now for *all* men; the humanities, in their indirect, slippery way, offer the raw materials from which the individual constructs a self—a self *distinct* from others. The sciences, to push the point a bit, produce people who study things, and who can therefore, presumably, make or fix or improve these things. The humanities don't.

One might, then, reasonably expect the two, each invaluable in its own right, to operate on an equal footing in the United States, to receive equal attention and respect. Not so. In fact, not even close. From the Sputnik-inspired emphasis on "science and math" to the pronouncements of our recently retired "Education President" (the jury is still out on Obama), the call is always for more investment in "math and science." And then a little more. The "American Competitiveness Initiative" calls for doubling federal spending on basic research grants in the physical sciences over ten years, at a cost of $50 billion. The federal government is asked to pay the cost of finding 30,000 new math and science teachers. Senator Bill Frist pushes for grants for students majoring in math and science.

Whether the bias trickles down or percolates up, it's systemic. The New York City Department of Education announces housing incentives worth up to $15,000 to lure teachers "in math and science" to the city's schools. Classes in history and art and foreign languages are cut back to make room for their more practical, "rigorous" cousins. The Howard Hughes Medical Institute announces its selection of twenty new professors who will use their million-dollar grants to develop fresh approaches to teaching science. Nothing remotely comparable exists in the humanities.

Popular culture, meanwhile, plays backup, cementing bias into cliché. Mathandscience becomes the all-purpose shorthand for intelligence; it has that all-American aura of money about it. The tax collector, to recall Mayakovsky, runs the show.

■ State of Play

We want our students to take into their interactions with others, into their readings, into their private thoughts, depth of experience and a willingness to be wrong. Only a study of the humanities provides that.
                                    —Marcus Eure, English teacher, Brewster High School

No assessment of the marginalized role of the humanities today is possible without first admitting the complicity of those in the fold. Outmanned, out-funded, perpetually on the defensive, we've adapted to the hostile environment by embracing a number of survival strategies, among them camouflage, mimicry, and—altogether too believably—playing dead. None of these is a strategy for success.

Which is not to say that the performance is without interest. Happily ignoring the fact that the whole point of reading is to force us into an encounter with the other, our high schools and colleges labor mightily to provide students with mirrors of their own experience, lest they be made uncomfortable, effectively undercutting diversity in the name of diversity. Some may actually believe in this. The rest, unable or unwilling to make the hard argument to parents and administrators, bend to the prevailing winds, shaping their curricula to appeal to the greatest number, a strategy suitable to advertising, not teaching.

Since it's not just the material itself but what's done with it that can lead to trouble (even the most staid "classic," subjected to the right pressures by the right teacher, can yield its measure of discomfort), how we teach must be adjusted as well. Thus we encourage anemic discussions about Atticus Finch and racism but race past the bogeyman of miscegenation; thus we debate the legacy of the founders but tactfully sidestep their issues with Christianity; thus we teach *Walden,* if we teach it at all, as an ode to Nature and ignore its full-frontal assault on the tenets of capitalism. Thus we tiptoe through the minefield, leaving the mines intact and loaded.

Still, the evasions and capitulations made by those on the secondary-school level are nothing compared with the tactics of their university counterparts, who, in a pathetic attempt to ape their more successful colleagues in the sciences, have developed over time their own faux-scientific, isolating jargon, robbing themselves of their greatest virtue, their ability to influence (or infect) the general population. Verily, self-erasure is rarely this effective, or ironic. Not content with trivializing itself through the subjects it considers important, nor with having assured its irrelevance by making itself unintelligible, the study of literature, for example, has taken its birthright and turned it into a fetish; that is, adopted the word "politics"—God, the irony!—and cycled it through so many levels of metaphorical interpretation that nothing recognizable remains except the husk. Politically neuter, we now sing the politics of ocularcentric rhetoric. Safe in our tenured nests, we risk neither harm nor good.

If the self-portrait is unflattering, I can't apologize. Look at us! Look at how we've let the fashion for economic utility intimidate us, how we simultaneously cringe and justify ourselves, how we secretly despise the philistines, who could never understand the relevance of our theoretical flea circus, even as we rush, in a paroxysm of class guilt, to offer classes in Introductory Sit-Com Writing, in Clown 500, in *Seinfeld*; classes in which "everyone is a winner." Small wonder the sciences don't respect us; we shouldn't respect us.

And what have we gained from all this? Alas, despite our eagerness to fit in, to play ball, we *still* don't belong, we're still ignored or infantilized. What we've earned is the prerogative of going out with a whimper. Marginalized, self-righteous, we just keep on keeping on, insulted that no one returns our calls, secretly expecting no less.

Which makes it all the more impressive that there remain individuals who stubbornly hold the line, who either haven't noticed or don't care what's happened to the humanities in America, who daily fight for relevance and achieve it. Editors, journalists, university and foundation presidents, college and high school teachers, they neither apologize nor equivocate nor retreat a single inch. Seen rightly, what could be more in the American grain?

Let the few stand for the many. Historian Drew Faust seems determined to use her bully pulpit as president of Harvard to call attention to the distorting force of our vocational obsession. Don Randel, president of the Mellon Foundation, the single largest supporter of the humanities in America, speaks of the humanities' unparalleled ability to force us into "a rigorous cross-examination of our myths about ourselves." Poet, classicist, and former dean of humanities at the University of Chicago Danielle Allen patiently advances the argument that the work of the humanities doesn't reveal itself within the typical three- or five-year cycle, that the humanities work on a fifty-year cycle, a hundred-year cycle.

Public high school English teacher Marcus Eure, meanwhile, teaching in the single most conservative county in New York State, labors daily "to dislocate the complacent mind," to teach students to parse not only what they are being told but how they are being told. His course in rhetoric—enough to give a foolish man hope—exposes the discrete parts of effective writing and reading, then nudges students to redefine their notion of "correct" to mean precise, logical, nuanced, and inclusive. His unit on lying asks students to read the "Yes, Virginia, there is a Santa Claus" letter from *The Sun* and Stephanie Ericsson's "The Ways We Lie," then consider how we define lying, whether we condone it under certain circumstances, how we learn to do it. "Having to treat Santa Claus as a systemic lie," Eure notes, "even if we can argue for its necessity, troubles a lot of them."

As does, deliberately, Eure's unit on torture, which uses Michael Levin's "The Case for Torture" to complicate the "us versus them" argument, then asks students to consider Stephen King's "Why We Crave Horror Movies" and David Edelstein's article on "torture porn," "Now Playing at Your Local Multiplex." Inevitably, the question of morality comes up, as does the line between catharsis and desensitization. Eure allows the conversation to twist and complicate itself, to cut a channel to a video game called *The Sims*, which many of the students have played and in which most of them have casually killed the simulated human beings whose world they controlled. The students argue about what it means to watch a movie like *Saw,* what it means to live in a society that produces, markets, and supports such products.

Challenged to defend the utility of his classes, Eure asks his questioner to describe an American life in which the skills he is trying to inculcate are unnecessary. Invariably, he says, it becomes obvious that there is no such life, that *every* aspect of life—every marriage, every job, every parent-teacher meeting—hinges in some way on the ability to understand and empathize with others, to challenge one's beliefs, to strive for reason and clarity.

Muzzle the trumpets, still the drums. The market for reason is slipping fast. The currency of ignorance and demagoguery is daily gathering strength. The billboards in the Panhandle proclaim god, guns and guts made america free. Today, the Marcus Eures of America resemble nothing so much as an island ecosystem, surrounded by the times. Like that ecosystem, they are difficult, unamenable, and necessary, and, also like that ecosystem, their full value may not be fully understood until they've disappeared, forcing us into a bankruptcy none of us wish to contemplate.

Perhaps there's still time to reinstate the qualifier to its glory, to invest our capital in what makes us human.

Note

[1] There's something almost sublime about this level of foolishness. By giving his argument a measured, mathematical air (the students only achieve better adult outcomes "on average"), Brooks hopes that we will overlook both the fact that his constant (success) is a

variable and that this terms are way unequal, as the kids might say. One is reminded of the scene in the movie *Proof* in which the mathematician played by Anthony Hopkins, sliding into madness, begins a proof with "Let X equal the cold." Let higher SAT scores equal better adult outcomes.

■ WHAT?

1. Develop a definition of "the humanities" that you think would satisfy Slouka, based on your reading of his essay. Make sure you include a brief discussion of the function of the humanities—what it is they do for us— in your response. How does this compare with your own thinking about the humanities? Do you see them the same way Slouka does?

2. As part of his argument, Slouka writes that the humanities "teach us, incrementally, endlessly, not what to do but how to be." What does he mean by this? How do you think the humanities can teach us "how to be"?

3. Slouka acknowledges that "there are many things 'math and science' do well," but argues that one of the things "they don't do well is democracy." How does he explain the humanities' aptitude for "doing democracy"? How does he contrast this with the kinds of things that math and science do well?

■ WHAT ELSE? WHAT'S NEXT?

4. Research the various opinions that political leaders—the governor, cabinet members, legislators—in South Carolina have about higher education and the humanities. Summarize these opinions and then respond to one of them (you might agree, disagree, or something else).

5. Compose a brief argument in favor of increased funding for classes in the fine arts as part of a complete college education. Then, compose an argument that takes the opposite position. Find at least one reliable source to use in each argument.

■ WHO CARES?

6. Who do you think is Slouka's intended audience? Why do you think this? Are there others you think would benefit from reading Slouka's essay?

> *David Leonhardt is a columnist for the business section of* The New York Times, *where this piece was published in the summer of 2011. As you read Leonhardt's column, think about the kind of argument he makes for attending college and compare his reasoning with that of Mark Slouka, in the essay preceding this one.*

BEFORE YOU READ

Research the University of South Carolina website to determine how the school markets itself to potential students. What does USC say it can do for students? What kinds of outcomes does the university tout? Does the university talk about preparation for jobs? Life skills? Other things? How do different colleges and programs within the university try to recruit students?

EVEN FOR CASHIERS, COLLEGE PAYS OFF   David Leonhardt

Almost a century ago, the United States decided to make high school nearly universal. Around the same time, much of Europe decided that universal high school was a waste. Not everybody, European intellectuals argued, should go to high school.

It's clear who made the right decision. The educated American masses helped create the American century, as the economists Claudia Goldin and Lawrence Katz have written. The new ranks of high school graduates made factories more efficient and new industries possible.

Today, we are having an updated version of the same debate. Television, newspapers and blogs are filled with the case against college for the masses: It saddles students with debt; it does not guarantee a good job; it isn't necessary for many jobs. Not everybody, the skeptics say, should go to college.

The argument has the lure of counterintuition and does have grains of truth. Too many teenagers aren't ready to do college-level work. Ultimately, though, the case against mass education is no better than it was a century ago.

The evidence is overwhelming that college is a better investment for most graduates than in the past. A new study even shows that a bachelor's degree pays off for jobs that don't require one: secretaries, plumbers and cashiers. And, beyond money, education seems to make people happier and healthier.

"Sending more young Americans to college is not a panacea," says David Autor, an M.I.T. economist who studies the labor market. "Not sending them to college would be a disaster."

The most unfortunate part of the case against college is that it encourages children, parents and schools to aim low. For those families on the fence—often deciding whether a student will be the first to attend—the skepticism becomes one more reason to stop at high school. Only about 33 percent of young adults get a four-year degree today, while another 10 percent receive a two-year degree.

So it's important to dissect the anti-college argument, piece by piece. It obviously starts with money. Tuition numbers can be eye-popping, and student debt has increased significantly. But there are two main reasons college costs aren't usually a problem for those who graduate.

First, many colleges are not very expensive, once financial aid is taken into account. Average net tuition and fees at public four-year colleges this past year were only about $2,000 (though Congress may soon cut federal financial aid).

Second, the returns from a degree have soared. Three decades ago, full-time workers with a bachelor's degree made 40 percent more than those with only a high-school diploma. Last year, the gap reached 83 percent. College graduates, though hardly immune from the downturn, are also far less likely to be unemployed than non-graduates.

Skeptics like to point out that the income gap isn't rising as fast as it once was, especially for college graduates who don't get an advanced degree. But the gap remains enormous—and bigger than ever. Skipping college because the pace of gains has slowed is akin to skipping your heart medications because the pace of medical improvement isn't what it used to be.

The Hamilton Project, a research group in Washington, has just finished a comparison of college with other investments. It found that college tuition in recent decades has delivered an inflation-adjusted annual return of more than 15 percent. For stocks, the historical return is 7 percent. For real estate, it's less than 1 percent.

Another study being released this weekend—by Anthony Carnevale and Stephen J. Rose of Georgetown—breaks down the college premium by occupations and shows that college has big benefits even in many fields where a degree is not crucial.

Construction workers, police officers, plumbers, retail salespeople and secretaries, among others, make significantly more with a degree than without one. Why? Education helps people do higher-skilled work, get jobs with better-paying companies or open their own businesses.

This follows the pattern of the early 20th century, when blue- and white-collar workers alike benefited from having a high-school diploma.

When confronted with such data, skeptics sometimes reply that colleges are mostly a way station for smart people. But that's not right either. Various natural experiments—like teenagers' proximity to a campus, which affects whether they enroll—have shown that people do acquire skills in college.

Even a much-quoted recent study casting doubt on college education, by an N.Y.U. sociologist and two other researchers, was not so simple. It found that only 55 percent of freshmen and sophomores made statistically significant progress on an academic test. But the margin of error was large enough that many more may have made progress. Either way, the general skills that colleges teach, like discipline and persistence, may be more important than academics anyway.

None of this means colleges are perfect. Many have abysmal graduation rates. Yet the answer is to improve colleges, not abandon them. Given how much the economy changes, why would a high-school diploma forever satisfy most citizens' educational needs?

Or think about it this way: People tend to be clear-eyed about this debate in their own lives. For instance, when researchers asked low-income teenagers how much more college graduates made than non-graduates, the teenagers made excellent estimates. And in a national survey, 94 percent of parents said they expected their child to go to college.

Then there are the skeptics themselves, the professors, journalists and others who say college is overrated. They, of course, have degrees and often spend tens of thousands of dollars sending their children to expensive colleges.

I don't doubt that the skeptics are well meaning. But, in the end, their case against college is an elitist one—for me and not for thee. And that's rarely good advice.

■ WHAT?

1. After completing Leonhardt's column, read Mark Slouka's "Dehumanized" (if you haven't already). Then, write two fifty- to 100-word summaries, one of Slouka's argument and the other of Leonhardt's.

■ WHAT ELSE? WHAT'S NEXT?

2. With college costs rising and more students and parents falling into debt as a result, debate over the value of higher education has increased lately. Find two sources that you think are reliable and that present arguments that contradict Slouka's and/or Leonhardt's. In your response, explain why you think the sources you have chosen are reliable, then summarize the sources and compare them with what Slouka and/or Leonhardt say.

3. Research the following questions and write a response summarizing your findings: What percentage of high school graduates go to college each year in the United States? How about in South Carolina? What do those who don't go to college after high school do instead?

■ WHO CARES?

4. Using the information you gathered for the "Before you read" exercise at the beginning of this article, compose a brief analysis of USC's intended audience and its strategy for connecting with that audience. Make sure you support any assertions you make with evidence from the USC website.

CHAPTER **2** | # Reading Response

IMAGE 2.1
"I cannot see an outstretched hand and not put something there," Elie Wiesel says in "Am I My Brother's Keeper?" How do you respond when you see others in need?

What do we owe our fellow human beings? Compassion? Understanding? Action? What are our obligations when we learn of injustice or tragedy, whether it's across the hall or a world away? Is joining a Facebook group enough? Or wearing a bracelet? Or are we obligated to take action? Clearly, these are difficult questions. And as the essays and articles in this chapter show, answering them in meaningful ways is a complicated process.

Holocaust survivor and Nobel laureate Elie Wiesel is a teacher, a writer, and one of the world's most persistent and eloquent voices for peace and moral responsibility. His best-known book is Night, *a memoir about his time in a Nazi death camp as a child, though he has written scores of other books, speeches, and essays. Richard D. Heffner is a professor of communications and public policy at Rutgers University and the producer and longtime host of the radio program* The Open Mind. *The text that follows is from the 2001 book* Conversations with Elie Wiesel.

BEFORE YOU READ———————————————————————————
Write a paragraph or two in which you explain your thinking about the difference between information and knowledge and the responsibilities that each carries with it.

AM I MY BROTHER'S KEEPER?
Elie Wiesel and Richard D. Heffner

Elie, this is a question that perhaps is not understood too well by a good many people in our time. What does it mean to you?

It is a question that Cain asked of God, having killed Abel: "Am I my brother's keeper?" And the answer, of course, is, we are all our brothers' keepers. Why? Either we see in each other brothers, or we live in a world of strangers. I believe that there are no strangers in God's creation. There are no strangers in a world that becomes smaller and smaller. Today I know right away when something happens, whatever happens, anywhere in the world. So there is no excuse for us not to be involved in these problems. A century ago, by the time the news of a war reached another place, the war was over. Now people die and the pictures of their dying are offered to you and to me while we are having dinner. Since I know, how can I not transform that knowledge into responsibility? So the key word is "responsibility." That means I must keep my brother.

Yet it seems that despite the fact that we live in an age of rapid, immediate communications, we know so little about what is happening to our brothers.

We are careless. Somehow life has been cheapened in our own eyes. The sanctity of life, the sacred dimension of every minute of human existence, is gone. The main problem is that there are so many situations that demand our attention. There are so many tragedies that need our involvement. Where do you begin? We know *too* much. No, let me correct myself. We are *informed* about too many things. Whether information is transformed into knowledge is a different story, a different question.

But we are in the world of communication. Nothing has caught the fantasy, the imagination, of the world these last years as communication has. So many radio stations, so many television stations, so many publications, so many talk shows. It's always more and more information that is being fed. And I'm glad that these things are happening, because I think people should be informed.

However, let us say that on a given day a tragedy has taken place. For a day we are all glued to the television. Three days later, we are still glued. A week later, another tragedy occurs and then the first tragedy is overshadowed by the next one. I remember when I saw the hungry children of Biafra for the first time. I didn't sleep. I tried everything I could to address the problem—to write articles and call up people and organize activities to send food to those children. But if you had shown those pictures for a whole month, by the second month people would not have been moved by them. What happened to the information there? It is still stored, but yet we don't act upon it, because we are summoned by the current event.

There seems to be almost an inevitability about what you are describing, because extending and perfecting the means of communication is certainly a major thrust of our times.

I would like to be able to say to my students that there are so many things in the world that solicit your attention and your involvement that you can choose any one. I really don't mind where that particular event is taking place. But I would like my students to be fully involved in *some* event. Today, for instance, they will say, "I go to zone A, and then I go to zone B." But as long as zone A has not been covered fully, as long as it is a human problem, I don't think we can abandon it. All the areas must be covered. I would not want to live in a world today in which a person or a community, because of color, because of religion, because of ethnic origin, or because of social conditions, would feel totally neglected or abandoned. There must be someone who speaks to and for that group, every group.

Is there any question but that we have seen the faces of those who suffer and yet we are not moved sufficiently?

I plead your case: In 1945, all the newspapers and magazines in the United States showed the pictures of the concentration camps. And yet for another five years, displaced persons remained in those camps. How many were allowed to come to America? They were told, "Those who want to go to Palestine, good. All the others, come and we shall give you what you really need most—human warmth?" Furthermore, look at what happened in South Africa. Apartheid was a blasphemy. We saw these white racists killing. I remember images that moved me to anger—images of funeral processions. Whites had killed blacks because they were black. And then the whites disrupted the funerals, killing more black people. That is the limit of endurance, the limit of any tolerance. We should have protested louder. And yet we didn't.

We talk about a world that is, perhaps, too much with us, so much so that there is no time to focus. How do you help your students deal with that?

> I mentioned Cain and Abel. Why did Cain kill Abel? It is not because he was jealous. According to the text that we read and comment upon, it was because Cain spoke to Abel, his younger brother, and he told him of his pain, of his abandonment, of his solitude—that God didn't want to accept his offering. In the Bible it's said, "And Cain spoke to Abel." And we don't even know whether Abel listened. There was no dialogue. So the first act, really, among brothers, was a lack of communication.

> So what I would teach my students is communication. I believe in dialogue. I believe if people talk, and they talk sincerely, with the same respect that one owes to a close friend or to God, something will come out of that, something good. I would call it presence. I would like my students to be present whenever people need a human presence. I urge very little upon my students, but that is one thing I do. To people I love, I wish I could say, "I will suffer in your place." But I cannot. Nobody can. Nobody should. I can be present, though. And when you suffer, you need a presence.

When you say "communicate," you mean to accept communication, don't you?

> To be able to give and to receive at the same time.

Does it seem to you that we're not listening to the world around us, that we're so much involved in our individual pursuits?

> Absolutely. I think the noise around us has become deafening. People talk but nobody listens. People aren't afraid of that silence. Have you seen those youngsters and not-so-young people go around in the street with a Walkman on their ears? They don't want to hear anything. They want to hear only their own music. Which is the same music, by the way, that they heard yesterday. It's a kind of repetition which is deafening. People don't want to hear the world. The world is, I think, in need of being heard.

Elie, I find that as I get older and older still, I so often find that I want to shut things out, because I can't focus on what needs to be focused on if I'm listening to everything. That seems to me to be where we began, in a sense.

> To me too, of course. So often I want to turn off everything and say, "Look, it's easier to talk about *Romeo and Juliet* than to talk about what's happening today anywhere in the world." Naturally. Because in that play, there is a text and there is a story. It's a story I can turn in any direction I want, really. You think that *Romeo and Juliet* is a story of love. It's a story of hate. So whatever subject I discuss, I can always turn it one way or another. It's familiar, graspable. I prefer to discuss Plato, naturally. But we must open our eyes, and—

I don't want to be a devil's advocate here. I understand the subjective need not to feel that I am my brother's keeper, the subjective need to shut out the pain—

> Sure. You couldn't take it. There is a need to remember, and it may last only a day or a week at a time. We cannot remember all the time. That would be impossible; we would be numb. If I were to remember all the time, I wouldn't be able to function. A person who is sensitive, always responding, always listening, always ready to receive someone else's pain … how can one live? One must forget that we die; if not, we wouldn't live.

So what do we do? Can we both attend to our own needs and to the various needs of our family and friends and still extend the notion of "Am I my brother's keeper?" way beyond Abel to the far points of the world?

> Perhaps we cannot, but we must try. Because we cannot, we must, even though Kant used to say, "We can, therefore we must." There is so much forgetfulness, so much indifference today, that we must **fight** it. We must fight for the sake of our own future. Is this the nature of human beings? Yes, it's part of our nature.
>
> I know it all seems like too much—even in our own city, New York. There is so much hate and so much mistrust and distrust that you wonder what can reach these people who live together, who can live together, who after all must live together. Where do you begin? Now, I always feel very strongly about the person who needs me. I don't know who that person is, but if the person needs me, I somehow must think of that person more than about myself. Why? Because I see my own life in him or her. I remember there were times when I needed people, and they were not there. If there is a governing precept in my life, it is that: If somebody needs me, I must be there.

When I ask the question that we began with—"Am I my brother's keeper?"—I most often receive a blank stare. Obviously that stare comes from people for whom the concept is, if not anathema, at least terribly foreign. More so now, don't you think?

> More so, because it involves us more deeply, because it goes further. If I say yes, then I have to do something about it. Then it really goes further than that: What does it mean? Who is my brother? It's a definition. Who is my brother? Is any person in the street my brother? Is a person in Somalia my brother? Is a person in Armenia my brother? Come on. If I say, "My brother," what do I mean? Have I seen them? Have I met them? So of course it could be a poetic expression, which means very little. But if you say that there are people in the world who need a brother, I will say, "Then I would like to be that brother." I don't always succeed, of course. I cannot. I am only an individual. I am alone, as you are alone. What can we do? We can be the brother to one person and then another person, to ten people, a hundred people in our whole life. Does it mean that we are brothers to everybody in the world? No, we cannot be. So even if we say that at least we can

tell a story about a brother who is looking for a brother and finds one, I think that's quite enough.

Yes, but aren't we experiencing a new kind of isolationism today? "Please, I can't solve these problems. Don't burden me with them. I'm not my brother's keeper!"

Today brothers become strangers. How do you expect strangers to become brothers? People who live in the same country today are strangers to one another. Take what's happened in Eastern Europe when the reactionary, exclusionary forces rule. They are neighbors, close to one another, but they see in each other a threat, a source of suspicion, a conqueror, not a brother. I think it's an historical phenomenon, which is worrisome.

Elie, what's the scriptural response to the question "Am I my brother's keeper?"

It is actually written as a dialogue, a scenario. Cain kills Abel. And God says to him, "Hi, good morning, how are you?" "All right," says Cain. Then God says, "By the way, where is your brother?" "I don't know," is the answer. "What do you mean, you don't know?" asks God. The answer: "I don't know. Am I my brother's keeper?" And then God says, "Come on, you know. I hear the voice of your brother's blood coming from the bowels of the earth. And you want to cheat me." The whole thing is a little bit silly. Does it mean that God didn't know where Abel was? God is playing a game. It's simply a story which I like to interpret as meaning that it is possible, unfortunately, throughout history, for two brothers to be brothers and yet to become the victim and/or the assassin of the other. However, I go one step further and I try to teach my students that we learn another lesson: Whoever kills, kills his brother.

Kills his brother or kills some part of himself?

It's possible, as I interpret it, that Cain and Abel were only one person. Cain killed Abel in Cain.

The Darwinian response to "Am I my brother's keeper?" is: "Of course not. If you pretend to be, you are interfering with natural selection." How do we build again upon the more ancient notion that indeed we are our brothers' keepers in many, many, ways?

But remember again, Cain was *not* his brother's keeper. He killed him.

But the question asked by God—

The question is good.

I know that's your specialty—questions.

I love questions, true. Because there is "quest" in "question." I love that. But today, I would like to put a face on words. When I see words, I see a face. When you speak about, let's say, "my brother's keeper," I see faces of people I knew or know, or people I've just seen this morning. Crossing the street, there is an old man with his hand outstretched. Now, am I his keeper?

Are you?

I must tell you that when I see that, I always feel strange. Because on the one hand, reason tells me that if I give him a dollar, he will go and buy alcohol. But then I say to myself, So what? Who am I to decide what he will do with the money that I give him? I cannot see an outstretched hand and not put something there. It's impossible. I know sometimes it's a weakness. I want to feel better, not to feel bad about it. But in fact I cannot.

You talked about communications before. If we don't "listen" by providing, presumably our brother will rise up and strike us down.

Or we would strike him down. Who are we? Children of Cain or children of Abel?

What's your answer?

You know, in my tradition, there is a marvelous way out. We are neither the children of Cain nor the children of Abel. There was a third son that Adam and Eve had afterward called Seth. And we are children of Seth. Which means you can be both.

Is that a cop-out?

No, not really. I think we are always oscillating between the temptation for evil and an attraction to goodness. It's enough for me to close my eyes and remember what men are capable of doing, to become terribly, profoundly, totally pessimistic, because they haven't changed. But then again, I open my eyes and close them again and say, "It would be absurd not to absorb some images and turn them into good consciousness." And it's up to us to choose. We are free to choose.

Don't you think that in our country at this time we're less concerned with, have less compassion for, those who suffer?

Absolutely. But it's really about what you are doing all your life. Can we really help more than the people around us? I go around the world, I travel, and whenever I hear about someone suffering, I try to go there and bear witness. That's my role, at least to bear witness. To say, "I've seen, I was there." Sometimes it inspires others to do what I am doing. More often than not, it doesn't.

If the moral imperative that you pose is one that seemingly is rejected in our time, why do you maintain this posture: "We must be caring, rather than careless?"

Because I don't have a position of power. Maybe that's the reason. You and I can afford to speak on moral issues. We don't have to make a decision on them. I am sure that if you had someone facing you here who had power, a senator or a member of the Cabinet, he or she would say, "We cannot do this or that." Why? "Because so much money would be needed. We don't have the money. Housing would be required. We don't have the housing." So I can afford, really, only to pose questions, and I know that.

Yes, but I'm convinced that you raise questions because you know what the right moral answers are.

That's true.

And you believe that by raising those questions, we will come to those answers.

I would like to think that. But even if I knew that I would not succeed, I would still raise those questions.

Why?

Otherwise, why am I here? I have the feeling, honestly, that my life is an offering. I could have died every minute between '44 and '45. So once I have received this gift, I must justify it. And the only way to justify life is by affirming the right to life of anyone who needs such affirmation.

Aren't you affirming, too, a conviction that something will be done in response to your question?

Here and there one person might listen and do something. Another person might listen and not do something. But I prefer to think, that here and there, there are small miracles. And there are: a good student, a good reader, a friend. I think we spoke about it years ago: Once upon a time, I was convinced I could change the whole world. Now I'm satisfied with small measures of grace. If we could open the door of one jail and free one innocent person … if I could save one child from starvation, believe me, to me it would be worth as much as, if not more than, all the work that I am doing and all the recognition that I may get for it.

You've spoken about those who put people in the death camps and brought about their deaths directly. You also speak about others who stood around indifferently. Do you feel that that is increasingly a theme in our own times?

Oh, more and more. I have the feeling that everything I do is a variation on the same theme. I'm simply trying to pull the alarm and say, "Don't be indifferent." Simply because I feel that indifference now is equal to evil. Evil, we know more or less what it is. But indifference to disease, indifference to famine, indifference to dictators, somehow it's here and we accept it. And I have always felt that the opposite of culture is not ignorance; it is indifference. And the opposite of morality is not immorality; it's again indifference. And we don't realize how indifferent we are simply because we cannot *not* be a little indifferent. We cannot think all the time of all the people who die. If, while I sit with you, I could see the children who are dying now while we talk, we wouldn't be able to talk, you and I. We would have to take a plane, go there and do something. We wouldn't be able to continue to try to be logical and rational.

You've said that if we ignore suffering, we become accomplices, as so many did during the Holocaust. Where is it written that we are not moral accomplices?

But we are.

But what can you expect of us?

Learning. After all, I don't compare situations. I don't compare any period to the period of the Second World War. But we have learned something. I have the feeling that sometimes it takes a generation for an event to awaken our awareness. But if now, so many years after that event, we are still behaving as though it did not occur, then what is the purpose of our work as teachers, as writers, as men and women who are concerned with one another's lives?

We have a tradition in this country of extending ourselves through our wealth, our material well-being. That tradition was set aside somewhat for some time. Do you think we will recapture it more fully?

I hope so. I hope that there will be enough students and teachers and writers and poets and communicators to bring back certain values. If a father cannot feed his children, then his human rights are violated. We are such a wealthy society. I think of the United States and am overtaken by gratitude. This nation has gone to war twice in its history to fight for other people's freedoms. Then, after the wars, consider the economic help, the billions of dollars that we have given to those poor countries ravaged, destroyed by the enemy. And even now, what would the free world do without us? We have always been ready to help.

So why not? It would show that we still have compassion. Now, those are nice words, I know. But what else do we have? We have words, and sometimes we try to act upon them.

WHAT?

1. Definitions play an important role in Wiesel's comments. What does he mean when he distinguishes between information and knowledge? How does he define responsibility? How does he link knowledge and responsibility? How does he define presence?
2. What role does listening play in Wiesel's world view?
3. How does Wiesel use references to God, religion, and religious texts in argument? Think especially about his audience and his ethos.
4. Weisel's comments about our responsibilities, and our desensitization to those responsibilities, implicate technology and the media. Technology allows us to know more than ever before about the sufferings of our "brothers and sisters" throughout the world, he argues, but it also can overwhelm us to the point that a kind of numbness sets in. How, according to Wiesel, can we deal with this conundrum?

WHAT ELSE? WHAT'S NEXT?

5. Wiesel sets the bar pretty high when he says that "we are all our brothers' keepers." How do you think this belief can play out in day-to-day life? As a starting point for your answer, research Wiesel's responses to specific events—wars, natural disasters, terrorist attacks—but also think about your responses.

WHO CARES?

6. Do you feel like Wiesel is speaking to you in his responses to Heffner's questions? Explain your answer.

Jacqueline Olds and Richard S. Schwartz are professors of psychiatry at Harvard Medical School. This piece, an excerpt from their book The Lonely American: Drifting Apart in the 21st Century, *was published by a magazine called the* Utne Reader *in the spring of 2009 as part of a package of articles and essays on "the golden age of re-engagement."*

BEFORE YOU READ

Define "friend." Include in your definition examples that fit the criteria you establish and examples that do not fit.

excerpt from
THE LONELY AMERICAN
Jacqueline Olds and Richard S. Schwartz

Americans in the 21st century devote more technology to staying connected than any society in history, yet somehow the devices fail us: Studies show that we feel increasingly alone. Our lives are spent in a tug-of-war between conflicting desires—we want to stay connected, and we want to be free. We lurch back and forth, reaching for both. How much of one should we give up in order to have more of the other? How do we know when we've got it right?

Two recent studies suggest that our society is in the midst of a dramatic and progressive slide toward disconnection. In the first, using data from the General Social Survey (GSS), Duke University researchers found that between 1985 and 2004 the number of people with whom the average American discussed "important matters" dropped from three to two. Even more stunning, the number of people who said there was *no one* with whom they discussed important matters tripled: In 2004 individuals without a single confidant made up a quarter of those surveyed. Our country is now filled with them.

The second study was the 2000 U.S. census. One of the most remarkable facts to emerge from this census is that one of four households consists of one person only. The number of one-person households has been increasing steadily since 1940, when they accounted for roughly 7 percent of households. Today, there are more people living alone than at any point in U.S. history. Placing the census data and the GSS side by side, the evidence that this country is in the midst of a major social change is overwhelming.

The significance of this increased aloneness is amplified by a very different body of research. There is now a clear consensus among medical researchers that social connection has powerful effects on health. Socially connected people live longer, respond better to stress, have more robust immune systems, and do better at fighting a variety of specific illnesses. Health and happiness, the two things we all say matter most, are certifiably linked to social connectedness.

Yet people in this country continue to drift apart. We need to know why.

First, let's look at the frenetic busyness of our lives. Americans may be the only people in the world who believe that each individual has the right and the capacity to fit whatever he or she wants into one small life. America is the original "You can be anything you want if you really try, and it's never too late to start trying!" country.

A good friend described the impact of busyness on our neighborhoods brilliantly: "Being neighborly used to mean visiting people. Now being nice to your neighbors means not bothering them." People's lives are shaped by how busy they are. Lives also are shaped by the respect and deference that is given to busyness—especially when it is valued above connection and community. If people are considerate, they assume that their neighbors are very busy and so try not to intrude on them. Dropping by is no longer neighborly. It is simply rude.

We treat socializing as if it's a frivolous diversion from the tasks at hand rather than an activity that is essential to our well-being as individuals and as a community. Soon our not bothering to call people (or even e-mail them) gets read by others as a sign that we are too caught up in the busy sweep of our own lives to have time for them. Our friends are not surprised. Our relatives may be indignant, but even they know how hard it is. An unspoken understanding develops. *It's too bad that we've lost touch, but that's just the way it is.*

The pace of everyday life may push us toward isolation, but there is a pull, as well: a very seductive picture of standing apart as a victory, not a retreat. Ever since Ralph Waldo Emerson wrote his famous essay and Henry David Thoreau set out to embody the concept in his cabin on Walden Pond, a long series of American icons have idealized the concept of self-reliance.

A culture's attitude toward the ties that bind pervasively shapes how its members interact with the world. These cultural blinders are made clear by a favorite question in cross-cultural research. People are asked to complete the sentence "I love my mother but . . ." In Western countries, the usual response is critical and distancing, something along the lines of "I love my mother but . . . she's just so difficult." In Southeast Asia, the usual response is "I love my mother but . . . I can never repay all that she has done for me." What makes the exercise so powerful is that most people cannot imagine the other response until they are presented with it. As self-reliant Americans, we are automatically prepared to question the value of our strongest bonds and to step away from them when necessary, relying instead on ourselves.

And when we do find ourselves isolated, by standing tall in our own minds, side by side with self-reliant heroes, each of us is suddenly no longer alone but part of a group—a great American tradition of lonesome cowboys and go-it-alone entrepreneurs. That psychological magic becomes the spoonful of sugar that makes painful experiences of finding ourselves left out easier to swallow. We may have isolated ourselves without entirely meaning to, but we also have ended up in a place that looks a lot like where we always knew that we were supposed to stand. On the outside, proud to be there.

It is also the last place on earth that a person would want to be.

The consequences of social disconnection are both extensive and remarkably diverse. To begin with, social support is an important determinant of overall health. It has significant effects on longevity, on an individual's response to stress, on immune functions, and on the incidence of a variety of specific illnesses. In diseases as varied as heart attacks and dementia, medical research repeatedly has found that social networks and social activity have a protective effect.

Social isolation damages ecological health, as well. The rising tide of single-person households strains the earth's resources. Additionally, in our consumer-oriented culture, a common solution to not having enough people in one's life is to turn to things, objects that will define one's identity through possessions rather than through one's place in a social world. (We once passed an elegant store in New York City whose name summed up the problem: More and More. We watched the shop from across the street, keeping a safe distance.)

Parents who don't have relatives or friends to help them gain perspective on their offspring are more likely to over-scrutinize the strange, quirky symptoms that are part of normal childhood development and to start wondering if their child will grow up to be a strange, quirky, and abnormal adult. This nervous, unchecked watching may be partially responsible for the fact that more American children and adolescents are on psychoactive medications than ever before.

Additionally, even seemingly trivial experiences of social exclusion have been shown to lead to an increase in aggressive behavior. Researchers hypothesize that aggressive impulses are normally held in check by social relationships and community norms—constraints that we usually refer to as a moral sense or conscience. People who lose the sense of belonging to a community are less likely to restrain their combative urges.

Unfortunately for many, the problem of feeling isolated and left out has an easy solution: Have a drink or a pill that makes you feel better. There is no need to call anyone up or make it clear that you're lonely. Some substances, like alcohol, even make it easier for shy and lonely strangers to enjoy one another's company. We frequently hear socially awkward college students say that they have to use alcohol or drugs because it's the only way they know to be part of a group. They are very clear that they are using substances to cure loneliness, but, as they poignantly explain, they can't find any other way. Sometimes, at least, the cure is successful and drug use does allow entry into a network of friends. But all too often, the drug itself becomes the friend.

Substance abuse is a complex phenomenon. It almost certainly does not have a single cause. But the substance abuse of a great many individuals is fueled by their experiences of social rejection and social isolation. The rising rate of depression and the rising numbers of both adults and children who use antidepressant medication are also fueled (again, in part) by experiences of social rejection and social isolation. These changes have occurred in the context of major social changes in the United States—as networks of confidants have fallen away, as the number of individuals living alone has skyrocketed, as social capital has declined. One study of 389 American cities found that deaths from alcoholism and suicide increase when people live alone. It would be foolish to ignore these correlations, even as we recognize that substance abuse is a complex phenomenon with more than one cause.

The truth is that if one can bring oneself to acknowledge loneliness, half the battle is won. It is not an easy half of a battle, however. When we began to talk about these ideas with friends, their first response was to passionately defend their styles of staying disconnected. Having chosen, like so many Americans, to step back, they explained how right the choice has been for them.

It is exactly that kind of reflexive claim—*we chose it, so it must make us happy*—that traps people. The argument that people are happier when they can spend more time alone seems to make so much sense, yet over the course of a life (and a country's life) it is simply wrong. The medical evidence tells us otherwise. The happiness research tells us otherwise. Statistics on crime and substance abuse tell us otherwise. Yes, we all need balance in our lives. We all need time away from the crowd. But we also need one another—and feeling left out, *even when one has chosen to be left out*, is not satisfying. It is painful.

Small daily choices—whether to go to a local store or order off the Internet, whether to pick up a ringing telephone or let it go to voice mail, whether to get together with a friend or pop in a DVD—end up defining one's social world. These little decisions are cumulative. You step back a little from others. They step back a little from you. You feel a little left out. Feeling left out, unexamined, leads you to step back further. But feeling left out, when it's examined, can lead people to work a little harder to reconnect.

Awareness of the risks of social disconnection can also change the bigger decisions that people make: whether to work from home or to work alongside others, whether to live alone or to live with others. People regularly make those choices based on what they think they are supposed to want, even when their own experiences tell them it is a mistake.

In the end, we as a nation must return to the ideals that shape the choices we make—the myths that we live by and the heroes of those myths in whose footsteps we long to follow. The ideal of the self-reliant outsider can supply a heroic gloss for a decision to give up on relationships, with all their difficulties, demands, and complications. It lets us spin an escape as an act of courage. But if we sell ourselves on the idea that our escapes ennoble us, we're much less likely to find our way back.

We need other heroes, those whose courage and creativity flow from their engagement and connection with others. And if we have stories about staying engaged that can also make us feel brave, if we include in our pantheon of heroes individuals who step into the fray of human entanglements, then we enhance both our awareness of the choices we make and our freedom to choose. We start to free the small but crucial decisions of everyday life from a set of glorious but too-rigid ideals that have not always served us well.

Loneliness was never the goal. It's just the spot where too many people wind up. We get stuck because the world we have wandered away from is so frantic and demanding. We get stuck because we have dreamed about lonesome heroes who stand defiantly apart. We get stuck because we feel left out and stop looking for ways back in. We should remember that the outside was not meant to be our final destination.

■ WHAT?

1. Summarize—accurately and thoroughly—the consequences of social isolation as Olds and Schwartz explain them in their essay. Do you agree with their conclusions? Explain your response.

2. Olds and Schwartz cite research from Duke University stating that "between 1985 and 2004 the number of people with whom the average American discussed 'important matters' dropped from three to two. . . . [and that] the number of people who said there was *no one* with whom they discussed important matters tripled" to a quarter of those surveyed. Do you see yourself or people you know in this portrait of social isolation? Based on your experience, do you think young adults have more than a couple of close confidantes?

3. The authors do not directly address the effects that social networking may have on isolation, but they do hint that the time we spend online takes away from time we could be interacting with people face to face. How do you think online social networking has affected personal relationships?

■ WHAT ELSE? WHAT'S NEXT?

4. What implicit argument do Olds and Schwartz make about the nature and value of face-to-face social networks versus connections made online? What evidence do they provide to support their argument? Conduct some research to find out what others have to say about this issue, and compare at least two other positions with the argument you identify in Olds and Schwartz.

5. Following the examples mentioned in the essay, complete the following statement: "I love my friends . . . but . . ." Then, complete either a, b, or c below. Make sure you explain your responses.
    a. "I love my cell phone . . . but . . ."
    b. "I love Facebook . . . but . . ."
    c. "I love my computer . . . but . . ."

> *Author, speaker, and blogger Courtney E. Martin has written five books, the most recent being* Project Rebirth: Survival and the Strength of the Human Spirit from 9/11 Survivors. *The following excerpt is from the introduction to her 2010 book* Do It Anyway: The New Generation of Activists, *a report on young people engaged in a variety of social justice projects.*

BEFORE YOU READ——————————————————————————

Write a brief response to the common claim that young Americans, in their late teens and twenties, are "entitled, self-absorbed, and apathetic." Make sure you include some examples to support your position.

excerpt from
DO IT ANYWAY: THE NEW GENERATION
OF ACTIVISTS Courtney E. Martin

Save the world.

Where were you the first time you heard those three little words?

It's a phrase that has slipped off the tongues of hippie parents and well-intentional teachers with a sort of cruel ease for the last three decades. In Evangelical churches and Jewish summer camps, on *3-2-1 Contact* and *Dora the Explorer,* even on MTV, we (America's youth) have been charged with the vaguest and most ethically dangerous of responsibilities: save the world. But what does it really mean? What has it ever really meant—when uttered by moms and ministers, by zany aunts and debate coaches—to save the whole wildly complex, horrifically hypocritical, overwhelmingly beautiful world?

I for one had no idea, but that didn't stop me from internalizing the message. I swallowed those three little words—a trio of radioactive seeds. They looked innocent enough when poured into my palm, but when swallowed, they buried themselves deep in my gut and started to grow. South African novelist, J.M. Coetzee wrote, "All creatures come into the world bringing with them the memory of justice." Shortly thereafter, if all is right, the world breeds in us an outrage over injustice.

At first I engaged my outrage like a true-blue white girl from the suburbs. I sent letters to the managers of Arby's and Wendy's in my hometown, begging them to stop using Styrofoam cups in their establishments for the good of our Mother Earth. No response.

I volunteered in an assisted living facility, screaming the letter-number combination for a comatose game of bingo. Though the residents attempted to adjust their hearing aids, my voice was too high to register. They screamed, "What? What did that girl say?" to one another, but everyone just shrugged and smiled at me sympathetically.

I worked at the local soup kitchen, dragging wet rags across Formica tables with my eyes diverted straight down, hoping none of the homeless people would actually speak to me. I was frightened by the ones that smelled, but even more frightened by the ones that didn't smell. The ones that looked like me and my mom. The ones that I'd seen walking around downtown and never even known I was supposed to save. I couldn't name it yet, but it was the first experience that called the conventional wisdom at the time—that there were savers and those to be saved, and that these were immutable categories—into question.

When Sally Struthers commercials came on, featuring little African babies with distended bellies and flies hovering around their eyes, I felt as if I had been punched in the stomach. I took it personally. After all, I had been charged with saving the world, as had my friends and little bike-riding neighbors. The adults in our lives had drawn a line directly between the suffering of the world—the African babies, the growing hole in the ozone layer, the homeless guy who lay listlessly on the bench outside the library—and our own nascent sense of purpose.

Once, agitated with one epiphany or another, I decided I would march around my neighborhood—middle class, suburban, white—and ask people for money for "the poor." I found an old glass jar in my playhouse, cleaned it fastidiously, and headed into the suburban wilderness for my first experience of fund-raising.

It went pretty well, actually. I was cute at the time—frizzy hair permanently set in a side ponytail, big blue-green eyes with dark, thick eyelashes, and a pair of magenta Converse high-tops (it was the eighties). I think that the smiling neighbors, pried from their daily dose of Oprah, took one look at me, heard my half-formed rationale, and sympathized with the familiar ache in my heart. They dropped quarters, sometimes even dollars, into my jar and set me on my way.

I rounded the block, growing more and more excited about the efficiency of my tactic. By the time I returned to my playhouse, I had over ten dollars. But as I sat on the wooden planks, my legs splayed, and pushed the coins around with my fingertips, a bad feeling started to creep over me. I realized that I had no idea who "the poor" really were.

I didn't know if I had met them before. There were kids at my school with less trendy clothes than all the others, but did this really mean they were poor or just that their parents were strict or stingy? There were those little babies with the bloated bellies on the commercial, but would ten dollars really help them? It seemed like they need much more. I could find some of the homeless guys near the library, but they might spend the money on drugs (by age eight, I'd already heard this warning many times). And how would I choose which people to give the money to anyway? Who was the most deserving? How could you predict that they'd use it for good? What if you gave money to someone and they were insulted—angry that you assumed they needed it?

The questions washed over me like a tidal wave, and suddenly everything about my initial intention—so pure, so heartfelt—was murky. I piled the money back into the jar and stared at it disapprovingly. There is, perhaps, nothing more paralyzing than a good intention suddenly proven naïve. I decided to bury the jar in the shadow of my playhouse until I knew what to do with it. If you go to 1718 North Tejon Street in Colorado Springs, you'll find that it's still buried there, along with my childhood illusions that "saving the world" is a simple or pure prospect.

Social scientists and the media seem to have made an ugly habit in the last few years of labeling my generation (defined in this book as those thirty-five years old and under) as entitled, self-absorbed, and apathetic. Psychologist Jean M. Twenge, in *Generation Me: Why Today's Young Americans Are More Confident, Assertive, Entitled—and More Miserable Than Ever Before,* argues that, largely because of the boom in self-esteem education in the eighties and nineties, young people today "speak the language of the self as their native tongue." Tom Friedman dubbed us Generation Q, for quiet, in the pages of the *New York Times*, writing that "Generation Q may be too quiet, too online, for its own good, and for the country's own good." And morning shows can't resist a segment on how entitled Gen Yers are in the workplace and what their bosses can do to tame their positively gargantuan egos.

I think they've got it wrong. They're missing a class analysis. And they've mistaken symptoms for the disease. We are not, on the whole, entitled, self-absorbed, and apathetic. We're overwhelmed, empathic, and paralyzed. The privileged among us are told over and over that it is our charge to "save the world," but once in it, we realize that it's not so simple. The less privileged are gifted their own empty rhetoric: American Dream ideology that charges them with saving, perhaps not necessarily the whole damn world, but at the very least their families, their countries, their honor. We are the most educated, most wanted, most diverse generation in American history, and we are also the most conscious of complexity.

In *Let Your Life Speak,* Parker Palmer writes, "Absolutism and relativism have ravaged not only the things of the world but our sense of the knowing self as well. We are whiplashed between an arrogant overestimation of ourselves and a servile underestimation of ourselves, but the outcome is always the same: a distortion of the humble yet exalted reality of the human self, a paradoxical pearl of price." In other words, we know that—simply by virtue of being born at this time, in this place—we are privileged, and furthermore, responsible for sharing that privilege. But we also know that making good on either promise—saving the world or saving our families—is not nearly as simple as our kindergarten teachers or our aspirational parents made it sound.

We know that soup ladling isn't enough, that Western values are sometimes imposed on other cultures in the guise of good works, that charity often serves to disempower a person in the long run, that too many nonprofits are joyless and ineffective places, that we have so much to give and yet so little. We've watched our own parents—many of them immigrants with big American Dreams in bright lights—be disrespected by the supposed promised land. We've taken human rights and women's studies classes where first-world arrogance was put in sharp relief to third-world ingenuity. We've experienced the painful irony of walking our donation check, earmarked for Indonesian hurricane relief, to the mailbox in our own poor Oakland neighborhood, which we were gentrifying by our mere existence.

Perhaps most significantly, we experienced 9/11 right as we were developing a political consciousness. I was a senior in college, poised to enter the real world with a sort of indestructible bravado on September 10. On September 11, everything I'd understood about my own safety, about the implications of America's reputation throughout the world, about violence and poverty and extremism, was transformed. I became simultaneously more humble and also more committed to really examining the beauty and ugliness of the country I'd been so blessed to be born in. But that examination has not lead to any clear answers. It's been worthwhile, but it's also been paralyzing. The war on terror may be an ill-conceived, inaccurate battle plan, but what do we do in the face of such hatred? Reinstating the draft would be a disaster, but how can we stand by as military recruiters prey on the most needy of young Americans? What is our individual responsibility to end war?

It's as if we each possess that glass jar, buried within, and it's growing heavier all the time, and we have no idea what the hell we're supposed to do with it.

When I first conceived of this book, it was out of very real desperation. I marched against the Iraq War, along with upwards of six million other people across the world, and President George Bush called it a "focus group." Despite all of my phone banking and wonky obsessing, he was reelected for a second term. The wars in Afghanistan and Iraq raged on. Abu Ghraib hit the headlines. The wealth disparity yawned larger and larger. My first nonprofit job was one long exercise in disillusion, and freelance writing was often alienating. I felt as if I had been sold a bill of goods. The world was a cruel, unjust place, and far from saving it, I felt stuck in it.

Looking for solace, I had lunch with my favorite professor from Barnard College, where I'd been an undergrad just a few years earlier. Professor Dalton was the one whose gospel of a true calling or *arête* (Plato), of a social contract (Rousseau), and of the power of love (King) had set me on fire at twenty years old. I would leave his class vibrating with grand notions of what it meant to live an ethical, examined life and how I might shape mine to reflect all this learning. Just five years later, I felt extinguished. The real world was not a place of perfect forms and pat answers. It was messy, bureaucratic, painful.

But instead of soothing me, my professor seemed to have his own desperation to battle. "Where is your generation's outrage?" he asked me. He told me stories of lecturing on the Holocaust, only to have one of his students ask, "Is this going to be on the test?" When I visited his classroom, slipping into a seat in the back, I saw laptop screens alight with Facebook and Zappos as he spoke passionately about the "miracle, mystery, and authority" of Dostoevsky.

The conspicuous lack of outrage, however, was not limited to the privileged. Consumerism and celebrity worship distracted the students that I worked with two afternoons a week at a low-income public high school. They were more interested in brand name bags and tight sneakers than fighting inequity. They wanted to know how they could get rich, not how the rich perpetuate systems of oppression.

And I couldn't really blame them. The political and cultural landscape circa 2005 prized status over courage, safety over innovation, and pre-professionalism over finding one's true calling. Anyone stubbornly dedicated to social change was destined for a harsh lesson in what Martin Seligman calls "learned helplessness": when one has grand expectations and finds them repeatedly unfulfilled, the unavoidable next stop is Despair. It was a time when the wind was knocked out of our collective sails. I was left standing on the shore of my own good intentions, wondering what ever happened to my dreams of "doing good."

And then a new day dawned.

It would be hard to overstate Barack Obama's significance in terms of his influence on young people and our notions of good works. I'm not talking exclusively about the thousands upon thousands of young people who joined his campaign—knocking on doors, sending text messages, descending on Iowa and Florida. Of course, those kids were transformed forever by their experience of standing up with a leader they finally believed in.

But Obama's leadership has had a broader, even more profound effect on us. It's given us an opportunity to see our own sensibilities, our own idealism, our own complex identities reflected at the highest level. Barack Obama is the America we dreamed about when we were little kids sitting in that classroom with Doritos cheese under our fingernails. He is the grand symbol, the big victory, the fireworks that we so longed for.

Which is a blessing and a curse. On one hand, his election has made a lot of young people believe the political process again, reflect on their own civic duty, and learn more about community organizing. On the other hand, all the hype that surrounded his candidacy has revived one of our more dangerous delusions—that "saving the world" is about heroics. In fact, the world will not be saved. It will be changed. It looks more like your mom— her palm on your fevered forehead, her handwritten schedule for sharing child care with neighbors, her letter to the editor of the local newspaper—than it does your president. Activism is a daily, even hourly, experiment in dedication, moral courage, and resilience.

This book is an exploration of that effort. Initially I conceived of it as a way out of my own desperation. I wanted to meet young people who had figured out how to feel efficacious in a world that seems to do its damnedest to make us feel otherwise. Interestingly, I found that much of the most effective social change comes, initially, from a self-interested place and radiates from there. My own vulnerability was not a bad place to start.

I also wanted to create a book that served as an answer to my professor's query— "Where is your generation's outrage?" I wanted it to be a collection of profiles that proved the skeptics like Tom Friedman wrong. This is not a quiet generation; it is a generation searching for its way. To older generations, that search is misinterpreted at best and invisible at worst—not because we aren't fighting, but because they don't recognize what the fight looks like anymore. It's rarely out in the streets. It's rarely dressed up in catchy slogans. But it's not all online either (a favorite misconception of boomer critics). It exists in defining moments—usually far from the glare of the television camera's eye or the flashing red light of the journalist's voice recorder.

As I began to meet my subjects—to spend hours with them in their offices, riding in their cars, sharing meals—I began to see some of the larger implications of my journey through their lives. I was examining the minutiae of existence in a way that rightfully honors it. The media rarely do this. Instead we focus on the extraordinary, the luminous, the booming finale. I was more interested in the in-between—the confusion, the contradictions, the quiet seconds when a person wrestles with his or her own instincts.

Like anthropologist Mary Catherine Bateson, who wrote *Composing a Life,* about the daily choices contemporary women make, I wanted to excavate the often overlooked and hugely important little moments that make a person an activist. This is not a book analyzing best practices or systemic change; some of that discussion comes up organically in the context of these activists' daily struggles, but I claim to be no expert on social work, civic engagement, or community organizing. Instead, this is a book that takes a psychological lens to the very human pursuit of making a life that mends, at least in some small way, a broken world.

It's so often not the protest march or the foundation grant that defines us, but the far more personal stuff of life—being disappointed by mentors, being uplifted by the tiniest of interpersonal victories, pulling ourselves off the edge. It is twenty-six-year-old Dena Simmons teaching her eighth-grade class how to solve for x. It is thirty-five-year-old Raul Diaz listening to a young man's fears about leaving prison. It is twenty-six-year-old Tyrone Boucher walking out of his way to get a wrap at the farmer's market instead of grabbing lunch at a corporate chain.

The eight young people featured in this book are not superhuman. They haven't cured cancer or donated their kidneys to strangers or won millions of dollars in prize money. They are, instead, breathtakingly ordinary. They are courageous and flawed and visionary. They are smart and powerful and sometimes insecure. What sets them apart is that they have found an intersection where, as Fredrick Buechner puts it, their "deep gladness and the world's deep hunger meet." Generally, they aren't satisfied. Or at least they are not any more satisfied than you and I. But they are satiated. Their work feeds them.

They are from a range of fields and geographical areas—a filmmaker in New York, a prison reentry social worker in East L.A., a radical philanthropist in Philly, an environmental justice advocate in D.C. They come from families where "save the world" was a charge by birth, and families where these words would never have been spoken, much less in English. Some of their activism was spurred by person trauma—a sexual assault, neighborhood violence, illness—and some of it grew from a more privileged, more intellectual place— the recognition of injustice, the desire to contribute to the solution, bad old-fashioned guilt.

I found them through a truly organic process. I met them at schools, in conferences, through blogs. They were recommended to me by friends, old professors, even strangers. Once I became intrigued by their official biographies, I took time to learn a bit about their personal stories—convinced that both had to be compelling in order to build engaging narratives, and of course drawing on my own feminist wisdom that the personal is always political.

I was very intentional about getting young people who work in a range of fields, from a range of demographic backgrounds, but I was also cognizant of my limits. These are just eight people out of thousands the country over who are doing incredible work. There are large fields left out that I would have loved to explore—among them medicine, social entrepreneurship, and law. I also had limited funding to travel, so I regret that the majority of the activists profiled here are from the West or East Coast. I hope that other documentarians will pick up where I've left off.

A word on the domestic focus of the majority of those profiled: it is my strong belief that globalization and its effects demand that we, as Americans, get clear about the unmet needs and unanswered injustices in our own backyard. Not only do many of these enduring inequities—global warming, militarization, economic disparity—have global impacts, but our moral integrity depends on our capacity to deal with the suffering that surrounds us before we point the finger at others.

I admire so much of the work that young Americans are doing throughout the world, but I also fear that too many of us seek sainthood abroad; Rachel Corries' profile illustrates the danger in this thinking, to some extent. Foreign problems can appear spuriously simple compared to those at home, which are so undeniably personal and seemingly intractable. I learned this when I studied abroad in Cape Town. I went eager to learn about the ways in which apartheid and its eventual defeat had affected the people there. Eventually I realized that part of my attraction to the place was that race relations seemed so black and white from an outsider's perspective, as opposed to the painful, gray shadows that made up my racialized American experience. I ended up learning far more about America than I did about South Africa in those six short months.

Thomas Merton wrote of an "invisible fecundity" and a "hidden wholeness" that exists within each of us. In these profiles, I aim to find the hidden wholeness in each of my subjects' lives. Writing about people inherently objectifies them. Though these profiles are substantial, they could never represent the true complexity of the human being they describe. Instead, I've tried to present a collage of moments and ideas that honors each of them and teaches the rest of us something important. These are not PR profiles. Each of these activists is too thoughtful, too honest, to feel truly honored by a portrait that doesn't acknowledge their complexity, so you'll find that I examine them scars and all, challenge them, and at times compassionately critique the impact of their work.

You will also find a hidden wholeness, if you look closely, among the group at large. I was delighted by the ways in which these totally disparate human beings—none of them working directly together, most of them complete strangers—echoed each other across great distances and divides. They have expressed parallel struggles, experienced the same places, asked the same questions. I'll revisit these larger trends and themes in the conclusion, but I encourage you to have fun spotting the moment when these perfect strangers appear exquisitely and unknowingly intertwined.

My gratitude toward them for allowing me to become part of their lives, and write it all down, is indescribable. It takes such confidence, such bravery, to allow a stranger— much less a journalist—inside. I would feel like a true cannibal unless I also know that this process can be healing for people, that activists—especially—are so rarely honored with the sort of listening ear and finely tuned attention that I have tried to introduce with my presence.

Bucking journalistic conventions, I also involved each of them in my writing process— giving them a chance to read their profiles, give me feedback, and correct any inaccuracies. It's something that most traditional journalists wouldn't do, for fear that their subjects' involvement would get in the way of the Truth, but I think that objectivity is an ideal all but impossible for an engaged writer (and what other kind is there, really?). I suspect that a lot of traditional journalists don't show their work to their subjects before publication not because of a lofty commitment to so-called objectivity, but out of plain old fear. It's incredibly difficult to write about real people—especially if you aim to do it honestly—and then face their reactions. It scares the shit out of me every time, but it's critical to my own integrity. I think it's not only disingenuous to hide behind journalistic convention, but—especially in long form pieces like these—actually immoral.

I hope that each of my subjects feels truly, deeply seen in this experience. And I hope that you, the reader, see yourself in them. You don't have to be a celebrity to relate to Rosario Dawson's struggle for authenticity within her activism. You don't have to have been in the military to identify with Maricela Guzman's silence. You don't have to have grown up in the Bronx to understand Dena Simmon's love affair with home. Alasdair Macintyre wrote, "I can only answer the question, 'What am I to do?' if I can answer the prior question, 'Of what story or stories do I find myself a part?'" I hope you find yourself a part of these stories, as I have so profoundly.

This book is dedicated to abandoning the "save the world" and American Dream rhetoric for a language that is still inspiring, but also pragmatic—a language that we can use like a bridge over the chasm between what our parents and teachers told us about good deeds, about success, and what the real world needs every day. It is a call to transcend school-required community service and résumé-padding activities in favor of the kind of work that keeps you up at night because you believe in it so deeply. It is a warning against paralysis and the sort of numbing our generation has made ourselves infamous for (drinking, drugging, shopping). It is an invitation.

I invite you to read about these eight ordinary human beings' lives and believe that your life has the potential to be no less powerful. I invite you to see yourself in them, your silly dreams in their brave acts, your buried instincts for kindness and outrage in their insistence on change. Because, of courage, they are no different from you and me—children of the eighties and nineties, inheritors of "save the world" anxiety, American dreamers, cynics, fragile and kind. They have just figured out a way to soothe the critics and pessimists in their own heads and act.

There are no real answers in this book, only insights and catharsis. None of these activists knows the "right way" to create a more just world, nor do I. What we do know is that it's still worthwhile to try. In these eight lives you will find thousands of noble attempts at healing the world's suffering, at making life more equitable and joyous for all. It is the smallness, not the largeness, of these attempts that make them worthy of examination.

Jane Addams once said, "We may either smother the divine fire of youth or we may feed it." I believe that outlandish expectations, crushing bureaucracies, out-of-touch political leaders, doomsday media coverage, and empty rhetoric about service and success only serve to suck the oxygen out of our hugely promising generation.

Instead we must look to one another for the spark. We must integrate lessons from the visionaries and pavement-pounders of yesteryear, but not become burned by waiting for their version of social change to manifest. Nor must we be relegated to sanitized point-and-click activism alone. Technology aids us, but it doesn't define us. Our work, our hearts, our ingenuity are what determine our legacy.

■ WHAT?

1. What does Martin argue is the problem with the command to "save the world," especially when it is delivered by adults to children?
2. How did the terrorist attacks of September 11, 2001, affect the development of Martin's political consciousness? What impact did 9/11 have on your thinking about the world?
3. Summarize the impact, as Martin explains it, that Barack Obama's election to the presidency has had on "young people and our notions of good works." Do you agree with Martin's claim about President Obama's influence? Explain your response.

■ WHAT ELSE? WHAT'S NEXT?

4. Use whatever resources you find helpful (the internet, interviews, informal surveys) to ascertain the state of student engagement and activism at the University of South Carolina. Are many students involved in campus and community service activities? What kinds of activities seem to attract student engagement? Is USC's level of involvement typical for a large university? Summarize your findings in a brief report that you can share with your classmates.

■ WHO CARES?

5. Based on your reading of this excerpt, who is Martin's target audience for her book? What does she do in the selection you read to connect with that audience? Do you think she is successful in reaching those readers? Explain your response.

Judith Lichtenberg, a professor of philosophy at Georgetown University, is working on a book on the idea of charity. She wrote this piece in October 2010 for the New York Times blog called The Stone, described by the newspaper as "a forum for contemporary philosophers on issues both timely and timeless."

BEFORE YOU READ
Visit The New York Times website and find The Stone blog. Take a look at the postings, and be prepared to discuss with your class the purpose of the blog, its audience, and its effectiveness as a public outlet for philosophers.

IS PURE ALTRUISM POSSIBLE?
Judith Lichtenberg

Who could doubt the existence of altruism?

True, news stories of malice and greed abound. But all around us we see evidence of human beings sacrificing themselves and doing good for others. Remember Wesley Autrey? On Jan. 2, 2007, Mr. Autrey jumped down onto the tracks of a New York City subway platform as a train was approaching to save a man who had suffered a seizure and fallen. A few months later the Virginia Tech professor Liviu Librescu blocked the door to his classroom so his students could escape the bullets of Seung-Hui Cho, who was on a rampage that would leave 32 students and faculty members dead. In so doing, Mr. Librescu gave his life.

Still, doubting altruism is easy, even when it seems at first glance to be apparent. It's undeniable that people sometimes act in a way that benefits others, but it may seem that they always get something in return—at the very least, the satisfaction of having their desire to help fulfilled. Students in introductory philosophy courses torture their professors with this reasoning. And its logic can seem inexorable.

Contemporary discussions of altruism quickly turn to evolutionary explanations. Reciprocal altruism and kin selection are the two main theories. According to reciprocal altruism, evolution favors organisms that sacrifice their good for others in order to gain a favor in return. Kin selection—the famous "selfish gene" theory popularized by Richard Dawkins—says that an individual who behaves altruistically towards others who share its genes will tend to reproduce those genes. Organisms may be altruistic; genes are selfish. The feeling that loving your children more than yourself is hard-wired lends plausibility to the theory of kin selection.

These evolutionary theories explain a puzzle: how organisms that sacrifice their own "reproductive fitness"—their ability to survive and reproduce—could possibly have evolved. But neither theory fully accounts for our ordinary understanding of altruism.

The defect of reciprocal altruism is clear. If a person acts to benefit another in the expectation that the favor will be returned, the natural response is: "That's not altruism!" Pure altruism, we think, requires a person to sacrifice for another without consideration of personal gain. Doing good for another person because something's in it for the do-er is the very opposite of what we have in mind. Kin selection does better by allowing that organisms may genuinely sacrifice their interests for another, but it fails to explain why they sometimes do so for those with whom they share no genes, as Professor Librescu and Mr. Autrey did.

When we ask whether human beings are altruistic, we want to know about their motives or intentions. Biological altruism explains how unselfish behavior might have evolved but, as Frans de Waal has suggested, it implies nothing about the motives or intentions of the agent: after all, birds and bats and bees can act altruistically. This fact helps to explain why, despite these evolutionary theories, the view that people never intentionally act to benefit others except to obtain some good for themselves still possesses a powerful lure over our thinking.

The lure of this view—egoism—has two sources, one psychological, the other logical. Consider first the psychological. One reason people deny that altruism exists is that, looking inward, they doubt the purity of their own motives. We know that even when we appear to act unselfishly, other reasons for our behavior often rear their heads: the prospect of a future favor, the boost to reputation, or simply the good feeling that comes from appearing to act unselfishly. As Kant and Freud observed, people's true motives may be hidden, even (or perhaps especially) from themselves. Even if we think we're acting solely to further another person's good, that might not be the real reason. (There might be no single "real reason"—actions can have multiple motives.)

So the psychological lure of egoism as a theory of human action is partly explained by a certain humility or skepticism people have about their own or others' motives. There's also a less flattering reason: denying the possibility of pure altruism provides a convenient excuse for selfish behavior. If "everybody is like that"—if everybody must be like that— we need not feel guilty about our own self-interested behavior or try to change it.

The logical lure of egoism is different: the view seems impossible to disprove. No matter how altruistic a person appears to be, it's possible to conceive of her motive in egoistic terms. On this way of looking at it, the guilt Mr. Autrey would have suffered had he ignored the man on the tracks made risking his life worth the gamble. The doctor who gives up a comfortable life to care for AIDS patients in a remote place does what she wants to do, and therefore gets satisfaction from what only appears to be self-sacrifice. So, it seems, altruism is simply self-interest of a subtle kind.

The impossibility of disproving egoism may sound like a virtue of the theory, but, as philosophers of science know, it's really a fatal drawback. A theory that purports to tell us something about the world, as egoism does, should be falsifiable. Not false, of course, but capable of being tested and thus proved false. If every state of affairs is compatible with egoism, then egoism doesn't tell us anything distinctive about how things are.

A related reason for the lure of egoism, noted by Bishop Joseph Butler in the 18th century, concerns ambiguity in the concepts of desire and the satisfaction of desire. If people possess altruistic motives, then they sometimes act to benefit others without the prospect of gain to themselves. In other words, they desire the good of others for its own sake, not simply as a means to their own satisfaction. It's obvious that Professor Librescu desired that his students not die, and acted accordingly to save their lives. He succeeded, so his desire was satisfied. But he was not satisfied—since he died in the attempt to save the students. From the fact that a person's desire is satisfied we can draw no conclusions about effects on his mental state or well-being.

Still, when our desires are satisfied we normally experience satisfaction; we feel good when we do good. But that doesn't mean we do good only in order to get that "warm glow"—that our true incentives are self-interested (as economists tend to claim). Indeed, as de Waal argues, if we didn't desire the good of others for its own sake, then attaining it wouldn't produce the warm glow.

Common sense tells us that some people are more altruistic than others. Egoism's claim that these differences are illusory—that deep down, everybody acts only to further their own interests—contradicts our observations and deep-seated human practices of moral evaluation.

At the same time, we may notice that generous people don't necessarily suffer more or flourish less than those who are more self-interested. Altruists may be more content or fulfilled than selfish people. Nice guys don't always finish last.

But nor do they always finish first. The point is rather that the kind of altruism we ought to encourage, and probably the only kind with staying power, is satisfying to those who practice it. Studies of rescuers show that they don't believe their behavior is extraordinary; they feel they must do what they do, because it's just part of who they are. The same holds for more common, less newsworthy acts—working in soup kitchens, taking pets to people in nursing homes, helping strangers find their way, being neighborly. People who act in these ways believe that they ought to help others, but they also want to help, because doing so affirms who they are and want to be and the kind of world they want to exist. As Prof. Neera Badhwar has argued, their identity is tied up with their values, thus tying self-interest and altruism together. The correlation between doing good and feeling good is not inevitable—inevitability lands us again with that empty, unfalsifiable egoism—but it is more than incidental.

Altruists should not be confused with people who automatically sacrifice their own interests for others. We admire Paul Rusesabagina, the hotel manager who saved over 1,000 Tutsis and Hutus during the 1994 Rwandan genocide; we admire health workers who give up comfortable lives to treat sick people in hard places. But we don't admire people who let others walk all over them; that amounts to lack of self-respect, not altruism.

Altruism is possible and altruism is real, although in healthy people it intertwines subtly with the well-being of the agent who does good. And this is crucial for seeing how to increase the amount of altruism in the world. Aristotle had it right in his "Nicomachean Ethics": we have to raise people from their "very youth" and educate them "so as both to delight in and to be pained by the things that we ought."

■ WHAT?

1. Explain how Lichtenberg answers the question she poses in the title of her essay: "Is True Altruism Possible?"
2. Lichtenberg writes that "doubting altruism is easy, even when it seems at first glance to be apparent." Why is this so? Do you agree with Lichtenberg's assertion?
3. Compare the way that Lichtenberg defines altruism with the definition implied in Elie Wiesel's discussion with Richard D. Heffner. Do you think Lichtenberg and Wiesel would agree in their thinking about helping others? Explain.

■ WHAT ELSE? WHAT'S NEXT?

4. In her essay, Lichtenberg mentions "the famous 'selfish gene' theory popularized by Richard Dawkins." Use whatever resources you need to compile an annotated bibliography in MLA format of four sources that help you understand what the "selfish gene" theory is and how it relates to Lichtenberg's claims about altruism. Your writing handbook can give you guidance on how to compose an annotated bibliography.

■ WHO CARES?

5. What does Lichtenberg do in her essay to make this topic matter to her readers? Do you think she does enough? Does she make you care about the topic?

Guy Horton blogs for Metropolis *and is author of* The Indicator, *a weekly column on the culture, business and economics of architecture, featured on* ArchDaily. *He is a frequent contributor to* Architectural Record, The Architect's Newspaper *and* Architect. *He wrote this article about the artist and photographer JR and his socially engaged work in March 2011 for the website* Good.

BEFORE YOU READ————————————————————————————
Do you think art can change the world for the better? Explain your response in a paragraph or two, and include at least one example to support your position.

WHY HE'S PUTTING YOUR FACE ALL OVER THE WORLD Guy Horton

What I am looking at while I write this is something I have never seen before. Taped to my wall is a poster-sized portrait of myself. In fact, It's a little disturbing, It's the largest image of myself I've ever seen. My whole life I have never been larger than I actually am. The biggest it gets is life-size in the mirror. We've all been conditioned to miniature representations of ourselves. More recently, I see myself reflected back in a tiny thumbnail profile image connected to my online life. I use the same little image for everything. This is how everybody else sees me, too. A few pixels across by a few pixels high. Now, here, in my living room, is my face rendered three feet across by five feet high in glorious, antiquated monochrome. It looks like a Nadar daguerreotype—oddly flattened—and it makes me look instantly historical and important. I like to think I'm important, but this portrait conveys importance on another level. I am forced to contemplate myself more directly when confronted by this black and white evidence.

The real story of this portrait is the story of the artist JR, the 2011 TED Prize-winner who on Wednesday revealed his TED Wish at the TED Conference in Long Beach, California. Each year, TED (Technology, Entertainment, Design), a global online-offline community made up of thinkers, dreamers, and innovators, awards the TED Prize to someone who has had a significant, positive impact on the world or has the potential to do so. The prize is $100,000 and "One Wish to Change the World." One of the highlights of the Conference is the unveiling of the prize-winner's "Wish."

Just before JR revealed his Wish, he recalled how he was terrified at first and didn't want to accept the prize. "How can I fix the world, I thought. I am just an artist." He called the prize director and said he didn't think this would work and that maybe he just wouldn't show up. "No, no," the director said. "You don't need to fix the world. You just need to change it." When he understood all he had to do was change the world, he realized he could probably handle that and accepted. He put the phone down and started wishing.

His initial hesitation was well-founded. Winning the TED Prize brings a lot of responsibility, and expectations are extremely high. Last year the prize went to celebrity chef Jamie Oliver for his mission to protect kids from obesity. Past winners include Bill Clinton, Bono, and author-publisher Dave Eggers. All brought change to significant numbers of people and have furthered the goals of human rights and justice.

I have followed JR's work and assumed I understood its relevance and social dimensions. I tried to imagine what he could possibly do along the lines of what he has been doing in different cities around the world, from the favelas of Rio de Janeiro to Shanghai. His massive art projects have empowered and made visible communities that historically remain invisible, impoverished, and disenfranchised. Could he take this to another level and what would this look like? Whatever it was, it was bound to be big and somehow involve photography, his passion since the age of 17, when he found a camera on the Paris subway.

After taking the audience on a tour of his earlier projects he made a drum-roll sound and said, in a dramatic made-for-TV moment, "I wish for you to stand up for what you care about by participating in a global art project, and together we'll turn the world...INSIDE OUT."

INSIDE OUT is the project that takes what JR usually does with small communities and distributes and decentralizes it to a global network. The project is set up so people can upload portraits of themselves, receive a poster-sized print by mail and then go and paste it out in their communities. As JR said, "This is not about me. The people become involved and the Wish becomes theirs."

"I am just the printer in this operation," he demurs. It's Thursday morning and I've managed to pull him away from Ashton and Demi, into a corner of the gallery where his Wish has just officially launched. He stands a little too close for American personal space, but this way I am able to peek behind his signature sunglasses. "Look. You can see my eyes," he says, as if to show he is a real person. "But I always keep the glasses on."

I asked him why the glasses even though, like his subjects, he has been made extremely visible through TED. "I wear them because I don't want to be seen when people photograph me." Ironic. But it makes perfect sense coming from the context of street art, where identities need to be hidden because of the subversive and illegal nature of the work. JR, however, does not easily fit into the category of stealth street artists. In fact, he considers the label "street art" derisive. "It's art."

His methods are of his own making. Rather than being a midnight bomber who subverts laws, property rights, and urban space, he enters the fray of the communities in which he works and builds trust and relationships. The people he comes to know become the basis of his photographs.

Perhaps the glasses are just part of the character "JR" (I still don't know his real name), a way to distance himself from the work. He likes to step aside and let the subjects tell their own stories with as little mediation as possible. For the TED Wish he steps back even further to let the masses do the photographing. So in this sense the Wish is the logical extension what came before.

"For me, I am an artist and I am just doing art," he says. "Whatever happens from that I do not control. I am not doing a humanitarian project. I'm not an NGO. It is an art project and if it goes beyond that to generate some change then that is good."

When I ask him how far he envisions the project going he says, "I would like it to go as far as possible, even to places without the internet. I would like to see people pasting wherever they can, showing what is important to them."

In my car in the free public parking space provided by the City of Long Beach (thank you broken machine!) I'm scrolling through my photographs. Not enough, I think. So I head back in. The celebrities have departed. The gallery is quiet and nearly empty. It's spooky with all those giant eyes staring at me. JR looks more relaxed, leaning against the wall chatting with some patrons. He seems just like a conference attendee rather than the center of attention and I think he prefers this. His assistant, Erin, approaches. "Have you tried the booth," she asks. I had been avoiding it, but now that the crowds had dissipated I didn't have an excuse anymore. The booth she is referring to is a giant portrait booth, like a blown-up version of the sort you find in amusement parks or malls. You sit behind a curtain, it takes your photo, and then spits out a huge black and white poster.

It was only after sitting in the machine and seeing my own portrait come put that I really began to understand JR's Wish. Before this, it was all abstract. Now that I have this thing, I need to figure out what to do with it. Should I paste it up on an overpass? Maybe I should reproduce it and put it up all over. What does it say? What would your poster say about you, about the world? Have one made and find out.

So, as I stare at my JR portrait, hanging by blue tape on my white wall, I think, This is the Wish. JR is facilitating presence, the re-presentation of ourselves, and he's challenging us to share this presence with the world in immediate and perhaps risky ways. "It is up to people to decide what to do with these, where to put them," he said. "People always ask me, will this change anything and I always say, 'I don't know. It's not up to me.'"

■ WHAT?

1. According to Horton's article, the photographer JR did not want to accept the TED prize he had won at first because he worried that he could not "fix the world." But then, as JR tells it, the prize director told the artist: "You don't need to fix the world. You just need to change it." How does this distinction between fixing and changing mesh with Elie Wiesel's thinking about responsibility and with Courtney E. Martin's ideas about civic and social engagement?

■ WHAT ELSE? WHAT'S NEXT?

2. Working with a group of classmates, visit the TED website (www.ted.com) and the TED Prize page (www.tedprize.org) to find out more about both. Use this information to prepare a brief report for the rest of the class about the purpose of the awards and how previous winners have spent their "wish." Finally, consider the following question: What effects have these wishes had?

WHO CARES?

3. Visit JR's wish page (www.insideoutproject.net/) and examine the responses his prompt has received. Who is participating? What kinds of things are they doing with their posters? What other modes of participation does the website provide? What do these responses say to you about art's ability to bring about change in the world?

© Michael Rubin/Shutterstock.com

IMAGE 2.2
"Women deserve to be safe from violent assault, no matter what they wear," Jessica Valenti writes in "SlutWalks and the Future of Feminism." Do you think the SlutWalks are an effective forum for conveying that message?

Jessica Valenti, the founder of Feministing.com, is the author of The Purity Myth: How America's Obsession With Virginity Is Hurting Young Women *and the forthcoming* Why Have Kids? The Truth About Parenting and Happiness. *She wrote this column about the SlutWalks protest movement in June 2011 for* The Washington Post. *For a look at how this protest is playing out in another setting, see Rama Lakshmi's article immediately following this one.*

BEFORE YOU READ
Use Google's "News" function and search for "SlutWalks." Then, prepare a brief report on recent developments (in the last year or so) in the SlutWalks campaign.

SLUTWALKS AND THE FUTURE OF FEMINISM Jessica Valenti

More than 40 years after feminists tossed their bras and high heels into a trash can at the 1968 Miss America pageant—kicking off the bra-burning myth that will never die—some young women are taking to the streets to protest sexual assault, wearing not much more than what their foremothers once dubbed "objects of female oppression" in marches called SlutWalks.

It's a controversial name, which is in part why the organizers picked it. It's also why many of the SlutWalk protesters are wearing so little (though some are sweatpants-clad, too). Thousands of women—and men—are demonstrating to fight the idea that what women wear, what they drink or how they behave can make them a target for rape. SlutWalks started with a local march organized by five women in Toronto and have gone viral, with events planned in more than 75 cities in countries from the United States and Canada to Sweden and South Africa. In just a few months, SlutWalks have become the most successful feminist action of the past 20 years.

In a feminist movement that is often fighting simply to hold ground, SlutWalks stand out as a reminder of feminism's more grass-roots past and point to what the future could look like.

The marches are mostly organized by younger women who don't apologize for their in-your-face tactics, making the events much more effective in garnering media attention and participant interest than the actions of well-established (and better funded) feminist organizations. And while not every feminist may agree with the messaging of SlutWalks, the protests have translated online enthusiasm into in-person action in a way that hasn't been done before in feminism on this scale.

The protests began after a police officer told students at Toronto's York University in January that if women want to avoid rape, they shouldn't dress like "sluts." (If you thought the days of "she was asking for it" were long gone, guess again.)

Heather Jarvis, a student in Toronto and a co-founder of SlutWalk, explained that the officer's comments struck her and her co-organizers as so preposterous and damaging that they demanded action. "We were fed up and pissed off, and we wanted to do something other than just be angry," she said. Bucking the oft-repeated notion that young women are apathetic to feminism, they organized. What Jarvis hoped would be a march of at least 100 turned out to be a rally of more than 3,000—some marchers with "slut" scrawled across their bodies, others with signs reading "My dress is not a yes" or "Slut pride."

The idea that women's clothing has some bearing on whether they will be raped is a dangerous myth feminists have tried to debunk for decades. Despite all the activism and research, however, the cultural misconception prevails. After an 11-year-old girl in Texas was gang-raped, the *New York Times* ran a widely criticized story this spring that included a description of how the girl dressed "older than her age" and wore makeup—as if either was relevant to the culpability of the 18 men accused of raping her. In Scotland, one secondary school is calling for uniforms to be baggier and longer in an attempt to dissuade pedophiles.

When I speak on college campuses, students will often say they don't believe that a woman's attire makes it justifiable for someone to rape her, but—and there almost always is a "but"—shouldn't women know better than to dress in a suggestive way?

What I try to explain to those students is part of what the SlutWalk protests are aiming to relay on a grander scale. That yes, some women dress in short, tight, "suggestive" clothing—maybe because it's hot outside, maybe because it's the style du jour or maybe just because they think they look sexy. And there's nothing wrong with that. Women deserve to be safe from violent assault, no matter what they wear. And the sad fact is, a miniskirt is no more likely to provoke a rapist than a potato sack is to deter one.

As one Toronto SlutWalk sign put it: "Don't tell us how to dress. Tell men not to rape." It's this—the proactive, fed-upness of SlutWalks—that makes me so hopeful for the future.

Feminism is frequently on the defensive. When women's activists fought the defunding of Planned Parenthood, for example, they didn't rally around the idea that abortion is legal and should be funded. Instead, advocates assured the public that Planned Parenthood clinics provide breast exams and cancer screenings. Those are crucial services, of course, but the message was far from the "free abortion on demand" rallying cry of the abortion rights movement's early days.

Established organizations have good reason to do their work in a way that's palatable to the mainstream. They need support on Capitol Hill and funding from foundations and donors. But a muted message will only get us so far.

"We called ourselves something controversial," Jarvis says. "Did we do it to get attention? Damn right we did!"

Nineteen year-old Miranda Mammen, who participated in SlutWalk at Stanford University, says the idea of "sluttiness" resonates with younger women in part because they are more likely than their older counterparts to be called sluts. "It's also loud, angry, sexy in a way that going to a community activist meeting often isn't," she says.

Emily May, the 30-year-old executive director of Hollaback, an organization that battles street harassment, plans to participate in SlutWalk in New York City in August. "Nonprofit mainstays like conferences, funding and strategic planning are essential to maintaining change—but they don't ignite change," she says. "It's easy to forget that change starts with anger, and that history has always been made by badasses."

Unlike protests put on by mainstream national women's organizations, which are carefully planned and fundraised for—even the signs are bulk-printed ahead of time—

SlutWalks have cropped up organically, in city after city, fueled by the raw emotional and political energy of young women. And that's the real reason SlutWalks have struck me as the future of feminism. Not because an entire generation of women will organize under the word "slut" or because these marches will completely eradicate the damaging tendency of law enforcement and the media to blame sexual assault victims (though I think they'll certainly put a dent in it). But the success of SlutWalks does herald a new day in feminist organizing. One when women's anger begins online but takes to the street, when a local step makes global waves and when one feminist action can spark debate, controversy and activism that will have lasting effects on the movement.

Established feminist groups have had tremendous success organizing feminist action in recent years. The 2004 March for Women's Lives—put on by the National Organization for Women, NARAL Pro-Choice America, the Feminist Majority Foundation and others— brought out more than 1 million people protesting President George W. Bush's anti-woman, anti-choice policies. It was an incredible event, but the momentum of the protest largely stopped when the march did.

It's too early to tell whether SlutWalks will draw people on that scale, but they are different in a key respect. Instead of young women being organized by established groups, SlutWalks have young women organizing themselves—something I believe makes these women more likely to stay involved once the protest is over.

SlutWalks aren't a perfect form of activism. Some feminist critics think that by attempting to reclaim the word "slut," the organizers are turning a blind eye to the many women who don't want to salvage what they see as an irredeemable term. As Harsha Walia wrote at the Canadian site Rabble: "I personally don't feel the whole 'reclaim slut' thing. I find that the term disproportionately impacts women of color and poor women to reinforce their status as inherently dirty and second-class."

Anti-pornography activist Gail Dines argued, along with victims rights advocate Wendy Murphy, that the SlutWalk organizers are playing into patriarchal hands. They say the protesters "celebrating" the word "slut" and dressing in risqué clothing are embracing a pornified consumer sexuality. Frankly, I don't think any of these women will be posing for the "Girls Gone Wild" cameras anytime soon. Yes, some protesters have worn lingerie, but others have worn jeans and T-shirts. Organizers encourage marchers to wear whatever they want because the point is that no matter what women wear, they have a right not to be raped. And if someone were to attack them, they have a right not to be blamed for it.

In the past, clothing designed to generate controversy has served to emphasize the message that women have a right to feel safe and participate fully in society. Suffragists wore pants called "bloomers," named for the women's rights activist Amelia Bloomer. They were meant to be more practical than the confining dresses of the times. But, echoing the criticism of SlutWalk participants today, the media did not take kindly to women wearing pants. The November 1851 issue of *International Monthly* called the outfits "ridiculous and indecent," deriding the suffragists as "vulgar women whose inordinate love of notoriety is apt to display itself in ways that induce their exclusion from respectable society."

The SlutWalkers, in outfits that could be grumpily labeled "ridiculous and indecent," are not inducing exclusion from respectable society. They're generating excitement, translating their anger into action and trying to change our supposedly respectable society into one that truly respects men, women and yes, even "sluts."

■ WHAT?

1. What are the SlutWalks? How did they begin?
2. What arguments for and against the use of the word "slut" do Valenti and Lakshmi (in the article that follows this one) list in their pieces? Do you think using a controversial and, to some, shocking term such as "slut" is an effective rhetorical strategy? Explain your response.
3. How do Valenti and Lakshmi (in the article that follows this one) explain the SlutWalks as feminist protests? What do the SlutWalks have to offer younger women who want to stand up for women's rights?

■ WHAT ELSE? WHAT'S NEXT?

4. How do those who have organized and participated in various SlutWalk protests explain their purpose? Is there any kind of centralized SlutWalk web presence (a Facebook page, for example, or a website) that lists the movement's mission and goals? If so, summarize these goals. If not, how do the protestors get their message out?
5. Valenti acknowledges that "SlutWalks aren't a perfect form of activism," and the protests have been received in a variety of ways. Research various reactions to and commentary about SlutWalks in the United States and elsewhere (see Rama Lakshmi's article following this one as a starting point). After you have gathered your research, write a brief report explaining public and political reaction to the protests.

■ WHO CARES?

6. How would you explain the SlutWalks movement and Valenti's argument to a religiously conservative audience? Remember, you're not sharing your opinion about the movement or Valienti's point.

Rama Lakshmi wrote the following article about the ways that Indian women are adapting SlutWalk tactics for The Washington Post. *See Jessica Valenti's essay that precedes this one for more on the SlutWalk movement and for writing prompts for both pieces.*

BEFORE YOU READ
Make sure you have read Jessica Valenti's "SlutWalks and the Future of Feminism" and answered Question 1 following the essay.

INDIAN WOMEN ALTER SLUTWALK
Rama Lakshmi

New Delhi—A young man follows a teenage girl along a street in India's capital on a recent muggy morning, leering. The girl, wearing jeans topped with a long tunic, quickens her steps. As the man closes in, she covers her mouth with her hands. Bystanders cover their eyes.

Then everybody freezes in place.

The two had just acted out the first scene of a street play about sexual harassment and social acquiescence that Indian university students have been performing across the city as part of the run-up to SlutWalk Delhi, India's version of the campus campaign that began in Toronto in April and has since spread to Argentina, Australia, Britain, Germany, South Korea and the United States.

The walk, designed as a protest against a Canadian police officer who advised women to "avoid dressing like sluts" if they want to be safe from sexual assault, has elsewhere involved women dressing as provocatively as they please. But in India, the SlutWalk set for this coming Sunday is getting a makeover, with student organizers saying they have tweaked the original concept to better match India's conservative social palette.

The confrontational "slut" has been softened by adding the Hindi word for "shamelessness" to the event's title. Women have been asked to march in their regular clothes. And weekly public debates and street theater are being promoted even more energetically than the walk itself.Rather than focusing on clothes, the campaign is questioning gender stereotypes embedded in ancient Hindu religious epics, Bollywood movies and sexist matrimonial classified ads.

"There will be no dress code" for the march, said UmangSabarwal, 19, the event's chief organizer. "In India, no matter what we wear, even if we are covered head to toe in a sari or a burqa, we get molested and raped. A woman's fight in India is more basic—it is a fight for the right to be born, education, nutritious food, work."

New Delhi, a city of about 16.7 million, has reported 258 cases of rape or molestation through June this year, and women in the city routinely face harassment in buses and on the metro system. SlutWalk Delhi has Twitter and Facebook accounts, but in an effort to be more inclusive, march organizers have also begun distributing pamphlets, titled "Speak Up," to women in the city. "We want to reach a larger audience, beyond the campus and the Facebook crowd," said Mishika Singh, 20, a law student and a walk coordinator.

The young English-speaking students also find themselves having to work hard to secure the backing of an older generation of feminists who prefer to be more culturally rooted. When they approached the government-run National Commission for Women and other women's organizations for funding and support, they were rebuffed.

"I agree with the cause, but the packaging is wrong," said RanjanaKumari, a leading feminist who heads the Center for Social Research. "I tried to counsel the students not to alienate the majority of Indian women. The Indian feminist movement took many decades to recover from the damage caused by the American bra-tossing campaigns. Let us not ape the West unnecessarily and trivialize our fight."

Still, India is urbanizing rapidly and embracing global culture. Two-thirds of the country's 1.2 billion people are younger than 35, and many young women say they are battling the same stereotypes as elsewhere.

ShefaleeVasudev, a fashion columnist for the *Indian Express* newspaper, wrote this month: "Damn the intellectuals. SlutWalk is actually about clothes, about what we wear and how. That's why if we all turn up in 'decent clothes' for the SlutWalk, we may not be able to make the point."

Amid rising crime against women, the city's police commissioner offered some advice last week. "You can't travel alone at 2 a.m. and then say Delhi is not safe," B.K. Gupta said. "It would be ideal if a woman takes her brother or driver along."

Two years ago, a young woman was killed while going home late from work. Delhi's chief minister, Sheila Dikshit, caused a public outcry at the time when she said that women should not be "adventurous."

Prateeka Nanda, 19, an undergraduate volunteer, said: "We hear such advice all the time from our parents. The restrictions are always put on women, never on the men. Men do not own the public space. We want to reclaim it."

Astrid Aafjes, who holds a Law degree from the University of Amsterdam and is founder and executive director of Women Win, has focused her career on gender and human rights and has gained extensive experience in advancing the lives of girls and women and in creating social change through innovative strategies. She has headed studies on women's microcredit for the UNDP, worked with the UN Special Rapporteur on Violence Against Women on a global report for the UN Commission on Human Rights in Geneva, and led the program department of Mama Cash, the first International Women's Fund. This essay was published in the summer of 2011 in The Fletcher Forum of World Affairs.

BEFORE YOU READ

Astrid Aafjes writes that "Title IX ... has established a valuable precedent as a strategy for increasing women's access to sports and, as such, is yielding data on positive outcomes from women's participation." Despite this, however, many people do not have a clear understanding of what Title IX is. Using the Internet and the resources available though Thomas Cooper Library, research Title IX and find two sources that provide ample background about the law. Then, write a brief report that explains the origins of the law, its purpose, and its requirements. Keep in mind that this is not a position piece about the value of Title IX; rather it is an explanatory report meant to inform. Include your sources, in MLA format, at the end of your report

SPORTS: A POWERFUL STRATEGY TO ADVANCE WOMEN'S RIGHTS Astrid Aafjes

On the 100th anniversary of International Women's Day, March 8, 2011, more than 1,000 supporters gathered in Washington, D.C., to celebrate and kick off CARE's Annual Conference.[1] Each year, CARE bestows their "I Am Powerful" Award upon a person who has had a profound effect upon his or her community or the community of others. This year, CARE presented the award to Peninah Nthenya Musyimi, the founder of Safe Spaces, a sports-for-women's-rights program in the Mathare slums of Nairobi, Kenya.

Safe Spaces provides an excellent example of a gender-targeted program that applies sports as a strategy to advance women's rights. In addition to basketball, yoga, and dance classes, Safe Spaces' leaders (who are all women) hold weekly discussions where participants talk about issues affecting girls and young women who live in the slums. Since its creation in 2008, Safe Spaces has worked with over 500 girls.

Nthenya Musyimi founded Safe Spaces when she returned to the community where she grew up, after she had escaped the slums and had attended university on a basketball scholarship. As a child, she had witnessed the injustices women faced in the slums, where "all women's rights are violated and nobody cares."[2] She realized she could be most effective as a role model, finding that girls who participate in the Safe Spaces program have an increased determination to escape from the slums.[3]

Like Nthenya Musyimi, international development agencies, donors, governments, universities, and nonprofits are turning to sports as an innovative and effective way to engage young women in achieving their rights. Well-designed sports programs are an effective platform for learning and building skills, increasing knowledge, improving health and fitness, and ultimately yielding positive behavioral and health outcomes. In the United States, Title IX, approaching its 40th anniversary in 2012, has established a valuable precedent as a strategy for increasing women's access to sports and, as such, is yielding data on positive outcomes from women's participation. This essay is not a discussion of whether girls should play sports—that is an unequivocal right—but rather an evaluation of how rights-based sports programs are effective in helping young women achieve their rights, and how additional resources within the women's rights and development sectors can be mobilized and targeted to improve outcomes for a woman and her community.

■ The Importance of Investing in Women and Girls

While the use of sports as a development tool and strategy to advance women's rights is growing, more funds must be targeted toward programs specifically geared toward women. In 2003, only 7.3 percent of total giving from foundations in the United States and 0.04 percent of total European Commission aid targeted "women and girls" programs and initiatives. Of the sixty-nine billion dollars distributed in 2003 in the category of "Official Development Assistance," approximately USD 2.5 billion, or 3.6 percent, had gender equality as part of the objective.[4]

Investment in young women yields significant returns, especially when considering population statistics. Young women make up more than twenty-five percent of the population of Asia, Latin America, the Caribbean, and sub-Saharan Africa, and the total global population of girls between the ages of ten and twenty-four is predicted to hit its peak in the next decade.[5] But when it comes to the development of communities and nations, investments in women are about more than raw numbers. The Girl Effect, an initiative sponsored by the Nike Foundation in partnership with the NoVo Foundation, the United Nations Foundation, and the Coalition for Adolescent Girls, reports, "an extra year of primary school boosts girls' eventual wages by ten to twenty percent. An extra year of secondary school: fifteen to twenty-five percent."[6]

Women Win, founded in 2007, targets funding specifically to rights-based sports programs for girls and young women. In the past four years, Women Win has worked with 26 programs in 19 countries, making direct contact with over 9,000 girls and young women. Through its work, Women Win is finding that the participation of girls and young women in high-quality, rights-based sports programs, such as Safe Spaces, decreases a young woman's tendency toward early pregnancy and marriage, and increases her chances of staying in school. Each additional year of schooling, and each year that childbirth or marriage is delayed, has a profound effect on a young woman's self-empowerment and earning potential—a high return on investments targeted toward women.

■ The Importance of Rights-Based Programming

Women Win supports rights-based programming. Rights-based programs start with the basic premise that every person has rights, and works to help each participant learn about and realize her rights. A well-known example of a rights-based approach is Title IX in the United States. Prior to 1972, universities and schools were distributing federal funding inequitably by gender. Title IX states:

> No person in the United States shall, on the basis of sex, be excluded from participation in, be denied the benefits of, or be subjected to discrimination under any education program or activity receiving Federal financial assistance...[7]

Although Title IX was not specifically directed at sports programs, Title IX's equitable funding mandate for all federally funded universities and schools made sports programming for girls and women immediately available. While many funding decisions rely upon extensive research to determine need, Title IX establishes a strong precedent for a funding decision based upon rights.

Rights-based programs, like those supported by Women Win, are designed to accomplish two major goals: first, to educate each participant about her rights; and, second, to help her build life skills that allow her to pursue the avenues necessary to realize her rights. For example, Safe Spaces' curriculum affirms for each participant that she has the right to realize economic empowerment. One way it does so is by emphasizing the importance of education in pursuing future employment. Musyimi's Safe Spaces program also includes team sports, such as basketball. Boxgirls, a rights-based sports program in Nairobi, engages participants through its curriculum on reproductive health and teaches girls how to box.

These programs are based upon the belief that when a girl or young woman learns about the rights to which she is entitled, she is able to develop the skills necessary to pursue her rights. If she also has a support system to which she can turn when she experiences a violation of her rights, she is more likely to seek support and legal redress when those rights are violated. Knowing about her rights is not enough; each girl must also have the inner strength and the self-confidence to take action. Educating a girl about her rights provides her the opportunity to envision a different path, and the physical challenges and mentoring inherent to sports programs gives her the skills and support to follow it.

Because Title IX is a rights-based approach to human development, it is particularly relevant to the implementation of sports programming in countries where the realities of women's lives do not reflect the rights to which they are entitled. Many programs in emerging economies and "low-income" countries are designed around need; they identify something that is lacking either in the environment or in the people, and then work to fill that gap. A rights-based approach is just the opposite: it begins with the premise that every person has rights, and then educates and empowers an individual to achieve his or her rights. Rights-based programs are not dependent upon research for implementation. There is enough information available today to guide the scaling up of rights-based sports programs for girls and young women in countries across the globe.

■ Areas in Which Rights-Based Programming Has Been Successful

Title IX provides evidence of the positive effect of rights-based programming upon a population whose rights had been denied. This has been particularly noticeable in regards to women and sports. After the passage of Title IX, the total number of girls playing high school sports increased from 300,000 in 1970 to almost three million today.[8] Studies are starting to demonstrate the successes in education and careers achieved by women who grew up playing sports in the United States.[9]

Women Win works with sports programs on the ground to provide quality programming that participants' knowledge and empowerment in three areas central to women's rights: 1) economic empowerment; 2) gender-based violence; and 3) sexual and reproductive rights and health. These three areas are essential and interconnected. If a woman is to achieve economic independence, she must be free from oppression inflicted through gender-based violence. She also must be aware of her sexual and reproductive rights and health so she can choose to delay childbirth until completing her education. The ultimate goal is to help a young woman escape from poverty, achieve economic independence, and become a fully-developed human being. Early pregnancy, sexual abuse, rape, lack of access to financial institutions, and inability to own property are just a few of the injustices that limit a young woman's ability to achieve independence and contribute to her community. Women Win has selected these three focus areas because they represent the "triangle of oppression." When a young woman is able to exercise her rights in these three critical areas, she is more likely to realize a life free from poverty.

Economic Empowerment

In 2010, the Population Council initiated a baseline survey of adolescent women participating in the Goal project in India. Goal, a "sports plus" program implemented by the Naz Foundation with support from Standard Chartered Bank, targets adolescent girls aged twelve to twenty from low-income families in urban areas. Population Council researchers K.G. Santhya and Komal Saxena found that only three-fifths of girls surveyed knew how to count money correctly, barely half were aware of savings institutions, and just one-fourth could identify one or two services or products provided by banks.[10] Goal's program is offered weekly, over a period of six to ten months, and includes a mix of sports- and life-skills-education modules that cover topics including financial literacy, communication skills, and health and hygiene. It is part of an increasingly large cadre of high-quality sports programs in which financial literacy is being integrated into curricula to assist young women in achieving economic independence. Since its founding in 2006 as a pilot program in Delhi, Goal has reached more than 14,000 girls in India, Nigeria, and Jordan. Its goal is to reach an additional 25,000 girls by the end of 2011.

Gender-Based Violence

Gender-based violence is pervasive and crippling for young women in countries around the world, and adolescent girls are particularly vulnerable. According to a 2005 report by the United Nations Population Fund (UNFPA), almost fifty percent of sexual assaults are against girls under the age of fifteen.[11]

Girls recognize the prevalence of violence in their communities. In 2010, Women Win worked with the Population Council to carry out a survey of 556 girls in four sports programs partnering with Women Win. They selected two programs in Kenya, one in Egypt, and one in Uganda. Seventy-six percent of girls surveyed believe that "violence against girls is a problem in their community."[12] A girl living with violence is often unaware that she has a choice to escape from it; programs must often teach the most basic aspects of human and legal rights. For example, the Population Council survey of adolescent girls in India for the Goal program found that only sixty-seven percent knew that eighteen is the legal minimum age for females in India to marry, and only thirty-seven percent knew that twenty-one is the legal minimum age for males.[13]

For a woman to live a life free from gender-based violence, she must first be aware that she has the right to live a life free from crimes inflicted upon her solely because of gender. Gender-based violence refers to a cluster of crimes, including sexual violence, trafficking, and property expropriation. Gender-based violence is inflicted at the domestic, community, and state levels. Quality sports programs for women's rights work on each of these levels. Nthenya Musyimi integrates lessons about gender-based violence into the Safe Spaces program because of her own experience in the Mathare slums.

A girl's need for mentors and positive peer groups makes quality sports programs, such as Safe Spaces in Kenya and Empowering Women of Nepal, particularly valuable because girls who do not have a personal network are more vulnerable to abuse. These sports programs create safe spaces. Eighty-nine percent of girls surveyed in the Population Council's survey of the four Women Win programs reported that they felt safe where they play sports; eighty-three percent reported they had made at least five new friends through the programs; and eighty-nine percent reported they had a female mentor they could confide in.[14]

Sexual and Reproductive Rights and Health

Adolescent girls are often forced to abandon schooling because of pregnancy. Every year, close to fourteen million adolescent girls give birth.[15] The 2005 Adolescent Fact Sheet from UNFPA states: "Based on data from 56 countries, girls aged 15 to 19 from the poorest groups are three times more likely than their better-off peers to give birth in adolescence, and bear twice as many children."[16] Women Win is working with sports programs to deliver information to girls about their sexual and reproductive rights.

Some girls have much to learn. As part of its baseline study for Standard Chartered's Goal program, researchers asked survey respondents about their knowledge of sex and pregnancy. Only twenty-five percent of respondents knew that a woman can become pregnant the first time she engages in sexual intercourse; sixty percent knew that there are ways to avoid pregnancy; and only seventy-six percent knew that a woman cannot get pregnant from kissing or hugging.[17]

The Population Council study of girls' perspectives from four programs found that over half of the girls surveyed know that it is okay to play sports while menstruating. The ten percent who noted they were "unsure" and the third who reported they felt that it was "not good" show that the program still has more work to do around education in this area.[18] Program leaders continue to find that cultural practices around menstruation often interfere with a girl's ability to play while menstruating, so each program's response must be qualified by the context of the community while still providing solid facts for participants. Program leaders also provide culturally relevant information about ovulation and pregnancy. Gender-specific sports programming provides a safe space for girls to initiate conversation about concerns, especially those that are often considered taboo. Women Win supports the training of peers as program leaders to provide information and support that aligns with cultural norms.

■ Women Win and the Work It Does

Women Win brings an asset-building approach to the field by supporting and strengthening women's organizations and sports-for-development organizations to deliver conceptually sound and culturally relevant sports programs. Women Win's theory of change is built on the belief that adolescent girls and women benefit from, and are empowered by, sports and sports programs that build assets, provide access to resources, and develop agency and leadership.

For a sports program to effectively support a young woman in achieving a self-fulfilling, empowered life free from violence, it must combine two powerful pieces: 1) education about her rights (the building of assets) within a supportive community; and 2) the provision of access to resources allowing her to build personal agency and leadership. Women Win refers to these as the "triple A's."

Assets

Assets may be social, human, or athletic. Social assets include social networks, positive peer groups, and female mentors. Human assets include physical strength and fitness, mental and emotional health, self-confidence, and information and knowledge about gender-based violence, reproductive health, and economic empowerment. Sports skills are also assets, as participants must develop discipline and concentration to master a sport, and build one's sense of competence to compete. Women Win is tracking an emerging body of research suggesting that asset-building programs can result in long-term gains for girls and women.

Access

Quality sports programming also provides access to resources not often available to girls and young women. Sports programs allow for access to institutional and community resources, such as playing fields, basketball courts, and even something as simple as a soccer ball or basketball. Programming can also provide access to community resources, such as health centers, financial institutions, and community development organizations. Sports programs additionally create access to safe, female-friendly public spaces where girls can gather to learn new skills, form friendships, expand social networks, and receive mentoring. Access to these safe spaces is an important strategy in overcoming the social isolation that many girls face and that further exacerbates discrimination and gender-based violence. A safe and supportive environment is a contributory factor in motivating young people to make healthy choices.

Agency

Finally, quality sports programming develops agency and leadership in young women. Sport is an ideal means to teach teamwork and goal-setting, and to develop and practice leadership skills. Sports programs help participants develop a sense of agency, empowering girls to act in their own best interest. Agency and leadership cultivated through sports programs for girls and women build a tremendous source of human capital by developing the maximum potential of each individual.

■ Gaps in Rights-Based Sports Programming

As funders look to increase their investments in girls and young women, Women Win encourages implementation of another lesson from Title IX: funding drives equity. Political structures and international resolutions are not enough. What if donors viewed funding of sports programs as an equity strategy and stipulated equitable access as a requirement for funds? What if they required communities to allow girls to play sports as a condition of receiving a grant? How would this stipulation propel a donor's overall goals for a community? Women Win believes that sports-programming-for-women is a strategy that has tremendous impact upon communities, and encourages funders to see it as such and target and leverage funds to increase overall impact.

Funding is needed at all levels, not the least of which is research. In the field of quality sports programming for girls and women, there is an urgent need for longitudinal studies. The studies cited in this essay are snapshots in time and provide valuable baseline information. Research is needed to track changes over time. Programs work in both engaging and educating young women, but longitudinal studies would help to ensure quality and effectiveness. As noted in a sports-for-development impact study conducted by the University of Stirling and funded by Comic Relief and UK Sport, "the data enable us to identify 'what' happened, but there is a need to develop a more in-depth understanding of process—the 'how' and 'why'—and the reasons for inter-program differences, in order to consider issues of 'good practice.'"[19] Women Win measures success by outcomes, not numbers. Women Win's interest is in seeing every young woman realize her rights, practicing economic and physical empowerment, and living a life free from gender-based violence.

■ Conclusion

Investors such as Comic Relief, the NoVo Foundation, the Inter-American Development Bank, Nike, and Standard Chartered are increasingly turning to sports as both a development strategy and a strategy for advancing women's rights. One must look no further than the positive outcomes that Title IX has reaped in the United States to acknowledge the benefits of increasing girls' access to sports. Yet, in communities where gender inequities are deeply embedded and oppressive, sports alone will not alter the outcome for girls and young women. Effective programming must marry human-rights education with the development of life skills. This pairing allows a young woman to both learn about her rights and to acquire the skills and mentors to forge her own path away from poverty and toward economic independence. To sustain the growing momentum of the sports-for-women's-rights movement, and to scale up current successes, investors should consider making the equitable delivery of services a requirement for funding, just as Title IX did almost 40 years ago.

Endnotes

[1] CARE is an international humanitarian organization that fights global poverty. CARE has found that working with women to rise out of poverty has a profound positive effect upon entire families and communities.

[2] "International Women's Day Celebrations: VOA's Ndimyake Mwakalyelye talks to Peninah Ntheya Musyimi," YouTube video, 4:40, from TV2Africa, March 11, 2011, <http://www.youtube.com/watch?v=LO26pT8ISic> (accessed April 19, 2011).

[3] Ibid.

[4] Cindy Clark, Ellen Sprenger, and Lisa Vene Klasan, Where is the Money for Women's Rights? (Toronto: Association for Women's Rights in Development, February 2006), 11.

[5] Ruth Levine et al., Girls Count: A Global Investment & Action Agenda, (Washington, DC: Center for Global Development, 2009), <http://www.cgdev.org/content/publications/ detail/15154> (accessed April 19, 2011), 16.

[6] "The Girl Effect Data: Why Should We Pay Attention to Girls," Girl Effect Media fact sheet, <http://www. girleffect.org/uploads/documents/1/Girl_Effect_Fact_Sheet. pdf> (accessed April 19, 2011), citing George Psacharopoulos and Harry Anthony Patrinos, Returns to Investment in Education: A Further Update, World Bank Policy Research Working Paper 2881, September 2002.

[7] Title IX, Education Amendments of 1972, 20 U.S.C. § 1681 (1972).

[8] Del Jones, "Many Successful Women Say Sports Teaches Valuable Lessons," USA Today, March 26, 2002.

[9] A 2002 study showed that fifty percent of the women who make USD 75,000 and above identify themselves as athletic, and 82 percent of executive businesswomen played organized sports after elementary school. See Danielle Friedman, "Female Jocks Rule the World," The Daily Beast, September 29, 2010, <http://www.thedailybeast.com/blogs-and-   stories/2010-09-29/women-and-sports-why-athletic-ladies-excel-in-business/> (accessed April 20, 2011); see also Betsey Stevenson, Beyond the Classroom: Using Title IX to Measure the Return to High School Sports, National Bureau of Economic Research working paper 15728, (February 2010). The abstract notes, "Analysis of differences in outcomes across states in changes between pre- and post-cohorts reveals that a 10-percentage point rise in state-level female sports participation generates a 1 percentage point increase in female college attendance and a 1 to 2 percentage point rise in female labor force participation."

[10] K.G. Santhya and Komal Saxena, Assessing the Effects of Standard Chartered Bank's Goal Project on Adolescent Girl's Lives, Population Council, 2010, 4.

[11] UNFPA State of the World Population 2005, The Promise of Equality: Gender Equity, Reproductive Health and the MDGs, United Nations Population Fund, 2005 <http:// www.unfpa.org/webdav/site/global/shared/documents/publications/2005/swp05_ eng.pdf> (accessed April 20, 2011), 66.

[12] Martha Brady, A Snapshot of Girls' Perspectives on Sports, Health, and Empowerment: A Descriptive Study of Women Win Program Partners in Egypt, Kenya, and Uganda, Population Council, 2010, iv.

[13] Santhya and Saxena, 14-15.

[14] Brady, iii.

[15] UNFPA State of the World Population 2005, The Promise of Equality: Gender Equity, Reproductive Health and the MDGs, 14.

[16] Ibid., 50.

[17] Santhya and Saxena, 14.

[18] Brady, iii-iv.

[19] Fred Coalter with John Taylor, Sport-for-Development Impact Study, Department of Sports Studies, University of Stirling, October 2010, <www.uksport.gov.uk/docLib/ MISC/FredCoaltersseminalMandEManual.pdf> (accessed April 20, 2011), xi.

■ WHAT?

1. Aafjes explains up front that she is writing "an evaluation of how rights-based sports programs are effective in helping young women achieve their rights, and how additional resources within the women's rights and development sectors can be mobilized and targeted to improve outcomes for a woman and her community." Summarize her argument.
2. Do you believe, as Aafjes writes, that girls around the world have "an unequivocal right" to play sports? Explain your response. What might prevent girls from exercising this right?
3. What is "rights-based programming"? What, according to Aefjes, are the two major goals of rights-based programs?

■ WHAT ELSE? WHAT'S NEXT?

4. Examine and analyze the list of sources Aefjes uses to support her argument. What kinds of texts does she cite? How does she deploy her sources in her essay? How do the words, data, and ideas of others help Aefjes make her case?

■ WHO CARES?

5. Visit the website for The Fletcher Forum of World Affairs, the journal that published this article. After studying the website, including what the journal has to say about itself and its mission, write a brief report characterizing Aefjes' intended audience. Some questions to consider: Who do you think reads The Fletcher Forum? Who are the primary stakeholders in the issue that Aefjes addresses? What does Aefjes do to reach her readers, to make them pay attention and care about the issue?

IMAGE 2.3
Can sports do more than provide diversion and entertainment?

Alexander Wolff has worked for Sports Illustrated *for more than 30 years and is now the longest-tenured writer on the staff. In addition to covering basketball at all levels, he has written from the Olympics, the World Cup, the World Series, the NBA Finals, every Grand Slam tennis event and the Tour de France.* Sports Illustrated, *which published "Sports Saves the World" in September 2011, introduced Wolff's article with the following: "In grassroots programs involving tens of thousands of participants around the globe, visionaries are using athletics to tackle the most pressing problems of the developing world—from AIDS in Africa to violence in Rio. Can such projects make a lasting difference, or is the dream of salvation through sports too grandiose? SI senior writer Alexander Wolff set off on a yearlong journey to find the answer."*

BEFORE YOU READ

Find at least two sources that help you understand the philosophical concept of ubuntu. *Using these sources, write a brief explanation of the term to share with the class.*

SPORTS SAVES THE WORLD   Alexander Wolff

▩ Vancouver

I ran into Johann Olav Koss again in February 2010, at the Olympic oval in Richmond, B.C. The sight of Koss, then a temporary coach with Norway's speedskating team, transported me back 16 years instantly, happily.

I can't help it: Listmaking is a male thing, even more a sportswriterly thing, and I fastidiously rank Olympic Games. With its glitch-filled first week, the trucked-in snow and the fatal crash of a Georgian luger, the Vancouver edition will forever be an also-ran. The Winter Games of 1994, on the other hand, still surmount my desert-island all-time top five list of Olympics. Lillehammer abides with me not just because Koss won three gold medals and set three world records in three races; Dan Jansen finally skated to a gold himself; and 100,000 Norwegians camped overnight in the snow so they could cheer cross-country skiers with cowbells the next morning. It was the harmonious vibe, the intimate scale, the clean Scandinavian lines of the venues, even the crisp weather—as if the Norse gods had dropped a membrane over the town, sealing it off from the world's impurities.

The only breach of this hermetic idyll was on the pedestrian mall of Lillehammer's main street, where a few people solicited for a charity called Olympic Aid. They invoked Sarajevo, the Yugoslavian city that had hosted the Winter Games a decade earlier and, as a result of the war in the Balkans, remained under what would be the longest siege in modern history. The looping anthem of Sarajevo's suffering, Albinoni's *Adagio in G Minor,* haunted me every time I walked by. It seemed to whisper that, even as nature re-created a little patch of Eden for the playing of games, mankind still ginned up reminders of its fallen state.

And then the Perfect Olympics delivered its own latter-day god, a man to go forth into the Imperfect World and set it right. I'd watched Koss skate his triple at the Vikingskipet Oval. I'd heard him pledge his bonus money to Olympic Aid and challenge his countrymen to give 10 kroner each for every Norwegian gold medal, inspiring his government and fellow citizens to give $18 million over 10 days. For this as much as anything else, *Sports Illustrated* named Koss its 1994 Sportsman of the Year, an award he shared with U.S. speedskater Bonnie Blair. My colleague E.M. Swift wrote the story about the Olympic champion from Norway with a "headful of dreams and almost a lifetime in which to accomplish them."

We were now 16 years into that life left to live. When I saw Koss at the Richmond Oval, I asked, How goes the battle?

Sport, Koss replied, is doing nothing less than trying to save the world. Olympic Aid, since renamed Right To Play, now reaches 700,000 children in 20 countries during any given week. But Koss's outfit is only one player among hundreds in a burgeoning global movement. Today the field known generally as Sport for Development and Peace (SDP) extends well beyond nongovernmental organizations (NGOs) such as Right To Play. It attracts growing support from foundations and corporations, while governments and international agencies are eager to serve as partners to groups on the ground. And as the effectiveness of programs is more precisely measured, SDP's value as a tool for good is becoming more widely acknowledged. Even the stodgiest onlookers agree that sport "plays the hidden social worker," in the words of former champion miler Sebastian Coe, now chairman of the London 2012 organizing committee.

That is a good thing, for almost half the world's population is considered poor, and a full 1.4 billion people—one fifth of humanity, including more than half of all Africans—are extremely poor, living on less than $1.25 a day. As maladies of plenty such as obesity, diabetes and heart disease afflict the developed world, and elite pro sports reek of excess, SDP is a sobering counterpoint, spreading health messages, pacifying communities in conflict, preparing refugees for resettlement and providing what experts consider the simplest means of promoting development: improved status for women. At the turn of this century, when the U.N. drew up its Millennium Development Goals to cut extreme poverty in half by 2015 and eliminate it entirely by '25, Koss and Right To Play led the way in determining how sport could best help.

On the morning of the 2010 Olympic opening ceremonies, across Vancouver at a symposium at the University of British Columbia, the former Canadian ambassador to the United Nations, Stephen Lewis, delivered a confession. Lewis, who had served the U.N. secretary general as an anti-AIDS adviser, had long been skeptical of the value of sports. But SDP had won him over. "[Koss] understood early that you could use play to convey messages that aren't available anywhere else," Lewis told his audience. "Sport has become a development philosophy. Who would have imagined that to be possible? What began as an instinct has now become a profound social cause."

I wanted to see how, exactly. So after the dousing of the Vancouver flame, I lit out for far corners of this Imperfect World in search of other friends of sport who, like Koss, had broken from their bubbles to heed the *Adagio* call of Lillehammer.

■ Rio de Janeiro

It's not a classic hillside slum, but Complexo da Maré is easily one of Rio's largest favelas—a sprawling neighborhood of 135,000 people hard by the route visitors will travel between the airport and the beaches when they come to this city for the 2014 World Cup and the 2016 Olympics. Rival drug gangs recruit kids as foot soldiers and sort out differences with gunplay. Luke Dowdney has driven me into the favela beneath weltering electrical wires and past huddled walk-ups. He parks our car and we stroll a block. A boy of no more than 15 preens in an intersection, automatic weapon slung over one shoulder.

Dowdney, a former British universities light middleweight boxing champion, came to Brazil in 1995 to study street children in the northern city of Recife for his dissertation in social anthropology. He was haunted by the murder of two kids he had grown close to and by the words of a 12-year-old drug trafficker who told him, "I'm going to die young, but I'm going to live well." One day a group of glue-sniffing boys asked him to show them some boxing moves. "When they'd get in a stance, they'd leave the glue behind," says Dowdney, 38, "and a light went off in my head."

In 2000, Dowdney founded a boxing and martial arts program in Maré called Luta Pela Paz, or Fight for Peace, and five years later he opened a training and educational center. On its first floor, boys and girls practice boxing, wrestling and the Brazilian martial art capoeira. In a suite of second-floor classrooms the same kids learn computer skills, citizenship and conflict resolution; they also practice martial arts in a third-floor matted dojo. Boxer Douglas Noronha, whose brother was shot to death in '01, is one of about 4,600 young Cariocas to go through the program. "You'd think I'd have become more violent," he tells me. "In fact, I've become a more controlled person. It's all about the self-confidence and discipline of not finding yourself in a position where, before you know it, somebody's got a gun."

Dowdney introduces me to another fighter, Roberto Custódio, who was 14 when his father was ordered out of the favela by a drug trafficker who was jealous of his relationship with a local woman. When he returned to look in on his family, which he supported as a bus driver, the drug lord settled the matter in his usual way, with bullets.

Figuring that fitness and martial arts would help him square accounts with his father's killer, Roberto turned to Luta Pela Paz. Then the unexpected happened. The program transformed his bloodlust into something altogether new. As he developed the discipline that boxing demands—and took the academic classes required of all participants—relatives marveled that his anger gradually drained away. Last October, Roberto, now 24, won the light welterweight gold medal at the Brazilian championships, and he is likely to qualify for the London Olympics as a welterweight. "Our program isn't just about getting rid of energy," Dowdney tells me. "It's also about rigor and values. The disciplined fighter will always beat the overwrought fighter. *Luta* means fight, but it also means struggle, in a good way."

Dowdney hopes to develop a funding stream from a new line of fightwear and lifestyle clothing called Luta (luta.co.uk). "If the line hits, it becomes the engine," says Dowdney, who runs a second Fight for Peace center in East London that has trained 1,700 boxers. "We're not about being a traditional charity. It's like boxing: You get out what you put in. If you're not trained, you don't win. That's life. You've got to step up."

Last spring, as a crew filmed a commercial for the Luta brand in a ring set up in a warehouse at the edge of the favela, a gunfight broke out between police and traffickers. The film crew dove under the ring for cover. That's what favela dwellers such as Roberto Custódio deal with. Says Dowdney, "Luta is about celebrating the real heroes in the favelas, young people born into extraordinary adversity who get painted as victims when they're actually aspirational heroes."

■ Port Elizabeth, South Africa

Tommy Clark figured his sojourn in Zimbabwe to play pro soccer after college would be a joyous homecoming. He'd spent part of his teens in that southern African nation while his father, former Scotland international Bobby Clark, coached Highlanders F.C. in Bulawayo. But what he found upon returning in 1992 left him mystified and heartbroken. Seven of his dad's finest players—seemingly invincible footballers whom Tommy had idolized—were dead or dying. Worst of all, no one dared say why. "I was there for a year," says Clark, who also taught school and coached, "and I didn't have a single conversation about HIV."

Clark hit upon the idea of using soccer to break down this wall of silence and educate Africans about HIV. He embarked on a medical career, with a residency in pediatrics and a fellowship in HIV research in the U.S. In 2002, Clark launched Grassroot Soccer with three ex-Highlanders, including Ethan Zohn, the *Survivor: Africa* champion who donated a chunk of his $1 million prize money to the cause. Today the organization operates in South Africa, Zambia and Zimbabwe and shares curriculum and resources with partners in nine other African countries. Studies confirm that graduates of the program wait longer to engage in sex; have fewer partners; and are more willing to talk about HIV with peers and relatives, take an HIV test and stay on treatment if they test positive. Those proven results have attracted such patrons as Elton John, whose AIDS foundation contributed $1.4 million last year to fund the program in Zambia. There's no way to tie the 50% drop in the HIV infection rate among South African teens from 2005 to '08 directly to Grassroot Soccer, but foundations are showing their confidence in the program with more grant money. This week the Clinton Global Initiative announced a $1 million commitment to a Grassroot program for South African girls.

Among the organization's most effective tools are the voluntary counseling and testing tournaments that it uses to reach the men who drive the disease. Clark invited me to a tournament in Motherwell, a township in the South African city of Port Elizabeth. For years locals had hidden behind euphemisms, saying of an HIV-positive woman, "She has a House in Veeplaas," a play on the name of a local neighborhood. But there had been a breakthrough a week before my visit, when South African president Jacob Zuma—a father of 22 children by multiple wives—announced the results of his own HIV test. (They were negative.)

The grounds outside a school teemed with players who ducked into a makeshift clinic between games, and Grassroot personnel touted a post-tournament dance contest to flush more prospects out of a nearby supermarket. By the end of the day 289 more people knew their HIV status. "Five years ago, if you'd bring up HIV, everyone would shut down," one of the tournament workers, 27-year-old Mkadi Nkopane, told me. "Now a 10-year-old will tell you of an uncle or mother who's positive. The stigma will always be there, but it's much less now."

As the game that launches countless conversations in Africa, soccer is a natural idiom to cut through the taboos surrounding one of the continent's most pressing problems. In one popular drill, each soccer ball stands for a sexual partner. A player dribbling two balls is easily chased down by a defender who represents the AIDS virus; a player dribbling only one ball eludes that defender much longer, and a memorable point is made. Grassroot Soccer distributed thousands of "red cards" during the 2010 World Cup to help teenage girls, who can be up to eight times more likely to become infected than their male counterparts, use sass and humor to fend off unwanted sexual approaches. "The culture soccer creates around this topic is our 'secret sauce,'" says Grassroot Soccer COO Bill Miles. "By focusing on intergenerational sex and multiple partners, you try to shift social norms. And if you shift social norms, you change the epidemic."

Clark and his fellow ex-Highlanders work in part to honor the dead of Bulawayo—men such as the former star of the Zimbabwean national team who was refused service by bank tellers because of the stigma of AIDS, and the ex-player who trained as one of Grassroot Soccer's first coaches only to die before he could work with kids. "We're trying to be both bold and humble," says Clark, 40, whose program is nearly halfway toward its goal of a million youth participants by '14. "We ask for millions of dollars, and we're trying to change behavior and norms on a huge scale. But we also know we're not always going to have the answer, and that there may be a better answer tomorrow."

■ Tel Aviv, Jerusalem and the West Bank

When it ventures to global trouble spots, basketball can flash a kind of diplomatic passport. In South Africa, hoops comes without the racial baggage of soccer (a largely black sport) or rugby (mostly white). In divided Cyprus it's loved equally by citizens of Turkish and Greek descent. In Northern Ireland it's regarded as neither a Gaelic game by Protestants nor a game of the British garrison by Catholics. All of which helps explain the success of Peace Players International (PPI), which has spent the past decade using basketball to build bridges among young people in divided communities.

In the Middle East such efforts face a challenge of another magnitude. Upon launching there in 2005, PPI easily found Israeli Arabs to mix with Jewish kids in its programs. But Palestinian parents in the Israeli-controlled West Bank balked at letting their boys and girls travel to Israel for integrated play. Meanwhile, poor coaching and inadequate facilities in the West Bank led kids there to fear that their lack of hoops competency would only bolster Israeli stereotypes of worthless Palestinians.

On a brilliant spring day in 2010, Brendan Tuohey flashes me a smile as he oversees a PPI youth tournament in a Tel Aviv park. "Five years ago we decided to build up the skills of Palestinian kids," says Tuohey, a former player at Colgate whose brother Sean had the idea for the organization. "It's a big breakthrough that players from [the Palestinian city of] Ramallah chose to get on the bus to come here today."

Some parents on both sides of the Israel-Palestine divide still hesitate to let their kids enter PPI's programs—Jews out of safety concerns and Arabs because of cultural norms for girls. But the chance to get good coaching at no cost, plus uniforms and occasional travel, has enticed some 5,600 participants. "They all come for sport," PPI Middle East director Karen Doubilet tells me. "'Meet the other side' is just something they put up with in order to do what they really want to do."

Children ages 10 to 14 participate in PPI's "twinning" program, in which Jews and Arabs at first practice regularly in their home communities, then combine into mixed teams under two coaches (one Arab and one Jewish) and meet weekly throughout the school year. At 15 they're eligible to become PPI coaches themselves; last season two teams of 15- and 16-year-old Arab and Jewish girls competed in the Israeli first division under the PPI banner. Meanwhile, in hoops-deprived parts of the West Bank such as Ramallah and nearby refugee camps, PPI continues to offer its "single-identity" program to boost the level of Palestinian basketball, provide constructive outlets for kids' energy and train coaches as leaders.

Once PPI gets them, most participants buy into the coexistence component. It's based on a curriculum, developed by a U.S.-based conflict-resolution think tank called the Arbinger Institute, that supplies strategies for exploring why one side stigmatizes the other and how to change those attitudes. "After Arbinger they might still clique up," says Heni Bizawi, who has played and coached in the program, "but according to different variables, like Jaffa versus Jerusalem instead of Arab versus Jew."

Peace Players has helped make a fan of Raneem Nashef, a 12-year-old Arab who lives in the West Jerusalem enclave of Beit Safafa. She'll wake up early to watch TV broadcasts involving her favorite player, Omri Casspi, the Jewish Israeli who plays for the Cleveland Cavaliers. Her mother, Lubna, who grew up despising the yellow and blue of Maccabi Tel Aviv, Casspi's old club, catches me by surprise: "My daughter feels Casspi represents her. She knows he comes from her part of the world."

In the seemingly intractable Arab-Israeli conflict, progress is measured in tiny steps. "A lot of people in my school don't like Arabs and don't know that I play PPI," says Naomi Goldstein, 14. "I don't tell them."

Amir Abu Dalu, 19, an Arab who's now a PPI coach, also keeps his counsel: "Otherwise I might get in trouble."

But a tiny step is a step just the same. First a bus ride, then a basketball game, ultimately the realization that someone you thought was your enemy makes a pretty good teammate. "In basketball it's easy to communicate," says Dalu. "You can play a game and connect, just like that."

■ Toronto

Johann Olav Koss runs Right To Play out of Canada's largest city, and University of Toronto professor and former Olympic distance runner Bruce Kidd has been a reliable sounding board for him. I've turned up at Kidd's office because SDP is one of his academic specialties, and I'm looking for a sense of where the movement has been and where it might go.

In the 19th century, English-speaking exporters of sport, freighted with ulterior motives such as imperialism and evangelism, held attitudes strikingly different from those of Luke Dowdney, Tommy Clark and Brendan Tuohey. The Victorians took their "Games Ethic" from the playing fields of Eton and sent it overseas to "civilize" the ancestors of many of the very people engaged by SDP today.

Fast-forward to 1987, to Kenya and the Eastlands of Nairobi. A Canadian environmental worker named Bob Munro looks on as a handful of kids play with a soccer ball made of discarded shopping bags tied with bits of string. "Clean up the field," Munro tells them, "and I'll give you a real ball." Soon Munro launches the Mathare Youth Sports Association (MYSA), a soccer league with a blunt message: *If you do something, MYSA does something; if you do nothing, MYSA does nothing.* To join elite teams, players must pledge to perform thousands of hours of community service together each season. Those who organize cleanups, counsel peers in AIDS-prevention activities and coach or referee younger kids become eligible for scholarships. Teams can't take a field unless they clear it of trash—but earn points in the standings for doing so. Today MYSA, which is owned and run by the youths themselves and was nominated for a Nobel Peace Prize in 2003 and '04, touches 25,000 young Kenyans at any given time with nested-in-sport programs in community building, health education and environmentalism.

Kidd points out that the recent rise of SDP coincides with the fall of apartheid as much as it follows from the efforts of Koss and MYSA. Activists who had led the international sports boycott that helped bring down the South African regime—Kidd among them—essentially asked, "What do we do now?" They rallied to the answer that came back from their allies in the new Africa: "Help us build sport."

Today even those in sport's sunlit uplands are responding to that cry. When he stood before the IOC in Singapore in 2005 to deliver the final pitch for London's 2012 Olympic bid, Sebastian Coe pledged millions in aid for SDP to benefit 12 million people in 20 countries. The IOC chose London over Paris, Moscow, Madrid and New York City in large part because of that commitment to "legacy." In its winning bid for the 2016 Olympics, Rio also distinguished itself over rivals such as Chicago with a superior commitment to grassroots sport. With the most recent World Cup and Commonwealth Games having taken place in South Africa and India, respectively, and the next World Cup and Olympics ticketed for Brazil, a legacy component for the developing world is the new normal for major global events.

But Kidd is among many students of the movement who sound cautionary notes. "It's woefully underfunded and highly uncoordinated," he tells me. "And it's completely unregulated and largely isolated from mainstream development efforts." At international conferences dedicated to SDP, delegates from the developing world complain about Westerners who parachute in with things that aren't wanted or needed. As Right To Play spearheads the handoff of responsibility to locals, such as a 500-person team in Liberia led by a former refugee who first encountered SDP in a displacement camp, Kidd credits Koss with leading a move away from "a top-down, we-know-what-you-need approach with First World volunteers."

Before the Brazilian national soccer team visited Port-au-Prince in 2004 to play its Haitian counterparts, organizers proposed offering free tickets to those who turned in a firearm, only to cancel the plan at the last minute out of security fears. Even so, without a long-term violence-reduction campaign, such an event would have been a one-off with limited impact. "More attention has to be paid to context," Kidd tells me. "It's got to be sport *plus*. Sport plus education, sport plus health, sport plus peace-building." For all its networking and digital platforms, SDP's biggest challenge may be coordination. "In Zambia, I saw kids in slums who'd been trained five or more times by different NGOs, while just outside the city there was nothing," Kidd says. "NGOs aren't just fighting for donors, they're fighting for kids."

Or as Eli Wolff of Brown University's Sport and Development Project, who also coordinates the International Sport for Development and Peace Association, puts it, "There's been this boom, lots of networks and groups, but not really a professionalization of the field. There's no credentialing process or quality control, the way there is for teachers or lawyers. And there's the question, Is it effective?"

It's a familiar demand in sports: Show me the numbers. Is a program actually creating a positive outcome or just coinciding with it? "Because there's so much evidence that participation is a good thing, it's easy to assume that programs work," says Amy Farkas, a former sport-for-development specialist with UNICEF. "It's a lot easier to simply justify your program's existence than to do the hard work of justifying the impact of the intervention. That's why all sport-for-development programs need rigorous monitoring and evaluation."

Kidd believes the clamor for M&E, as it's known, can be taken too far. "People who have personal trainers, who choose schools for their kids based on athletic opportunities, tell us, 'Prove it! Prove that sport has benefits!'" he says. "That's where Johann has made a huge contribution. He continues to argue on the rights-based front."

But practitioners of all types recognize that funders are increasingly insisting on proof of results. "You're tempted to do sport for sport's sake, because it's fun," says Miles, the Grassroot Soccer executive. "We like it. But you have to show donors the outcomes."

■ Chicago

The Beyond Sport Summit is a three-day mixer for all sides of SDP's triangle—problem, practitioner and patron. It's a place to shake loose funding and inspire others, and it serves as the Grammys of the field, a place to call attention to deserving programs. Dowdney,

Clark and Tuohey turned up for the 2010 edition in Chicago, but so too did scores of first-timers, many with little more than a notion and a dream.

Since its founding in 2008, Beyond Sport, a London-based firm that helps match practitioners with corporate sponsors, has had a particular eye for the modest initiative that would have an enormous impact if only it could be replicated or scaled up. But even Beyond Sport can't recognize every worthy project. Cambodia, for instance, is a country whose 40,000 amputees, victims of some of the millions of mines laid during a decade of war, were long considered unemployable. Now more than 60% of the players in the Cambodian National Volleyball League-Disabled (CNVL-D), mostly demobilized soldiers from both sides of the conflict, hold jobs. Even more notably, with its sponsors and broad fan following, the league has so transformed public attitudes that many disabled Cambodians, athletic and not, now wear shorts to show off their prostheses. A league like the CNVL-D could flourish in virtually any postconflict part of the world.

Moving the Goalposts is another initiative ready for its scale-up. It offers soccer to Kenyan girls, who are much more likely than boys to be HIV-positive. The program distributes packs of sanitary pads imprinted with health messages, but it operates only in the coastal region of Kilifi—which invites the question, What if it had the funding to expand throughout sub-Saharan Africa?

Similarly, in barely five years Globalbike has touched the lives of some 400,000 people by supplying bicycles to frontline aid workers in Africa and Asia. A microfinance loan officer serving village artisans in Ethiopia, an engineer working to ensure clean water in Bolivia, a health worker delivering vaccines in Zambia—each can see three times as many people and carry five times as much equipment by bike as on foot. A U.S.-based pro cycling team spreads word of Globalbike's impact so far, which suggests what could be accomplished if tens of thousands of bikes were delivered to the field.

No one in the developing world wants to depend on Western aid, so much buzz in the halls and breakout rooms in Chicago was about programs that have come up with their own revenue streams—groups such as Grupo Desportivo de Manica in Mozambique, a soccer club turned community hub that is building Futeco Park, three pitches girdled by 1,500 trees flush with mangos, lychees, oranges, avocados, guavas and papayas, which members will harvest and sell to fund the club's activities.

Indeed, there's a salutary realism amid all the idealism. John Sugden, an English sociologist who pioneered the "twinning" concept 25 years earlier with a mixed-faith soccer team in Belfast during the height of the Troubles and who is now the director of Football 4 Peace, doing in the Middle East with soccer what PPI does with basketball, puts it both wryly and well: "It's not as if you can sprinkle the pixie dust of sport and everything's going to be fine."

But sport does have its bewitching power, and for evidence a skeptic need only look at South Africa. Even in solitary confinement Nelson Mandela knew that many of his fellow black nationalists played soccer during their captivity on Robben Island. As he heard how the future leaders of his country brought the game to life with their own meticulously run Makana Football Association (MFA), Mandela recognized that soccer brought *them* to life—and he could imagine them in turn taking the obligations of democracy seriously. Since the fall of apartheid, former MFA players, referees and officials have served as South Africa's president, defense minister, minister for safety and security, deputy chief justice and sports minister, as well as provincial premiers and members of parliament. In prison Mandela began to recognize a truth he would articulate decades later as a free man: "Sport can create hope where once there was only despair. It is more powerful than governments in breaking down barriers. Sport has the power to change the world."

Mandela would demonstrate this masterfully as president of the new nation. Aware of the hold of rugby on the Afrikaaner imagination, he enlisted white captain François Pienaar to help him rally citizens of all races around the national team, the Springboks—long a symbol of white-minority rule—for the 1995 World Cup, which South Africa hosted and won. Says team manager Morne du Plessis of the story told in the film *Invictus:* "The very game that kept us apart for so long, he used to unite this country."

Thus modern South Africa owes its existence as a functioning, multiracial democracy partly to the braiding together of two epic sports stories—one from a largely black game, the other from a historically white one. Considering that sport, through the international boycott, helped do away with apartheid, it's not a bad showing for a few decades' work in one small corner of the globe.

Emmanuel Madonda grew up in Durban, South Africa's fourth-largest city, and now works for the Laureus Sport for Good Foundation. "I was 14 at the time of the '95 Rugby World Cup, and it was a pivotal moment for my country," he tells me during a break in the conference. "But even more powerful is the ongoing delivery of programming, of working deeply with young people. In Zulu we have this concept of *ubuntu:* 'I am because you are.' That is the essence of it."

Today sporting *ubuntu* extends from the street kid in Rio who, thanks to boxing, is transformed from avenging tough into potential Olympian; to the African AIDS orphan who, thanks to soccer, has a better chance of living long enough to raise children of her own; to the Arab girl in West Jerusalem who, thanks to basketball, feels bound to the fortunes of a Jewish Israeli player in the NBA. Yes, we look up to Mandela and Pienaar, and to former NBA star Dikembe Mutombo, the Congolese seven-footer who built a $29 million hospital in his hometown of Kinshasa and received Beyond Sport's Humanitarian in Sport Award. We will always look up, because as fans it's in our nature to do so.

But as human beings there's something else in our nature, which leads us to look around. Our eyes meet those of others, whom we engage as opponents, teammates, collaborators, neighbors and there-but-for-the-grace-of-God versions of ourselves. As Mutombo told the gathering in Chicago, quoting a proverb of his people: "When you take the elevator to the top, please remember to send it back down so someone else might use it."

WHAT?

1. Wolff sets out to investigate whether sports-based projects can bring about lasting social change, or whether "the dream of salvation through sports [is] too grandiose." What does he find on his yearlong exploration?
2. Explain the tension that Wolff examines between sports for sports sake—the benefits of participation—and the demand for proof that programs are actually making a difference beyond the playing fields.

WHAT ELSE? WHAT'S NEXT?

3. After reading Wolff's piece and the essay by Astrid Aafjes that precedes it, explain whether you believe that sports can truly change the world for the better. Be specific in your response.
4. Choose one of the places Wolff visits and do some follow-up research so that you can update his report. Think about the following questions as you report on your findings: Is the program Wolff wrote about still in operation? Were you able to find any reports on the effects that the program has had? Based on your research, would you call the program a success?

WHO CARES?

5. What does Wolff do in his essay to appeal to readers who have no interest in sports? Do you think he is successful in reaching a broad audience? Point to specific strategies Wolff uses and to places in the essay where Wolff deploys these strategies in your response.

> *Monica Potts is associate editor for the* American Prospect, *where this article was published in September of 2011. Her work has appeared in* The New York Times, *the* Connecticut Post, *and the* Stamford Advocate. *She also blogs at* PostBourgie. *As you read this article, consider whether you think the acts of sharing it describes are a valid response to the calls for social action that many of the readings in this chapter make.*

BEFORE YOU READ

Make a list of things in your life that you would be willing to share with others—not necessarily people you know—in exchange for things that they have and that you need. Would you be willing, for example, to barter the use of your car? How about textbooks? Or your apartment? What would be your biggest concern about taking part in what Potts calls the "social market"?

HOW MUCH ARE WE WILLING TO SHARE?
Monica Potts

In the late 1990s, when Robin Chase and her co-founders started testing names for what would become the car-sharing network Zipcar, they quickly learned to avoid the word "sharing." "Every one that had the word 'share' in it," she says, "about 40 percent of the people hated. They thought, 'It's going to be dirty—crummy—like the 1960s, and I'm going to have to wait.' Imagine if hotels were called bed-sharing."

If Chase found users reluctant to embrace the concept of sharing, it might have been because hers was one of the first businesses to try it. To sell the Zipcar idea, the company highlighted its convenience: Rather than check out with an agent, customers reserve a car online for however long they need it. Rentals can be as short as an hour. The cars are parked in public lots, and users unlock the vehicles by waving their membership card over an electronic reader behind the windshield. The ignition keys and a gas card are inside. When done, customers wave their card over the reader again, which is how the company knows the car has been returned on time.

For Chase, a mother of three living in Cambridge, Massachusetts, this was as much a personal need as a business idea. She was among a generation of college graduates who didn't flee to the suburbs when they got married and had children. In the 1990s, urban-revitalization projects encouraged middle-class families to live in downtown neighborhoods. That meant consumption patterns were ripe for change. In a cramped city, space is expensive and rare, especially when it comes to owning a car.

Unlike traditional car-rental companies, Zipcar relies on members to be neat, honest, and punctual. Fees are charged for late returns, but Zipcar also appeals to users' sense of obligation to one another. It borrows some elements of what any type of sharing requires—

that we understand others need to use the good, too—and translates them into a capitalist enterprise. People have responded. After 2003, when Chase left the company, Zipcar began expanding rapidly. About four years ago, Zipcar swallowed its closest competitor, Flexcar, and now it's in 102 locations. Revenues went from $2 million in 2003 to more than $186 million in 2010. Nearly every major rental-car company is jumping in with a Zipcar-like program.

Zipcar is the most successful example of a new type of sharing that has exploded in the past decade. Five U.S. cities now have similar services with bikes. By September 2010, when Washington, D.C., began its city-run Capital Bikeshare program, the largest of its kind in the country, potential customers reacted enthusiastically to the notion of sharing. "Since Zipcar and Flexcar, it's a pretty easy step to bike-sharing," says Chris Holben, Capital Bikeshare's project manager. In focus groups, a host of names were floated, and people liked the one with "share" in the title. Holben also says that names like WeBike tested better than names like UBike: "Most people seemed to like the more inclusive name."

Go online today and you'll find even more sharing. Chase's new venture, Buzzcar, uses a social network that allows car owners to rent out their private vehicles for a short period of time. Airbnb and Couchsurfing.org let users stay in other users' apartments, and the terms of the transactions are negotiated informally between the two parties; users vouch for each other through online networks. In many cities, groups of businesses or residences pay for wireless Internet networks that are free to anyone within range. People swap old clothes and old books online. New mothers even share breast milk.

All of these services draw on the notion of sharing, but they vary greatly. Zipcar and Airbnb look a lot like traditional rental businesses but are less formal, while others are digitalized versions of an old-fashioned yard sale. Still others involve giving away items for free. They all, though, change our idea of ownership. Instead of buying a car or bike, we can belong to a network that allows us to rent one almost whenever we want. We can open up our homes. When we're finished using a good, we can increase its value by sharing it with others, and we're often happy to do so free of charge.

There are a number of names for this: the empathy economy, distributed capitalism, collaborative consumption and its counterpart, collaborative production. Yochai Benkler, a professor at Harvard Law School who has written two books on the subject, calls this type of economic model the social market, because it draws upon the obligations we feel to one another. The incentives to join and share go beyond monetary compensation.

Increased urbanization worked in tandem with other cultural shifts to trigger this phenomenon. Growing awareness of global climate change makes activities like driving a car every day less socially desirable. This coincided with new attitudes in Western countries that emphasized quality-of-life choices over the acquisition of material assets. The movement of young, well-educated adults back to cities doesn't just mean they lack the space to buy a car; it also means they're accustomed to sharing space. Most important, the rise of the Internet lowered transaction costs and created a new brand of community building.

The idea of communal property was built into the Internet itself. The programs that make our online lives possible—like Apache and Linux—were created through a system of collaborative production, brought together by uncompensated volunteers around the world. The first services to take advantage of the sharing ethos allowed users to swap music and movies, and now both legal and illegal sites have picked up where programs like Napster left off. Social networks created a new kind of wealth. In the past, we might have shown off by buying a new car, but today we show off on Facebook. "We have a new way of attaining status that doesn't have to do with assets," Chase says. "How many friends do I have? How many people are tweeting or commenting about me? What is my score on *World of Warcraft?*"

Not that we're suddenly willing to share everything. The idea breaks down somewhere along what Benkler describes as a conceptual continuum between oranges and apples. "Apples are harder to share than oranges. They require a little more intimacy or physical capability with a knife," he says. "Oranges just beg to be shared." Benkler believes that whether home-sharing services like Airbnb survive will test how far we're willing to go.

For some customers, the idea of sharing space and meeting new people is the biggest draw for joining these sites. When Ron Zucker, a 46-year-old who works in food policy in D.C., and his wife planned a trip to New York in December 2009, they decided to forgo traditional hotels and use Airbnb for the first time. Zucker found an apartment he liked near Times Square, but the regular tenant would be in town during the couple's planned trip. They decided to be roommates for the weekend.

Zucker lucked out. "My wife walked in, and the guy had this huge, hand-drawn image of Buddy Rich up on the wall, and she looked up and said, 'My husband is going to love you.'" Zucker had worked as a jazz drummer for four years. When he signed up for Airbnb, he hadn't expected to make a new friend who would share his love for one of the world's most famous jazz drummers. When the couple visited New York a second time, they wanted to stay with the same person, but his spare bedroom was taken. Instead, he offered to sleep on the couch so they could have his bed. (These types of interactions are more common with Couchsurfing, a nonprofit network of people in 230 countries who let guests sleep on their couch for a night for free.)

Other, more cautious Airbnb users can sublet their apartments when they're away without meeting their temporary tenants and leave parts of their apartment locked. There are good reasons not to share. Airbnb recently suffered a spate of bad press when a couple of San Francisco users described how their apartments were burglarized and vandalized. A woman who blogs as "EJ" said of the incident: "They smashed a hole through a locked closet door, and found the passport, cash, credit card, and grandmother's jewelry I had hidden inside. They took my camera, my iPod, an old laptop, and my external backup drive filled with photos, journals … my entire life." Airbnb at first didn't offer to compensate for the damages; now, though, it has an insurance policy, operates a 24-hour helpline, and requires verifiable identifying information when users sign up. The company also issued a mea culpa and sent all of its users an e-mail explaining its new policies, which satisfied Zucker. "I think they were probably a little bit naive," he says.

For Benkler, the rise and persistence of all of these services just shows that the social market is fundamental to human nature. Its existence is only surprising because economists have done such a good job of convincing us that people need top-down control systems, as in state-run communist economies, or market incentives like raises or bonuses, to work for the benefit of a larger group. "They said everything could be understood through rational self-interest," he says, but it isn't true. "We are more like how we tell our kids to be on the playground than what the economists say."

■ WHAT?

1. What, according to Potts, has led to the recent wider acceptance of economic models that involve sharing?
2. Would you be willing to engage in the kinds of sharing that Potts describes? Explain why you would or why you would not.
3. How, according to Potts' article, are economic transactions based on sharing a form of positive social engagement? How does sharing benefit the people who participate and their communities?

■ WHAT ELSE? WHAT'S NEXT?

4. Potts explains that Yochai Benkler, who has researched and written about the phenomenon, calls the sharing-based economic model the "social market." Using the Internet, interviews, and whatever other sources you need, look for examples of the social market at the University of South Carolina and around Columbia. Prepare a brief report of your findings. And if you see no evidence of a social market on campus or in Columbia, explain why you think this idea hasn't caught on here.

■ WHO CARES?

5. Write a complete and accurate summary of Potts' piece that you tailor for an audience of USC students. Imagine that you are trying to sell the idea of the "social market" on USC's campus, using the Potts article as your primary support.

3 | Reading.com

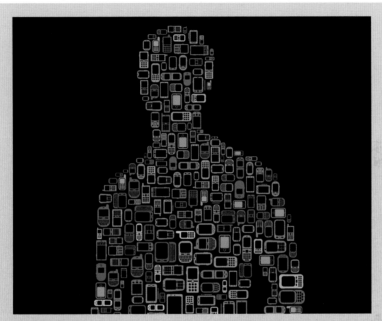

IMAGE 3.1
In "Liking is for Cowards. Go for What Hurts," Jonathan Franzen writes:
"Our lives look a lot more interesting when they're filtered through the sexy
Facebook interface. We star in our own movies, we photograph ourselves
incessantly, we click the mouse and a machine confirms our sense of
mastery." Is there anything wrong with this?

Are you ready for the intelligence-augmented 'You+' that futurist
Jamais Cascio argues is already in the works? Can you imagine a
future in which "teme" machines—as psychologist Susan Blackmore
envisions them—thrive with less and less help from humans? Do you
worry—as Jaron Lanier does—that who we are is being overwhelmed
by the technologies we use? The readings in this chapter examine
the evolution of digital technologies and present a variety of opinions
about what these technologies are doing to us.

Susan Blackmore is a psychologist and writer researching consciousness, memes, and anomalous experiences, and a Visiting Professor at the University of Plymouth. She is the author of several books, including The Meme Machine *(1999),* Conversations on Consciousness *(2005) and* Ten Zen Questions *(2009). Blackmore wrote this piece in August 2010 for the* New York Times *blog called* The Stone, *described by the newspaper as "a forum for contemporary philosophers on issues both timely and timeless." In this essay, Blackmore presents an argument about memes, ideas that replicate themselves, and a new kind of meme called the teme, which spreads via technology.*

BEFORE YOU READ——————————————————————————

Research Susan Blackmore and her ideas. Highlight anything you find that you think might help your classmates get a better handle on Blackmore's argument.

THE THIRD REPLICATOR   Susan Blackmore

All around us information seems to be multiplying at an ever-increasing pace. New books are published, new designs for toasters and i-gadgets appear, new music is composed or synthesized and, perhaps above all, new content is uploaded into cyberspace. This is rather strange. We know that matter and energy cannot increase, but apparently information can.

It is perhaps rather obvious to attribute this to the evolutionary algorithm or Darwinian process, as I will do, but I wish to emphasize one part of this process—copying. The reason information can increase like this is that, if the necessary raw materials are available, copying creates more information. Of course it is not new information, but if the copies vary (which they will if only by virtue of copying errors), and if not all variants survive to be copied again (which is inevitable given limited resources), then we have the complete three-step process of natural selection (Dennett, 1995). From here novel designs and truly new information emerge. None of this can happen without copying.

I want to make three arguments here.

The first is that humans are unique because they are so good at imitation. When our ancestors began to imitate they let loose a new evolutionary process based not on genes but on a second replicator, memes. Genes and memes then coevolved, transforming us into better and better meme machines.

The second is that one kind of copying can piggy-back on another: that is, one replicator (the information that is copied) can build on the products (vehicles or interactors) of another. This multilayered evolution has produced the amazing complexity of design we see all around us.

The third is that now, in the early 21st century, we are seeing the emergence of a third replicator. I call these temes (short for technological memes, though I have considered other names). They are digital information stored, copied, varied and selected by machines. We humans like to think we are the designers, creators and controllers of this newly emerging world, but really we are steppingstones from one replicator to the next.

As I try to explain this I shall make some assertions and assumptions that some readers may find outrageous, but I am deliberately putting my case in its strongest form so that we can debate the issues people find most interesting or most troublesome.

Some may entirely reject the notion of replicators, and will therefore dismiss the whole enterprise. Others will accept that genes are replicators but reject the idea of memes. For example, Eva Jablonka and Marion J. Lamb (2005) refer to "the dreaded memes" while Peter J. Richerson and Robert Boyd (2005), who have contributed so much to the study of cultural evolution, assert that "cultural variants are not replicators." They use the phrase "selfish memes" but still firmly reject memetics (Blackmore 2006). Similarly, in a previous "On The Human" post, William Benzon explains why he does not like the term "meme," yet he needs some term to refer to the things that evolve and so he still uses it. As John S. Wilkins points out in response, there are several more classic objections: memes are not discrete (I would say *some* are not discrete), they do not form lineages (*some* do), memetic evolution appears to be Lamarckian (but only *appears* so), memes are not replicated but re-created or reproduced, or are not copied with sufficient fidelity (see discussions in Aunger 2000, Sterelny 2006, Wimsatt 2010). I have tackled all these, and more, elsewhere and concluded that the notion is still valid (Blackmore 1999, 2010a).

So I will press on, using the concept of memes as originally defined by Dawkins who invented the term; that is, memes are "that which is imitated" or whatever it is that is copied when people imitate each other. Memes include songs, stories, habits, skills, technologies, scientific theories, bogus medical treatments, financial systems, organizations—everything that makes up human culture. I can now, briefly, tell the story of how I think we arrived where we are today.

First there were genes. Perhaps we should not call genes the first replicator because there may have been precursors worthy of that name and possibly RNA-like replicators before the evolution of DNA (Maynard Smith and Szathmary 1995). However, Dawkins (1976), who coined the term "replicator," refers to genes this way and I shall do the same.

We should note here an important distinction for living things based on DNA, that the genes are the replicators while the animals and plants themselves are vehicles, interactors, or phenotypes: ephemeral creatures constructed with the aid of genetic information coded in tiny strands of DNA packaged safely inside them. Whether single-celled bacteria, great oak trees, or dogs and cats, in the gene-centered view of evolution they are all gene machines or Dawkins's "lumbering robots." The important point here is that the genetic information is faithfully copied down the generations, while the vehicles or interactors live and die without actually being copied. Put another way, this system copies the instructions for making a product rather than the product itself, a process that has many advantages (Blackmore 1999, 2001). This interesting distinction becomes important when we move on to higher replicators.

So what happened next? Earth might have remained a one-replicator planet but it did not. One of these gene machines, a social and bipedal ape, began to imitate. We do not know why, although shifting climate may have favored stealing skills from others rather than learning them anew (Richerson and Boyd 2005). Whatever the reason, our ancestors began to copy sounds, skills and habits from one to another. They passed on lighting fires, making stone tools, wearing clothes, decorating their bodies and all sorts of skills to do with living together as hunters and gatherers. The critical point here is, of course, that they *copied* these sounds, skills and habits, and this, I suggest, is what makes humans unique. No other species (as far as we know) can do this. Songbirds can copy some sounds, some of the other great apes can imitate some actions, and most notably whales and dolphins can imitate, but none is capable of the widespread, generalized imitation that comes so easily to us. Imitation is not just some new minor ability. It changes everything. It enables a new kind of evolution.

This is why I have called humans "Earth's Pandoran species." They let loose this second replicator and began the process of memetic evolution in which memes competed to be selected by humans to be copied again. The successful memes then influenced human genes by gene-meme co-evolution (Blackmore 1999, 2001). Note that I see this process as somewhat different from gene-culture co-evolution, partly because most theorists treat culture as an adaptation (e.g. Richerson and Boyd 2005), and agree with Wilson that genes "keep culture on a leash." (Lumsden and Wilson 1981 p 13).

Benzon, in responding to Peter Railton's post here at The Stone, points out the limits of this metaphor and proposes the "chess board and game" instead. I prefer a simple host-parasite analogy. Once our ancestors could imitate they created lots of memes that competed to use their brains for their own propagation. This drove these hominids to become better meme machines and to carry the (potentially huge and even dangerous) burden of larger brain size and energy use, eventually becoming symbiotic. Neither memes nor genes are a dog or a dog-owner. Neither is on a leash. They are both vast competing sets of information, all selfishly getting copied whenever and however they can.

To help understand the next step we can think of this process as follows: one replicator (genes) built vehicles (plants and animals) for its own propagation. One of these then discovered a new way of copying and diverted much of its resources to doing this instead, creating a new replicator (memes) which then led to new replicating machinery (big-brained humans). Now we can ask whether the same thing could happen again and—aha—we can see that it can, and is.

A sticking point concerns the equivalent of the meme-phenotype or vehicle. This has plagued memetics ever since its beginning: some arguing that memes must be inside human heads while words, technologies and all the rest are their phenotypes, or "phemotypes"; others arguing the opposite. I disagree with both (Blackmore 1999, 2001). By definition, whatever is copied is the meme, and I suggest that, until very recently, there was no meme-phemotype distinction because memes were so new and so poorly replicated that they had not yet constructed stable vehicles. Now they have.

Think about songs, recipes, ways of building houses or clothes fashions. These can be copied and stored by voice, by gesture, in brains, or on paper with no clear replicator/vehicle distinction. But now consider a car factory or a printing press. Thousands of near-identical copies of cars, books, or newspapers are churned out. Those actual cars or books are not copied again but they compete for our attention and if they prove popular then more copies are made from the same template. This is much more like a replicator-vehicle system. It is "copy the instructions" not "copy the product."

Of course cars and books are passive lumps of metal, paper and ink. They cannot copy, let alone vary and select information themselves. So could any of our modern meme products take the step our hominid ancestors did long ago and begin a new kind of copying? Yes. They could and they are. Our computers, all linked up through the Internet, are beginning to carry out all three of the critical processes required for a new evolutionary process to take off.

Computers handle vast quantities of information with extraordinarily high-fidelity copying and storage. Most variation and selection is still done by human beings, with their biologically evolved desires for stimulation, amusement, communication, sex and food. But this is changing. Already there are examples of computer programs recombining old texts to create new essays or poems, translating texts to create new versions, and selecting between vast quantities of text, images and data. Above all there are search engines. Each request to Google, Alta Vista or Yahoo! elicits a new set of pages—a new combination of items selected by that search engine according to its own clever algorithms and depending on myriad previous searches and link structures.

This is a radically new kind of copying, varying and selecting, and means that a new evolutionary process is starting up. This copying is quite different from the way cells copy strands of DNA or humans copy memes. The information itself is also different, consisting of highly stable digital information stored and processed by machines rather than living cells. This, I submit, signals the emergence of temes and teme machines, the third replicator.

What should we expect of this dramatic step? It might make as much difference as the advent of human imitation did. Just as human meme machines spread over the planet, using up its resources and altering its ecosystems to suit their own needs, so the new teme machines will do the same, only faster. Indeed we might see our current ecological troubles not as primarily our fault, but as the inevitable consequence of earth's transition to being a three-replicator planet. We willingly provide ever more energy to power the Internet, and there is enormous scope for teme machines to grow, evolve and create ever more extraordinary digital worlds, some aided by humans and others independent of them. We are still needed, not least to run the power stations, but as the temes proliferate, using ever more energy and resources, our own role becomes ever less significant, even though we set the whole new evolutionary process in motion in the first place.

Whether you consider this a tragedy for the planet or a marvelous, beautiful story of creation, is up to you.

References

Aunger, R.A. (Ed) (2000) "Darwinizing Culture: The Status of Memetics as a Science," Oxford University Press

Benzon, W.L. (2010) "Cultural Evolution: A Vehicle for Cooperative Interaction Between the Sciences and the Humanities." Post for On the Human.

Blackmore, S. 1999 "The Meme Machine," Oxford and New York, Oxford University Press

Blackmore, S. 2001 "Evolution and memes: The human brain as a selective imitation device." Cybernetics and Systems, 32, 225-255

Blackmore, S. (2006) "Memetics by another name?" Review of "Not by Genes Alone" by P.J. Richerson and R. Boyd. Bioscience, 56, 74-5

Blackmore, S. (2010a) Memetics does provide a useful way of understanding cultural evolution. In "Contemporary Debates in Philosophy of Biology", Ed. Francisco Ayala and Robert Arp, Chichester, Wiley-Blackwell, 255-72.

Blackmore (2010b) "Dangerous Memes; or what the Pandorans let loose." In "Cosmos and Culture: Cultural Evolution in a Cosmic Context," Ed. Steven Dick and Mark Lupisella, NASA 297-318

Dawkins, R. (1976) "The Selfish Gene," Oxford, Oxford University Press (new edition with additional material, 1989)

Dennett, D. (1995) "Darwin's Dangerous Idea," London, Penguin

Jablonka, E. and Lamb, M.J. (2005) "Evolution in Four Dimensions: Genetic, Epigenetic, Behavioral and Symbolic Variation in the History of Life." Bradford Books

Lumsden, C. J. and Wilson, E. O. (1981) "Genes, Mind and Culture." Cambridge, Mass., Harvard University Press.

Maynard-Smith, J. and Szathmáry, E. (1995) "The Major Transitions in Evolution." Oxford, Freeman

Richerson, P. J. and Boyd, R. (2005) "Not by Genes Alone: How Culture Transformed Human Evolution," Chicago, University of Chicago Press

Sterelny, K. (2006). "Memes Revisited." British Journal for the Philosophy of Science 57 (1)

Wimsatt, W. (2010) "Memetics does not provide a useful way of understanding cultural evolution: A developmental perspective." In "Contemporary Debates in Philosophy of Biology" Ed. Francisco Ayala and Robert Arp, Chichester, Wiley-Blackwell, 255-72.

■ WHAT?

1. Blackmore uses several terms that may be unfamiliar but that are vital to understanding her argument. How, for example, does she define the following: replicator, meme, and teme. How are the three terms related?
2. Briefly—but thoroughly—summarize Blackmore's argument.
3. How does Blackmore anticipate and address possible objections to her argument about temes? Do you think her method of dealing with those who might not agree with her is effective? Explain your response.

■ WHAT ELSE? WHAT'S NEXT?

4. What else do you need to know in order to more fully understand Blackmore's essay? Where might you look to find this information?
5. What do you think are the consequences of the evolution of temes and teme machines, what Blackmore calls the "third replicator"? Find at least two sources that speculate on a future in which technology functions with less and less help from humans, and use these in your response.
6. Go online and search for Blackmore's TED Talk on memes and temes. Then, review the responses posted in the "comments" area. How would you characterize reaction to Blackmore's theory, based on these comments?

■ WHO CARES?

7. Who do you think is the intended audience for Blackmore's essay? Explain your response.

According to his website, Jaron Lanier is a "computer scientist, composer, visual artist, and author" who, in the 1980s, led a team that developed "the first implementations of multi-person virtual worlds using head mounted displays, ... as well as the first 'avatars'." The following excerpt is from his 2010 book You Are Not a Gadget: A Manifesto, which one journalist called "a provocative critique of digital technologies, including Wikipedia (which [Lanier] called a triumph of 'intellectual mob rule') and social-networking sites like Facebook and Twitter, which he has described as dehumanizing and designed to encourage shallow interactions." In the preface to You Are Not a Gadget, Lanier writes, "The words in this book are written for people, not computers."

BEFORE YOU READ

Jaron Lanier ends his preface to You Are Not a Gadget, from which "Trolls" is excerpted, with these words: "You have to be somebody before you can share yourself." What do you think he means?

TROLLS   Jaron Lanier

"Troll" is a term for an anonymous person who is abusive in an online environment. It would be nice to believe that there is only a minute troll population living among us. But in fact, a great many people have experienced being drawn into nasty exchanges online. Everyone who has experienced that has been introduced to his or her inner troll.

I have tried to learn to be aware of the troll within myself. I notice that I can suddenly become relieved when someone else in an online exchange is getting pounded or humiliated, because that means I'm safe for the moment. If someone else's video is being ridiculed on YouTube, then mine is temporarily protected. But that also means I'm complicit in a mob dynamic. Have I ever planted a seed of mob-beckoning ridicule in order to guide the mob to a target other than myself? Yes, I have, though I shouldn't have. I observe others doing that very thing routinely in anonymous online meeting places.

I've also found that I can be drawn into ridiculous pissing matches online in ways that just wouldn't happen otherwise, and I've never noticed any benefit. There is never a lesson learned, or a catharsis of victory or defeat. If you win anonymously, no one knows, and if you lose, you just change your pseudonym and start over, without having modified your point of view one bit.

If the troll is anonymous and the target is known, then the dynamic is even worse than an encounter between anonymous fragmentary pseudo-people. That's when the hive turns against personhood. For instance, in 2007 a series of "Scarlet Letter" postings in China incited online throngs to hunt down accused adulterers. In 2008, the focus shifted to Tibet sympathizers. Korea has one of the most intense online cultures in the world, so it has also suffered some of the most extreme trolling. Korean movie star Choi Jin-sil, sometimes described as the "Nation's Actress," committed suicide in 2008 after being hounded online by trolls, but she was only the most famous of a series of similar suicides.

In the United States, anonymous internet users have ganged up on targets like Lori Drew, the woman who created a fake boy persona on the internet in order to break the heart of a classmate of her daughter's, which caused the girl to commit suicide.

But more often the targets are chosen randomly, following the pattern described in the short story "The Lottery" by Shirley Jackson. In the story, residents of a placid small town draw lots to decide which individual will be stoned to death each year. It is as if a measure of human cruelty must be released, and to do so in a contained yet random way limits the damage by using the fairest possible method.

Some of the better-known random victims of troll mobs include the blogger Kathy Sierra. She was suddenly targeted in a multitude of ways, such as having images of her as a sexually mutilated corpse posted prominently, apparently in the hopes that her children would see them. There was no discernible reason Sierra was targeted. Her number was somehow drawn from the lot.

Another famous example is the tormenting of the parents of Mitchell Henderson, a boy who committed suicide. They were subjected to gruesome audio-video creations and other tools at the disposal of virtual sadists. Another occurrence is the targeting of epileptic people with flashing web designs in the hope of inducing seizures.

There is a vast online flood of videos of humiliating assaults on helpless victims. The culture of sadism online has its own vocabulary and has gone mainstream. The common term "lulz," for instance, refers to the gratification of watching others suffer over the cloud.*

When I criticize this type of online culture, I am often accused of being either an old fart or an advocate of censorship. Neither is the case. I don't think I'm necessarily any better, or more moral, than the people who tend the lulzy websites. What I'm saying, though, is that the user interface designs that arise from the ideology of the computing cloud make people—all of us— less kind. Trolling is not a string of isolated incidents, but the status quo in the online world.

■ The Standard Sequence of Troll Invocation

There are recognizable stages in the degradation of anonymous, fragmentary communication. If no pack has emerged, then individuals start to fight. This is what happens all the time in online settings. A later stage appears once a pecking order is established. Then the members of the pack become sweet and supportive of one another, even as they goad one another into ever more intense hatred of nonmembers.

---

*The Bible can serve as a prototypical example. Like Wikipedia, the Bible's authorship was shared, largely anonymous, and cumulative, and the obscurity of the individual authors served to create an oracle-like ambience for the document as "the literal word of God." If we take a non-metaphysical view of the Bible, it serves as a link to our ancestors, a window into human nature and our cultural origins, and can be used as a source of solace and inspiration. Someone who believes in a personal God can felicitously believe that the Bible reflects that God indirectly, through the people who wrote it. But when people buy into the oracle illusion, the Bible just turns into a tool to help religious leaders and politicians manipulate them.

*A website called the Encyclopedia Dramatica brags on its main page that it "won the 2nd Annual Mashable Open Web Awards for the wiki category." As I check it today, in late 2008, just as this book is about to leave my hands, the headlining "Article of the Now" is described in this way: "[Three guys] decided that the best way to commemorate their departing childhood was to kill around 21 people with hammers, pipes and screwdrivers, and record the whole thing on their [video recording] phones." This story was also featured on Boing Boing—which went to the trouble of determining that it was not a hoax—and other top sites this week.

This suggests a hypothesis to join the ranks of ideas about how the circumstances of our evolution influenced our nature. We, the big-brained species, probably didn't get that way to fill a single, highly specific niche. Instead, we must have evolved with the ability to switch between different niches. We evolved to be *both* loners *and* pack members. We are optimized not so much to be one or the other, but to be able to switch between them.

New patterns of social connection that are unique to online culture have played a role in the spread of modern networked terrorism. If you look at an online chat about anything, from guitars to poodles to aerobics, you'll see a consistent pattern: jihadi chat looks just like poodle chat. A pack emerges, and either you are with it or against it. If you join the pack, then you join the collective ritual hatred.

If we are to continue to focus the powers of digital technology on the project of making human affairs less personal and more collective, then we ought to consider how that project might interact with human nature.

The genetic aspects of behavior that have received the most attention (under rubrics like sociobiology or evolutionary psychology) have tended to focus on things like gender differences and mating behaviors, but my guess is that clan orientation and its relationship to violence will turn out to be the most important area of study.

■ Design Underlies Ethics in the Digital World

People are not universally nasty online. Behavior varies considerably from site to site. There are reasonable theories about what brings out the best or worst online behaviors: demographics, economics, child-rearing trends, perhaps even the average time of day of usage could play a role. My opinion, however, is that certain details in the design of the user interface experience of a website are the most important factors.

People who can spontaneously invent a pseudonym in order to post a comment on a blog or on YouTube are often remarkably mean. Buyers and sellers on eBay are a little more civil, despite occasional disappointments, such as encounters with flakiness and fraud. Based on those data, you could conclude that it isn't exactly anonymity, but *transient* anonymity, coupled with a lack of consequences, that brings out online idiocy.

With more data, that hypothesis can be refined. Participants in Second Life (a virtual online world) are generally not quite as mean to one another as are people posting comments to Slashdot (a popular technology news site) or engaging in edit wars on Wikipedia, even though all allow pseudonyms. The difference might be that on Second Life the pseudonymous personality itself is highly valuable and requires a lot of work to create.

So a better portrait of the troll-evoking design is effortless, consequence-free, transient anonymity in the service of a goal, such as promoting a point of view, that stands entirely apart from one's identity or personality. Call it drive-by anonymity.

Computers have an unfortunate tendency to present us with binary choices at every level, not just at the lowest one, where the bits are switching. It is easy to be anonymous or fully revealed, but hard to be revealed just enough. Still, that does happen, to varying degrees. Sites like eBay and Second Life give hints about how design can promote a middle path.

Anonymity certainly has a place, but that place needs to be designed carefully. Voting and peer review are pre-internet examples of beneficial anonymity. Sometimes it is desirable for people to be free of fear of reprisal or stigma in order to invoke honest opinions. To have a substantial exchange, however, you need to be fully present. That is why facing one's accuser is a fundamental right of the accused.

■ Could Drive-by Anonymity Scale Up the Way Communism and Fascism Did?

For the most part, the net has delivered happy surprises about human potential. As I pointed out earlier, the rise of the web in the early 1990s took place without leaders, ideology, advertising, commerce, or anything other than a positive sensibility shared by millions of people. Who would have thought that was possible? Ever since, there has been a constant barrage of utopian extrapolations from positive online events. Whenever a blogger humiliates a corporation by posting documentation of an infelicitous service representative, we can expect triumphant hollers about the end of the era of corporate abuses.

It stands to reason, however, that the net can also accentuate negative patterns of behavior or even bring about unforeseen social pathology. Over the last century, new media technologies have often become prominent as components of massive outbreaks of organized violence.

For example, the Nazi regime was a major pioneer of radio and cinematic propaganda. The Soviets were also obsessed with propaganda technologies. Stalin even nurtured a "Manhattan Project" to develop a 3-D theater with incredible, massive optical elements that would deliver perfected propaganda. It would have been virtual reality's evil twin if it had been completed. Many people in the Muslim world have only gained access to satellite TV and the internet in the last decade. These media certainly have contributed to the current wave of violent radicalism. In all these cases, there was an intent to propagandize, but intent isn't everything.

It's not crazy to worry that, with millions of people connected through a medium that sometimes brings out their worst tendencies, massive, fascist-style mobs could rise up suddenly. I worry about the next generation of young people around the world growing up with internet-based technology that emphasizes crowd aggregation, as is the current fad. Will they be more likely to succumb to pack dynamics when they come of age?

What's to prevent the acrimony from scaling up? Unfortunately, history tells us that collectivist ideals can mushroom into large-scale social disasters. The *fascias* and communes of the past started out with small numbers of idealistic revolutionaries.

I am afraid we might be setting ourselves up for a reprise. The recipe that led to social catastrophe in the past was economic humiliation combined with collectivist ideology. We already have the ideology in its new digital packaging, and it's entirely possible we could face dangerously traumatic economic shocks in the coming decades.

■ An Ideology of Violation

The internet has come to be saturated with an ideology of violation. For instance, when some of the more charismatic figures in the online world, including Jimmy Wales, one of the founders of Wikipedia, and Tim O'Reilly, the coiner of the term "web 2.0," proposed a voluntary code of conduct in the wake of the bullying of Kathy Sierra, there was a widespread outcry, and the proposals went nowhere.

The ideology of violation does not radiate from the lowest depths of trolldom, but from the highest heights of academia. There are respectable academic conferences devoted to methods of violating sanctities of all kinds. The only criterion is that researchers come up with some way of using digital technology to harm innocent people who thought they were safe.

In 2008, researchers from the University of Massachusetts at Amherst and the University of Washington presented papers at two of these conferences (called Defcon and Black Hat), disclosing a bizarre form of attack that had apparently not been expressed in public before, even in works of fiction. They had spent two years of team effort figuring out how to use mobile phone technology to hack into a pacemaker and turn it off by remote control, in order to kill a person. (While they withheld some of the details in their public presentation, they certainly described enough to assure protégés that success was possible.)

The reason I call this an expression of ideology is that there is a strenuously constructed lattice of arguments that decorate this murderous behavior so that it looks grand and new. If the same researchers had done something similar without digital technology, they would at the very least have lost their jobs. Suppose they had spent a couple of years and significant funds figuring out how to rig a washing machine to poison clothing in order to (hypothetically) kill a child once dressed. Or what if they had devoted a lab in an elite university to finding a new way to imperceptibly tamper with skis to cause fatal accidents on the slopes? These are certainly doable projects, but because they are not digital, they don't support an illusion of ethics.

A summary of the ideology goes like this: All those nontechnical, ignorant, innocent people out there are going about their lives thinking that they are safe, when in actuality they are terribly vulnerable to those who are smarter than they are. Therefore, we smartest technical people ought to invent ways to attack the innocents, and publicize our results, so that everyone is alerted to the dangers of our superior powers. After all, a clever evil person might come along.

There are some cases in which the ideology of violation does lead to practical, positive outcomes. For instance, any bright young technical person has the potential to discover a new way to infect a personal computer with a virus. When that happens, there are several possible next steps. The least ethical would be for the "hacker" to infect computers. The most ethical would be for the hacker to quietly let the companies that support the computers know, so that users can download fixes. An intermediate option would be to publicize the "exploit" for glory. A fix can usually be distributed before the exploit does harm.

But the example of the pacemakers is entirely different. The rules of the cloud apply poorly to reality. It took two top academic labs two years of focused effort to demonstrate the exploit, and that was only possible because a third lab at a medical school was able to procure pacemakers and information about them that would normally be very hard to come by. Would high school students or terrorists, or any other imaginable party, have been able to assemble the resources necessary to figure out whether it was possible to kill people in this new way?

The fix in this case would require many surgeries—more than one of each person who wears a pacemaker. New designs of pacemakers will only inspire new exploits. There will always be a new exploit, because there is no such thing as perfect security. Will each heart patient have to schedule heart surgeries on an annual basis in order to keep ahead of academic do-gooders, just in order to stay alive? How much would it cost? How many would die from the side effects of surgery? Given the endless opportunity for harm, no one will be able to act on the information the researchers have graciously provided, so everyone with a pacemaker will forever be at greater risk than they otherwise would have been. No improvement has taken place, only harm.

Those who disagree with the ideology of violation are said to subscribe to a fallacious idea known as "security through obscurity." Smart people aren't supposed to accept this strategy for security, because the internet is supposed to have made obscurity obsolete.

Therefore, another group of elite researchers spent years figuring out how to pick one of the toughest-to-pick door locks, and posted the results on the internet. This was a lock that thieves had not learned to pick on their own. The researchers compared their triumph to Turing's cracking of Enigma. The method used to defeat the lock would have remained obscure were it not for the ideology that has entranced much of the academic world, especially computer science departments.

Surely obscurity is the only fundamental form of security that exists, and the internet by itself doesn't make it obsolete. One way to deprogram academics who buy into the pervasive ideology of violation is to point out that security through obscurity has another name in the world of biology: biodiversity.

The reason some people are immune to a virus like AIDS is that their particular bodies are obscure to the virus. The reason that computer viruses infect PCs more than Macs is not that a Mac is any better engineered, but that it is relatively obscure. PCs are more commonplace. This means that there is more return on the effort to crack PCs.

There is no such thing as an unbreakable lock. In fact, the vast majority of security systems are not too hard to break. But there is always effort required to figure out how to break them. In the case of pacemakers, it took two years at two labs, which must have entailed a significant expense.

Another predictable element of the ideology of violation is that anyone who complains about the rituals of the elite violators will be accused of spreading FUD—fear, uncertainty, and doubt. But actually it's the ideologues who seek publicity. The whole point of publicizing exploits like the attack on pacemakers is the glory. If that notoriety isn't based on spreading FUD, what is?

■ The MIDI of Anonymity

Just as the idea of a musical note was formalized and rigidified by MIDI, the idea of drive-by, trollish, pack-switch anonymity is being plucked from the platonic realm and made into immoveable eternal architecture by software. Fortunately, the process isn't complete yet, so there is still time to promote alternative designs that resonate with human kindness. When people don't become aware of, or fail to take responsibility for, their role, accidents of time and place can determine the outcomes of the standards wars between digital ideologies. Whenever we notice an instance when history was swayed by accident, we also notice the latitude we have to shape the future.

Hive mind ideology wasn't running the show during earlier eras of the internet's development. The ideology became dominant *after* certain patterns were set, because it sat comfortably with those patterns. The origins of today's outbreaks of nasty online behavior go back quite a way, to the history of the counterculture in America, and in particular to the war on drugs.

Before the World Wide Web, there were other types of online connections, of which Usenet was probably the most influential. Usenet was an online directory of topics where anyone could post comments, drive-by style. One portion of Usenet, called "alt," was reserved for nonacademic topics, including those that were oddball, pornographic, illegal, or offensive. A lot of the alt material was wonderful, such as information about obscure musical instruments, while some of it was sickening, such as tutorials on cannibalism.

To get online in those days you usually had to have an academic, corporate, or military connection, so the Usenet population was mostly adult and educated. That didn't help. Some users still turned into mean idiots online. This is one piece of evidence that it's the design, not the demographic, that concentrates bad behavior. Since there were so few people online, though, bad "netiquette" was then more of a curiosity than a problem.

Why did Usenet support drive-by anonymity? You could argue that it was the easiest design to implement at the time, but I'm not sure that's true. All those academic, corporate, and military users belonged to large, well-structured organizations, so the hooks were immediately available to create a non-anonymous design. If that had happened, today's websites might not have inherited the drive-by design aesthetic.

So if it wasn't laziness that promoted online anonymity, what was it?

■ Facebook Is Similar to No Child Left Behind

Personal reductionism has always been present in information systems. You have to declare your status in reductive ways when you file a tax return. Your real life is represented by a silly, phony set of database entries in order for you to make use of a service in an approximate way. Most people are aware of the difference between reality and database entries when they file taxes.

But the order is reversed when you perform the same kind of self-reduction in order to create a profile on a social networking site. You fill in the data: profession, marital status, and residence. But in this case digital reduction becomes a causal element, mediating contact between new friends. This is new. It used to be that government was famous for being impersonal, but in a post-personal world, that will no longer be a distinction.

It might at first seem that the experience of youth is now sharply divided between the old world of school and parents, and the new world of social networking on the internet, but actually school now belongs on the new side of the ledger. Education has gone through a parallel transformation, and for similar reasons.

Information systems need to have information in order to run, but information underrepresents reality. Demand more from information than it can give, and you end up with monstrous designs. Under the No Child Left Behind Act of 2002, for example, U.S. teachers are forced to choose between teaching general knowledge and "teaching to the test." The best teachers are thus often disenfranchised by the improper use of educational informational systems.

What computerized analysis of all the country's school tests has done to education is exactly what Facebook has done to friendships. In both cases, life is turned into a database. Both degradations are based on the same philosophical mistake, which is the belief that computers can presently represent human thought or human relationships. These are things computers cannot currently do.

Whether one expects computers to improve in the future is a different issue. In a less idealistic atmosphere it would go without saying that software should only be designed to perform tasks that can be successfully performed at a given time. That is not the atmosphere in which internet software is designed, however.

If we build a computer model of an automobile engine, we know how to test whether it's any good. It turns out to be easy to build bad models! But it is possible to build good ones. We must model the materials, the fluid dynamics, the electrical subsystem. In each case, we have extremely solid physics to rely on, but we have lots of room for making mistakes in the logic or conception of how the pieces fit together. It is inevitably a long, unpredictable grind to debug a serious simulation of any complicated system. I've worked on varied simulations of such things as surgical procedures, and it is a humbling process. A good surgical simulation can take years to refine.

When it comes to people, we technologists must use a completely different methodology. We don't understand the brain well enough to comprehend phenomena like education or friendship on a scientific basis. So when we deploy a computer model of something like learning or friendship in a way that has an effect on real lives, we are relying on faith. When we ask people to live their lives through our models, we are potentially reducing life itself. How can we ever know what we might be losing?

■ The Abstract Person Obscures the Real Person

What happened to musical notes with the arrival of MIDI is happening to people.

It breaks my heart when I talk to energized young people who idolize icons of the new digital ideology, like Facebook, Twitter, Wikipedia, and free/Creative Commons mashups. I am always struck by the endless stress they put themselves through. They must manage their online reputations constantly, avoiding the ever-roaming evil eye of the hive mind, which can turn on an individual at any moment. A "Facebook generation" young person who suddenly becomes humiliated online has no way out, for there is only one hive.

I would prefer not to judge the experiences or motivations of other people, but surely this new strain of gadget fetishism is driven more by fear than by love.

At their best, the new Facebook/Twitter enthusiasts remind me of the anarchists and other nutty idealists who populated youth culture when I grew up. The ideas might be silly, but at least the believers have fun as they rebel against the parental-authority quality of entities like record companies that attempt to fight music piracy.

The most effective young Facebook users, however—the ones who will probably be winners if Facebook turns out to be a model of the future they will inhabit as adults—are the ones who create successful online fictions about themselves.

They tend their doppelgängers fastidiously. They must manage offhand remarks and track candid snapshots at parties as carefully as a politician. Insincerity is rewarded, while sincerity creates a lifelong taint. Certainly, some version of this principle existed in the lives of teenagers before the web came along, but not with such unyielding, clinical precision.

The frenetic energy of the original flowering of the web has reappeared in a new generation, but there is a new brittleness to the types of connections people make online.

This is a side effect of the illusion that digital representations can capture much about actual human relationships.

The binary character at the core of software engineering tends to reappear at higher levels. It is far easier to tell a program to run or not to run, for instance, than it is to tell it to sort-of run. In the same way, it is easier to set up a rigid representation of human relationships on digital networks: on a typical social networking site, either you are designated to be in a couple or you are single (or you are in one of a few other predetermined states of being)—and that reduction of life is what gets broadcast between friends all the time. What is communicated between people eventually becomes their truth. Relationships take on the troubles of software engineering.

■ Just a Reminder That I'm Not Anti-Net

It seems ridiculous to have to say this, but just in case anyone is getting the wrong idea, let me affirm that I am not turning against the internet. I love the internet.

For just one example among many, I have been spending quite a lot of time on an online forum populated by oud players. (The oud is a Middle Eastern string instrument.) I hesitate to mention it, because I worry that any special little place on the internet can be ruined if it gets too much attention.

The oud forum revives the magic of the early years of the internet. There's a bit of a feeling of paradise about it. You feel each participant's passion for the instrument, and we help one another become more intense. It's amazing to watch oud players from around the world cheer on an oud builder as he posts pictures of an instrument under construction. It's thrilling to hear clips from a young player captured in midair just as she is getting good.

The fancy web 2.0 designs of the early twenty-first century start off by classifying people into bubbles, so you meet your own kind. Facebook tops up dating pools, LinkedIn corrals careerists, and so on.

The oud forum does the opposite. There you find Turks and Armenians, elders and kids, Israelis and Palestinians, rich professionals and struggling artists, formal academics and bohemian street musicians, all talking with one another about a shared obsession. We get to know one another; we are not fragments to one another. Inner trolls most definitely appear now and then, but less often than in most online environments. The oud forum doesn't solve the world's problems, but it does allow us to live larger than them.

When I told Kevin Kelly about this magical confluence of obsessive people, he immediately asked if there was a particular magical person who tended the oud forum. The places that work online always turn out to be the beloved projects of individuals, not the automated aggregations of the cloud. In this case, of course, there is such a magical person, who turns out to be a young Egyptian American oud player in Los Angeles.

The engineer in me occasionally ponders the rather crude software that the forum runs on. The deep design mystery of how to organize and present multiple threads of conversation on a screen remains as unsolved as ever. But just when I am about to dive into a design project to improve forum software, I stop and wonder if there really is much room for improvement.

It's the people who make the forum, not the software. Without the software, the experience would not exist at all, so I celebrate that software, as flawed as it is. But it's not as if the forum would really get much better if the software improved. Focusing too much on the software might even make things worse by shifting the focus from the people.

There is huge room for improvement in digital technologies overall. I would love to have telepresence sessions with distant oudists, for instance. But once you have the basics of a given technological leap in place, it's always important to step back and focus on the people for a while.

■ WHAT?

1. What is a manifesto? Explain how "Trolls" does or does not fit that definition.
2. Explain what you think Lanier means when he writes that "the user interface designs that arise from the ideology of the computing cloud make people—all of us—less kind. Trolling is not a string of isolated incidents, but the status quo in the online world." Do you agree with this assertion?
3. What, according to Lanier, is "drive-by anonymity"? How does it contribute to what Lanier calls trollish behavior?
4. How does Lanier's argument implicate Facebook and other social networking and crowd-sourcing sites? Do you see a danger in what Lanier calls "internet-based technology that emphasizes crowd aggregation"? Explain your response.

■ WHAT ELSE? WHAT'S NEXT

5. In his essay, Lanier writes: "If we are to continue to focus the powers of digital technology on the project of making human affairs less personal and more collective, then we ought to consider how that project might interact with human nature." Part of what Lanier is concerned with in his essay is responsibility—our social obligations to one another and how digital technology might be transforming these obligations. Working with a group of classmates, propose a code of conduct and responsibility for a social networking site with which you are familiar. Keep in mind that any code of this kind must balance a variety of issues, among them anonymity, free speech, accountability, and the differences between face-to-face and digital encounters. As a starting point, you and your group mates should research existing codes at a few sites online.

■ WHO CARES?

6. Analyze Lanier's tone in "Trolls"—not necessarily what he says, but *how* he says it. How would you characterize his tone? What kind of language does he use? Is he talking *with* his readers or *at* them? What rhetorical effect does his tone have on you, as a reader?

> *Leon Neyfakh writes for the* Boston Globe, *where this article was published in May of 2011. Neyfakh uses his piece to report on a "small chorus of voices from law, technology, and government—united under the banner of a movement known as open data—who are already arguing that the benefits of opening up government records and generally disseminating as much data as possible outweigh the costs."*

BEFORE YOU READ———————————————————————————
Research Jane Yakowitz's concept of the "data commons" and write a brief explanation of the concept. Cite at least two sources, following MLA guidelines, in your response.

WHAT IF PRIVACY IS KEEPING US FROM REAPING THE REAL BENEFITS OF THE INFOSPHERE? Leon Neyfakh

If you're obsessive about your health, and you have $100 to spare, the Fitbit is a portable tracking device you can wear on your wrist that logs, in real time, how many calories you've burned, how far you've walked, how many steps you've taken, and how many hours you've slept. It generates colorful graphs that chart your lifestyle and lets you measure yourself against other users. Essentially, the Fitbit is a machine that turns your physical life into a precise, analyzable stream of data.

If this sounds appealing—if you're the kind of person who finds something seductive about the idea of leaving a thick plume of data in your wake as you go about your daily business—you'll be glad to know that it's happening to you regardless of whether you own a fancy pedometer. Even if this thought terrifies you, there's not much you can do: As most of us know by now, we're all leaving a trail of data behind us, generating 0s and 1s in someone's ledger every time we look something up online, make a phone call, go to the doctor, pay our taxes, or buy groceries.

Taken together, the information that millions of us are generating about ourselves amounts to a data set of unimaginable size and growing complexity: a vast, swirling cloud of information about all of us and none of us at once, covering everything from the kind of car we drive to the movies we've rented on Netflix to the prescription drugs we take.

Who owns the data in that cloud has been the subject of ferocious debate. It's not all stored in one place, of course—our lives are tracked and documented by a diffuse assortment of entities that includes private companies like Google and Visa, as well as governmental agencies like the IRS, the Department of Education, and the Census Bureau.

Up to now, the public conversation on this kind of data has taken the form of an argument about privacy rights, with legal scholars, computer scientists, and others arguing for tighter restrictions on how our data is used by companies and the government, and consumer advocates instructing us on how to prevent our information from being collected and misused.

But a small group of thinkers is suggesting an entirely new way of understanding our relationship with the data we generate. Instead of arguing about ownership and the right to privacy, they say, we should be imagining data as a public resource: a bountiful trove of information about our society which, if properly managed and cared for, can help us set better policy, more effectively run our institutions, promote public health, and generally give us a more accurate understanding of who we are. This growing pool of data should be public and anonymous, they say—and each of us should feel a civic responsibility to contribute to it.

In a paper forthcoming in the Harvard Journal of Law & Technology, Brooklyn Law School professor Jane Yakowitz introduces the concept of a "data commons"—a sort of public garden where everyone brings their data to be anonymized and made available to researchers working in the public interest. In the paper, she argues that the societal benefits of a thriving data commons outweigh the potential risks from the crooks and hackers who might use it for harm.

Yakowitz's paper has found support among a wider movement of thinkers who believe that, while protecting people's privacy is certainly important, it should not be our only priority when it comes to managing information. This position might be a hard sell at a time when consumers are increasingly worried about mass data leaks and identity theft, but Yakowitz and others argue that we shouldn't let fear of such inevitable accidents cloud our ability to see just how necessary data collection is to our progress as a society.

"There are patterns and trends that none of us can discern by looking at our own individual experiences," Yakowitz said. "But if we pooled our information, then these patterns can emerge very quickly and irrefutably. So, we should want that sort of knowledge to be made publicly available."

The idea of sharing one's personal information with researchers and policy makers for the good of society has a long history in the United States, dating back to the early years of the national census in the 1790s. Back then, a failure to comply with the census was considered a serious abdication of one's duty to the state. According to Douglas Sylvester, a law professor at Arizona State University, that attitude was grounded in a fundamental belief that in order to run a fair democracy, the country's leaders needed a detailed knowledge of the people they were governing. Anyone who stood in the way of that was publicly shamed.

"During the early years of the census, your name and your economic information were posted—literally posted, on a sheet of paper—in the public square, for anyone to come and see," said Sylvester, who has written extensively on the history of data-collection and privacy in America. "The idea was that if your name did not appear, your peers would know that you had not cooperated. Providing this information was a civic obligation."

Of course, census workers still speak of responsible citizenship and good government when they knock on your door and implore you to fill out their forms, and technically, not doing so is still illegal. But the idea that we owe it to our fellow men to share our information with the public is long gone—and the fact that we think of it as "our" information provides a hint as to what has changed. At some point, privacy experts say, Americans started thinking of their personal data as a form of property, something that could be stolen from them if they didn't vigilantly protect it.

It's hard to pinpoint exactly when this transformation began, but its roots lie in the dramatic expansion of administrative data-collection that began around the turn of the last century. A more urban and industrialized nation with more public programs meant that more information was being submitted to government agencies, and eventually, people started getting possessive. Then, during the 1960s, according to Sylvester, the Watergate scandal and advancements in computing power made people even more nervous about government monitoring, and the notion that one's personal information required protection from hostile outside forces became deeply ingrained in the nation's psyche.

"Property rules are where people end up going when something is new and uncertain," said Yakowitz. "When we aren't sure what to do with something new, there are always a lot of stakeholders who claim a property interest in it. And I think that's sort of what happened with data."

Yakowitz came face-to-face with this attitude, and realized how severely it might impede scholarship, as a researcher at UCLA four years ago, when she was working on a study on affirmative action and student performance. Trying to obtain the data sets she needed for her work proved to be an immensely frustrating experience, the 31-year-old said: Some of the schools that kept the records she was after were uncooperative, and in one case, individual graduates who had heard about her research objected to having their information included in her analysis despite the fact that it had been scrubbed of anything that personally identified them.

Yakowitz was disturbed by the fact that her research could be thwarted just because a few people didn't want "their" data being used in ways they hadn't anticipated or agreed to. The experience had a galvanizing effect on Yakowitz, causing her to think more pointedly about how Americans understood their relationship to data, and how their attitudes might be at odds with the public interest. Her concept of a "data commons" came out of that thought process. The underlying goal is to revive the idea that sharing our information—this time, without our names attached—should be seen as a civic duty, like a tax that each of us pays in exchange for enjoying the benefits of what researchers learn from it.

Yakowitz began giving presentations on the data commons in February—she visited Google earlier this month to discuss the idea—and although it won't officially be published until the fall, her paper has already begun attracting attention among people who care about data and privacy law. In it, she reviews the literature on so-called re-identification techniques—the ways that hackers and criminals might cross-reference big, anonymous data sets to figure out information about specific individuals. Yakowitz concludes that these risks have been overblown, and don't outweigh the social benefits of having lots of anonymized data publicly available. The importance currently placed on privacy in our culture, she says, is the result of a "moral panic" that ultimately hurts us.

She joins a small chorus of voices from law, technology, and government—united under the banner of a movement known as open data—who are already arguing that the benefits of opening up government records and generally disseminating as much data as possible outweigh the costs.

"If you look at the kinds of concerns that we have as a society, they involve questions about health and our economy, and these are all issues which, if they're to be addressed from an empirical point of view, require actual data on individuals and organizations," said George T. Duncan, a professor emeritus at Carnegie Mellon University's Heinz College, who has written about the tension between privacy and the social benefits of data. "Privacy advocates are so locked into their own ideological viewpoint … that they fail to appreciate the value of the data."

The potential value of data has arguably never been greater, for the simple reason that there's never been as much of it collected as there is today. According to a report published this month by the consulting firm McKinsey & Co., 15 out of 17 sectors of the American economy have more data stored per company than the entire Library of Congress. One example of data being leveraged for the public good in a way that would have been unthinkable a short time ago is Google Flu Trends, a tool that helps users track the spread of flu by telling them where, and how often, people are typing in flu-related search terms. The Global Viral Forecasting Initiative, based in San Francisco, uses large data sets provided by cellphone and credit card companies to detect and predict epidemics around the world. In Boston recently, a group of researchers commissioned by the governor to study local greenhouse emissions obtained data from the Registry for Motor Vehicles—which keeps inspection records on every car in the city—to find out how much Bostonians were driving.

But advocates of the open data movement see these applications as just a hint of its potential: The more access researchers have to the vast amount of data that is being generated every day, the more accurate and wide-ranging the insights they'll be able to produce about how to organize our cities, educate our children, fight crime, and stay healthy.

Marc Rodwin, a professor at Suffolk University Law School, has argued for a system in which patient records collected by hospitals and insurance companies—which are currently considered private property, and are routinely purchased in aggregate by pharmaceutical companies—are managed by a central authority and made available, in anonymized form, to researchers. "You can find out about dangerous drugs, you can find out about trends, you can compare effectiveness of different therapies, and the like," he said. "But if you don't have that database, you can't do it."

Even as such ideas ripen in some corners of the academy and government, proponents of open data are the first to admit that the culture as a whole seems to be heading in the opposite direction. More and more, people are bristling as they realize that everything they do online—including the e-mails they send their friends and the words they search for on Google—is being tracked and turned into data for the benefit of advertisers. And they are made understandably nervous by large-scale data breaches like the one reported last week in Massachusetts, which resulted in as many as 210,000 residents having their financial information exposed to computer hackers. In light of such perceived threats, it's no wonder the words of privacy advocates are resonating.

Yakowitz and the open data advocates acknowledge that these are reasonable fears, but point out that they won't be solved by locking down data further. The most damaging breaches, they argue, happen when thieves hack into private sources like credit card processors that are supposedly secure. When we respond by imposing tighter controls on the dissemination of anonymized data, we're just ensuring that it can't be used where it might do the most public good.

"The same groups that get really concerned about privacy issues are also the groups that call for more efficiently targeted government resources," said Holly St. Clair, the director of data services at the Metropolitan Area Planning Council in Boston, where she works on procuring governmental data sets for research purposes. "The only way to do that is with more information—with better information, with more timely information."

The problem with this vision of the future, according to some privacy experts, is not that large amounts of data don't come with obvious public benefits. It's that Yakowitz's argument presumes a level of anonymization that not only doesn't exist, but never will. Given enough outside information to draw on, they say, bad actors will always be able to cross-reference data sets with each other, figure out who's who, and harm individuals who never explicitly agreed to be included in the first place.

In one famous case back in 1997, Carnegie Mellon professor of computer science Latanya Sweeney was able to match publicly available voter rolls to a set of supposedly anonymized medical data, and successfully identify former Massachusetts Governor William F. Weld. According to Sweeney, currently a visiting professor at Harvard and an affiliate of the Berkman Center for Internet and Society, 87 percent of the US population can be identified by name in this way, based only on birthday, ZIP code, and gender. Sweeney called Yakowitz's paper on the data commons "irresponsible" for dismissing the risk of re-identification.

There are other practical obstacles as well: Data, in today's economy, is extremely valuable. Even if data sets could be made truly anonymous, Sweeney asks, why should we expect the huge private collectors of data—companies like Google and Facebook, whose business rather depends on their ability to maintain an exclusive trove of data on their customers—to share what they have for the public good? As data-gathering becomes bigger and bigger business, it might become more valuable to society—but also becomes an asset that companies will fight harder to protect.

As far as Yakowitz is concerned, that's all the more reason to try to bring about a shift in the way our culture views data. To that end, she proposes granting legal immunity to any entity that releases data into the commons, protecting them from privacy litigation under the condition that they follow a set of strictly enforced standards for anonymization. She also hopes that framing data as a public resource—something that belongs, collectively, to all of us who generate it—will give the public some leverage over big private companies to make their information public.

"Right now I feel like the public gets the rawest deal, because a lot of data is collected, and it's shared with any company that the private data-collector cares to share it with. But there's no guarantee that they'll share it with researchers who are working in the public interest," Yakowitz said. "Maybe I don't go far enough—maybe we should force these companies to share with researchers. But that's for another day, I guess."

■ WHAT?

1. How do concerns about anonymization and the commercial value of personal data complicate discussions of online privacy?
2. What personal data do you willingly make available online? (Think about information you post on Facebook, for example, tweets you send, comments you post, and forms you fill out when you shop online.) What privacy expectations do you have when you post, tweet, search, or respond online?
3. Summarize the positions for and against Jane Yakowitz's "data commons" idea that Neyfakh explains in his article. Which position do you find more compelling? Why?

■ WHAT ELSE? WHAT'S NEXT?

4. Research the privacy policies of some of the communities (online and off) in which you live and participate. You might examine, for example, your privacy rights as a student at the University of South Carolina, as a student-athlete, as a member of a fraternity or a sorority, as a pedestrian in Five Points, or at your job. Online, you might consider the privacy policies of social networking sites in which you participate, websites where you shop, and search engines that you use. After compiling your research, write a brief analysis of the differences you see between what it means to protect individual privacy in the online world vs. our offline lives.

■ WHO CARES?

5. What does Leon Neyfakh do in his article to make his readers care about this issue? Does he do enough? Did he make you care? Explain your response.

Matt Richtel, who writes about technology for The New York Times, *won the 2010 Pulitzer Prize for National Reporting for "Driven to Distraction," a series about driving and multitasking that spurred legislative efforts across the nation to deal with the problem. He wrote this piece for the June 6, 2010, edition of* The Times.

BEFORE YOU READ————————————————————————————————
Make a list of all of the digital technologies you use each day and of the ways in which you multitask using these technologies. Be prepared to share your list with the class.

HOOKED ON TECHNOLOGY, AND PAYING A PRICE   Matt Richtel

When one of the most important e-mail messages of his life landed in his in-box a few years ago, Kord Campbell overlooked it. Not just for a day or two, but 12 days. He finally saw it while sifting through old messages: a big company wanted to buy his Internet start-up. "I stood up from my desk and said, 'Oh my God, oh my God, oh my God,' " Mr. Campbell said. "It's kind of hard to miss an e-mail like that, but I did."

The message had slipped by him amid an electronic flood: two computer screens alive with e-mail, instant messages, online chats, a Web browser and the computer code he was writing.

While he managed to salvage the $1.3 million deal after apologizing to his suitor, Mr. Campbell continues to struggle with the effects of the deluge of data. Even after he unplugs, he craves the stimulation he gets from his electronic gadgets. He forgets things like dinner plans, and he has trouble focusing on his family.

His wife, Brenda, complains, "It seems like he can no longer be fully in the moment." This is your brain on computers.

Scientists say juggling e-mail, phone calls and other incoming information can change how people think and behave. They say our ability to focus is being undermined by bursts of information. These play to a primitive impulse to respond to immediate opportunities and threats. The stimulation provokes excitement—a dopamine squirt—that researchers say can be addictive. In its absence, people feel bored.

The resulting distractions can have deadly consequences, as when cellphone-wielding drivers and train engineers cause wrecks. And for millions of people like Mr. Campbell, these urges can inflict nicks and cuts on creativity and deep thought, interrupting work and family life.

While many people say multitasking makes them more productive, research shows otherwise. Heavy multitaskers actually have more trouble focusing and shutting out irrelevant information, scientists say, and they experience more stress. And scientists are discovering that even after the multitasking ends, fractured thinking and lack of focus persist. In other words, this is also your brain off computers.

"The technology is rewiring our brains," said Nora Volkow, director of the National Institute of Drug Abuse and one of the world's leading brain scientists. She and other researchers compare the lure of digital stimulation less to that of drugs and alcohol than to food and sex, which are essential but counterproductive in excess.

Technology use can benefit the brain in some ways, researchers say. Imaging studies show the brains of Internet users become more efficient at finding information. And players of some video games develop better visual acuity.

More broadly, cellphones and computers have transformed life. They let people escape their cubicles and work anywhere. They shrink distances and handle countless mundane tasks, freeing up time for more exciting pursuits.

For better or worse, the consumption of media, as varied as e-mail and TV, has exploded. In 2008, people consumed three times as much information each day as they did in 1960. And they are constantly shifting their attention. Computer users at work change windows or check e-mail or other programs nearly 37 times an hour, new research shows.

The nonstop interactivity is one of the most significant shifts ever in the human environment, said Adam Gazzaley, a neuroscientist at the University of California, San Francisco. "We are exposing our brains to an environment and asking them to do things we weren't necessarily evolved to do," he said. "We know already there are consequences."

Mr. Campbell, 43, came of age with the personal computer, and he is a heavier user of technology than most. But researchers say the habits and struggles of Mr. Campbell and his family typify what many experience—and what many more will, if trends continue.

For him, the tensions feel increasingly acute, and the effects harder to shake.

The Campbells recently moved to California from Oklahoma to start a software venture. Mr. Campbell's life revolves around computers. He goes to sleep with a laptop or iPhone on his chest, and when he wakes, he goes online. He and Mrs. Campbell, 39, head to the tidy kitchen in their four-bedroom hillside rental in Orinda, an affluent suburb of San Francisco, where she makes breakfast and watches a TV news feed in the corner of the computer screen while he uses the rest of the monitor to check his e-mail.

Major spats have arisen because Mr. Campbell escapes into video games during tough emotional stretches. On family vacations, he has trouble putting down his devices. When he rides the subway to San Francisco, he knows he will be offline 221 seconds as the train goes through a tunnel.

Their 16-year-old son, Connor, tall and polite like his father, recently received his first C's, which his family blames on distraction from his gadgets. Their 8-year-old daughter, Lily, like her mother, playfully tells her father that he favors technology over family.

"I would love for him to totally unplug, to be totally engaged," says Mrs. Campbell, who adds that he becomes "crotchety until he gets his fix." But she would not try to force a change. "He loves it. Technology is part of the fabric of who he is," she says. "If I hated technology, I'd be hating him, and a part of who my son is too."

■ Always On

Mr. Campbell, whose given name is Thomas, had an early start with technology in Oklahoma City. When he was in third grade, his parents bought him Pong, a video game. Then came a string of game consoles and PCs, which he learned to program. In high school, he balanced computers, basketball and a romance with Brenda, a cheerleader with a gorgeous singing voice. He studied too, with focus, uninterrupted by e-mail. "I did my homework because I needed to get it done," he said. "I didn't have anything else to do."

He left college to help with a family business, then set up a lawn mowing service. At night he would read, play video games, hang out with Brenda and, as she remembers it, "talk a lot more." In 1996, he started a successful Internet provider. Then he built the start-up that he sold for $1.3 million in 2003 to LookSmart, a search engine.

Mr. Campbell loves the rush of modern life and keeping up with the latest information. "I want to be the first to hear when the aliens land," he said, laughing. But other times, he fantasizes about living in pioneer days when things moved more slowly: "I can't keep everything in my head."

No wonder. As he came of age, so did a new era of data and communication.

At home, people consume 12 hours of media a day on average, when an hour spent with, say, the Internet and TV simultaneously counts as two hours. That compares with five hours in 1960, say researchers at the University of California, San Diego. Computer users visit an average of 40 Web sites a day, according to research by RescueTime, which offers time-management tools.

As computers have changed, so has the understanding of the human brain. Until 15 years ago, scientists thought the brain stopped developing after childhood. Now they understand that its neural networks continue to develop, influenced by things like learning skills.

So not long after Eyal Ophir arrived at Stanford in 2004, he wondered whether heavy multitasking might be leading to changes in a characteristic of the brain long thought immutable: that humans can process only a single stream of information at a time.

Going back a half-century, tests had shown that the brain could barely process two streams, and could not simultaneously make decisions about them. But Mr. Ophir, a student-turned-researcher, thought multitaskers might be rewiring themselves to handle the load.

His passion was personal. He had spent seven years in Israeli intelligence after being weeded out of the air force—partly, he felt, because he was not a good multitasker. Could his brain be retrained? Mr. Ophir, like others around the country studying how technology bent the brain, was startled by what he discovered.

■ The Myth of Multitasking

The test subjects were divided into two groups: those classified as heavy multitaskers based on their answers to questions about how they used technology, and those who were not.

In a test created by Mr. Ophir and his colleagues, subjects at a computer were briefly shown an image of red rectangles. Then they saw a similar image and were asked whether any of the rectangles had moved. It was a simple task until the addition of a twist: blue rectangles were added, and the subjects were told to ignore them.

The multitaskers then did a significantly worse job than the non-multitaskers at recognizing whether red rectangles had changed position. In other words, they had trouble filtering out the blue ones—the irrelevant information. So, too, the multitaskers took longer than non-multitaskers to switch among tasks, like differentiating vowels from consonants and then odd from even numbers. The multitaskers were shown to be less efficient at juggling problems.

Other tests at Stanford, an important center for research in this fast-growing field, showed multitaskers tended to search for new information rather than accept a reward for putting older, more valuable information to work. Researchers say these findings point to an interesting dynamic: multitaskers seem more sensitive than non-multitaskers to incoming information.

The results also illustrate an age-old conflict in the brain, one that technology may be intensifying. A portion of the brain acts as a control tower, helping a person focus and set priorities. More primitive parts of the brain, like those that process sight and sound, demand that it pay attention to new information, bombarding the control tower when they are stimulated.

Researchers say there is an evolutionary rationale for the pressure this barrage puts on the brain. The lower-brain functions alert humans to danger, like a nearby lion, overriding goals like building a hut. In the modern world, the chime of incoming e-mail can override the goal of writing a business plan or playing catch with the children.

"Throughout evolutionary history, a big surprise would get everyone's brain thinking," said Clifford Nass, a communications professor at Stanford. "But we've got a large and growing group of people who think the slightest hint that something interesting might be going on is like catnip. They can't ignore it." Mr. Nass says the Stanford studies are important because they show multitasking's lingering effects: "The scary part for guys like Kord is, they can't shut off their multitasking tendencies when they're not multitasking."

Melina Uncapher, a neurobiologist on the Stanford team, said she and other researchers were unsure whether the muddied multitaskers were simply prone to distraction and would have had trouble focusing in any era. But she added that the idea that information overload causes distraction was supported by more and more research.

A study at the University of California, Irvine, found that people interrupted by e-mail reported significantly increased stress compared with those left to focus. Stress hormones have been shown to reduce short-term memory, said Gary Small, a psychiatrist at the University of California, Los Angeles.

Preliminary research shows some people can more easily juggle multiple information streams. These "supertaskers" represent less than 3 percent of the population, according to scientists at the University of Utah.

Other research shows computer use has neurological advantages. In imaging studies, Dr. Small observed that Internet users showed greater brain activity than nonusers, suggesting they were growing their neural circuitry. At the University of Rochester, researchers found that players of some fast-paced video games can track the movement of a third more objects on a screen than nonplayers. They say the games can improve reaction and the ability to pick out details amid clutter.

"In a sense, those games have a very strong both rehabilitative and educational power," said the lead researcher, Daphne Bavelier, who is working with others in the field to channel these changes into real-world benefits like safer driving.

There is a vibrant debate among scientists over whether technology's influence on behavior and the brain is good or bad, and how significant it is.

"The bottom line is, the brain is wired to adapt," said Steven Yantis, a professor of brain sciences at Johns Hopkins University. "There's no question that rewiring goes on all the time," he added. But he said it was too early to say whether the changes caused by technology were materially different from others in the past.

Mr. Ophir is loath to call the cognitive changes bad or good, though the impact on analysis and creativity worries him. He is not just worried about other people. Shortly after he came to Stanford, a professor thanked him for being the one student in class paying full attention and not using a computer or phone. But he recently began using an iPhone and noticed a change; he felt its pull, even when playing with his daughter. "The media is changing me," he said. "I hear this internal ping that says: check e-mail and voice mail."

"I have to work to suppress it."

Kord Campbell does not bother to suppress it, or no longer can.

■ Interrupted by a Corpse

It is a Wednesday in April, and in 10 minutes, Mr. Campbell has an online conference call that could determine the fate of his new venture, called Loggly. It makes software that helps companies understand the clicking and buying patterns of their online customers.

Mr. Campbell and his colleagues, each working from a home office, are frantically trying to set up a program that will let them share images with executives at their prospective partner. But at the moment when Mr. Campbell most needs to focus on that urgent task, something else competes for his attention: "Man Found Dead Inside His Business."

That is the tweet that appears on the left-most of Mr. Campbell's array of monitors, which he has expanded to three screens, at times adding a laptop and an iPad. On the left screen, Mr. Campbell follows the tweets of 1,100 people, along with instant messages and group chats. The middle monitor displays a dark field filled with computer code, along with Skype, a service that allows Mr. Campbell to talk to his colleagues, sometimes using video. The monitor on the right keeps e-mail, a calendar, a Web browser and a music player.

Even with the meeting fast approaching, Mr. Campbell cannot resist the tweet about the corpse. He clicks on the link in it, glances at the article and dismisses it. "It's some article about something somewhere," he says, annoyed by the ads for jeans popping up.

The program gets fixed, and the meeting turns out to be fruitful: the partners are ready to do business. A colleague says via instant message: "YES."

Other times, Mr. Campbell's information juggling has taken a more serious toll. A few weeks earlier, he once again overlooked an e-mail message from a prospective investor. Another time, Mr. Campbell signed the company up for the wrong type of business account on Amazon.com, costing $300 a month for six months before he got around to correcting it. He has burned hamburgers on the grill, forgotten to pick up the children and lingered in the bathroom playing video games on an iPhone.

Mr. Campbell can be unaware of his own habits. In a two-and-a-half hour stretch one recent morning, he switched rapidly between e-mail and several other programs, according to data from RescueTime, which monitored his computer use with his permission. But when asked later what he was doing in that period, Mr. Campbell said he had been on a long Skype call, and "may have pulled up an e-mail or two."

The kind of disconnection Mr. Campbell experiences is not an entirely new problem, of course. As they did in earlier eras, people can become so lost in work, hobbies or TV that they fail to pay attention to family.

Mr. Campbell concedes that, even without technology, he may work or play obsessively, just as his father immersed himself in crossword puzzles. But he says this era is different because he can multitask anyplace, anytime. "It's a mixed blessing," he said. "If you're not careful, your marriage can fall apart or your kids can be ready to play and you'll get distracted."

■ The Toll on Children

Father and son sit in armchairs. Controllers in hand, they engage in a fierce video game battle, displayed on the nearby flat-panel TV, as Lily watches. They are playing Super Smash Bros. Brawl, a cartoonish animated fight between characters that battle using anvils, explosives and other weapons.

"Kill him, Dad," Lily screams. To no avail. Connor regularly beats his father, prompting expletives and, once, a thrown pillow. But there is bonding and mutual respect. "He's a lot more tactical," says Connor. "But I'm really good at quick reflexes."

Screens big and small are central to the Campbell family's leisure time. Connor and his mother relax while watching TV shows like "Heroes." Lily has an iPod Touch, a portable DVD player and her own laptop, which she uses to watch videos, listen to music and play games.

Lily, a second-grader, is allowed only an hour a day of unstructured time, which she often spends with her devices. The laptop can consume her. "When she's on it, you can holler her name all day and she won't hear," Mrs. Campbell said.

Researchers worry that constant digital stimulation like this creates attention problems for children with brains that are still developing, who already struggle to set priorities and resist impulses.

Connor's troubles started late last year. He could not focus on homework. No wonder, perhaps. On his bedroom desk sit two monitors, one with his music collection, one with Facebook and Reddit, a social site with news links that he and his father love. His iPhone availed him to relentless texting with his girlfriend.

When he studied, "a little voice would be saying, 'Look up' at the computer, and I'd look up," Connor said. "Normally, I'd say I want to only read for a few minutes, but I'd search every corner of Reddit and then check Facebook."

His Web browsing informs him. "He's a fact hound," Mr. Campbell brags. "Connor is, other than programming, extremely technical. He's 100 percent Internet savvy." But the parents worry too. "Connor is obsessed," his mother said. "Kord says we have to teach him balance."

So in January, they held a family meeting. Study time now takes place in a group setting at the dinner table after everyone has finished eating. It feels, Mr. Campbell says, like togetherness.

■ No Vacations

For spring break, the family rented a cottage in Carmel, Calif. Mrs. Campbell hoped everyone would unplug. But the day before they left, the iPad from Apple came out, and Mr. Campbell snapped one up. The next night, their first on vacation, "We didn't go out to dinner," Mrs. Campbell mourned. "We just sat there on our devices."

She rallied the troops the next day to the aquarium. Her husband joined them for a bit but then begged out to do e-mail on his phone. Later she found him playing video games.

The trip came as Mr. Campbell was trying to raise several million dollars for his new venture, a goal that he achieved. Brenda said she understood that his pursuit required intensity but was less understanding of the accompanying surge in video game.

His behavior brought about a discussion between them. Mrs. Campbell said he told her that he was capable of logging off, citing a trip to Hawaii several years ago that they called their second honeymoon. "What trip are you thinking about?" she said she asked him. She recalled that he had spent two hours a day online in the hotel's business center.

On Thursday, their fourth day in Carmel, Mr. Campbell spent the day at the beach with his family. They flew a kite and played whiffle ball. Connor unplugged too. "It changes the mood of everything when everybody is present," Mrs. Campbell said.

The next day, the family drove home, and Mr. Campbell disappeared into his office.

Technology use is growing for Mrs. Campbell as well. She divides her time between keeping the books of her husband's company, homemaking and working at the school library. She checks e-mail 25 times a day, sends texts and uses Facebook.

Recently, she was baking peanut butter cookies for Teacher Appreciation Day when her phone chimed in the living room. She answered a text, then became lost in Facebook, forgot about the cookies and burned them. She started a new batch, but heard the phone again, got lost in messaging, and burned those too. Out of ingredients and shamed, she bought cookies at the store.

She feels less focused and has trouble completing projects. Some days, she promises herself she will ignore her device. "It's like a diet—you have good intentions in the morning and then you're like, 'There went that,' " she said.

Mr. Nass at Stanford thinks the ultimate risk of heavy technology use is that it diminishes empathy by limiting how much people engage with one another, even in the same room.

"The way we become more human is by paying attention to each other," he said. "It shows how much you care." That empathy, Mr. Nass said, is essential to the human condition. "We are at an inflection point," he said. "A significant fraction of people's experiences are now fragmented."

■ WHAT?

1. Richtel quotes one researcher as saying that "technology is rewiring our brains." Explain what this means, in the context of Richtel's article, and summarize the evidence that Richtel uses to support this contention.

2. Explain what Richtel calls the "myth of multitasking." Does he change your thinking about multitasking? Why? Or why not?

■ WHAT ELSE? WHAT'S NEXT?

3. In this article, Richtel engages in explanatory writing—that is, he introduces and explains information and ideas with which the audience may not be familiar. Explanatory writing, as the name implies, has a specific purpose: It is meant to help readers understand something new. The news media engage in explanatory writing every day as they try to help their audiences make sense of what's going on in the world. With Richtel's article in mind, read the two essays that follow—"Is Google Making Us Stupid" and "Get Smarter." Then, select a concept or a technology from one of these three pieces that you would like to learn more about. Research the topic—find at least two reliable sources—and then write a brief essay in which you explain it to your classmates. Make sure you document your sources using MLA guidelines.

■ WHO CARES?

4. How does Richtel use the Campbell family to help connect with his readers and to drive home the importance of this issue?

Nicholas Carr, whose most recent book is The Big Switch: Rewiring the World, From Edison to Google *(2008), writes on the social, intellectual, and business implications of technology. He uses his own experience as a starting point in this examination of how digital technologies such as Google's search engines affect intelligence. He wrote this essay for the July/August 2008 issue of* Atlantic Monthly.

BEFORE YOU READ
Answer the following question: Has using the Internet made you smarter? Support your response with specific examples based on your experience.

IS GOOGLE MAKING US STUPID? Nicholas Carr

"Dave, stop. Stop, will you? Stop, Dave. Will you stop, Dave?" So the supercomputer HAL pleads with the implacable astronaut Dave Bowman in a famous and weirdly poignant scene toward the end of Stanley Kubrick's *2001: A Space Odyssey*. Bowman, having nearly been sent to a deep-space death by the malfunctioning machine, is calmly, coldly disconnecting the memory circuits that control its artificial "brain." "Dave, my mind is going," HAL says, forlornly. "I can feel it. I can feel it."

I can feel it, too. Over the past few years I've had an uncomfortable sense that someone, or something, has been tinkering with my brain, remapping the neural circuitry, reprogramming the memory. My mind isn't going—so far as I can tell—but it's changing. I'm not thinking the way I used to think. I can feel it most strongly when I'm reading. Immersing myself in a book or a lengthy article used to be easy. My mind would get caught up in the narrative or the turns of the argument, and I'd spend hours strolling through long stretches of prose. That's rarely the case anymore. Now my concentration often starts to drift after two or three pages. I get fidgety, lose the thread, begin looking for something else to do. I feel as if I'm always dragging my wayward brain back to the text. The deep reading that used to come naturally has become a struggle.

I think I know what's going on. For more than a decade now, I've been spending a lot of time online, searching and surfing and sometimes adding to the great databases of the Internet. The Web has been a godsend to me as a writer. Research that once required days in the stacks or periodical rooms of libraries can now be done in minutes. A few Google searches, some quick clicks on hyperlinks, and I've got the telltale fact or pithy quote I was after. Even when I'm not working, I'm as likely as not to be foraging in the Web's info-thickets reading and writing emails, scanning headlines and blog posts, watching videos and listening to podcasts, or just tripping from link to link to link. (Unlike footnotes, to which they're sometimes likened, hyperlinks don't merely point to related works; they propel you toward them.)

For me, as for others, the Net is becoming a universal medium, the conduit for most of the information that flows through my eyes and ears and into my mind. The advantages of having immediate access to such an incredibly rich store of information are many, and they've been widely described and duly applauded. "The perfect recall of silicon memory," *Wired*'s Clive Thompson has written, "can be an enormous boon to thinking." But that boon comes at a price. As the media theorist Marshall McLuhan pointed out in the 1960s, media are not just passive channels of information. They supply the stuff of thought, but they also shape the process of thought. And what the Net seems to be doing is chipping away my capacity for concentration and contemplation. My mind now expects to take in information the way the Net distributes it: in a swiftly moving stream of particles. Once I was a scuba diver in the sea of words. Now I zip along the surface like a guy on a Jet Ski.

I'm not the only one. When I mention my troubles with reading to friends and acquaintances—literary types, most of them—many say they're having similar experiences. The more they use the Web, the more they have to fight to stay focused on long pieces of writing. Some of the bloggers I follow have also begun mentioning the phenomenon. Scott Karp, who writes a blog about online media, recently confessed that he has stopped reading books altogether. "I was a lit major in college, and used to be [a] voracious book reader," he wrote. "What happened?" He speculates on the answer: "What if I do all my reading on the web not so much because the way I read has changed, i.e. I'm just seeking convenience, but because the way I THINK has changed?"

Bruce Friedman, who blogs regularly about the use of computers in medicine, also has described how the Internet has altered his mental habits. "I now have almost totally lost the ability to read and absorb a longish article on the web or in print," he wrote earlier this year. A pathologist who has long been on the faculty of the University of Michigan Medical School, Friedman elaborated on his comment in a telephone conversation with me. His thinking, he said, has taken on a "staccato" quality, reflecting the way he quickly scans short passages of text from many sources online. "I can't read *War and Peace* anymore," he admitted. "I've lost the ability to do that. Even a blog post of more than three or four paragraphs is too much to absorb. I skim it."

Anecdotes alone don't prove much. And we still await the long-term neurological and psychological experiments that will provide a definitive picture of how Internet use affects cognition. But a recently published study of online research habits, conducted by scholars from University College London, suggests that we may well be in the midst of a sea change in the way we read and think. As part of the five-year research program, the scholars examined computer logs documenting the behavior of visitors to two popular research sites, one operated by the British Library and one by a U.K. educational consortium, that provide access to journal articles, e-books, and other sources of written information. They found that people using the sites exhibited "a form of skimming activity," hopping from one source to another and rarely returning to any source they'd already visited. They typically read no more than one or two pages of an article or book before they would "bounce" out to another site. Sometimes they'd save a long article, but there's no evidence that they ever went back and actually read it. The authors of the study report:

It is clear that users are not reading online in the traditional sense; indeed there are signs that new forms of "reading" are emerging as users "power browse" horizontally through titles, contents pages and abstracts going for quick wins. It almost seems that they go online to avoid reading in the traditional sense.

Thanks to the ubiquity of text on the Internet, not to mention the popularity of text-messaging on cell phones, we may well be reading more today than we did in the 1970s or 1980s, when television was our medium of choice. But it's a different kind of reading, and behind it lies a different kind of thinking—perhaps even a new sense of the self. "We are not only what we read," says Maryanne Wolf, a developmental psychologist at Tufts University and the author of *Proust and the Squid: The Story and Science of the Reading Brain*. "We are how we read." Wolf worries that the style of reading promoted by the Net, a style that puts "efficiency" and "immediacy" above all else, may be weakening our capacity for the kind of deep reading that emerged when an earlier technology, the printing press, made long and complex works of prose commonplace. When we read online, she says, we tend to become "mere decoders of information." Our ability to interpret text, to make the rich mental connections that form when we read deeply and without distraction, remains largely disengaged.

Reading, explains Wolf, is not an instinctive skill for human beings. It's not etched into our genes the way speech is. We have to teach our minds how to translate the symbolic characters we see into the language we understand. And the media or other technologies we use in learning and practicing the craft of reading play an important part in shaping the neural circuits inside our brains. Experiments demonstrate that readers of ideograms, such as the Chinese, develop a mental circuitry for reading that is very different from the circuitry found in those of us whose written language employs an alphabet. The variations extend across many regions of the brain, including those that govern such essential cognitive functions as memory and the interpretation of visual and auditory stimuli. We can expect as well that the circuits woven by our use of the Net will be different from those woven by our reading of books and other printed works.

Sometime in 1882, Friedrich Nietzsche bought a typewriter—a Malling-Hansen Writing Ball, to be precise. His vision was failing, and keeping his eyes focused on a page had become exhausting and painful, often bringing on crushing headaches. He had been forced to curtail his writing, and he feared that he would soon have to give it up. The typewriter rescued him, at least for a time. Once he had mastered touch-typing, he was able to write with his eyes closed, using only the tips of his fingers. Words could once again flow from his mind to the page.

But the machine had a subtler effect on his work. One of Nietzsche's friends, a composer, noticed a change in the style of his writing. His already terse prose had become even tighter, more telegraphic. "Perhaps you will through this instrument even take to a new idiom," the friend wrote in a letter, noting that, in his own work, his "'thoughts' in music and language often depend on the quality of pen and paper."

"You are right," Nietzsche replied, "our writing equipment takes part in the forming of our thoughts." Under the sway of the machine, writes the German media scholar Friedrich

A. Kittler, Nietzsche's prose "changed from arguments to aphorisms, from thoughts to puns, from rhetoric to telegram style."

The human brain is almost infinitely malleable. People used to think that our mental meshwork, the dense connections formed among the 100 billion or so neurons inside our skulls, was largely fixed by the time we reached adulthood. But brain researchers have discovered that that's not the case. James Olds, a professor of neuroscience who directs the Krasnow Institute for Advanced Study at George Mason University, says that even the adult mind "is very plastic." Nerve cells routinely break old connections and form new ones. "The brain," according to Olds, "has the ability to reprogram itself on the fly, altering the way it functions."

As we use what the sociologist Daniel Bell has called our "intellectual technologies"— the tools that extend our mental rather than our physical capacities—we inevitably begin to take on the qualities of those technologies. The mechanical clock, which came into common use in the 14th century, provides a compelling example. In *Technics and Civilization*, the historian and cultural critic Lewis Mumford described how the clock "disassociated time from human events and helped create the belief in an independent world of mathematically measurable sequences." The "abstract framework of divided time" became "the point of reference for both action and thought."

The clock's methodical ticking helped bring into being the scientific mind and the scientific man. But it also took something away. As the late MIT computer scientist Joseph Weizenbaum observed in his 1976 book, *Computer Power and Human Reason: From Judgment to Calculation*, the conception of the world that emerged from the widespread use of timekeeping instruments "remains an impoverished version of the older one, for it rests on a rejection of those direct experiences that formed the basis for, and indeed constituted, the old reality." In deciding when to eat, to work, to sleep, to rise, we stopped listening to our senses and started obeying the clock.

The process of adapting to new intellectual technologies is reflected in the changing metaphors we use to explain ourselves to ourselves. When the mechanical clock arrived, people began thinking of their brains as operating "like clockwork." Today, in the age of software, we have come to think of them as operating "like computers." But the changes, neuroscience tells us, go much deeper than metaphor. Thanks to our brain's plasticity, the adaptation occurs also at a biological level.

The Internet promises to have particularly far-reaching effects on cognition. In a paper published in 1936, the British mathematician Alan Turing proved that a digital computer, which at the time existed only as a theoretical machine, could be programmed to perform the function of any other information-processing device. And that's what we're seeing today. The Internet, an immeasurably powerful computing system, is subsuming most of our other intellectual technologies. It's becoming our map and our clock, our printing press and our typewriter, our calculator and our telephone, and our radio and TV.

When the Net absorbs a medium, that medium is re-created in the Net's image. It injects the medium's content with hyperlinks, blinking ads, and other digital gewgaws, and it surrounds the content with the content of all the other media it has absorbed. A new e-mail message, for instance, may announce its arrival as we're glancing over the latest headlines at a newspaper's site. The result is to scatter our attention and diffuse our concentration.

The Net's influence doesn't end at the edges of a computer screen, either. As people's minds become attuned to the crazy quilt of Internet media, traditional media have to adapt to the audience's new expectations. Television programs add text crawls and pop-up ads, and magazines and newspapers shorten their articles, introduce capsule summaries, and crowd their pages with easy-to-browse info-snippets. When, in March of this year, *The New York Times* decided to devote the second and third pages of every edition to article abstracts, its design director, Tom Bodkin, explained that the "shortcuts" would give harried readers a quick "taste" of the day's news, sparing them the "less efficient" method of actually turning the pages and reading the articles. Old media have little choice but to play by the new-media rules.

Never has a communications system played so many roles in our lives—or exerted such broad influence over our thoughts—as the Internet does today. Yet, for all that's been written about the Net, there's been little consideration of how, exactly, it's reprogramming us. The Net's intellectual ethic remains obscure.

About the same time that Nietzsche started using his typewriter, an earnest young man named Frederick Winslow Taylor carried a stopwatch into the Midvale Steel plant in Philadelphia and began a historic series of experiments aimed at improving the efficiency of the plant's machinists. With the approval of Midvale's owners, he recruited a group of factory hands, set them to work on various metalworking machines, and recorded and timed their every movement as well as the operations of the machines. By breaking down every job into a sequence of small, discrete steps and then testing different ways of performing each one, Taylor created a set of precise instructions—an "algorithm," we might say today—for how each worker should work. Midvale's employees grumbled about the strict new regime, claiming that it turned them into little more than automatons, but the factory's productivity soared.

More than a hundred years after the invention of the steam engine, the Industrial Revolution had at last found its philosophy and its philosopher. Taylor's tight industrial choreography—his "system," as he liked to call it—was embraced by manufacturers throughout the country and, in time, around the world. Seeking maximum speed, maximum efficiency, and maximum output, factory owners used time-and-motion studies to organize their work and configure the jobs of their workers. The goal, as Taylor defined it in his celebrated 1911 treatise, *The Principles of Scientific Management*, was to identify and adopt, for every job, the "one best method" of work and thereby to effect "the gradual substitution of science for rule of thumb throughout the mechanic arts." Once his system was applied to all acts of manual labor, Taylor assured his followers, it would bring about a restructuring not only of industry but of society, creating a utopia of perfect efficiency. "In the past the man has been first," he declared; "in the future the system must be first."

Taylor's system is still very much with us; it remains the ethic of industrial manufacturing. And now, thanks to the growing power that computer engineers and software coders wield over our intellectual lives, Taylor's ethic is beginning to govern the realm of the mind as well. The Internet is a machine designed for the efficient and automated collection, transmission, and manipulation of information, and its legions of programmers are intent on finding the "one best method"—the perfect algorithm—to carry out every mental movement of what we've come to describe as "knowledge work."

Google's headquarters, in Mountain View, California—the Googleplex—is the Internet's high church, and the religion practiced inside its walls is Taylorism. Google, says its chief executive, Eric Schmidt, is "a company that's founded around the science of measurement," and it is striving to "systematize everything" it does. Drawing on the terabytes of behavioral data it collects through its search engine and other sites, it carries out thousands of experiments a day, according to the *Harvard Business Review*, and it uses the results to refine the algorithms that increasingly control how people find information and extract meaning from it. What Taylor did for the work of the hand, Google is doing for the work of the mind.

The company has declared that its mission is "to organize the world's information and make it universally accessible and useful." It seeks to develop "the perfect search engine," which it defines as something that "understands exactly what you mean and gives you back exactly what you want." In Google's view, information is a kind of commodity, a utilitarian resource that can be mined and processed with industrial efficiency. The more pieces of information we can "access" and the faster we can extract their gist, the more productive we become as thinkers.

Where does it end? Sergey Brin and Larry Page, the gifted young men who founded Google while pursuing doctoral degrees in computer science at Stanford, speak frequently of their desire to turn their search engine into an artificial intelligence, a HAL-like machine that might be connected directly to our brains. "The ultimate search engine is something as smart as people—or smarter," Page said in a speech a few years back. "For us, working on search is a way to work on artificial intelligence." In a 2004 interview with *Newsweek*, Brin said, "Certainly if you had all the world's information directly attached to your brain, or an artificial brain that was smarter than your brain, you'd be better off." Last year, Page told a convention of scientists that Google is "really trying to build artificial intelligence and to do it on a large scale."

Such an ambition is a natural one, even an admirable one, for a pair of math whizzes with vast quantities of cash at their disposal and a small army of computer scientists in their employ. A fundamentally scientific enterprise, Google is motivated by a desire to use technology, in Eric Schmidt's words, "to solve problems that have never been solved before," and artificial intelligence is the hardest problem out there. Why wouldn't Brin and Page want to be the ones to crack it?

Still, their easy assumption that we'd all "be better off" if our brains were supplemented, or even replaced, by an artificial intelligence is unsettling. It suggests a belief that intelligence is the output of a mechanical process, a series of discrete steps that can be isolated, measured, and optimized. In Google's world, the world we enter when we go online, there's little place for the fuzziness of contemplation. Ambiguity is not an opening for insight but a bug to be fixed. The human brain is just an outdated computer that needs a faster processor and a bigger hard drive.

The idea that our minds should operate as high-speed data-processing machines is not only built into the workings of the Internet, it is the network's reigning business model as well. The faster we surf across the Web—the more links we click and pages we view—the more opportunities Google and other companies gain to collect information about us and to feed us advertisements. Most of the proprietors of the commercial Internet have a financial stake in collecting the crumbs of data we leave behind as we flit from link to link—the more crumbs, the better. The last thing these companies want is to encourage leisurely reading or slow, concentrated thought. It's in their economic interest to drive us to distraction.

Maybe I'm just a worrywart. Just as there's a tendency to glorify technological progress, there's a countertendency to expect the worst of every new tool or machine. In Plato's *Phaedrus*,

Socrates bemoaned the development of writing. He feared that, as people came to rely on the written word as a substitute for the knowledge they used to carry inside their heads, they would, in the words of one of the dialogue's characters, "cease to exercise their memory and become forgetful." And because they would be able to "receive a quantity of information without proper instruction," they would "be thought very knowledgeable when they are for the most part quite ignorant." They would be "filled with the conceit of wisdom instead of real wisdom." Socrates wasn't wrong—the new technology did often have the effects he feared—but he was shortsighted. He couldn't foresee the many ways that writing and reading would serve to spread information, spur fresh ideas, and expand human knowledge (if not wisdom).

The arrival of Gutenberg's printing press, in the 15th century, set off another round of teeth gnashing. The Italian humanist Hieronimo Squarciafico worried that the easy availability of books would lead to intellectual laziness, making men "less studious" and weakening their minds. Others argued that cheaply printed books and broadsheets would undermine religious authority, demean the work of scholars and scribes, and spread sedition and debauchery. As New York University professor Clay Shirky notes, "Most of the arguments made against the printing press were correct, even prescient." But, again, the doomsayers were unable to imagine the myriad blessings that the printed word would deliver.

So, yes, you should be skeptical of my skepticism. Perhaps those who dismiss critics of the Internet as Luddites or nostalgists will be proved correct, and from our hyperactive, data-stoked minds will spring a golden age of intellectual discovery and universal wisdom. Then again, the Net isn't the alphabet, and although it may replace the printing press, it produces something altogether different. The kind of deep reading that a sequence of printed pages promotes is valuable not just for the knowledge we acquire from the author's words but for the intellectual vibrations those words set off within our own minds. In the quiet spaces opened up by the sustained, undistracted reading of a book, or by any other act of contemplation, for that matter, we make our own associations, draw our own inferences and analogies, foster our own ideas. Deep reading, as Maryanne Wolf argues, is indistinguishable from deep thinking.

If we lose those quiet spaces, or fill them up with "content," we will sacrifice something important not only in our selves but in our culture. In a recent essay, the playwright Richard Foreman eloquently described what's at stake:

> I come from a tradition of Western culture, in which the ideal (my ideal) was the complex, dense and "cathedral-like" structure of the highly educated and articulate personality—a man or woman who carried inside themselves a personally constructed and unique version of the entire heritage of the West. [But now] I see within us all (myself included) the replacement of complex inner density with a new kind of self—evolving under the pressure of information overload and the technology of the "instantly available."

As we are drained of our "inner repertory of dense cultural inheritance," Foreman concluded, we risk turning into "'pancake people'—spread wide and thin as we connect with that vast network of information accessed by the mere touch of a button."

I'm haunted by that scene in *2001*. What makes it so poignant, and so weird, is the computer's emotional response to the disassembly of its mind: its despair as one circuit after another goes dark, its childlike pleading with the astronaut—"I can feel it. I can feel it. I'm afraid"—and its final reversion to what can only be called a state of innocence. HAL's outpouring of feeling contrasts with the emotionlessness that characterizes the human figures in the film, who go about their business with an almost robotic efficiency. Their thoughts and actions feel scripted, as if they're following the steps of an algorithm. In the world of *2001*, people have become so machinelike that the most human character turns out to be a machine. That's the essence of Kubrick's dark prophecy: as we come to rely on computers to mediate our understanding of the world, it is our own intelligence that flattens into artificial intelligence.

■ WHAT?

1. What, according to Carr, is the difference between assimilating information and learning?

2. Carr writes that the "Web has been a godsend to me as a writer" but also that this "boon comes at a price." Summarize the advantages that Carr says the Internet offers as well as the drawbacks that he worries might accompany long-term use.

3. Carr uses Google's desire to develop the "perfect search engine" to discuss two kinds of intelligence. How would you describe these? Do you see any reason for concern about the influence technology might be having on intelligence?

4. Do you think Carr presents an effective argument? Why or why not? Does he address possible counterarguments? What are they?

■ WHAT ELSE? WHAT'S NEXT?

5. Carr's essay was published in 2008, nearly a lifetime ago in the world of digital technology. Research the ways in which the concerns Carr raises have evolved since then. Do more people believe technology is changing the way we read and think for the worse? Has Carr written anything else about the subject? Can you find any expert research or opinion about the issue? Compile your findings in a brief report, complete with a bibliography in MLA style.

■ WHO CARES?

6. Who reads the *Atlantic Monthly* and its website, www.TheAtlantic.com? Research online—starting with the website itself—and compose a brief portrait of the publications' readership. Then, explain whether you think Carr's piece is a good fit for that audience.

> *According to his biography at TED.com, Jamais Cascio rejects the "nightmare scenarios of global catastrophe and social meltdown" we so often hear from other futurists in favor of "a different, often surprising alternative: What if human beings, and all of our technology, could actually manage to change things for the better?" In this article, first published in the July/August 2009 issue of* Atlantic Monthly, *Cascio argues that humans have the means, right now, to overcome just about anything by harnessing technology and pharmacology to boost intelligence.*

BEFORE YOU READ—————————————————————————
Find Jamais Cascio's video titled "The Future We Will Create" online and watch it. What does this tell you about his worldview?

GET SMARTER Jamais Cascio

Seventy-four thousand years ago, humanity nearly went extinct. A super-volcano at what's now Lake Toba, in Sumatra, erupted with a strength more than a thousand times that of Mount St. Helens in 1980. Some 800 cubic kilometers of ash filled the skies of the Northern Hemisphere, lowering global temperatures and pushing a climate already on the verge of an ice age over the edge. Some scientists speculate that as the Earth went into a deep freeze, the population of *Homo sapiens* may have dropped to as low as a few thousand families.

The Mount Toba incident, although unprecedented in magnitude, was part of a broad pattern. For a period of 2 million years, ending with the last ice age around 10,000 B.C., the Earth experienced a series of convulsive glacial events. This rapid-fire climate change meant that humans couldn't rely on consistent patterns to know which animals to hunt, which plants to gather, or even which predators might be waiting around the corner.

How did we cope? By getting smarter. The neurophysiologist William Calvin argues persuasively that modern human cognition—including sophisticated language and the capacity to plan ahead—evolved in response to the demands of this long age of turbulence. According to Calvin, the reason we survived is that our brains changed to meet the challenge: we transformed the ability to target a moving animal with a thrown rock into a capability for foresight and long-term planning. In the process, we may have developed syntax and formal structure from our simple language.

Our present century may not be quite as perilous for the human race as an ice age in the aftermath of a super-volcano eruption, but the next few decades will pose enormous hurdles that go beyond the climate crisis. The end of the fossil-fuel era, the fragility of the global food web, growing population density, and the spread of pandemics, as well as the emergence of radically transformative bio- and nanotechnologies—each of these threatens us with broad disruption or even devastation. And as good as our brains have become at planning ahead, we're still biased toward looking for near-term, simple threats. Subtle, long-term risks, particularly those involving complex, global processes, remain devilishly hard for us to manage.

But here's an optimistic scenario for you: if the next several decades are as bad as some of us fear they could be, we can respond, and survive, the way our species has done time and again: by getting smarter. But this time, we don't have to rely solely on natural evolutionary processes to boost our intelligence. We can do it ourselves.

Most people don't realize that this process is already under way. In fact, it's happening all around us, across the full spectrum of how we understand intelligence. It's visible in the hive mind of the Internet, in the powerful tools for simulation and visualization that are jump-starting new scientific disciplines, and in the development of drugs that some people (myself included) have discovered let them study harder, focus better, and stay awake longer with full clarity. So far, these augmentations have largely been outside of our bodies, but they're very much part of who we are today: they're physically separate from us, but we and they are becoming cognitively inseparable. And advances over the next few decades, driven by breakthroughs in genetic engineering and artificial intelligence, will make today's technologies seem primitive. The nascent jargon of the field describes this as "intelligence augmentation." I prefer to think of it as "You+."

Scientists refer to the 12,000 years or so since the last ice age as the Holocene epoch. It encompasses the rise of human civilization and our co-evolution with tools and technologies that allow us to grapple with our physical environment. But if intelligence augmentation has the kind of impact I expect, we may soon have to start thinking of ourselves as living in an entirely new era. The focus of our technological evolution would be less on how we manage and adapt to our physical world, and more on how we manage and adapt to the immense amount of knowledge we've created. We can call it the Nöocene epoch, from Pierre Teilhard de Chardin's concept of the Nöosphere, a collective consciousness created by the deepening interaction of human minds. As that epoch draws closer, the world is becoming a very different place.

Of course we've been augmenting our ability to think for millennia. When we developed written language, we significantly increased our functional memory and our ability to share insights and knowledge across time and space. The same thing happened with the invention of the printing press, the telegraph, and the radio. The rise of urbanization allowed a fraction of the populace to focus on more-cerebral tasks—a fraction that grew inexorably as more complex economic and social practices demanded more knowledge work, and industrial technology reduced the demand for manual labor. And caffeine and nicotine, of course, are both classic cognitive-enhancement drugs, primitive though they may be.

With every technological step forward, though, has come anxiety about the possibility that technology harms our natural ability to think. These anxieties were given eloquent expression in these pages by Nicholas Carr, whose essay "Is Google Making Us Stupid?" (July/August 2008 *Atlantic*) argued that the information-dense, hyperlink-rich, spastically churning Internet medium is effectively rewiring our brains, making it harder for us to engage in deep, relaxed contemplation.

Carr's fears about the impact of wall-to-wall connectivity on the human intellect echo cyber-theorist Linda Stone's description of "continuous partial attention," the modern phenomenon of having multiple activities and connections under way simultaneously. We're becoming so accustomed to interruption that we're starting to find focusing difficult, even when we've achieved a bit of quiet. It's an induced form of ADD—a "continuous partial attention-deficit disorder," if you will.

There's also just more information out there—because unlike with previous information media, with the Internet, creating material is nearly as easy as consuming it. And it's easy to mistake more voices for more noise. In reality, though, the proliferation of diverse voices may actually improve our overall ability to think. In *Everything Bad Is Good for You*, Steven Johnson argues that the increasing complexity and range of media we engage with have, over the past century, made us smarter, rather than dumber, by providing a form of cognitive calisthenics. Even pulp-television shows and video games have become extraordinarily dense with detail, filled with subtle references to broader subjects, and more open to interactive engagement. They reward the capacity to make connections and to see patterns—precisely the kinds of skills we need for managing an information glut.

Scientists describe these skills as our "fluid intelligence"—the ability to find meaning in confusion and to solve new problems, independent of acquired knowledge. Fluid intelligence doesn't look much like the capacity to memorize and recite facts, the skills that people have traditionally associated with brainpower. But building it up may improve the capacity to think deeply that Carr and others fear we're losing for good. And we shouldn't let the stresses associated with a transition to a new era blind us to that era's astonishing potential. We swim in an ocean of data, accessible from nearly anywhere, generated by billions of devices. We're only beginning to explore what we can do with this knowledge-at-a-touch.

Moreover, the technology-induced ADD that's associated with this new world may be a short-term problem. The trouble isn't that we have too much information at our fingertips, but that our tools for managing it are still in their infancy. Worries about "information overload" predate the rise of the Web (Alvin Toffler coined the phrase in 1970), and many of the technologies that Carr worries about were developed precisely to help us get some control over a flood of data and ideas. Google isn't the problem; it's the beginning of a solution.

In any case, there's no going back. The information sea isn't going to dry up, and relying on cognitive habits evolved and perfected in an era of limited information flow—and limited information access—is futile. Strengthening our fluid intelligence is the only viable approach to navigating the age of constant connectivity.

When people hear the phrase *intelligence augmentation*, they tend to envision people with computer chips plugged into their brains, or a genetically engineered race of post-human super-geniuses. Neither of these visions is likely to be realized, for reasons familiar to any Best Buy shopper. In a world of ongoing technological acceleration, today's cutting-edge brain implant would be tomorrow's obsolete junk—and good luck if the protocols change or you're on the wrong side of a "format war" (anyone want a Betamax implant?). And then there's the question of stability: Would you want a chip in your head made by the same folks that made your cell phone, or your PC?

Likewise, the safe modification of human genetics is still years away. And even after genetic modification of adult neurobiology becomes possible, the science will remain in flux; our understanding of how augmentation works, and what kinds of genetic modifications are possible, would still change rapidly. As with digital implants, the brain modification you might undergo one week could become obsolete the next. Who would want a 2025-vintage brain when you're competing against hotshots with Model 2026?

Yet in one sense, the age of the cyborg and the super-genius has already arrived. It just involves external information and communication devices instead of implants and genetic modification. The bioethicist James Hughes of Trinity College refers to all of this as "exocortical technology," but you can just think of it as "stuff you already own." Increasingly, we buttress our cognitive functions with our computing systems, no matter that the connections are mediated by simple typing and pointing. These tools enable our brains to do things that would once have been almost unimaginable:

- powerful simulations and massive data sets allow physicists to visualize, understand, and debate models of an 11-dimension universe;

- real-time data from satellites, global environmental databases, and high-resolution models allow geophysicists to recognize the subtle signs of long-term changes to the planet;

- cross-connected scheduling systems allow anyone to assemble, with a few clicks, a complex, multimodal travel itinerary that would have taken a human travel agent days to create.

If that last example sounds prosaic, it simply reflects how embedded these kinds of augmentation have become. Not much more than a decade ago, such a tool was outrageously impressive—and it destroyed the travel-agent industry.

That industry won't be the last one to go. Any occupation requiring pattern-matching and the ability to find obscure connections will quickly morph from the domain of experts to that of ordinary people whose intelligence has been augmented by cheap digital tools. Humans won't be taken out of the loop—in fact, many, many *more* humans will have the capacity to do something that was once limited to a hermetic priesthood. Intelligence augmentation decreases the need for specialization and increases participatory complexity.

As the digital systems we rely upon become faster, more sophisticated, and (with the usual hiccups) more capable, we're becoming more sophisticated and capable too. It's a form of co-evolution: we learn to adapt our thinking and expectations to these digital systems, even as the system designs become more complex and powerful to meet more of our needs—and eventually come to adapt to *us*.

Consider the Twitter phenomenon, which went from nearly invisible to nearly ubiquitous (at least among the online crowd) in early 2007. During busy periods, the user can easily be overwhelmed by the volume of incoming messages, most of which are of only passing interest. But there is a tiny minority of truly valuable posts. (Sometimes they have extreme value, as they did during the October 2007 wildfires in California and the November 2008 terrorist attacks in Mumbai.) At present, however, finding the most-useful bits requires wading through messages like "My kitty sneezed!" and "I hate this taco!"

But imagine if social tools like Twitter had a way to learn what kinds of messages you pay attention to, and which ones you discard. Over time, the messages that you don't really care about might start to fade in the display, while the ones that you do want to see could get brighter. Such attention filters—or focus assistants—are likely to become important parts of how we handle our daily lives. We'll move from a world of "continuous partial attention" to one we might call "continuous augmented awareness."

As processor power increases, tools like Twitter may be able to draw on the complex simulations and massive data sets that have unleashed a revolution in science. They could become individualized systems that augment our capacity for planning and foresight, letting us play "what-if" with our life choices: where to live, what to study, maybe even where to go for dinner. Initially crude and clumsy, such a system would get better with more data and more experience; just as important, we'd get better at asking questions. These systems, perhaps linked to the cameras and microphones in our mobile devices, would eventually be able to pay attention to what we're doing, and to our habits and language quirks, and learn to interpret our sometimes ambiguous desires. With enough time and complexity, they would be able to make useful suggestions without explicit prompting.

And such systems won't be working for us alone. Intelligence has a strong social component; for example, we already provide crude cooperative information-filtering for each other. In time, our interactions through the use of such intimate technologies could dovetail with our use of collaborative knowledge systems (such as Wikipedia), to help us not just to build better data sets, but to filter them with greater precision. As our capacity to provide that filter gets faster and richer, it increasingly becomes something akin to collaborative intuition—in which everyone is effectively augmenting everyone else.

In pharmacology, too, the future is already here. One of the most prominent examples is a drug called modafinil. Developed in the 1970s, modafinil—sold in the U.S. under the brand name Provigil—appeared on the cultural radar in the late 1990s, when the American military began to test it for long-haul pilots. Extended use of modafinil can keep a person awake and alert for well over 32 hours on end, with only a full night's sleep required to get back to a normal schedule.

While it is FDA-approved only for a few sleep disorders, like narcolepsy and sleep apnea, doctors increasingly prescribe it to those suffering from depression, to "shift workers" fighting fatigue, and to frequent business travelers dealing with time-zone shifts. I'm part of the latter group: like more and more professionals, I have a prescription for modafinil in order to help me overcome jet lag when I travel internationally. When I started taking the drug, I expected it to keep me awake; I didn't expect it to make me feel smarter, but that's exactly what happened. The change was subtle but clear, once I recognized it: within an hour of taking a standard 200-mg tablet, I was much more alert, and thinking with considerably more clarity and focus than usual. This isn't just a subjective conclusion.

A University of Cambridge study, published in 2003, concluded that modafinil confers a measurable cognitive-enhancement effect across a variety of mental tasks, including pattern recognition and spatial planning, and sharpens focus and alertness.

I'm not the only one who has taken advantage of this effect. The Silicon Valley insider webzine *Tech Crunch* reported in July 2008 that some entrepreneurs now see modafinil as an important competitive tool. The tone of the piece was judgmental, but the implication was clear: everybody's doing it, and if you're not, you're probably falling behind.

This is one way a world of intelligence augmentation emerges. Little by little, people who don't know about drugs like modafinil or don't want to use them will face stiffer competition from the people who do. From the perspective of a culture immersed in athletic doping wars, the use of such drugs may seem like cheating. From the perspective of those who find that they're much more productive using this form of enhancement, it's no more cheating than getting a faster computer or a better education.

Modafinil isn't the only example; on college campuses, the use of ADD drugs (such as Ritalin and Adderall) as study aids has become almost ubiquitous. But these enhancements are primitive. As the science improves, we could see other kinds of cognitive-modification drugs that boost recall, brain plasticity, even empathy and emotional intelligence. They would start as therapeutic treatments, but end up being used to make us "better than normal." Eventually, some of these may become over-the-counter products at your local pharmacy, or in the juice and snack aisles at the supermarket. Spam e-mail would be full of offers to make your brain bigger, and your idea production more powerful.

Such a future would bear little resemblance to *Brave New World* or similar narcomantic nightmares; we may fear the idea of a population kept doped and placated, but we're more likely to see a populace stuck in overdrive, searching out the last bits of competitive advantage, business insight, and radical innovation. No small amount of that innovation would be directed toward inventing the next, more powerful cognitive-enhancement technology.

This would be a different kind of nightmare, perhaps, and cause waves of moral panic and legislative restriction. Safety would be a huge issue. But as we've found with athletic doping, if there's a technique for beating out rivals (no matter how risky), shutting it down is nearly impossible. This would be yet another pharmacological arms race—and in this case, the competitors on one side would just keep getting smarter.

The most radical form of superhuman intelligence, of course, wouldn't be a mind augmented by drugs or exocortical technology; it would be a mind that isn't human at all. Here we move from the realm of extrapolation to the realm of speculation, since solid predictions about artificial intelligence are notoriously hard: our understanding of how the brain creates the mind remains far from good enough to tell us how to construct a mind in a machine.

But while the concept remains controversial, I see no good argument for why a mind running on a machine platform instead of a biological platform will forever be impossible; whether one might appear in five years or 50 or 500, however, is uncertain. I lean toward 50, myself. That's enough time to develop computing hardware able to run a high-speed neural network as sophisticated as that of a human brain, and enough time for the kids who will have grown up surrounded by virtual-world software and household robots—that is, the people who see this stuff not as "Technology," but as everyday tools—to come to dominate the field.

Many proponents of developing an artificial mind are sure that such a breakthrough will be the biggest change in human history. They believe that a machine mind would soon modify itself to get smarter—and with its new intelligence, then figure out how to make itself smarter still. They refer to this intelligence explosion as "the Singularity," a term applied by the computer scientist and science-fiction author Vernor Vinge. "Within thirty years, we will have the technological means to create superhuman intelligence," Vinge wrote in 1993. "Shortly after, the human era will be ended." The Singularity concept is a secular echo of Teilhard de Chardin's "Omega Point," the culmination of the Nöosphere at the end of history. Many believers in Singularity—which one wag has dubbed "the Rapture for nerds"—think that building the first real AI will be the last thing humans do. Some imagine this moment with terror, others with a bit of glee.

My own suspicion is that a stand-alone artificial mind will be more a tool of narrow utility than something especially apocalyptic. I don't think the theory of an explosively self-improving AI is convincing—it's based on too many assumptions about behavior and the nature of the mind. Moreover, AI researchers, after years of talking about this prospect, are already ultra-conscious of the risk of runaway systems.

More important, though, is that the same advances in processor and process that would produce a machine mind would also increase the power of our own cognitive-enhancement technologies. As intelligence augmentation allows us to make *ourselves* smarter, and then smarter still, AI may turn out to be just a sideshow: we could always be a step ahead.

So what's life like in a world of brain doping, intuition networks, and the occasional artificial mind?

Banal.

Not from our present perspective, of course. For us, now, looking a generation ahead might seem surreal and dizzying. But remember: people living in, say, 2030 will have lived every moment from now until then—we won't jump into the future. For someone going from 2009 to 2030 day by day, most of these changes wouldn't be jarring; instead, they'd be incremental, almost overdetermined, and the occasional surprises would quickly blend into the flow of inevitability.

By 2030, then, we'll likely have grown accustomed to (and perhaps even complacent about) a world where sophisticated foresight, detailed analysis and insight, and augmented awareness are commonplace. We'll have developed a better capacity to manage both partial attention and laser-like focus, and be able to slip between the two with ease—perhaps by popping the right pill, or eating the right snack. Sometimes, our augmentation assistants will handle basic interactions on our behalf; that's okay, though, because we'll increasingly see those assistants as extensions of ourselves.

The amount of data we'll have at our fingertips will be staggering, but we'll finally have gotten over the notion that accumulated information alone is a hallmark of intelligence. The power of all of this knowledge will come from its ability to inform difficult decisions, and to support complex analysis. Most professions will likely use simulation and modeling in their day-to-day work, from political decisions to hairstyle options. In a world of augmented intelligence, we will have a far greater appreciation of the consequences of our actions.

This doesn't mean we'll all come to the same conclusions. We'll still clash with each other's emotions, desires, and beliefs. If anything, our arguments will be more intense, buttressed not just by strongly held opinions but by intricate reasoning. People in 2030 will look back aghast at how ridiculously unsubtle the political and cultural disputes of our present were, just as we might today snicker at simplistic advertising from a generation ago.

Conversely, the debates of the 2030s would be remarkable for us to behold. Nuance and multiple layers will characterize even casual disputes; our digital assistants will be there to catch any references we might miss. And all of this will be everyday, banal reality. Today, it sounds mind-boggling; by then, it won't even merit comment.

What happens if such a complex system collapses? Disaster, of course. But don't forget that we already depend upon enormously complex systems that we no longer even think of as technological. Urbanization, agriculture, and trade were at one time huge innovations. Their collapse (and all of them are now at risk, in different ways, as we have seen in recent months) would be an even greater catastrophe than the collapse of our growing webs of interconnected intelligence.

A less apocalyptic but more likely danger derives from the observation made by the science-fiction author William Gibson: "The future is already here, it's just unevenly distributed." The rich, whether nations or individuals, will inevitably gain access to many augmentations before anyone else. We know from history, though, that a world of limited access wouldn't last forever, even as the technology improved: those who sought to impose limits would eventually face angry opponents with newer, better systems.

Even as competition provides access to these kinds of technologies, though, development paths won't be identical. Some societies may be especially welcoming to biotech boosts; others may prefer to use digital tools. Some may readily adopt collaborative approaches; others may focus on individual enhancement. And around the world, many societies will reject the use of intelligence-enhancement technology entirely, or adopt a cautious wait-and-see posture.

The bad news is that these divergent paths may exacerbate cultural divides created by already divergent languages and beliefs. National rivalries often emphasize cultural differences, but for now we're all still standard human beings. What happens when different groups quite literally think in very, very different ways?

The good news, though, is that this diversity of thought can also be a strength. Coping with the various world-historical dangers we face will require the greatest possible insight, creativity, and innovation. Our ability to build the future that we want—not just a future we can survive—depends on our capacity to understand the complex relationships of the world's systems, to take advantage of the diversity of knowledge and experience our civilization embodies, and to fully appreciate the implications of our choices. Such an ability is increasingly within our grasp. The Nöocene awaits.

WHAT?

1. According to Cascio, how have we been "augmenting our ability to think for millennia"?
2. How do you feel about evolving into what Cascio calls "You+"?
3. In explaining the use of drugs to augment intelligence, Cascio writes: "From the perspective of a culture immersed in athletic doping wars, the use of such drugs may seem like cheating. From the perspective of those who find that they're much more productive using this form of enhancement, it's no more cheating than getting a faster computer or a better education." Do you agree with Cascio's point? Explain your response.
4. In "The Allegory of the Cave," Plato writes that "in the world of knowledge the idea of good appears last of all, and is seen only with an effort..." How might Cascio respond to this concept of knowledge and "the idea of good"?

WHAT ELSE? WHAT'S NEXT?

5. "Get Smart" is, in part, a response to Nicholas Carr's "Is Google Making Us Stupid?" How does Cascio address Carr's concerns about technology's ill effects on learning and concentration? Do you find Cascio's counterarguments persuasive? Why or why not?
6. Research the response to Cascio's essay. How, in particular, have others addressed Cascio's discussion of performance- and intelligence-enhancing technologies (including drugs)? Summarize your findings in a brief report, accompanied by a bibliography of the sources you use.

WHO CARES?

7. What does Cascio do to lead his readers to believe that he knows what he's talking about? In other words, how does he establish his authority and expertise on the topic?

> The Onion *is a satirical news source that began as a print newspaper in Madison, Wisconsin, but that is now available online at TheOnion.com. The following article was published March 9, 2010.*

BEFORE YOU READ
Write a brief explanation of satire and how it works (or is supposed to work). Use at least two sources to help you compose your response, and make sure you document them correctly.

NATION SHUDDERS AT LARGE BLOCK OF UNINTERRUPTED TEXT *The Onion*

WASHINGTON—Unable to rest their eyes on a colorful photograph or boldface heading that could be easily skimmed and forgotten about, Americans collectively recoiled Monday when confronted with a solid block of uninterrupted text.

Dumbfounded citizens from Maine to California gazed helplessly at the frightening chunk of print, unsure of what to do next. Without an illustration, chart, or embedded YouTube video to ease them in, millions were frozen in place, terrified by the sight of one long, unbroken string of English words.

"Why won't it just tell me what it's about?" said Boston resident Charlyne Thomson, who was bombarded with the overwhelming mass of black text late Monday afternoon. "There are no bullet points, no highlighted parts. I've looked everywhere—there's nothing here but words."

"Ow," Thomson added after reading the first and last lines in an attempt to get the gist of whatever the article, review, or possibly recipe was about.

At 3:16 p.m., a deafening sigh was heard across the country as the nation grappled with the daunting cascade of syllables, whose unfamiliar letter-upon-letter structure stretched on for an endless 500 words. Children wailed for the attention of their bewildered parents, businesses were shuttered, and local governments ground to a halt as Americans scanned the text in vain for a web link to click on.

Sources also reported a 450 percent rise in temple rubbing and under-the-breath cursing around this time.

"It demands so much of my time and concentration," said Chicago resident Dale Huza, who was confronted by the confusing mound of words early Monday afternoon. "This large block of text, it expects me to figure everything out on my own, and I hate it."

"I've never seen anything like it," said Mark Shelton, a high school teacher from St. Paul, MN who stared blankly at the page in front of him for several minutes before finally holding it up to his ear. "What does it want from us?"

As the public grows more desperate, scholars are working to randomly italicize different sections of the text, hoping the italics will land on the important parts and allow everyone to go on with their day. For now, though, millions of panicked and exhausted Americans continue to repetitively search the single column of print from top to bottom and right to left, looking for even the slightest semblance of meaning or perhaps a blurb.

Some have speculated that the never-ending flood of sentences may be a news article, medical study, urgent product recall notice, letter, user agreement, or even a binding contract of some kind. But until the news does a segment in which they take sections of the text and read them aloud in a slow, calm voice while highlighting those same words on the screen, no one can say for sure.

There are some, however, who remain unfazed by the virtual hailstorm of alternating consonants and vowels, and are determined to ignore it.

"I'm sure if it's important enough, they'll let us know some other way," Detroit local Janet Landsman said. "After all, it can't be that serious. If there were anything worthwhile buried deep in that block of impenetrable English, it would at least have an accompanying photo of a celebrity or a large humorous title containing a pop culture reference."

Added Landsman, "Whatever it is, I'm pretty sure it doesn't even have a point."

■ WHAT?

1. What is being argued here? How can you tell?
2. How does this article use hyperbole? How does this technique help the author advance the argument?
3. The large block of text is described as a "virtual hailstorm of alternating consonants and vowels." What does this mean? Do you think this accurately describes an encounter with an unfamiliar text?

■ WHAT ELSE? WHAT'S NEXT?

4. *The Onion* quotes one person as saying: "Why won't it just tell me what it's about? … There are no bullet points, no highlighted parts. I've looked everywhere—there's nothing here but words." Compare this piece with "Is Google Making Us Stupid?" by Nicholas Carr and "Hooked on Technology" by Matt Richtel, elsewhere in this chapter. How does *The Onion* use humor to illustrate some of the same points that Carr and Richtel make? Which approach do you find more persuasive? Why?

■ WHO CARES?

5. What does *The Onion* need from its readers to make this satire work? In other words, what is the audience expected to bring to the table? How does this piece ensure that the audience is invested in the satire?

IMAGE 3.2
In his essay "Wall of Sound," Nikil Saval writes: "In light of the epoch-making iPod, we need a way to find out what all this music listening is doing to us, or what we're doing with it."

Nikil Saval is an assistant editor at n+1 magazine, where this essay was published in March 2011 (it was also posted at Slate.com). He uses his essay to examine how the iPod—and other digital listening devices—is changing just about everything about how and why we listen to (or are subjected to) music. His argument has social implications that go far beyond the music industry.

BEFORE YOU READ———————————————————————————
Take a look around campus and make note of how many people are plugged in to their smartphones, iPods, or other electronic devices as they go through their days.

WALL OF SOUND   Nikil Saval

Two years ago, at the nadir of the financial crisis, the urban sociologist Sudhir Venkatesh wondered aloud in the *New York Times* why no mass protests had arisen against what was clearly a criminal coup by the banks. Where were the pitchforks, the tar, the feathers? Where, more importantly, were the crowds? Venkatesh's answer was the iPod: "In public spaces, serendipitous interaction is needed to create the 'mob mentality.' Most iPod-like devices separate citizens from one another; you can't join someone in a movement if you can't hear the participants. Congrats Mr. Jobs for impeding social change."Venkatesh's suggestion was glib, tossed off—yet it was also a rare reminder, from the quasi-left, of how urban life has been changed by recording technologies.

The concern that recorded music promotes solipsism and isolation isn't new. Before the invention of the record and the gramophone (1887), the only form of listening people knew was social; the closest thing to a private musical experience was playing an instrument for yourself, or silently looking over a score. More often, if you had the means, you got to sit in the panopticon of the concert hall, seeing and being seen to the accompaniment of Verdi—an experience most fully described by Edith Wharton in the opening scene of *The Age of Innocence* (1920), just as it was going out of style. With mechanical reproduction came the hitherto unimaginable phenomenon of listening to multi-instrumental music by *yourself*. How, a contributor to *Gramophone* magazine asked in 1923, would you react if you stumbled upon somebody in the midst of this private rapture? It would be "as if you had discovered your friend sniffing cocaine, emptying a bottle of whisky, or plaiting straws in his hair. People, we think, should not do things 'to themselves,' however much they may enjoy doing them in company."

But it wasn't only solitary hyper-listening that recording facilitated. By 1960, recorded popular music had begun, in mysterious ways, to promote new social movements. Former Black Panther Bobby Seale recounts in his memoir how Huey Newton developed an elaborate reading of Dylan's "Ballad of a Thin Man" as an allegory of race: "This song Bobby Dylan was singing became a very big part of that whole publishing operation of the Black Panther paper. And in the background, while we were putting this paper out, this record came up and I guess a number of papers were published, and many times we would play that record." The song wasn't overtly political but its mood of stately menace seems to have insinuated itself into the politics of the Panthers.

The '60s were a decade of both mass protests and mass concerts, and this was more than a coincidence. Barbara Ehrenreich has suggested that the roots of second-wave feminism could be found in the tens of thousands of shrieking girls who filled arenas and ballparks at the Beatles' American stops, from the Hollywood Bowl to Shea. These girls, unladylike, insistent, were going to scream for what they wanted. Social change drove musical experimentation, and—more remarkably—vice versa.

The music of this era was—it's worth repeating—an incitement to social change. It was the sound of not going reflexively to war, of mingling across class and racial lines, of thinking it might be all right to sleep around a little, of wanting to work a job that didn't suck.

Of course the radical hopes of the '60s collapsed. The highest-rated YouTube comment on a video of Joan Baez singing "We Shall Overcome" manages to be both smug and glum: "Though we obviously failed, I am so glad that I am of a generation that believed we could make a difference." By the early '70s, popular music had more or less forfeited its capacity to promote social movements. From then on its different varieties would be associated with defining lifestyle niches, consumer habits, and subcultural affiliations. In this way the make-it-new modernist imperative, which seized pop music several decades late, came to seem little different from the program of advertisers launching fresh product lines. Jadedness swept pop music enthusiasts, many of whom, heartbroken by their brief glimpse of collective life, would discount the whole era of the '60s as history's cunning preparation for a descent into hellish consumerism. Welcome to dystopia, a counterfeit heaven where music plays all the time.

The first to ring the alarm about the omnipresence of recorded music were classical music snobs who, as part of their contracted duties as university professors, had to spend time on college campuses. "This is being written in a study in a college of one of the great American universities," wrote George Steiner in 1974. "The walls are throbbing gently to the beat of music coming from one near and several more distant amplifiers. The walls quiver to the ear or to the touch roughly eighteen hours per day, sometimes twenty-four." Allan Bloom picked up the beat in *The Closing of the American Mind* (1987): "Though students do not have books, they most emphatically do have music. ... Nothing is more singular about this generation than its addiction to music." Steiner: "It matters little whether it is that of pop, folk or rock. What counts is the all-pervasive pulsation, morning to night and into night, made indiscriminate by the cool burn of electronic timbre." The only historical analogy Bloom could think of was to the Wagner cult of the late 19th century. Yet even world-conquering Wagner appealed to a limited class, who could only hear his works in opera houses. By contrast the music of the late-20th-century world was truly ubiquitous. Steiner: "When a young man walks down a street in Vladivostok or Cincinnati with his transistor blaring, when a car passes with its radio on at full blast, the resulting sound-capsule encloses the individual." Bloom: "There is the stereo in the home, in the car; there are concerts; there are music videos, with special channels devoted to them, on the air, nonstop; there are the Walkmans so that no place—not public transportation, not the library—prevents students from communing with the Muse, even while studying." Steiner: "What tissues of sensibility are being numbed or exacerbated?"

Yadda, yadda. Yet Bloom and Steiner were right! In fact they had no idea how right they would become. If the spread of home stereo equipment in the 1970s, followed by that of portable devices (the boom box, the Walkman, briefly the Discman), brought music to the masses in a new way, digitization and the iPod have made recorded music even more plentiful and ubiquitous. The fears in Bloom's time that cassette tapes would bring down the music industry are quaint now, in the face of trillions of bytes of music traded brazenly over the Internet every minute. So, too, does the disc mania of record collectors pale in the face of digital collections measured in weeks of music. A DJ's crate of 100 LPs amounts to about three days of straight listening; your standard 60-gigabyte iPod, 50 days. Has anyone these days listened to all of their music, even once through?

Nobody knows how much music we listen to, since so often we're not even listening. The American Time Use Survey, performed every year by the Bureau of Labor Statistics, throws up its hands. Does music playing in the background at a cafe count? Music in a film? Music played to drown out other music? Music played while reading, writing, cleaning, exercising, eating, sleeping—all of this has to count in some way. Stumbling into a college dorm now to ask the kids to turn it down, Steiner would find them all earmuffed with headphones as they stare at their computers, each listening to his own private playlist while something else plays on the stereo loud enough for a communal spirit to be maintained. And this is true not only of colleges but the world at large.

If it's easier than ever to listen to other people's music, it's also more tempting than ever to do so all alone. Walkman listening never lost the stigma of the juvenile; the sophistication—and expense—of the iPod have made adulthood safe for solipsism as never before. What does it mean for us, on the listening end, as we pad around the world with our iPods, trying to keep those shitty white earbuds from falling out of our ears? Public music criticism—a wasteland—isn't much help. It mainly focuses on individual works or single performances, when it isn't giving us drooling profiles of artists. This has nothing to do with our current mode of listening, which only rarely obsesses on particular works or genres, let alone worships particular figures. In light of the epoch-making iPod, we need a way to find out what all this music listening is doing to us, or what we're doing with it.

In the 20th century, the two most considered attempts to connect music and society were those of the philosopher Theodor Adorno and the sociologist Pierre Bourdieu.

Among the main philosophers of Western music—Schopenhauer, Nietzsche, Kierkegaard—Adorno knew the most about music and worked hardest to figure out its relationship to history. For Adorno, it wasn't just that historical forces circumscribed the production and reception of musical works; it was that historical conflicts appeared in music in mediated form. Thus a seemingly autonomous, nonrepresentational, and non linguistic art transfigured the world and returned it to the listener in a way that oriented him ideologically. The huge melodic conflicts animating Beethoven's symphonies and the brassy, thumping triumphs with which they concluded announced the era of bourgeois ascendancy after the French Revolution. The "emancipation of dissonance" in the atonal works of Schoenberg suggested a crisis of the bourgeoisie in which the self-evidence of tonality, like that of human progress, began to crack up.

Infamously, when society began to produce new forms of music that accompanied unrest by workers and students, the old Marxist turned a deaf ear. His essays on jazz and pop music are notorious classics of "bad"Adorno. The syncopations of bebop were only a mirage of liberty, and the relentless repetitiveness of rock and roll a virtual embodiment of a reified, historyless, mythological consciousness. The problem here was not exactly snobbism or even unconscious racism. It's that Adorno seemed only to understand and accept a model of listening in which music solicits and rewards the listener's whole attention. This is a musical sociology of the concert hall and the study, not the street, store, workplace, block party, or demonstration. From its standpoint, contemporary music of less-than-Schoenbergian melodic complexity can only seem simple, in the sense of dumb.

Bourdieu was a kind of anti-Adorno, his sociology a negation of the traditional aesthetics Adorno had mastered. Bourdieu practiced a deliberate and heroic philistinism. He seemed to know virtually nothing about music; it's not even clear he liked it. "Music is the 'pure' art par excellence," he wrote in *Distinction*."It says nothing and it has *nothing to say*."Adorno would have recognized this ostensibly timeless aperçu as a historically specific statement, the product of a whole century (the 19th) of debate over precisely this question: What and how does music communicate? Yet out of this falsehood Bourdieu came to a startling conclusion, the truth of which we've all had to concede: "Nothing more clearly affirms one's 'class,' nothing more infallibly classifies, than tastes in music." In the mid-1960s, he conducted a giant survey of French musical tastes, and what do you know? The haute bourgeoisie loved *The Well-Tempered Clavier*; the upwardly mobile got high on "jazzy" classics like "Rhapsody in Blue"; while the working class dug what the higher reaches thought of as schmaltzy trash, the "Blue Danube" waltz and Petula Clark. Bourdieu drew the conclusion that judgments of taste reinforce forms of social inequality, as individuals imagine themselves to possess superior or inferior spirit and perceptiveness, when really they just like what their class inheritance has taught them to. *Distinction* appeared in English in 1984, cresting the high tide of the culture wars about to hit the universities. Adorno had felt that advanced art-music was doing the work of revolution. *Are you kidding, Herr Professor?*might have been Bourdieu's response. And thus was Adorno dethroned, all his passionate arguments about history as expressed in musical form recast as moves in the game of taste, while his dismissal of jazz became practically the most famous cultural mistake of the 20th century.

In Adorno and Bourdieu we have two radically different perspectives, inhabiting each other's blind spots, with a convergence in both authors' political sympathy with socialism. We can agree with Adorno that music has immanent, formal properties that are connected, somehow, to large-scale historical forces. And we can agree with Bourdieu that musical taste is an instrument in the legitimation of class hierarchies.

So Bourdieu is helpful when we ask what the iPod has wrought in the realm of musical classification. The social world of opera-going may be headed the way of polar bears and ice caps, but *society* hasn't disappeared. A hierarchical social world has managed to absorb the omnipresence of music pretty effortlessly. You can see this in the violent intragenre squabbling that animates indie rock circles, and in the savage takedowns of avant-garde opera performances in art-music magazines. Meanwhile the proliferation of genre names represents an ever finer process of social differentiation, each genre's acolytes determining (as Serge Gainsbourg put it) *qui est*"in," *qui est*"out." The rise of generic distinctions has lately reached a climax of absurdity, such that we can name off the top of our heads: house, witch house, dub, dubstep, hardstep, dancehall, dance-floor, punk, post-punk, noise, "Noise," new wave, nu wave, No Wave, emo, post-emo, hip-hop, conscious hip-hop, alternative hip- hop, jazz hip-hop, hardcore hip-hop, nerd-core hip-hop, Christian hip-hop, crunk, crunkcore, metal, doom metal, black metal, speed metal, thrash metal, death metal, Christian death metal, and, of course, shoe-gazing, among others. (Meanwhile, 1,000 years of European art music is filed under "classical.") Some people listen to some of these; others, to only one; and others still, to nearly all. And this accomplishes a lot of handy social sorting, especially among the young, whenever music is talked about or played so that more than one person can hear it.

At the same time, modes of listening seem to be moving toward the (apparent) opposite of micro-differentiation: a total pluralism of taste. This has become the most celebrated feature of the iPod era. "I have seen the future," Alex Ross, music critic of *TheNew Yorker*, wrote in 2004, "and it is called the Shuffle—the setting on the iPod that skips randomly from one track to another." Here the iPod, or the digitization of musical life it represents, promises emancipation from questions of taste. Differences in what people listen to, in a Shuffled world, may have less and less to do with social class and purchasing power. Or, better yet, taste won't correlate to class distinction: The absence of taste will. As certain foodies score points by having eaten everything—blowfish, yak milk tea, haggis, hot dogs—so the person who knows and likes all music achieves a curious sophistication-through-indiscriminateness.

Adorno would be more at home analyzing the uses to which the omnipresence of music has been put in the service of "the administered life"—the background Muzak and easy listening, the somehow consolingly melancholy shopping pop, that we hear in malls and supermarkets almost without noticing. "I do love a new purchase!" says the Gang of Four outright—while all the other songs merely insinuate it. Around the holidays, Banana Republic will alternate familiar hits like George Michael's "Last Christmas" with pounding C-grade techno, lulling you into a state of sickly nostalgia before ramping up your heart rate—a perfect way to goose you into an impulse buy. So, too, as Adorno would have been unsurprised to find out, has music become a common way for people to get through the workday. Your local cafe's barista may literally depend on Bon Iver's reedy lugubriousness to palliate a dreary job as you depend on coffee.

On the other hand, Adorno's prejudice against empirical research—as Brecht said, Adorno"never took a trip in order to see"—meant that he never understood how music could be used for different purposes by the very people it was supposed to manage and administer. People not only use music to help them swallow an unpalatable life, but to enhance and enlarge their capacities for action. If a bass line of a standard 12-bar blues, repeating with machinelike regularity, keeps you clicking through the data entry sheet, a sharp post-punk squall can move you to sabotage and revolt, and vice versa. Of course music can also move you in less obviously political ways, filling you with romantic enthusiasm or unshakable sorrow. Then there are all the uses of music that are beneath good and evil, that neither shore up nor undermine the system. In utopia, as under late capitalism, there will still be a lot of cooking and cleaning to do, as well as long drives to take in our electric cars. These slightly boring parts of life are made less so by listening to slightly boring music.

If Adorno, in his emphasis on the immanent unfolding of musical works as cognition, didn't understand the mixed uses of distracted listening, Bourdieu missed something even more important. His empiricism blinded him to the utopian potential in music. You would never guess, to read his books, that they were published *after* the '60s, an extraordinary period that demonstrated the capacity of musical taste to break down as well as reinforce social boundaries. Shoveled at us now as commodities played ad nauseam on Clear Channel, the "classic rock" of the '60s no longer discloses its role in the social movements of that time. And yet—Hendrix, Joplin; Coltrane, Davis, Coleman; the Stones, the Beatles; and Riley, Young, Reich—even if they didn't sing a single revolutionary word, even if they chastised you for "carrying pictures of Chairman Mao," they were all either directly involved with social movements or deeply implicated in them.

The great 1990s magazine the *Baffler* spent its first half-decade analyzing how the culture industry managed, with increasing success, to recognize new musical trends and package them and sell them back at a markup to the people who'd pioneered them. The *Baffler* looked back to the punk scene of the early '80s for inspiration; it spoke up for small labels that sold music to local constituencies. If you couldn't get what you wanted on the radio, you would have to find it left of the dial—and keep looking over your shoulder for the man.

The danger now is different. The man no longer needs a monopoly on musical taste. He just wants a few cents on the dollar of every song you download, he doesn't care what that song says. Other times he doesn't even care if you pay that dollar, as long as you listen to your stolen music on his portable MP3 player, store it on his Apple computer, send it to your friends through his Verizon network. To paraphrase Yeltsin's famous offer to the Chechens, take as much free music as you can stomach. We'll see where it gets you.

If recording and mechanical reproduction opened up the world of musical pluralism—of listening to other people's music until you and they became other people yourselves—digital reproduction expanded that pluralism to the point where it reversed itself. You have all the world's music on your iPod, in your earphones. Now it's "other people's music"—which should be very exciting to encounter—as played in cafes and stores that is the problem. In any public setting, it acquires a coercive aspect. The iPod is the thing you have to buy in order not to be defenseless against the increasingly sucky music played to make you buy things.

One radical option remains: abnegation—some "Great Refusal" to obey the obscure social injunction that condemns us to a lifetime of listening. *Silence*: The word suggests the torture of enforced isolation, or a particularly monkish kind of social death. But it was the tremendously congenial avant-garde gadabout John Cage who showed, just as the avalanche of recorded music was starting to bury us, how there was "no such thing as silence," that listening to an absence of listener-directed sounds represented a profounder and far more heroic submission than the regular attitude adopted in concert halls—a willingness to "let sounds be," as he put it. Such were Cage's restrictions that he needed to herd everyone into their seats in order to make his point—an authoritarian gesture toward an anarchic result. But now in conditions of relative freedom we can listen to 4'33" on record, or on our iPods, and the change in attention it demands is exactly the opposite of our endless contemporary communing with music, our neurotic search for the right sound, the exact note that never comes. What if we tried to listen to nothing? Silence is the feature of our buzzing sound-world we enjoy least, whose very existence we threaten to pave over track by track. Silence is the most endangered musical experience in our time. Turning it up, we might figure out what all our music listening is meant to drown out, the thing we can't bear to hear.

■ WHAT?

1. Do you listen to music when you study or write? Did you listen to music (or was music playing) as you read Saval's essay? Do you study in places where you can hear the music of other people (in a residence hall, for example, or a coffee shop)?

2. Early in his essay, Saval asks: "What does it mean for us, on the listening end, as we pad around the world with our iPods, trying to keep those shitty white earbuds from falling out of our ears?" How does he answer this question? Compare his response—which isn't necessarily direct— with your own experience.

3. How does Saval use the philosopher Theodor Adorno and the sociologist Pierre Bourdieu in his essay? Do you think including them is an effective persuasive strategy? Explain your response.

■ WHAT ELSE? WHAT'S NEXT?

4. What terms, names, or concepts did you look up as you read Saval's piece? If you didn't look up anything, what should you have researched to help you better understand Saval's text?

5. Working with a group of classmates, conduct an informal survey of family, friends, classmates, and anyone else you wish to include to find out when and where people listen to music through headphones or ear buds. Compile your findings in a brief report to be shared with the class. Do your results support or contradict Saval's arguments about the ubiquity of the iPod and other listening devices and their isolating effects?

■ WHO CARES?

6. Who do you think is Saval's intended audience for this essay? Do you consider yourself to be part of that target readership? What in the text supports your position?

"Jonathan Franzen is the author of several books, most recently, Freedom. *The following piece, published in May 2011 in* The New York Times, *is adapted from a commencement speech Franzen delivered that month at Kenyon College.*

BEFORE YOU READ

Find Facebook's "Like" page (it's part of the Help Center, or you can Google "liking Facebook"). Look over what's there, and then write a brief explanation of what it means to "like" something on the social networking site.

LIKING IS FOR COWARDS. GO FOR WHAT HURTS. Jonathan Franzen

A couple of weeks ago, I replaced my three-year-old BlackBerry Pearl with a much more powerful BlackBerry Bold. Needless to say, I was impressed with how far the technology had advanced in three years. Even when I didn't have anybody to call or text or e-mail, I wanted to keep fondling my new Bold and experiencing the marvelous clarity of its screen, the silky action of its track pad, the shocking speed of its responses, the beguiling elegance of its graphics.

I was, in short, infatuated with my new device. I'd been similarly infatuated with my old device, of course; but over the years the bloom had faded from our relationship. I'd developed trust issues with my Pearl, accountability issues, compatibility issues and even, toward the end, some doubts about my Pearl's very sanity, until I'd finally had to admit to myself that I'd outgrown the relationship.

Do I need to point out that—absent some wild, anthropomorphizing projection in which my old BlackBerry felt sad about the waning of my love for it—our relationship was entirely one-sided? Let me point it out anyway.

Let me further point out how ubiquitously the word "sexy" is used to describe late-model gadgets; and how the extremely cool things that we can do now with these gadgets—like impelling them to action with voice commands, or doing that spreading-the-fingers iPhone thing that makes images get bigger—would have looked, to people a hundred years ago, like a magician's incantations, a magician's hand gestures; and how, when we want to describe an erotic relationship that's working perfectly, we speak, indeed, of magic.

Let me toss out the idea that, as our markets discover and respond to what consumers most want, our technology has become extremely adept at creating products that correspond to our fantasy ideal of an erotic relationship, in which the beloved object asks for nothing and gives everything, instantly, and makes us feel all powerful, and doesn't throw terrible scenes when it's replaced by an even sexier object and is consigned to a drawer.

To speak more generally, the ultimate goal of technology, the telos of techne, is to replace a natural world that's indifferent to our wishes—a world of hurricanes and hardships and breakable hearts, a world of resistance—with a world so responsive to our wishes as to be, effectively, a mere extension of the self.

Let me suggest, finally, that the world of techno-consumerism is therefore troubled by real love, and that it has no choice but to trouble love in turn.

Its first line of defense is to commodify its enemy. You can all supply your own favorite, most nauseating examples of the commodification of love. Mine include the wedding industry, TV ads that feature cute young children or the giving of automobiles as Christmas presents, and the particularly grotesque equation of diamond jewelry with everlasting devotion. The message, in each case, is that if you love somebody you should buy stuff.

A related phenomenon is the transformation, courtesy of Facebook, of the verb "to like" from a state of mind to an action that you perform with your computer mouse, from a feeling to an assertion of consumer choice. And liking, in general, is commercial culture's substitute for loving. The striking thing about all consumer products—and none more so than electronic devices and applications—is that they're designed to be immensely likable. This is, in fact, the definition of a consumer product, in contrast to the product that is simply itself and whose makers aren't fixated on your liking it. (I'm thinking here of jet engines, laboratory equipment, serious art and literature.)

But if you consider this in human terms, and you imagine a person defined by a desperation to be liked, what do you see? You see a person without integrity, without a center. In more pathological cases, you see a narcissist—a person who can't tolerate the tarnishing of his or her self-image that not being liked represents, and who therefore either withdraws from human contact or goes to extreme, integrity-sacrificing lengths to be likable.

If you dedicate your existence to being likable, however, and if you adopt whatever cool persona is necessary to make it happen, it suggests that you've despaired of being loved for who you really are. And if you succeed in manipulating other people into liking you, it will be hard not to feel, at some level, contempt for those people, because they've fallen for your shtick. You may find yourself becoming depressed, or alcoholic, or, if you're Donald Trump, running for president (and then quitting).

Consumer technology products would never do anything this unattractive, because they aren't people. They are, however, great allies and enablers of narcissism. Alongside their built-in eagerness to be liked is a built-in eagerness to reflect well on us. Our lives look a lot more interesting when they're filtered through the sexy Facebook interface. We star in our own movies, we photograph ourselves incessantly, we click the mouse and a machine confirms our sense of mastery.

And, since our technology is really just an extension of ourselves, we don't have to have contempt for its manipulability in the way we might with actual people. It's all one big endless loop. We like the mirror and the mirror likes us. To friend a person is merely to include the person in our private hall of flattering mirrors.

I may be overstating the case, a little bit. Very probably, you're sick to death of hearing social media disrespected by cranky 51-year-olds. My aim here is mainly to set up a contrast between the narcissistic tendencies of technology and the problem of actual love. My friend Alice Sebold likes to talk about "getting down in the pit and loving somebody." She has in mind the dirt that love inevitably splatters on the mirror of our self-regard.

The simple fact of the matter is that trying to be perfectly likable is incompatible with loving relationships. Sooner or later, for example, you're going to find yourself in a hideous, screaming fight, and you'll hear coming out of your mouth things that you yourself don't like at all, things that shatter your self-image as a fair, kind, cool, attractive, in-control, funny, likable person. Something realer than likability has come out in you, and suddenly you're having an actual life.

Suddenly there's a real choice to be made, not a fake consumer choice between a BlackBerry and an iPhone, but a question: Do I love this person? And, for the other person, does this person love me?

There is no such thing as a person whose real self you like every particle of. This is why a world of liking is ultimately a lie. But there is such a thing as a person whose real self you love every particle of. And this is why love is such an existential threat to the techno-consumerist order: it exposes the lie.

This is not to say that love is only about fighting. Love is about bottomless empathy, born out of the heart's revelation that another person is every bit as real as you are. And this is why love, as I understand it, is always specific. Trying to love all of humanity may be a worthy endeavor, but, in a funny way, it keeps the focus on the self, on the self's own moral or spiritual well-being. Whereas, to love a specific person, and to identify with his or her struggles and joys as if they were your own, you have to surrender some of your self.

The big risk here, of course, is rejection. We can all handle being disliked now and then, because there's such an infinitely big pool of potential likers. But to expose your whole self, not just the likable surface, and to have it rejected, can be catastrophically painful. The prospect of pain generally, the pain of loss, of breakup, of death, is what makes it so tempting to avoid love and stay safely in the world of liking.

And yet pain hurts but it doesn't kill. When you consider the alternative—an anesthetized dream of self-sufficiency, abetted by technology—pain emerges as the natural product and natural indicator of being alive in a resistant world. To go through a life painlessly is to have not lived. Even just to say to yourself, "Oh, I'll get to that love and pain stuff later, maybe in my 30s" is to consign yourself to 10 years of merely taking up space on the planet and burning up its resources. Of being (and I mean this in the most damning sense of the word) a consumer.

When I was in college, and for many years after, I liked the natural world. Didn't love it, but definitely liked it. It can be very pretty, nature. And since I was looking for things to find wrong with the world, I naturally gravitated to environmentalism, because there were certainly plenty of things wrong with the environment. And the more I looked at what was wrong—an exploding world population, exploding levels of resource consumption, rising global temperatures, the trashing of the oceans, the logging of our last old-growth forests—the angrier I became.

Finally, in the mid-1990s, I made a conscious decision to stop worrying about the environment. There was nothing meaningful that I personally could do to save the planet, and I wanted to get on with devoting myself to the things I loved. I still tried to keep my carbon footprint small, but that was as far as I could go without falling back into rage and despair.

But then a funny thing happened to me. It's a long story, but basically I fell in love with birds. I did this not without significant resistance, because it's very uncool to be a birdwatcher, because anything that betrays real passion is by definition uncool. But little by little, in spite of myself, I developed this passion, and although one-half of a passion is obsession, the other half is love.

And so, yes, I kept a meticulous list of the birds I'd seen, and, yes, I went to inordinate lengths to see new species. But, no less important, whenever I looked at a bird, any bird, even a pigeon or a robin, I could feel my heart overflow with love. And love, as I've been trying to say today, is where our troubles begin.

Because now, not merely liking nature but loving a specific and vital part of it, I had no choice but to start worrying about the environment again. The news on that front was no better than when I'd decided to quit worrying about it—was considerably worse, in fact—but now those threatened forests and wetlands and oceans weren't just pretty scenes for me to enjoy. They were the home of animals I loved.

And here's where a curious paradox emerged. My anger and pain and despair about the planet were only increased by my concern for wild birds, and yet, as I began to get involved in bird conservation and learned more about the many threats that birds face, it became easier, not harder, to live with my anger and despair and pain.

How does this happen? I think, for one thing, that my love of birds became a portal to an important, less self-centered part of myself that I'd never even known existed. Instead of continuing to drift forward through my life as a global citizen, liking and disliking and withholding my commitment for some later date, I was forced to confront a self that I had to either straight-up accept or flat-out reject.

Which is what love will do to a person. Because the fundamental fact about all of us is that we're alive for a while but will die before long. This fact is the real root cause of all our anger and pain and despair. And you can either run from this fact or, by way of love, you can embrace it.

When you stay in your room and rage or sneer or shrug your shoulders, as I did for many years, the world and its problems are impossibly daunting. But when you go out and put yourself in real relation to real people, or even just real animals, there's a very real danger that you might love some of them.

And who knows what might happen to you then?

■ WHAT?

1. Briefly summarize the argument that Franzen presents in his speech.
2. How does Franzen differentiate between "liking" and "loving"? Make sure you point to specific examples from his speech as you explain his definitions.
3. How, according to Franzen, does "real love" trouble the world of techno-consumerism? How does techno-consumerism, in turn, trouble real love?

■ WHAT ELSE? WHAT'S NEXT?

4. Research the backlash against "liking." How have others criticized this phenomenon? Does anyone online step up to defend "liking"? Do you see anything wrong with "liking"? Explain your response.

■ WHO CARES?

5. At one point in his speech, Franzen says to the audience, gathered for a college commencement: "Very probably, you're sick to death of hearing social media disrespected by cranky 51-year-olds." Why do you think Franzen says this? How does this statement function rhetorically?

6. Does Franzen convince you that all this fuss over "liking" is warranted? If so, how does he do this? If not, what could he have done differently to make you care?

IMAGE 3.3
In her essay, Caitlin Dewey writes: "The Internet brings ... people together with hash tags and message boards, but it never satisfies them. No matter how much you love someone's blog or Twitter feed, it isn't their posts you actually want." How would you characterize the dynamic between the online and in-real-life aspects of relationships?

Caitlin Dewey was a senior at Syracuse University majoring in magazine journalism when the following piece won the 2011 Modern Love Essay Contest sponsored by The New York Times. *According to the newspaper, the contest "asked college students nationwide to tell us—through their own stories, in their own voices—what love is like for them." Responses came from scores of colleges and universities, including the University of South Carolina. Dewey's essay was published in May 2011 in* The Times.

BEFORE YOU READ

How does digital technology—the Internet, smartphones, social networking—affect the way you think about and pursue relationships?

EVEN IN REAL LIFE, THERE WERE SCREENS BETWEEN US Caitlin Dewey

Curled up at the foot of my bed, my face inches from the laptop screen, I stared anxiously at the Google chat box. "Will is typing," the box told me, helpfully.

I forced myself to read e-mail while I waited for his message. Then I refreshed my Twitter feed, scrolled through my blog posts and began brushing my teeth.

Still the box said, "Will is typing."

"Don't you dare get hurt by this," I muttered around my toothpaste. "This was a stupid idea, and you knew that from the start."

But recognizing the stupidity of falling for someone on the Internet does not prevent you from doing it. My friend Jeanette, a college radio D.J., chats constantly with some music blogger she met on Tumblr. My friend Tuan, who lives in Los Angeles, stays up until after 3 to talk to his London-based girlfriend.

And I had just driven nearly 1,100 miles round trip to visit Will, a guy I met in October at a Web journalism conference and got to know almost entirely on Skype.

I noticed him across the table at a noisy hotel bar. Will owns thick black-frame glasses but no hairbrush or comb, traits that lend him the look of a basement-bound hacker. If you have ever attended an Internet conference, you understand how pale skin, thick glasses and scruffy hair can be attractive; otherwise, I can't explain it to you.

In either case, I liked Will's weirdly overconfident smirk and his obsession with WordPress. He regaled me with the merits of plug-ins and PHP until I became tired and went to bed.

"I'll find you on Twitter," I joked when I left.

I didn't expect or even want to see Will again after that weekend. Since he lived three states away, further face time seemed unlikely. I followed his Twitter posts with detached curiosity; in January, he G-chatted me to complain about work. Then he got drunk and messaged me again, sometime near midnight, as I uploaded photos and otherwise wasted bandwidth.

With obvious sarcasm, he wrote, "Do you have that Skype thing kids talk about these days?"

I've read that 90 percent of human communication is nonverbal. Skype captures that 90 percent on a low-resolution video camera, compresses it, funnels it to a node computer and reproduces it on a screen anywhere in the world. Skype eliminates distance; that's why it works.

And that's exactly what it did for us. With my Skype screen open and my webcam on, I viscerally felt that Will was sitting a foot away on my bed. Ignoring the times the picture froze or his voice cut out, I thought he looked and sounded exactly as he had in person. Sometimes, when he leaned into the computer to read an article I had sent him, I could see the pores of his face.

We started video chatting for hours every night—he from an ascetic all-white bedroom, me from the cupcake-print corner of my studio apartment. I learned that he ate take-out for every meal, slept in a series of identical white V-neck T-shirts and smirked with one side of his mouth when I said something clever. I knew his preferred coding languages, his least favorite content management system, and his general hatred of dancing, small talk and girls in bars.

One night, when we talked too late, I fell asleep with my laptop open and woke up seven hours later, tangled in cords. He was still there, asleep in the light from an open window, pale and young and pixelated.

Eventually he stirred, blinked at the camera and said, "Hey, you."

"Hey," I said easily. "How did you sleep?"

As the weeks went on, I told Will about my last boyfriend, a guy I had met in psychology class and dated for almost two years. He listened quietly, his glasses reflecting my image from his computer, and gave good, clear-eyed advice about letting go.

I couldn't remember the last time I met somebody that smart and talented in ways I certainly wasn't. He told me about his ex-girlfriend, who never appreciated his work. I texted him from classes when I was frustrated or bored.

In the safety of my apartment, I could see Will, but I couldn't touch him. I could summon him when I wanted to talk, but I never knew him in any light other than the one from his bedside lamp. This phenomenon worked in my favor as well. I could call him after a few drinks, when I felt sufficiently talkative and social; I could avoid him if I had videos to edit or blog posts to write. I could say whatever I wanted and risk awkwardness, because at the end of the conversation, one click of the mouse would shut him out of my room.

The irony is that we flock to the Internet for this type of safe, sanitized intimacy, but we want something entirely different. "In real life," or IRL, is a popular term in online parlance. At Internet conferences like the one where I met Will, Twitter explodes with people celebrating IRL meetings: "So nice to finally see @so-and-so IRL." "Hey @so-and-so, I can't believe we hadn't met IRL yet!"

The Internet brings these people together with hash tags and message boards, but it never satisfies them. No matter how much you love someone's blog or Twitter feed, it isn't their posts you actually want.

And so—slowly, cautiously—Will and I began circling the question of what it all meant.

"I really like you," he said one night, after getting home from the bar.

"I really like you too," I said. "I don't know what that means."

I wanted to find out. So in early March I rented a car, begged my professors to let me out of class a day early, and drove 540 miles to spend a long weekend in the midsize city where Will lives. When I got close, I called my friend Tuan from a rest stop, where I fixed my makeup and chewed gum and generally tried to calm down.

"What if it's terrible?" I demanded. "What if he's nothing like I expect?"

In fact, Will was almost exactly as I expected: thin lips, straight nose, small hazel eyes, glasses. He stood waiting at the side of the street while I parked my car—going forward and back, forward and back, until I nervously got within two feet of the curb. We kissed on the cold, blustery sidewalk as the wind whipped my thoughts around. Mostly, I felt relieved. I thought: "This works in real life. This means something."

But after we kissed and ate pizza and went back to his house, we struggled for things to talk about. In real life, Will stared off at nothing while I talked. In real life, he had no questions about the drive or my work or the stuff that waited for me when I went back to school.

He took me out for dinner and read his e-mail while we waited for our food. He apologized profusely, but still checked his Web site's traffic stats while we sat in his living room.

He took me to a party at his friend's house where they proceeded to argue for hours about Web design while I sat on a futon and stared at the ceiling, drunk and bored and terribly concerned that I looked thinner online. At points, he grabbed my hand and gave me small, apologetic smiles. It seemed like a strategy game: a constant dance of reaching for me and pulling back, of intimacy and distance, of real life and Internet make-believe.

On the last day of my visit, Will overslept. He rushed around the apartment with his hair wet and his tie untied, looking for his laptop. According to the plan we made the night before, he would go to work and I would leave when it suited me, dropping his spare keys in the mailbox.

In the front hallway, where I stood rubbing my eyes, Will hugged me goodbye and told me to drive safely. He struggled for a closing statement.

"It was great to see you," he said at last.

I didn't leave right away. After I showered and packed and studied the books near his fireplace, I sat for a long time at his kitchen counter, trying to work out what happened. I didn't like being surrounded by his things. I felt more comfortable in my room, with my things, and with his presence confined to a laptop screen.

I wrote him a note before I left: "Dear Will: Thank you so much for having me this weekend. It meant a lot to me to spend time with you in person."

I signed my name and left it on the counter. Then, willing myself not to cry, I dropped his keys in the mailbox and gunned it home. In real life, getting there took nine hours.

■ WHAT?

1. Dewey's piece is a memoir essay, grounded in personal experience, yet it also presents an argument not unlike Jonathan Franzen's in "Liking Is for Cowards. Go for What Hurts." What do you think Dewey is saying in her essay about online and in-real-life relationships? Do you agree with her perspective? Why or why not?
2. What effects does Skype have on the evolving relationship between Dewey and Will?
3. Dewey ends her essay by pointing out the following about her return home: "In real life, getting there took nine hours." What does this mean—beyond the temporal accounting and given the context of Dewey's essay as a whole?

■ WHAT ELSE? WHAT'S NEXT?

4. Write a brief essay suitable for submission to the opinion pages of *The Gamecock* in response to the following statement: "Social networking sites are destroying our ability to develop and maintain personal relationships." In your essay, you should clearly state your position on the statement and support your position with specific and suitable examples. Keep in mind that opinion columns in *The Gamecock* rarely exceed 300 words and are meant for an audience that includes the entire campus community.

■ WHO CARES?

5. What does Dewey do rhetorically to make her personal experience relevant to others? Is she successful? Explain.

4 | Reading Green

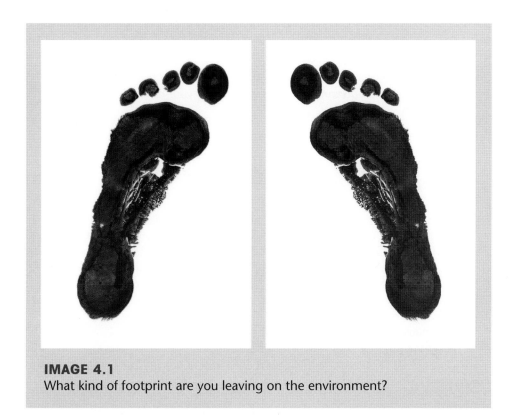

IMAGE 4.1
What kind of footprint are you leaving on the environment?

Though experts may debate the best way to address the threats to our environment, most agree that the situation is dire and that we cannot maintain our present course. Against this backdrop, this chapter provides a path through the myriad perspectives on environmental issues. Rooted in philosophy, science, politics, history, pop culture, and personal experience, the texts collected in the pages that follow consider the environmental crises we face and argue about how and why we should try to do something to protect the planet—and ourselves.

One of the world's greatest and most influential living scientists, biologist Edward O. Wilson has written numerous books and won two Pulitzer Prizes. "For the Love of Life" is the penultimate chapter of his 2002 book The Future of Life, which one reviewer called "a meditation on the splendor of our biosphere and the dangers we pose to it."

BEFORE YOU READ

Research the concept of "biophilia." Find at least two sources that help you understand what the concept means and how it is used, and then write a brief report, with proper MLA documentation, summarizing your research.

FOR THE LOVE OF LIFE   Edward O. Wilson

Have you ever wondered how we will be remembered a thousand years from now, when we are as remote as Charlemagne? Many would be satisfied with a list that includes the following: *the technoscientific revolution continued, globalized, and unstoppable; computer capacity approaching that of the human brain; robotic auxiliaries proliferating; cells rebuilt from molecules; space colonized; population growth slackening; the world democratized; international trade accelerated; people better fed and healthier than ever before; life span stretched; religion holding firm.*

In this buoyant vision of the twenty-first century, what might we have overlooked about our place in history? What are we neglecting and at risk of forever losing? The answer most likely in the year 3000 is: *much of the rest of life, and part of what it means to be a human being.*

A few technophiles, I expect, will beg to differ. What, after all, in the long term does it mean to be human? We have traveled this far; we will go on. As to the rest of life, they continue, we should be able to immerse fertilized eggs and clonable tissues of endangered species in liquid nitrogen and use them later to rebuild the destroyed ecosystems. Even that may not be necessary: in time entirely new species and ecosystems, better suited to human needs than the old ones, can be created by genetic engineering. *Homo sapiens* might choose to redesign itself along the way, the better to live in a new biological order of our own making.

Such is the extrapolated endpoint of technomania applied to the natural world. The compelling response, in my opinion, is that to travel even partway there would be a dangerous gamble, a single throw of the dice with the future of life on the table. To revive or synthesize the thousands of species needed—probably millions when the still largely unknown microorganisms have been cataloged—and put them together in functioning ecosystems is beyond even the theoretical imagination of existing science. Each species is adapted to particular physical and chemical environments within the habitat. Each species has evolved to fit together with certain other species in ways biologists are only beginning to understand. To synthesize ecosystems on bare ground or in empty water is no more practicable than the reanimation of deep-frozen human corpses. And to redesign the human genotype better to fit a ruined biosphere is the stuff of science horror fiction. Let us leave it there, in the realm of imagination.

Another reason exists not to take the gamble, not to let the natural world slip away. Suppose, for the sake of argument, that new species can be engineered and stable ecosystems built from them. With that distant potential in mind, should we go ahead, and for short-term gain, allow the original species and ecosystems to slip away? Yes? Erase Earth's living history? Then also burn the libraries and art galleries, make cordwood of the musical instruments, pulp the musical scores, erase Shakespeare, Beethoven, and Goethe, and the Beatles too, because all these—or at least fairly good substitutes—can be re-created.

The issue, like all great decisions, is moral. Science and technology are what we can do; morality is what we agree we should or should not do. The ethic from which moral decisions spring is a norm or standard of behavior in support of a value, and value in turn depends on purpose. Purpose, whether personal or global, whether urged by conscience or graven in sacred script, expresses the image we hold of ourselves and our society. In short, ethics evolve through discrete steps, from self-image to purpose to value to ethical precepts to moral reasoning.

A conservation ethic is that which aims to pass on to future generations the best part of the nonhuman world. To know this world is to gain a proprietary attachment to it. To know it well is to love and take responsibility for it.

Each species—American eagle, Sumatran rhinoceros, flat-spined three-toothed land snail, furbish lousewort, and on down the roster of ten million or more still with us—is a masterpiece. The craftsman who assembled them was natural selection, acting upon mutations and recombinations of genes, through vast numbers of steps over long periods of time. Each species, when examined closely, offers an endless bounty of knowledge and aesthetic pleasure. It is a living library. The number of genes prescribing a eukaryotic life form such as a Douglas fir or a human being runs into the tens of thousands. The nucleotide pairs composing them—in other words, the genetic letters that encode the life-giving enzymes—vary among species from one billion to ten billion. If the DNA helics in one cell of a mouse, a typical animal species, were placed end on end and magically enlarged to have the same width as wrapping string, they would extend for over nine hundred kilometers, with about four thousand nucleotide pairs packed into every meter. Measured in bits of pure information, the genome of a cell is comparable to all editions of the *Encyclopedia Britannica* published since its inception in 1768.

The creature at your feet dismissed as a bug or a weed is a creation in and of itself. It has a name, a million-year history, and a place in the world. Its genome adapts it to a special niche in an ecosystem. The ethical value substantiated by close examination of its biology is that the life forms around us are too old, too complex, and potentially too useful to be carelessly discarded.

Biologists point to another ethically potent value; the genetic unity of life. All organisms have descended from the same distant ancestral life form. The reading of the genetic codes has shown thus far that the common ancestor of all living species was similar to present-day bacteria and Achaeans, single-celled microbes with the simplest known anatomy and molecular composition. Because of this single ancestry, which arose on Earth over 3.5 billion years ago, all species today share certain fundamental molecular traits. Their tissue is divided into cells, whose enveloping lipid membranes regulate exchange with the outside environment. The molecular machinery that generates energy is similar. The genetic information is stored in DNA, transcribed into RNA, and translated into proteins. Finally, a large array of mostly similar protein catalysts, the enzymes, accelerate all the life processes.

Still another intensely felt value is stewardship, which appears to arise from emotions programmed in the very genes of human social behavior. Because all organisms have descended from a common ancestor, it is correct to say that the biosphere as a whole began to think when humanity was born. If the rest of life is the body, we are the mind. Thus, our place in nature, viewed from an ethical perspective, is to think about the creation and to protect the living planet.

As cognitive scientists have focused on the nature of the mind, they have come to characterize it not just as a physical entity, the brain at work, but more specifically as a flood of scenarios. Whether set in the past, present, or future, whether based on reality or entirely fictive, these free-running narratives are all churned out with equal facility. The present is constructed from the avalanche of sensations that pour into the wakened brain. Working at a furious pace, the brain summons memories to screen and make sense of the incoming chaos. Only a minute part of the information is selected for higher-order processing. From that part, small segments are enlisted through symbolic imagery to create the white-hot core of activity we call the conscious mind.

During the story-building process the past is reworked and then returned to storage. The repeated cycles allow the brain to hold on to only small but shrinking fragments of these former conscious states. Over a lifetime the details of real events are increasingly distorted by editing and supplementation. Across generations the most important among them turn into history, and finally legend and myth.

Each culture has its own creation myth, the primary functions of which are to place the tribe that contrived it at the center of the universe, and to portray history as a noble epic. The ultimate epic unfolding through science is the genetic history both of *Homo sapiens* and of all our antecedents. Traced back far enough through time, across more than three billion years, all organisms on Earth share a common ancestry. That genetic unity is a fact-based history confirmed with increasing exactitude by the geneticists and paleontologists who reconstruct evolutionary genealogy. If *Homo sapiens* as a whole must have a creation myth—and emotionally in the age of globalization it seems we must—none is more solid and unifying for the species than evolutionary history. That is another value favoring stewardship of the natural world.

To summarize: a sense of genetic unity, kinship, and deep history are among the values that bond us to the living environment. They are survival mechanisms for ourselves and our species. To conserve biological diversity is an investment in immortality.

Do other species therefore have inalienable rights? There are three reaches of altruism possible from which a response can be made. The first is anthropocentrism: nothing matters except that which affects humanity. Then pathocentrism: intrinsic rights should be extended to chimpanzees, dogs, and other intelligent animals for whom we can legitimately feel empathy. And finally biocentrism: all kinds of organisms have an intrinsic right at least to exist. The three levels are not as exclusive as they first seem. In real life they often coincide, and when in life-or-death conflict, they can be ordered in priority as follows: first humanity, next intelligent animals, and then other forms of life.

The influence of the biocentric view, expressed institutionally through quasi-religious movements such as Deep Ecology and the Epic of Evolution, is growing worldwide. The philosopher Holmes Rolston III tells a story that can serve as a parable of this trend. For years, trailside signs at a sub alpine campground in the Rocky Mountains he occasionally visited read, "Please leave the flowers for others to enjoy." When the wooden signs began to erode and flake, they were replaced by new ones that read, "Let the flowers live!"

It is not so difficult to love nonhuman life, if gifted with knowledge about it. The capacity, even the proneness to do so, may well be one of the human instincts. The phenomenon has been called biophilia, defined as the innate tendency to focus upon life and lifelike forms, and in some instances to affiliate with them emotionally. Human beings sharply distinguish the living from the inanimate. We esteem novelty and diversity in other organisms. We are thrilled by the prospect of unknown creatures, whether in the deep sea, the unbroken forest, or remote mountains. We are riveted by the idea of life on other planets. Dinosaurs are our icons of vanished biodiversity. More people visit zoos in the United States than attend professional sports events. Their favorite site in the National Zoo of Washington, D.C., is the insect exhibit, representing maximum novelty and diversity.

A prominent component of biophilia is habitat selection. Studies conducted in the relatively new field of environmental psychology during the past thirty years point consistently to the following conclusion: people prefer to be in natural environments, and especially in savanna or park-like habitats. They like a long depth of view across a relatively smooth, grassy ground surface dotted with trees and copses. They want to be near a body of water, whether ocean, lake, river, or stream. They try to place their habitations on a prominence, from which they can safely scan the savanna and watery environment. With nearly absolute consistency, these landscapes are preferred over urban settings that are either bare or clothed in scant vegetation. To a relative degree people dislike woodland views that possess restricted depth of vision, a disordered complexity of vegetation, and rough ground structures—in short, forests with small, closely spaced trees and dense undergrowth. They want a topography and openings that improve their line of sight.

People prefer to look out over their ideal terrain from a secure position framed by the semi-enclosure of a domicile. Their choice of home and environs, if made freely, combines a balance of refuge for safety and a wide visual prospect for exploration and foraging. There may be small gender differences: among Western landscape painters at least, women stress refuges with small prospect spaces, and men stress large prospect spaces. Women also tend to place human figures in or near the refuges, while men place them more consistently in the open spaces beyond.

The ideal natural habitat is intuitively understood by landscape architects and real-estate entrepreneurs. Even when it offers no practical value, the setting commands a relatively high price, reaching its maximum if also located conveniently near cities.

I once described the principle of the ideal habitat to a wealthy friend as we looked down from his New York penthouse to the open woodland and lake of Central Park. His terrace, I also noticed, was ringed by potted plants. I thought of him as a convincing experimental subject. It has since often occurred to me that to see most clearly the manifestations of human instinct, it is useful to start with the rich, who among us enjoy the widest range of options in response, and most readily follow their emotional and aesthetic inclinations.

No direct evidence has yet been sought for a genetic basis of the human habitat preference, but its presence is suggested by a consistency in its manifestation across cultures, including those in North America, Europe, Korea, and Nigeria.

A similar convergence occurs in the aesthetics of tree form. Subjects in cross-cultural psychological tests prefer moderate-sized and sturdy trees with broad, layered canopies close to the ground. The species considered most attractive include acacias, which are dominant elements of healthy African savannas.

Tree aesthetics brings us to the question of the origin of the biophilic instincts. The human habitat preference is consistent with the "savanna hypothesis," that humanity originated in the savannas and transitional forests of Africa. Almost the full evolutionary history of the genus *Homo,* including *Homo sapiens* and its immediate ancestors, was spent in or near these habitats or others similar to them. If that amount of time, about two millions years, were to be compressed into a span of seventy years, humanity occupied the ancestral environment for sixty-nine years and eight months, whereupon some of the populations took up agriculture and moved into villages to spend the last 120 days.

The savanna hypothesis extended to include behavior stipulates that *Homo sapiens* is likely to be genetically specialized for the ancestral environment so that today, even in the most sequestered stone-and-glass cities, we still prefer it. Part of human nature is a residue of bias in mental development that causes us to gravitate back to savannas or their surrogates.

The savanna hypothesis of habitat preference may strike some readers as evolutionism run amok. But is the idea really so strange? Not at all: just a glance at the world of animal behavior suggests otherwise. Every species that moves under its own power, from protozoans to chimpanzees, instinctively seeks the habitat it must occupy in order to survive and reproduce. The behavioral steps for which it is genetically programmed are usually complex and exactly executed. The study of habitat selection is an important branch of ecology, and no species ever lets down the researcher who chooses to examine this part of its life cycle. To take one of a multitude of excellent examples, the African mosquito *Anopheles gambiae* is a species specialized to feed on human blood. (As a result it is a carrier of the malignant malarial parasite *Plasmodium falciparum.*) Each female, in order to complete her life cycle, finds her way from the stagnant pool of her birth and larval growth to a nearby village. In the daytime she hides in crevices of the house. At night she flies directly to one of the inhabitants, moving upwind through a plume of the chemically distinctive odor of the human body. She accomplishes all this with no experience and a brain the size of a grain of salt.

So it should be no great surprise that human beings, a biological species dependent on certain natural environments until very recently in its evolutionary history, should retain an aesthetic preference for savannas and transitional woodland among an array of natural and artificial environments laid before them. In general, what we call aesthetics may be just the pleasurable sensations we get from the particular stimuli to which our brains are inherently adapted.

To say that there is an instinct, or more accurately an array of instincts, that can be labeled biophilia is not to imply that the brain is hardwired. We do not ambulate like robots to the nearest lakeshore meadow. Instead, the brain is predisposed to acquire certain preferences as opposed to others. Psychologists who study mental development say that we are hereditarily *prepared* to learn certain behaviors and *counter-prepared* to learn others. The vast majority of humans, to use a familiar example, are prepared to learn the lyrics of a song but counter-prepared to learn calculus. We delight in the first and are fearful and begrudging of the second. Also, true to the pattern of instinct thus broadly defined, there are sensitive periods during childhood and early maturity in which learning and distaste are most easily picked up. In a manner also true to the conception, the timing varies among categories of behavior. Fluency in language comes earlier than fluency in mathematics.

The critical stages in the acquisition of biophilia have been worked out by psychologists during studies of childhood mental development. Under the age of six, children tend to be egocentric, self-serving, and domineering in their responses to animals and nature. They are also most prone to be uncaring or fearful of the natural world and of all but a few familiar animals. Between six and nine, children become interested in wild creatures for the first time, and aware that animals can suffer pain and distress. From nine to twelve their knowledge and interest in the natural world rises sharply, and between thirteen and seventeen they readily acquire moral feeling toward animal welfare and species conservation.

A single study in the United States devoted to the subject suggests that a parallel sequence unfolds in the development of habitat preference. Children between the ages of eight and eleven, when given a choice of environmental photographs spread before them, favored savanna over hardwood forest, north-temperate conifer forest, rainforest, and desert. In contrast, older children preferred hardwood forest and savanna equally—in other words, habitats with which they had the most direct experience during their adolescence. Both of these environments were chosen over the remaining three. From this one set of data at least, the evidence supports the savanna hypothesis. In other words, children are evidently predisposed to favor the ancestral human habitat, but then increasingly favor the environment in which they have grown up.

Another sequence occurs in the way children explore the environment. At four they confine themselves to the immediate vicinity of their home and to small creatures readily found there, the "worms, chipmunks and pigeons" of neighboring yards and streets, as David Sobel expressed it in *Children's Special Places*. At eight to eleven they head for nearby woods, fields, ditches, and other unclaimed spots they can claim as their own. There they often build some kind of shelter such as a tree house, fort, or cave where they can read magazines, eat lunch, conspire with a friend or two, play games, and spy on the world. If natural wild environments are available, so much the better, but they are not essential. In urban East Harlem, children were observed building forts in culverts, alleyways, basements, abandoned warehouses, railroad right-of-ways, and hedges.

The secret places of childhood, whether a product of instinct or not, at the very least predispose us to acquire certain preferences and to undertake practices of later value in survival. The hideaways bond us with place, and they nourish our individuality and self-esteem. They enhance joy in the construction of habitation. If played out in natural environments, they also bring us close to the earth and nature in ways that can engender a lifelong love of both. Such was my own experience as a boy of eleven to thirteen, when I sought little Edens in the forest of Alabama and Florida. On one occasion I built a small hut of saplings in a remote off-trail spot. Unfortunately, I didn't notice until later that some of the saplings were poison oak, a virulent relative of poison ivy. That was the last of my secret-house constructions, but my love of the natural world nevertheless grew even stronger.

If biophilia is truly part of human nature, if it is truly an instinct, we should be able to find evidence of a positive effect of the natural world and other organisms on health. In fact, the annals of physiology and medicine contain abundant and diverse studies affirming just such a connection, at least when health is broadly defined, to use the words of the World Health Organization, as "a state of complete physical, mental and social well-being and not merely the absence of disease and infirmity." The following results of published studies are representative:

- A population of 120 volunteers were shown a stressful movie, followed by videotapes of either natural or urban settings. By their own subjective rating, they recovered from the feeling of stress more quickly while experiencing the natural settings. Their opinion was supported by four standard physiological measures of stress: heartbeat, systolic blood pressure, facial muscle tension, and electrical skin conductance. The results suggest, although don't prove, the involvement of the parasympathetic nerves, that part of the autonomic system whose activation induces a state of relaxed awareness. The same result was obtained in a different group of student volunteers stressed by a difficult mathematical examination, and then shown videotapes that stimulated automobile rides through natural as opposed to urban settings.

- Studies of response prior to surgery and dental work have consistently revealed a significant reduction of stress in the presence of plants and aquaria. Natural environments viewed through windows or merely displayed in wall-mounted pictures produce the same effect.

- Post-surgical patients recover more quickly, suffer fewer minor complications, and need smaller dosages of painkillers if given a window view of open terrain or waterscape.

- In one Swedish study covering fifteen years of records, clinically anxious psychiatric patients responded positively to wall pictures of natural environments, but negatively, occasionally even violently, to most other decorations (especially those containing abstract art).

- Comparable studies in prisons revealed that inmates provided window views of nearby farmlands and forest, as opposed to prison yards, reported fewer stress-related symptoms such as headaches and indigestion.

- In a different category, the popular notion that owning pets reduces stress-related problems has been well supported by research conducted independently in Australia, England, and the United States. In one Australian study, which factored out variation in exercise levels, diet, and social class, pet ownership accounted for a statistically significant reduction of cholesterol, triglycerides, and systolic blood pressure. In a parallel U.S. study, survivors of heart attacks (myocardial infarction) who owned dogs had a survival rate six times higher than those who did not. The same benefit was not, I am sorry to report, enjoyed by cat owners.

The implications of biophilia for preventive medicine are substantial. The biophilic instinct can be counted as one of humanity's fortunate irrationalities, like women's choice to have fewer children when economically secure, that deserve to be understood better and put to more practical use. It is a remarkable fact that while average life expectancy in the leading industrialized countries has risen to nearly eighty years, the contribution of preventive medicine, including the design of healthful and curative environments, has remained far below potential. Obesity, diabetes, melanoma, asthma, depression, hip fracture, and breast cancer have risen in frequency since 1980. Further, despite advances in scientific knowledge and public awareness, neither coronary atherosclerosis among young people nor acute myocardial infarction among the middle-ages and old has declined. All of these conditions can be delayed or even avoided by preventive measures that include, in most cases and to the point I wish to make, a reconnection to the natural world. As such they are cost-effective, amounting to no more than salvage of natural habitats, improvements in landscape design, and relocation of windows in public buildings.

Of course nature has a dark side too. The face it presents to humanity is not always friendly. Throughout most of human deep history there have been predators eager to snatch us for dinner; venomous snakes ready with a fatal, defensive strike to the ankle; spiders and insects that bite, sting, and infect; and microbes designed to reduce the human body to malodorous catabolic chemicals. The reverse side of nature's green-and-gold is the black-and-scarlet of disease and death. The companion of biophilia is therefore biophobia. Like the responses of biophilia, those of biophobia are acquired by prepared learning. They vary in intensity among individuals according to heredity and experience. At one end of the scale are mild distaste and feelings of apprehension. At the other end are full-blown clinical phobias that fire the sympathetic nervous system and produce panic, nausea, and cold sweat. The innate biophobic intensities are most readily evoked by sources of peril that have existed in the natural world throughout humanity's evolutionary past. They include heights, close spaces, running water, snakes, wolves, rats and mice, bats, spiders, and blood. In contrast, prepared learning is unknown in response to knives, frayed electric wires, automobiles, and guns, although far deadlier today than the ancient perils of humankind, are too recent in evolutionary history to have been targeted by genetically prepared learning.

The defining properties of hereditary predisposition are multiple. One negative experience may be enough to trigger the response and permanently instill the fear. The critical stimulus can be unexpected and very simple—for example, the abrupt approach of an animal face, or the writhing of a serpent or serpent-like object nearby. The likelihood of imprinting is enhanced by already existing stressful conditions that surround the event. The learning can even be vicarious: just witnessing panic in another person or listening to a scary story can induce it in some people.

Those in whom the fear has been implanted respond almost instantly and subconsciously to subliminal images. When psychologists flashed pictures of snakes or spiders to subjects for only fifteen to thirty milliseconds, intervals too brief to be processed by the conscious mind, those previously conditioned adversely to these animals reacted with automatic muscle changes in the face within less than half a second. Although the response was easily detectable by the researchers, the subjects remained unaware that anything had happened at all.

Because aversive responses are so well defined, it has been possible to apply standard tests used in human genetics to determine whether variation in them among people has at least a partly genetic basis. The measure of choice is heritability, the standard used in studies of personality, obesity, neuroticism, and other traits that display complex variation in human populations. Heritability of a given trait is the percentage of variation among individuals in a population due to differences in genes among the individuals, as opposed to the percentage caused by differences in their environment. The heritability of innate aversion to snakes, spiders, insects, and bats respectively has been estimated to be about 30 percent, a common figure for human behavioral traits in general. The heritability of proneness to agoraphobia, an extreme aversion to crowds or open areas, is about 40 percent.

Another characteristic of prepared aversion is the existence of a sensitive period, which as in biophilic behavior is the interval in the normal life cycle when learning is easiest and the trait most apt to be established. In the case of ophidiophobia (snake), arachnophobia (spider), and other animal phobias, the onset occurs during childhood, with about 70 percent of cases occurring by ten years of age. In contrast, agoraphobia is an affliction of adolescents and young adults, triggered in 60 percent of the cases between fifteen and thirty years of age.

If elements of the natural world can sometimes paralyze modern humans by the evocation of ancient instincts, human instinct can and does wreak havoc on the natural world. Finding themselves surrounded by forests that once covered most of Earth's habitable land, Neolithic peoples set out ten thousand years ago to convert them into cropland, pasture, corrals, and scattered woodlots. What they could not chop down, they burned. Successive generations, their populations growing, continued the process until today only half the original cover is left. They needed the food, of course, but there is another way of looking at the relentless deforestation. People then as now instinctively wanted the ancestral habitat. So they proceeded to create savanna crafted to human needs. *Homo sapien* did not evolve to be a forest dweller, like chimpanzees, gorillas, and other great apes. Rather, it became a specialist of open spaces. The aesthetically ideal environment of today's transformed world is the much-treasured pastoral landscape, for better or worse our ersatz savanna.

Where does attachment to that habitat leave wilderness? No question in environmental ethics cuts more deeply. Before agriculture and villages were invented, people lived in or very close to nature. They were part of it, and had no need for the concept of wilderness. Pastoral settlers drew a line between cultivated and virgin land. As they pushed back virgin land and built more complex societies with the aid of agricultural surpluses, they sharpened the distinction. Those in more advanced cultures imagined themselves to be above the untamed world around them. They were destined, they thought, to dwell among the gods. The word "wilderness" acquired the meaning expressed in its Old English progenitor *wil(d) dēornes:* wild, savage. To pastoral and urban sensibilities, it was the impenetrable dark woods, the mountain fastness, the thorn bush desert, the open sea, and any other part of the world that had not been and might never be tamed. It was the realm of beasts, savages, evil spirits, magic, and the menacing, amorphous unknown.

The European conquest of the New World established the concept of wilderness as a frontier region waiting to be rolled back. The image was most clearly formed in the United States, whose early history is geographically defined as a westward march across an undeveloped and fertile continent.

Then came a tipping point. By the time the American frontier closed, around 1890, wilderness had become a scarce resource at risk of being eliminated altogether and hence worth saving. American environmentalism was born, rising upon the new conservation ethic created by Henry David Thoreau, John Muir, and other nineteenth-century prophets. It spread slowly through the United States, Europe, and elsewhere. It argued that humanity would be foolish to wager its future on a wholly transformed planet. Wild lands in particular, the early environmentalists said, have a unique value for humankind. The warrior king of the movement was Theodore Roosevelt, who declared, "I hate a man who skins the land."

What is a wilderness today in our largely humanized world? What it has always been: a space that sustains itself, was here before humanity, and where, in the words of the Wilderness Act of 1964, "the Earth and its community of life are untrammeled by man and where man himself is a visitor who does not remain." The true great wildernesses of the world include the rainforests of the Amazon, the Congo, and New Guinea; the evergreen coniferous forests of northern North America and Eurasia; and Earth's ancient deserts, polar regions, and open seas.

A few contrarians like to claim that true wilderness is a thing of the past. They point out, correctly, that very few places on land have remained untrodden by human feet. Moreover, 5 percent of Earth's land surface is burned every year, and the plumes of nitrous oxide produced travel most of the way around the world. Greenhouse gases thicken, global temperatures rise, and glaciers and montane forests retreat up mountain peaks. With the exception of a few places in tropical Asia and Africa, terrestrial environments everywhere have lost most of their largest mammals, birds, and reptiles, destabilizing the populations of many other kinds of plants and animals. As the remnant wild areas shrink, they are invaded by more and more alien species, diminishing the native plants and animals yet more. The smaller the area of the natural reserves, the more we are forced to intervene to avoid the partial collapse of their ecosystems.

All true. But to claim that the surviving wildernesses are less than the name implies, and have in some sense become part of the human domain, is false. The argument is specious. It is like flattening the Himalayas to the level of the Ganges Delta by saying that all the planet's surface is but a geometer's plane. Walk from a pasture into a tropical rainforest, sail from a harbor marina to a coral reef, and you will see the difference. The glory of the primeval world is still there to protect and savor.

The exact perception of wilderness is a matter of scale. Even in disturbed environments, with most of their native plants and vertebrates long vanished, bacteria, protozoans, and miniature invertebrates still maintain the ancient substratum. The micro-wildernesses are more accessible than full-scale wildernesses. They are usually only minutes away, waiting to be visited by microscope instead of jetliner. A single tree in a city park, harboring thousands of species, is an island, complete with miniature mountains, valleys, lakes, and subterranean caverns. Scientists have only begun to explore these compacted worlds. Educators have made surprisingly little use of them in introducing the wonders of life to students. Micro aesthetics based upon them is still an unexplored wilderness to the creative mind.

A strong case can be made for the creation of micro-reserves. A one-hectare patch of rainforest still clinging to a Honduran hillside, a road strip of native grasses in Iowa, and a muddy natural pond on the edge of a Florida golf course are to be valued and preserved even if the large native organisms that once lived in and around them have disappeared.

Still, while micro-reserves are infinitely better than nothing at all, they are no substitute for macro- and mega-reserves, where full-blown biotas with sizable animals continue to live. People can acquire an appreciation for savage carnivorous nematodes and shape-shifting rotifers in a drop of pond water, but they need life on the large scale to which the human intellect and emotion most naturally respond. No one of my acquaintance, except a few microbiologists, would visit a town dump upon being told it harbors a dazzling variety of bacteria. But tourists and locals alike travel to the dumps of sub-arctic Canadian towns to watch scavenging polar bears.

To the multiple valorizations of wild environments can be added mystery. Without mystery life shrinks. The completely known is a numbing void to all active minds. Even a laboratory rat seeks the advantage of the maze.

So we are drawn to the natural world, aware that it contains structure and complexity and length of history as well, at orders of magnitude greater than anything yet conceived in human imagination. Mysteries solved within it merely uncover more mysteries beyond. For the naturalist every entrance into a wild environment rekindles an excitement that is childlike in spontaneity, often tinged with apprehension—in short, the way life ought to be lived, all the time.

I will offer one such personal remembrance out of hundreds forever fresh in my mind. It is the summer of 1965, in the Dry Tortugas, at the tip of the Florida Keys. I stand at the water's edge on Garden Key, with Fort Jefferson at my back, looking across a narrow channel to Bush Key, where the littoral scrub and mangrove swamp are alive with thousands of nesting sooty terns. I have a boat, and I will go there soon, but right now I have an inexplicable urge to swim across instead. The channel is about a hundred feet across, maybe less, and the tidal current from the Gulf of Mexico to Florida Bay is for the moment too slow to pose a risk. There will be no problem if I choose to swim, it seems. Then I look more closely at the moving water. How deep is the channel center? What might come up from below to meet me? A barracuda? I saw a five-footer circling the nearby dock pilings that morning. And what do I know about the local sharks? Hammerheads and bull sharks are common in deeper water, for sure, and have been known to attack humans. Great whites are occasionally seen. Shark attacks in this region are very rare, yet—would I be the dramatic exception? Now, reflecting as I hesitate, I feel an urge not just to cross, but to dive and explore the bottom of the channel. I want to know it inch by inch as I know the soil surface of the islands I have been studying, to see what else lives there and comes in sporadically from the Gulf.

The impulse to swim fades as quickly as it arose, but I make a resolution to come back someday and become an intimate of the channel and its inhabitants and to bond with this place on which I have randomly fixated, to make it part of my life. There is something crazy about the episode, but also something real, primal, and deeply satisfying.

At some time in our lives—for the naturalist always—we long for the gate to the paradisiacal world. It is the instinctive after-image that comes to us in daydreams, and a wellspring of hope. Its mysteries, if ignited in our minds and solved, grant more control over existence. If ignored, they leave an emotional void. How did such a strange quality of human nature come about? No one knows for sure, but evolutionary genetics tells us that even if just one person in a thousand survived because of a genetic predisposition to explore the unknown and persevere in daunting circumstances, then over many generations, natural selection would have installed the predisposition in the whole human race to wonder and take the dare.

We need nature, and particularly its wilderness strongholds. It is the alien world that gave rise to our species, and the home to which we can safely return. It offers choices our spirit was designed to enjoy.

■ WHAT?

1. Wilson cites the World Health Organization's definition of health: "a state of complete physical, mental, and social well-being and not merely the absence of disease and infirmity." According to Wilson, how does biophilia promote this state of being? What do you think is the environment's role in promoting the health of humans?

2. Wilson recounts philosopher Holmes Rolston III's telling of a brief story: "For years, trailside signs at a sub alpine campground in the Rocky Mountains … read, 'Please leave the flowers for others to enjoy.' When the wooden signs began to erode and flake, they were replaced by new ones that read, 'Let the flowers live!'" What does this anecdote mean? How does Wilson use it to explain the nature of biocentrism?

■ WHAT ELSE? WHAT'S NEXT?

3. Wilson writes that "micro-wildernesses are more accessible than full-scale wildernesses. They are usually only minutes away, waiting to be visited by the microscope instead of jetliner." By way of example, Wilson likens a single tree in a city park to an island. With this metaphor in mind, explore the USC campus, your back yard, or a local park, forest, or lake. What micro-wildernesses make up your local environment? Your instructor may ask you to work with a small group or as a class to develop a list of these locations and discuss how they might introduce you and others to what Wilson characterizes as "the wonders of life."

4. Research the practical applications of Wilson's ideas about conservation and biophilia. Are people and/or organizations using these concepts in their environmental work? Do these concepts show up in policy debates? Based on your research, explain whether you think Wilson's ideas could be useful in developing an environmental ethos for individuals or groups.

■ WHO CARES?

5. Summarize—accurately and completely—Wilson's piece for an audience of oil industry executives. Think specifically about how—using language, style, tone, and other rhetorical elements—you can make them care about and consider Wilson's point of view.

Maywa Montenegro, an editor at Seed *magazine, likes to write about agriculture, biodiversity, and sustainable development. Terry Glavin, a journalist, editor, and author of numerous books, teaches in the Creative Writing Department at University of British Columbia and maintains the blog "Chronicles and Dissent." They wrote this piece for the October 2008 print edition of* Seed; *it was published on* Seed's *website in July 2010.*

BEFORE YOU READ

Search online for other articles, essays, blog posts, and books written by Maywa Montenegro and Terry Glavin (individually or together). Based on this research, compile a bibliography, following MLA guidelines, of a few of their publications that help you get a better idea of who these authors are and what they think and care about.

IN DEFENSE OF DIFFERENCE

Maywa Montenegro and Terry Glavin

In January 2008, at the St. Innocent Russian Orthodox Cathedral in Anchorage, Alaska, friends and relatives gathered to bid their last farewell to Marie Smith Jones, a beloved matriarch of her community. At 89 years old, she was the last fluent speaker of the Eyak language. In May 2007 a cavalry of the Janjaweed—the notorious Sudanese militia responsible for the ongoing genocide of the indigenous people of Darfur—made its way across the border into neighboring Chad. They were hunting for 1.5 tons of confiscated ivory, worth nearly $1.5 million, locked in a storeroom in Zakouma National Park. Around the same time, a wave of mysterious frog disappearances that had been confounding herpetologists worldwide spread to the US Pacific Northwest. It was soon discovered that Batrachochytrium dendrobatidis, a deadly fungus native to southern Africa, had found its way via such routes as the overseas trade in frog's legs to Central America, South America, Australia, and now the United States. One year later, food riots broke out across the island nation of Haiti, leaving at least five people dead; as food prices soared, similar violence erupted in Mexico, Bangladesh, Egypt, Cameroon, Ivory Coast, Senegal and Ethiopia.

All these seemingly disconnected events are the symptoms, you could say, of a global epidemic of sameness. It has no precise parameters, but wherever its shadow falls, it leaves the landscape monochromatic, monocultural, and homogeneous. Even before we've been able to take stock of the enormous diversity that today exists—from undescribed microbes to undocumented tongues—this epidemic carries away an entire human language every two weeks, destroys a domesticated food-crop variety every six hours, and kills off an entire species every few minutes. The fallout isn't merely an assault to our aesthetic or even ethical values: As cultures and languages vanish, along with them go vast and ancient storehouses of accumulated knowledge. And as species disappear, along with them go not just valuable genetic resources, but critical links in complex ecological webs.

Experts have long recognized the perils of biological and cultural extinctions. But they've only just begun to see them as different facets of the same phenomenon, and to tease out the myriad ways in which social and natural systems interact. Catalyzed in part by the urgency that climate change has brought to all matters environmental, two progressive movements, incubating already for decades, have recently emerged into fuller view. Joining natural and social scientists from a wide range of disciplines and policy arenas, these initiatives are today working to connect the dots between ethnosphere and biosphere in a way that is rapidly leaving behind old unilateral approaches to conservation. Efforts to stanch extinctions of linguistic, cultural, and biological life have yielded a "biocultural" perspective that integrates the three. Efforts to understand the value of diversity in a complex systems framework have matured into a science of "resilience." On parallel paths, though with different emphases, different lexicons, and only slightly overlapping clouds of experts, these emergent paradigms have created space for a fresh struggle with the tough questions: What kinds of diversity must we consider, and how do we measure them on local, regional, and global scales? Can diversity be buffered against the streamlining pressures of economic growth? How much diversity is enough? From a recent biocultural diversity symposium in New York City to the first ever global discussion of resilience in Stockholm, these burgeoning movements are joining biologist with anthropologist, scientist with storyteller, in building a new framework to describe how, why, and what to sustain.

The biological diversity crisis is often called the "Sixth Extinction" because an event of this magnitude has occurred only five times in the history of life on Earth. The last was at the end of the Cretaceous period, when the dinosaurs disappeared. In the past couple hundred years, humans have increased species extinction rates by as much as 10,000 times the background rates that have been typical over Earth's history. This is a crash that, within the scientific community, is causing a slow panic and a wide belief that the dangers of biodiversity loss are woefully underestimated by most everyone outside of science. Yet even those who grasp extinction's severity haven't made much of a noticeable contribution to its containment. On May 16, 2008, the Zoological Society of London released a report suggesting that since contemporary environmentalism emerged with the declaration of the first Earth Day in 1970, close to one-third of all the wild species on Earth have disappeared. Language conservationists have fared no better: Of the world's roughly 6,800 languages, fully half—though some experts say closer to 90 percent—are expected to disappear before the end of the century.

Our collective failure to recognize and impede this rampant winnowing of diversity can in part be blamed on the sheer rapidity with which it has advanced. Since only 1900, the human population has increased by a factor of four, water use by a factor of nine, carbon dioxide emissions by 17, marine-fish catch by 35, and industrial output by 40. It's this expanding human footprint, and the global commerce on which it depends, that unifies the stories of Marie Smith Jones, the Janjaweed horsemen, the disappearing frogs, and the food riots. The transnational flow of people and products, media and information, crops and commodities has never in the history of the planet been so heavy or so fast. But as globalized trade expands across horizons, it both uproots local cultures and kills off vulnerable species of animals and plants. If it's not the literal extinction of a language when its last speaker dies or the spread of a devastating invasive fungus, it's the trafficking of such exotic commodities as elephant tusks, which only get more precious as the animals' numbers dwindle. A world increasingly calibrated on consumption, efficiency, and convenience is perhaps most apparent in modern industrial agriculture, which churns out mass quantities of food but also demands ever greater uniformity and standardization. And deep flaws within the system are beginning to show. This year a potent mix of drought, flooding, high fuel prices, and an increased developing-world demand for meat caused supplies of many staple crops to plummet and their prices to surge. But as scientists and farmers consider how to breed and engineer the next generation of higher-yielding, climate-resilient plants, they confront an alarmingly shallow gene pool. Addressing the audience at the World Food Summit in May, Alexander Müller, assistant director-general of the UN Food and Agriculture Organization, warned that most of the global food supply had narrowed to just a dozen crops and 14 animal species. According to the FAO, three-quarters of the world's critically important food-crop varieties have disappeared during the 20th century, and hundreds of locally adapted livestock breeds are on the verge of doing so. "The erosion of biodiversity for food and agriculture severely compromises global food security," said Müller.

The tether between linguistic, cultural, and biological extinction is, however, far more complex than its common, top-down driver of globalization. Once set in motion, the extinctions themselves also become drivers, creating a dense network of positive feedback loops. That we are beginning to understand the intricacies of these relationships is due in no small measure to the work of Italian-born anthropologist and linguist Luisa Maffi. Thirty years ago, fresh out of the University of Rome, Maffi was doing fieldwork in Somalia when she first began to surmise a connection between language and ecology. She moved to the University of California at Berkeley and began working toward a PhD in anthropology doing research on ethnomedicine in Chiapas, Mexico. It was in Chiapas that Maffi had a kind of epiphany.

The way Maffi tells the story, she was interviewing Tzeltal Mayan people waiting in line at a medical clinic in the village of Tenejapa when she met a man who had walked for hours, carrying his two-year-old daughter, who was suffering from diarrhea. It turned out that the man had only a dim memory of the "grasshopper leg herb" that was once well known as a perfectly effective diarrhea remedy in the Tzeltal ethnomedical pharmacopeia. Because he'd nearly forgotten the words for the herb, he'd lost almost any trace of the herb's utility, or even of its existence.

This is when the full impact of current global trends dawned on her, Maffi recalls. It's not just species or languages that are vanishing from the world. The world is losing knowledge, too, of the most useful and precious kinds. If the world was losing local knowledge, what else was slipping away?

Maffi began to cast her net broadly, reaching out to indigenous leaders, academics in the natural and social sciences, development experts, and, of course, linguists. In 1996 she and her colleagues organized a pivotal conference at Berkeley, "Endangered Knowledge, Endangered Environments," and one year later, Maffi founded Terralingua, an international organization dedicated to research, education, and advocacy for "linguistic human rights." Thanks in large part to Maffi, the term "biocultural diversity" started showing up with increasing frequency in the lexicon of a wide variety of scientists and academics concerned with the phenomenon of extinction.

The biocultural perspective is now gaining a high profile on the international scene. Last October, when United Nations Environment Program (UNEP) released its Global Outlook 4 report, reiterating the scientific consensus that, ultimately, humans are to blame for current global extinctions, UNEP for the first time made an explicit connection between the ongoing collapse of biological diversity and the rapid, global-scale withering of cultural and linguistic diversity: "Global social and economic change is driving the loss of biodiversity and disrupting local ways of life by promoting cultural assimilation and homogenization," the report noted. "Cultural change, such as loss of cultural and spiritual values, languages, and traditional knowledge and practices, is a driver that can cause increasing pressures on biodiversity...In turn, these pressures impact human well-being."

A second major milestone—arguably even more significant—came earlier this year, when more than 300 leading thinkers in nature conservation, linguistics, anthropology, and biology gathered at the American Museum of Natural History in New York City for a symposium entitled "Sustaining Cultural and Biological Diversity in a Rapidly Changing World: Lessons for Global Policy." Co-organized by the museum's Center for Biodiversity Conservation, Maffi's Terralingua, and a handful of other groups, the symposium was an attempt to begin rectifying what those involved identified as two gaping handicaps: a "mutual isolation" between the natural and social sciences and a "limited appreciation of the relevance of the vast variety of approaches to human-environment relationships that have developed across the world's diverse cultures." Through four days of panels, presentations, and informal "ubuntu" sessions (in the spirit of the African "humanity towards others" ethic), the forum highlighted a renewed interest in transdisciplinary fields such as enthnolinguistics, ethnozoology, ethnobotany, ethnobiology, and ethnoecology— all of which focus on documenting, describing, and understanding how other peoples perceive, use, and manage their environments.

The symposium ended on a firm and high note: a formal resolution to be put before the International Union for the Conservation of Nature (IUCN) when it convenes this October in Barcelona, Spain. The resolution calls on the IUCN—which until now has focused solely on nonhuman aspects of conservation—to begin integrating into its policies and programs efforts to preserve cultural diversity.

"If it all happens the way we want, this would be a really huge shift," says Eleanor Sterling, director of the Center for Biodiversity Conservation. "It would mean a focus not just on biodiversity, but also on how people have traditionally shaped the land. It would be a major shift in the way the world thinks about what it is we're trying to conserve."

Maffi agrees that if the Barcelona resolution is adopted, it will completely change the way the IUCN operates. A key contributor to the biodiversity sections of last year's UNEP Global Outlook report, Maffi says the concept of biocultural diversity appears to have finally hit its stride. "When I think about where we were 12 years ago," Maffi says, "this sort of thing just wasn't what people were talking about. It was difficult to open a clearing for these discussions to take place. But now we are getting to this important understanding that nature and culture are one thing. It's gone from being a really obscure issue to having an important place in international forums."

It is one thing, of course, to recognize on paper that culture and nature, language and landscape, are intimately connected. Discerning what those relationships are, in a rigorous manner, is infinitely more challenging, and it's the sort of research that Maffi and others are just delving into. Some patterns, however, have already emerged—the most remarkable being a striking geographic overlap: Epicenters of global biodiversity, it turns out, tend to be situated in exactly the same places as the epicenters of high cultural, linguistic, and food-crop diversity. One of these so-called "megadiversity" hotspots sits on the borderlands of Burma, India, and China, in the tropical forests of the Eastern Himalayas. In just one small corner of the region, more than 30 Tibeto-Burman languages are spoken; in the gardens of just three small villages within one tribal district, more than 150 domesticated food-plant varieties are under cultivation.

Indeed, if it were possible for a person to hover over the Earth and to somehow detect biocultural richness, they would see, on every continent save Antarctica, regions where nature and culture seem to have spilled all their riches in concentrated drops. Why this overlap exists, however, makes for an ongoing riddle, for the lines of cause and effect can— and often do—run in many directions. Habitat loss through deforestation, for example, is widely known to result in language death and mass extinction of animal and plant species. But sometimes, as in the case of Canada's pine forests, the causality is inverted. Over the past decade, mountain pine beetles have killed off about 7 million hectares of British Columbia's forests—an area roughly equal in size to the state of New York. But the story really begins with smallpox, which swept through the interior about 150 years ago, decimating tribal communities that had for thousands of years regularly burned the forests in order to regulate berry production and deer abundance. When that management scheme came to an end, the result was a landscape of dense forests and even-aged stands of pine. A government policy of fire suppression, coupled with fewer winter cold snaps, and the pine forests became increasingly susceptible to insect infestations and massive fires.

That the Earth is becoming more homogeneous—less of a patchwork quilt and more of a melting pot—is only partly due to the extinction of regionally unique languages or life forms. The greater contributing factor is invasiveness. According to the 2005 Millennium Ecosystem Assessment report, as rapidly as regionally unique species are dying out, rates of species introductions in most regions of the world actually far exceed current rates of extinction. Similarly, the spread of English, Spanish, and, to a lesser extent, Chinese, into all corners of the world easily dwarfs the rate of global language loss. This spread of opportunistic species and prodigal tongues thrives on today's anthropogenic conduits of commerce and communications.

Bringing new organisms or new languages into a community nearly always results in an increase of global homogeneity. Its effect on diversity is, however, more complex, raising an important point about the very concept of diversity: It makes sense only as a matter of scale. If, for example, you introduce several weedy species to an African veldt, you will increase local biodiversity. Introduce English into a multidialect Alaskan community, and you will increase local linguistic diversity—you are, after all, just adding more to the mix. But gains in local diversity due to new introductions are likely to be short-lived. Just as languages often become overwhelmed by more dominant ones, invasive plants, animals, and microbes often eventually outcompete and replace native life. If even one native grass or one native dialect perishes as a result of these introductions—as is almost always the case—global biodiversity suffers. Thus, homogeneity, while not synonymous with extinction, reflects both extinctions in the past and ones likely to ensue.

But what, ultimately, is the value in diversity? What merits the colossal efforts required to preserve it? According to biologist E.O. Wilson's often-cited "biophilia" hypothesis, humans have an innate attraction to other kinds of creatures and a desire to live in a world of diverse and abundant forms of life. Pose questions on the value of diversity to a group of people, and some will certainly emerge as biophiles, citing the intrinsic worth of other life forms and other ways of knowing, and therefore, their inherent right to exist. Others will take a more utilitarian tack, mentioning the carbon sink services of a forest or the role of local languages as records of human history. Still others will be hard-pressed to find any value at all. But amid the philosophical, the pragmatic, and the nonexistent, there's a new paradigm emerging to describe the importance of diversity. For a small group of forward-thinking biologists, ecologists, physicists, and economists who assembled earlier this year in Stockholm, the answer is simple: It's all about resilience.

Resilience theory, and the nascent field of resilience science associated with it, begins with the basic premise that human and natural systems act as strongly coupled, integrated systems. These so-called "social-ecological" systems are understood to be in constant flux and highly unpredictable. And unlike standard ecological theory, which holds that nature responds to gradual changes in a correspondingly steady fashion, resilience thinking holds that systems often respond to stochastic events—things like storms or fires—with dramatic shifts into completely different states from which it is difficult, if not impossible, to recover. Numerous studies of rangelands, coral reefs, forests, lakes, and even human political systems show this to be true: A clear lake, for instance, seems hardly affected by fertilizer runoff until a critical threshold is passed, at which point the pond abruptly turns murky. A reef dominated by hard coral can, in the aftermath of a hurricane, flip into a state dominated by algae. A democratic nation stricken by drought, disease, or stock market crashes can descend into political chaos.

It's the ability of a system—whether a tide pool or township—to withstand environmental flux without collapsing into a qualitatively different state that is formally defined as "resilience." And that is where diversity enters the equation. The more biologically and culturally variegated a system is, the more buffered, or resilient, it is against disturbance. Take the Caribbean Sea, where a wide variety of fish once kept algae on the coral reef in check. Because of overfishing in recent years, these grazers gradually gave way to sea urchins, which continued to keep algae levels down. Then in 1983 a pathogen moved in and decimated the urchin population, sending the reef into a state of algal dominance. Thus, the loss of diversity through overfishing eroded the resilience of the system, making it vulnerable to an attack it likely could have withstood in the past.

For Crawford "Buzz" Holling, widely acknowledged as the father of resilience theory and founding director of the Resilience Alliance, a small international network of academics who collaborate to explore the dynamics of social-ecological systems, this year marked a definite coming of age of an idea. At the first annual Resilience 2008 summit, held at the newly opened Resilience Center at the University of Stockholm, Holling delivered the keynote address to more than 600 scientists, policymakers, and artists, convened for a four-day brainstorm session. As was the case at the AMNH symposium just weeks earlier, the focus was on how to move from theory to practice. And once one starts thinking through the lens of resilience, the policy implications are indeed enormous. Economics necessarily morphs into its social-ecological analogue, "ecological economics"—so that a city seeking to expand its boundaries, for example, must consider not only costs and benefits in human terms, but also the same calculus as applied to the environment. Efficiency at the expense of diversity becomes anathema, so that a company struggling to stay afloat thinks twice before replacing five human workers with one seemingly smarter machine. Redundancy is encouraged, rather than quashed, on the grounds that more genes and more memes ultimately provide insurance against a time when changing conditions overwhelm the dominant paradigm of the day. There is no "sacred balance" in nature, says Holling. "That is a very dangerous idea."

Resilience science can get bogged down in its own specific lexicon: a cloud of "adaptive capacities," "functional groups," and "self-organizing principles." But pull back from the jargon and the essence is simple: Homogeneous landscapes—whether linguistic, cultural, biological, or genetic—are brittle and prone to failure. The evidence peppers human history, as Jared Diamond so meticulously catalogued in his aptly named book, Collapse. Whether it was due to a shifting climate that devastated a too-narrow agricultural base, a lack of cultural imagination in how to deal with the problem, or a devastating combination of the two, societies insufficiently resilient enough to cope with the demands of a changing environment invariably crumbled. The idea is perhaps best summed up in the pithy standard, "What doesn't bend, breaks."

By the reckoning of ecological economist Robert Costanza, the value of all Earth's ecosystem services amounts to a staggering $33 trillion. When this figure was published in Nature back in 1997 the impact rippled widely—for the first time people had a sense of what an intact biosphere contributes to the economy, and, on the flip side, what the fallout of its destruction would be. Decelerating the biological and the cultural extinctions we now understand to be close affiliates is the only logical response to this kind of calculation. And yet no one seems to have even a vague figure in mind when it comes to a goal. Just how much diversity—biological, linguistic, or social—is enough?

The first difficulty is inherent in the question itself: "Enough for what?" To be resilient against 75 percent of environmental change? Against 90 percent? Enough to fulfill how much of the aesthetic, utilitarian, and scientific value it encompasses? The second problem, more concrete though equally intractable, is that in 2008 we still have only a partial record of the biological and linguistic diversity that exists on the planet. On geneticist Craig Venter's recent two-year cruise aboard the Sorcerer II, he more than doubled all the genes known so far to science. During an interview upon returning, Venter said, "We're finding as many as 40,000 new species of bacteria in a barrel of seawater. And that's not counting viruses. There may be as many as 400,000 of those." Wilson estimates that humans have named only about 1.5 to 1.8 million species, among a total number that scientists put somewhere between 3.6 and 112 million. While no reliable data concerning the level of documentation of the world's languages exists, a plausible estimate is that fewer than 10 percent are "well documented," meaning that they have comprehensive grammars, extensive dictionaries, and abundant texts in a variety of genres and media. The remaining 90 percent are, to varying degrees, underdocumented, or, for all intents and purposes, not documented at all.

Perhaps the closest anyone has come to an explicit goal for conserving diversity is the "2010 Biodiversity Target," a decision approved in 2002 by the 188 (now 191) member nations of the UN Convention on Biological Diversity. Its aim is ambitious: "to achieve by 2010 a significant reduction of the current rate of biodiversity loss at the global, regional, and national level as a contribution to poverty alleviation and to the benefit of all life on earth." But despite marked progress, including the 2006 incorporation of the objective into the UN Millennium Development Goals and a recent redoubled commitment to it by global leaders at the 2008 World Biodiversity Summit in Bonn, by the UN's own reckoning, the target is unlikely to be met by 2010 without "unprecedented additional efforts." A less lofty, though perhaps more feasible, approach has focused on the shoring up of the world's biological hot spots. With organizations such as Conservation International and the World Wildlife Fund, Wilson has spent the past several years advocating for the urgent protection of 25 tracts of land that account for only 1.4 percent of the Earth's terrestrial surface but house 44 percent of its plant species and more than one-third of all species of birds, mammals, reptiles, and amphibians. He estimates that the cost of this project would amount to around $25 billion—or roughly 5 percent of the US defense budget for 2008. Given the clear geographic overlap between biodiversity and language hotspots—and more crucially, what Maffi and others are identifying as the coevolution of language and ecology—that $25 billion could quite possibly be the best bargain on Earth.

The emergent paradigms of biocultural diversity and resilience science are not, however, without their detractors. In a 2005 paper, University of Chicago linguist and evolutionary biologist Salikoko Mufwene said he wondered whether bioculturalists weren't "simply being paternalistic and not making an effort to learn what has led speakers to give up their languages." He argued that people routinely exchange their native languages for perfectly rational social and economic benefits, and "ethnolinguistic segregation" is no remedy to the economic conditions at the root of language loss. "The embarrassment," he said, "is that language rights advocates have given little thought to the revolution that is entailed by their discourse."

Perhaps Mufwene has a point. After all, more than 96 percent of the world's languages are spoken by just 4 percent of its people. If all the planet's endangered tongues disappeared tomorrow, hardly anyone, relatively speaking, would notice. And who, really, would mourn the loss of a few million undiscovered microbes? We might accept that some extinction is the justifiable trade-off for the many advantages of a globalized society—that to maintain a world rapidly becoming hotter, smaller, and more crowded, the luxuries of heterogeneity may have to go.

That argument might be more convincing if our current trajectory didn't look so precarious. For all that modern, industrialized civilization has produced—from more-abundant food and better medicines to near-instantaneous communications—it is built on what Jules Pretty calls a fundamental "deceit." In a session on the opening day of the AMNH symposium, Pretty, who heads the biological sciences department at University of Essex, told the audience, "There is an underlying assumption in much of the literature that the world can be saved from these problems that we face—poverty, lack of food, environmental problems—if we bring consumption levels across the world up to the same levels [of] North America and Europe." But this sort of convergence, says Pretty, would require the resources of six to eight planets. "How can we move from convergence to divergence, and hence diversity?"

Traditional environmentalism, with its tendency to erect impermeable theoretical barriers between nature and culture, between the functions of artificial and natural selection, hasn't been able to accommodate the perspective necessary to see larger patterns at work. Its distinction—as the writer Lewis Lapham recently put it—"between what is 'natural' (the good, the true, the beautiful) and what is 'artificial' (wicked, man-made, false)" has obscured their profound interrelatedness. Whether expressed as biocultural diversity or as diverse social-ecological systems, the language of these new paradigms reframes the very concept of "environment." Explicit in both terms is a core understanding that as human behavior shapes nature in every instant, nature shapes human behavior. Also explicit is that myth, legend, art, literature, and science are not only themselves reflections of the environment, passed through the filter of human cognition, but that they are indeed the very means we have for determining the road ahead.

■ WHAT?

1. A causal argument, "In Defense of Difference" begins with a problem and then makes a series of claims about causes and consequences. What is the problem at the heart of this argument? How do Montenegro and Glavin try to make their readers understand and care about this problem?
2. Montenegro and Glavin introduce two terms that are vital to their argument: "biocultural diversity" and "resilience theory." How do they define these terms? How are they related?
3. What, according to this text, are some of the consequences of what Montenegro and Glavin call a "world increasingly calibrated on consumption, efficiency, and convenience"?

■ WHAT ELSE? WHAT'S NEXT?

4. In their piece, which was first published in 2008, Montenegro and Glavin write: "Perhaps the closest anyone has come to an explicit goal for conserving diversity is the '2010 Biodiversity Target,' a decision approved in 2002 by the 188 (now 191) member nations of the UN Convention on Biological Diversity. Its aim is ambitious: 'to achieve by 2010 a significant reduction of the current rate of biodiversity loss at the global, regional, and national level as a contribution to poverty alleviation and to the benefit of all life on earth.'" Using resources available online and

through the library, find out the status of this effort. Did the world hit the "2010 Biodiversity Target"?

◼ WHO CARES?

5. Visit the website for *Seed* magazine, where this essay was first published, and spend some time examining the site—look at other articles and essays, links, ads, and anything else you find interesting or helpful. Then, decide which elements on the site are the best indicators of who *Seed's* audience is; in other words, identify what helped you figure out who the readers are. Write a brief report explaining your conclusions.

Though he died nearly a century ago, naturalist and writer John Muir, according to a Sierra Club biography, is still teaching Americans "the importance of experiencing and protecting our natural heritage. ... His personal and determined involvement in the great conservation questions of the day was and remains an inspiration for environmental activists everywhere." "The American Forests," from which this piece was excerpted, was first published in August 1897 in the Atlantic Monthly.

BEFORE YOU READ
Research the state of America's forests at the time Muir was writing (including percentage of forested land, percentage of protected forests, threats to the forests, and the like), and summarize your findings in a brief report.

excerpts from
THE AMERICAN FORESTS John Muir

The forests of America, however slighted by man, must have been a great delight to God; for they were the best he ever planted. The whole continent was a garden, and from the beginning it seemed to be favored above all the other wild parks and gardens of the globe. To prepare the ground, it was rolled and sifted in seas with infinite loving deliberation and forethought, lifted into the light, submerged and warmed over and over again, pressed and crumpled into folds and ridges, mountains and hills, subsoiled with heaving volcanic fires, ploughed and ground and sculptured into scenery and soil with glaciers and rivers,—every feature growing and changing from beauty to beauty, higher and higher. And in the fullness of time it was planted in groves, and belts, and broad, exuberant, mantling forests, with the largest, most varied, most fruitful, and most beautiful trees in the world. Bright seas made its border with wave embroidery and icebergs; gray deserts were outspread in the middle of it, mossy tundras on the north, savannas on the south, and blooming prairies and plains; while lakes and rivers shone through all the vast forests and openings, and happy birds and beasts gave delightful animation. Everywhere, everywhere over all the blessed continent, there were beauty, and melody, and kindly, wholesome, foodful abundance.

These forests were composed of about five hundred species of trees, all of them in some way useful to man, ranging in size from twenty-five feet in height and less than one foot in diameter at the ground to four hundred feet in height and more than twenty feet in diameter,—lordly monarchs proclaiming the gospel of beauty like apostles. For many a century after the ice-ploughs were melted, nature fed them and dressed them every day; working like a man, a loving, devoted, painstaking gardener; fingering every leaf and flower and mossy furrowed bole; bending, trimming, modeling, balancing, painting them with the loveliest colors; bringing over them now clouds with cooling shadows and showers, now sunshine; fanning them with gentle winds and rustling their leaves; exercising them in every fibre with storms, and pruning them; loading them with flowers and fruit, loading them with snow, and ever making them more beautiful as the years rolled by. Wide-branching oak and elm in endless variety, walnut and maple, chestnut and beech, ilex and locust, touching limb to limb, spread a leafy translucent canopy along the coast of the Atlantic over the wrinkled folds and ridges of the Alleghanies,—a green billowy sea in summer, golden and purple in autumn, pearly gray like a steadfast frozen mist of interlacing branches and sprays in leafless, restful winter.

To the southward stretched dark, level-topped cypresses in knobby, tangled swamps, grassy savannas in the midst of them like lakes of light, groves of gay sparkling spice-trees, magnolias and palms, glossy-leaved and blooming and shining continually. To the northward, over Maine and the Ottawa, rose hosts of spiry, rosiny evergreens,—white pine and spruce, hemlock and cedar, shoulder to shoulder, laden with purple cones, their myriad needles sparkling and shimmering, covering hills and swamps, rocky headlands and domes, ever bravely aspiring and seeking the sky; the ground in their shade now snow-clad and frozen, now mossy and flowery; beaver meadows here and there, full of lilies and grass; lakes gleaming like eyes, and a silvery embroidery of rivers and creeks watering and brightening all the vast glad wilderness.

Thence westward were oak and elm, hickory and tupelo, gum and liriodendron, sassafras and ash, linden and laurel, spreading on ever wider in glorious exuberance over the great fertile basin of the Mississippi, over damp level bottoms, low dimpling hollows, and round dotting hills, embosoming sunny prairies and cheery park openings, half sunshine, half shade; while a dark wilderness of pines covered the region around the Great Lakes. Thence still westward swept the forests to right and left around grassy plains and deserts a thousand miles wide: irrepressible hosts of spruce and pine, aspen and willow, nut-pine and juniper, cactus and yucca, caring nothing for drought, extending undaunted from mountain to mountain, over mesa and desert, to join the darkening multitudes of pines that covered the high Rocky ranges and the glorious forests along the coast of the moist and balmy Pacific, where new species of pine, giant cedars and spruces, silver firs and sequoias, kings of their race, growing close together like grass in a meadow, poised their brave domes and spires in the sky three hundred feet above the ferns and the lilies that enameled the ground; towering serene through the long centuries, preaching God's forestry fresh from heaven.

Here the forests reached their highest development. Hence they went wavering northward over icy Alaska, brave spruce and fir, poplar and birch, by the coasts and the rivers, to within sight of the Arctic Ocean. American forests! the glory of the world! Surveyed thus from the east to the west, from the north to the south, they are rich beyond thought, immortal, immeasurable, enough and to spare for every feeding, sheltering beast and bird, insect and son of Adam; and nobody need have cared had there been no pines in Norway, no cedars and deodars on Lebanon and the Himalayas, no vine-clad selvas in the basin of the Amazon. With such variety, harmony, and triumphant exuberance, even nature, it would seem, might have rested content with the forests of North America, and planted no more.

So they appeared a few centuries ago when they were rejoicing in wildness. The Indians with stone axes could do them no more harm than could gnawing beavers and browsing moose. Even the fires of the Indians and the fierce shattering lightning seemed to work together only for good in clearing spots here and there for smooth garden prairies, and openings for sunflowers seeking the light. But when the steel axe of the white man rang out in the startled air their doom was sealed. Every tree heard the bodeful sound, and pillars of smoke gave the sign in the sky.

I suppose we need not go mourning the buffaloes. In the nature of things they had to give place to better cattle, though the change might have been made without barbarous wickedness. Likewise many of nature's five hundred kinds of wild trees had to make way for orchards and cornfields. In the settlement and civilization of the country, bread more than timber or beauty was wanted; and in the blindness of hunger, the early settlers, claiming Heaven as their guide, regarded God's trees as only a larger kind of pernicious weeds, extremely hard to get rid of. Accordingly, with no eye to the future, these pious destroyers waged interminable forest wars; chips flew thick and fast; trees in their beauty fell crashing by millions, smashed to confusion, and the smoke of their burning has been rising to heaven more than two hundred years. After the Atlantic coast from Maine to Georgia had been mostly cleared and scorched into melancholy ruins, the overflowing multitude of bread and money seekers poured over the Alleghanies into the fertile middle West, spreading ruthless devastation ever wider and farther over the rich valley of the Mississippi and the vast shadowy pine region about the Great Lakes. Thence still westward the invading horde of destroyers called settlers made its fiery way over the broad Rocky Mountains, felling and burning more fiercely than ever, until at last it has reached the wild side of the continent, and entered the last of the great aboriginal forests on the shores of the Pacific.

Surely, then, it should not be wondered at that lovers of their country, bewailing its baldness, are now crying aloud, "Save what is left of the forests!" Clearing has surely now gone far enough; soon timber will be scarce, and not a grove will be left to rest in or pray in. The remnant protected will yield plenty of timber, a perennial harvest for every right use, without further diminution of its area, and will continue to cover the springs of the rivers that rise in the mountains and give irrigating waters to the dry valleys at their feet, prevent wasting floods and be a blessing to everybody forever. [...]

[...] Emerson says that things refuse to be mismanaged long. An exception would seem to be found in the case of our forests, which have been mismanaged rather long, and now come desperately near being like smashed eggs and spilt milk. Still, in the long run the world does not move backward. The wonderful advance made in the last few years, in creating four national parks in the West, and thirty forest reservations, embracing nearly forty million acres; and in the planting of the borders of streets and highways and spacious parks in all the great cities, to satisfy the natural taste and hunger for landscape beauty and righteousness that God has put, in some measure, into every human being and animal, shows the trend of awakening public opinion. The making of the far-famed New York Central Park was opposed by even good men, with misguided pluck, perseverance, and ingenuity; but straight right won its way, and now that park is appreciated. So we confidently believe it will be with our great national parks and forest reservations. There will be a period of indifference on the part of the rich, sleepy with wealth, and of the toiling millions, sleepy with poverty, most of whom never saw a forest; a period of screaming protest and objection from the plunderers, who are as unconscionable and enterprising as Satan. But light is surely coming, and the friends of destruction will preach and bewail in vain.

The United States government has always been proud of the welcome it has extended to good men of every nation, seeking freedom and homes and bread. Let them be welcomed still as nature welcomes them, to the woods as well as to the prairies and plains. No place is too good for good men, and still there is room. They are invited to heaven, and may well be allowed in America. Every place is made better by them. Let them be as free to pick gold and gems from the hills, to cut and hew, dig and plant, for homes and bread, as the birds are to pick berries from the wild bushes, and moss and leaves for nests. The ground will be glad to feed them, and the pines will come down from the mountains for their homes as willingly as the cedars came from Lebanon for Solomon's temple. Nor will the woods be the worse for this use, or their benign influences be diminished any more than the sun is diminished by shining. Mere destroyers, however, tree-killers, spreading death and confusion in the fairest groves and gardens ever planted, let the government hasten to cast them out and make an end of them. For it must be told again and again, and be burningly borne in mind, that just now, while protective measures are being deliberated languidly, destruction and use are speeding on faster and farther every day. The axe and saw are insanely busy, chips are flying thick as snowflakes, and every summer thousands of acres of priceless forests, with their underbrush, soil, springs, climate, scenery, and religion, are vanishing away in clouds of smoke, while, except in the national parks, not one forest guard is employed.

All sorts of local laws and regulations have been tried and found wanting, and the costly lessons of our own experience, as well as that of every civilized nation, show conclusively that the fate of the remnant of our forests is in the hands of the federal government, and that if the remnant is to be saved at all, it must be saved quickly.

Any fool can destroy trees. They cannot run away; and if they could, they would still be destroyed,—chased and hunted down as long as fun or a dollar could be got out of their bark hides, branching horns, or magnificent bole backbones. Few that fell trees plant them; nor would planting avail much towards getting back anything like the noble primeval forests. During a man's life only saplings can be grown, in the place of the old trees— tens of centuries old—that have been destroyed. It took more than three thousand years to make some of the trees in these Western woods,—trees that are still standing in perfect strength and beauty, waving and singing in the mighty forests of the Sierra. Through all the wonderful, eventful centuries since Christ's time—and long before that—God has cared for these trees, saved them from drought, disease, avalanches, and a thousand straining, leveling tempests and floods; but he cannot save them from fools,—only Uncle Sam can do that.

■ WHAT?

1. Write a 100-word summary of Muir's piece.
2. Muir's piece is remarkable in its use of highly descriptive language. Why do you think he makes such an effort to vividly describe the forests? How does this language help him persuade readers of his claim?
3. Think about the forests, mountains, swamps, beaches, valleys, or lakes (among other possible natural landscapes) that make up your local surroundings. With one of these sites in mind, write a short passage in which you imitate Muir's descriptive prose.

■ WHAT ELSE? WHAT'S NEXT?

4. Muir's "The American Forests" was originally published in 1897, but its message—that we need to better manage our natural resources—does not seem so dated. Using online search engines or the library's databases, find a modern editorial or letter to the editor that shares a message similar to Muir's. What similarities do you notice? Why do you think this message stands the test of time?
5. Using the research you conducted on the state of America's forests at the time Muir was writing (which you did before reading), compare those conditions with today's. What has changed in the past century? Has anything remained the same?

■ WHO CARES?

6. Write a detailed letter to Muir in which you advise him on how to update his argument for an audience of 21st-century college students. Consider language, style, tone, choice of examples—anything you think would need to be revised to make his text effective.

> *In these excerpts from her 1999 memoir* Ecology of a Cracker Childhood, *author and environmental activist Janisse Ray writes eloquently of her family's deep-rooted ties to the longleaf pine forests of southern Georgia and of her fears about the destruction of these irreplaceable ecosystems.*

BEFORE YOU READ

Find at least two sources that help you more fully understand what memoirs and memoir essays are and what they do. Summarize your findings and document your sources using MLA guidelines.

excerpts from
ECOLOGY OF A CRACKER CHILDHOOD
Janisse Ray

■ Introduction

In south Georgia everything is flat and wide. Not empty. My people live among the mobile homes, junked cars, pine plantations, clearcuts, and fields. They live among the lost forests.

The creation ends in south Georgia, at the very edge of the sweet earth. Only the sky, widest of the wide, goes on, flatness a gainst flatness. The sky appears so close that, with a long-enough extension ladder, you think you could touch it, and sometimes you do, when clouds descend in the night to set a fine pelt of dew on the grasses, leaving behind white trails of fog and mist.

At night the stars are thick and bright as a pint jar of fireflies, the moon at full a pearly orb, sailing through them like an egret. By day the sun, close in a paper sky, laps moisture from the land, then gives it back, always an exchange. Even in drought, when each dawn a parched sun cracks against the horizon's griddle, the air is thick with water.

It is a land of few surprises. It is a land of routine, of cycle, and of constancy. Many a summer afternoon a black cloud builds to the southwest, approaching until you hear thunder and spot lightning, and even then there's time to clear away tools and bring in the laundry before the first raindrops spatter down. Everything that comes you see coming.

That's because the land is so wide, so much of it open. It's wide open, flat as a book, vulnerable as a child. It's easy to take advantage of, and yet it is also a land of dignity. It has been the way it is for thousands of years, and it is not wont to change.

I was born from people who were born from people who were born from people who were born here. The Crackers crossed the wide Altamaha into what had been Creek territory and settled the vast, fire-loving uplands of the coastal plains of southeast Georgia, surrounded by a singing forest of tall and widely spaced pines whose history they did not know, whose stories were untold. The memory of what they entered is scrawled on my bones, so that I carry the landscape inside like an ache. The story of who I am cannot be severed from the story of the flatwoods.

To find myself among what has been and what remains, I go where my grandmother's name is inscribed on a clay hill beside my grandfather. The cemetery rests in a sparse stand of remnant longleaf pine, where clumps of wiregrass can still be found. From the grave I can see a hardwood drain, hung with Spanish moss, and beyond to a cypress swamp, and almost to the river, but beyond that, there is only sky.

■ Child of Pine

When my parents had been married five years and my sister was four, they went out searching among the pinewoods through which the junkyard had begun to spread. It was early February of 1962, and the ewes in the small herd of sheep that kept the grass cropped around the junked cars were dropping lambs.

On this day, Candlemas, with winter half undone, a tormented wind bore down from the north and brought with it a bitter wet cold that cut through my parents' sweaters and coats and sliced through thin socks, stinging their skin and penetrating to the bone. Tonight the pipes would freeze if the faucets weren't left dripping, and if the fig tree wasn't covered with quilts, it would be knocked back to the ground.

It was dark by six, for the days lengthened only by minutes, and my father had gone early to shut up the sheep. Nights he penned them in one end of his shop, a wide, tin-roofed building that smelled both acrid and sweet, a mixture of dry dung, gasoline, hay, and grease. That night when he counted them, one of the ewes was missing. He had bought the sheep to keep weeds and snakes down in the junkyard, so people could get to parts they needed; now he knew all the animals by name and knew also their personalities. Maude was close to her time.

In the hour they had been walking, the temperature had fallen steadily. It would soon be dark. Out of the grayness Mama heard a bleating cry.

"Listen," she said, touching Daddy's big arm and stopping so suddenly that shoulder-length curls of dark hair swung across her heart-shaped face. Her eyes were a deep, rich brown, and she cut a fine figure, slim and strong, easy in her body. Her husband was over six feet tall, handsome, his forehead wide and smart, his hair thick and wiry as horsetail.

Again came the cry. It sounded more human than sheep, coming from a clump of palmettos beneath a pine. The sharp-needled fronds of the palmettos stood out emerald against the gray of winter, and the pine needles, so richly brown when first dropped, had faded to dull sienna. Daddy slid his hands—big, rough hands—past the bayonet-tipped palmetto fronds, their fans rattling urgently with his movements, him careful not to rake against saw-blade stems. The weird crying had not stopped. He peered in.

It was a baby. Pine needles cradled a long-limbed newborn child with a duff of dark hair, its face red and puckered. And that was me, his second-born. I came into their lives easy as finding a dark-faced merino with legs yet too wobbly to stand.

My sister had been found in a big cabbage in the garden; a year after me, my brother was discovered under the grapevine, and a year after that, my little brother appeared beside a huckleberry bush. From as early as I could question, I was told this creation story. If they'd said they'd found me in the trunk of a '52 Ford, it would have been more believable. I was raised on a junkyard on the outskirts of a town called Baxley, the county seat of Appling, in rural south Georgia. [...]

■ Below the Fall Line

The landscape that I was born to, that owns my body: the uplands and lowlands of southern Georgia. The region lies below what's called the fall line, a half-imaginary demarcation avouched by a slight dip in the land, above which the piedmont climbs to the foothills of the Blue Ridge, then up that mountain chain to the eastern continental divide. The fall line separates the piedmont from the Atlantic coastal plain—a wide flat plateau of piney-woods that sweeps to a marble sea.

My homeland is about as ugly as a place gets. There's nothing in south Georgia, people will tell you, except straight, lonely roads, one-horse towns, sprawling farms, and tracts of planted pines. It's flat, monotonous, used-up, hotter than hell in summer and cold enough in winter that orange trees won't grow. No mountains, no canyons, no rocky streams, no waterfalls. The rivers are muddy, wide and flat, like somebody's feet. The coastal plain lacks the stark grace of the desert or the umber panache of the pampas. Unless you look close, there's little majesty.

It wasn't always this way. Even now, in places, in the Red Hills near Thomasville, for example, and on Fort Stewart Military Reservation near Hinesville, you can see how south Georgia used to be, before all the old longleaf pine forests that were our sublimity and our majesty were cut. Nothing is more beautiful, nothing more mysterious, nothing more breathtaking, nothing more surreal.

Longleaf pine is the tree that grows in the upland flatwoods of the coastal plains. Miles and miles of longleaf and wiregrass, the ground cover that coevolved with the pine, once covered the left hip of North America—from Virginia to the Florida peninsula, west past the Mississippi River: longleaf as far in any direction as you could see. In a longleaf forest, miles of trees forever fade into a brilliant salmon sunset and reappear the next dawn as a battalion marching out of fog. The tip of each needle carries a single drop of silver. The trees are so well spaced that their limbs seldom touch and sunlight streams between and within them. Below their flattened branches, grasses arch their tall, richly dun heads of seeds, and orchids and lilies paint the ground orange and scarlet. Purple liatris gestures across the landscape. Our eyes seek the flowers like they seek the flash of birds and the careful crossings of forest animals.

You can still see this in places.

Forest historians estimate that longleaf covered 85 of the 156 million acres in its southeastern range. By 1930, virtually all of the virgin longleaf pine had been felled. Now, at the end of the twentieth century, about two million acres of longleaf remain. Most is first-and second-growth, hard-hit by logging, turpentining, grazing, and the suppression of fire.

Less than 10,000 acres are virgin—not even 0.001 percent of what was. There's none known in Virginia, none in Louisiana, non in Texas, none in South Carolina. About 200 old-growth acres remain in Mississippi, about 300 in Alabama, and almost 500 in North Carolina, in four separate tracts. The rest survives in Georgia and Florida. An estimated 3,000 acres of old-growth in Georgia lie on private land, precariously, and the largest holding of virgin longleaf, about 5,000 acres, belongs to Eglin Air Force Base in Florida.

In a 1995 National Biological Service assessment of biological loss, ecologist Reed Noss classified the longleaf/wiregrass community as "critically endangered." Ninety-eight percent of the presettlement longleaf pine barrens in the southeastern coastal plains were lost by 1986, he said. Natural stands—meaning not planted—have been reduced by about 99 percent.

Apocalyptic.

This was not a loss I knew as a child. *Longleaf* was a word I never heard. But it is a loss that as an adult shadows every step I take. I am daily aghast at how much we have taken, since it does not belong to us, and how much as a people we have suffered in consequence.

Not long ago I dreamed of actually cradling a place, as if something so amorphous and vague as a region, existing mostly in imagination and idea, suddenly took form. I held its shrunken relief in my arms, a baby smelted from a plastic topography map, and when I gazed down into its face, as my father had gazed into mine, I saw the pine flatwoods of my homeland.

■ Clearcut

If you clear a forest, you'd better pray continuously. While you're pushing a road through and rigging the cables and moving between trees on the dozer, you'd better be talking to God. While you're cruising timber and marking trees with a blue slash, be praying; and pray while you're peddling the chips and logs and writing Friday's checks and paying the diesel bill—even if it's under your breath, a rustling at the lips. If you're manning the saw head or the scissors, snipping the trees off at the ground, going from one to another, approaching them brusquely and laying them down, I'd say, pray extra hard; and pray hard when you're hauling them away.

God doesn't like a clearcut. It makes his heart turn cold, makes him wince and wonder what went wrong with his creation, and sets him to thinking about what spoils the child.

You'd better be pretty sure that the cut is absolutely necessary and be at peace with it, so you can explain it to God, for it's fairly certain he's going to question your motives, want to know if your children are hungry and your oldest boy needs asthma medicine—whether you deserve forgiveness or if you're being greedy and heartless. You'd better pay good attention to the saw blade and the runners and the falling trees; when a forest is falling, it's easy for God to determine to spank. Quid pro quo.

Don't ever look away or daydream and don't, no matter what, plan how you will spend your tree money while you are in among toppling trees.

For a long time God didn't worry about the forests. Some trees got cut, which was bad enough, of course, and he would be sick about the cutting awhile, but his children needed houses and warmth, so he stepped in right after they had gone and got some seeds in the ground. The clear-cutting had come so fast he'd been unprepared. One minute the loggers were axmen, with their crosscut saws and oxen and rafts, and when he looked again, they were in helicopters.

When people started to replant, it was a good thing, but there was no way to re-create a forest. Not quickly. And the trees would just be cut again.

Before God knew it, his trees were being planted in rows, like corn, and harvested like corn. That was 1940, when the tree farming started, but it seems like yesterday to God.

Not longleaf. It was quirky in habit, its taproot cumbersome to deal with and slow-growing, so most of the tree farmers abandoned it. They could plant slash or loblolly and in twenty-five years be able to cut again.

Plant for the future, the signs said.

To prepare ground, they chopped, disked, rootraked, herbicided, windrowed. In wetter soils they bedded, plowing and heaping the soil into wide racks with drainage furrows between. The land was laid bare as a vulture's pate, and the scriveners came on their tree-planting tractors, driving down new words to replace the old one, *forest*.

The trees were planted close, five or six feet between, in phalanxes. They were all the same age and size, unlike the woodland that had been, with its old-growth and its saplings, as well as every age in between. The old forest had snags where woodpeckers fed and it had pine cones eager to burst open on bare ground.

Because slash and loblolly are intolerant of fire, the tree farmers, with Smokey as mascot, kept fire back. Within ten years a canopy would close, and the commercial plantation was dark within, darker than you can imagine a forest being. The limbs and needles of the overcrowded pines drank every inch of sky. Any native vegetation that survived land preparation did not survive loss of light.

The diversity of the forest decreased exponentially the more it was altered. In autumn, the flatwoods salamander no longer crossed the plantation to breed, and the migrating redstart no longer stopped, and the pine snake was not to be found. The gopher frog was a thirsty pool of silence.

Pine plantations dishearten God. In them he aches for blooming things, and he misses the sun trickling through the tree crowns, and he pines for the crawling, spotted, scale-backed, bushy-tailed, leaf-hopping, chattering creatures. Most of all he misses the bright-winged, singing beings he cast as angels.

The wind knocking limbs together is a jeremiad.

God likes to prop himself against a tree in a forest and study the plants and animals. They all please him. He has to drag himself through a pine plantation, looking for light on the other side, half-crazy with darkness, half-sick with regret. He refuses to go into clearcuts at all. He thought he had given his children everything their hearts would desire; what he sees puts him in a quarrelsome mood, wondering where he went wrong.

■ WHAT?

1. Ray characterizes herself as a "child of pine" and re-tells the "creation stories" told to her and her sister about how they came into the world. What are these "creation stories" and why do you think Ray includes them in her memoir? What do they tell you about her? How do these make her message more concrete and compelling?
2. Although Ray's piece is not an argumentative essay, it does present a point of view. What ideas do you think Ray is trying to convey to her readers about the environment?

■ WHAT ELSE? WHAT'S NEXT?

3. Ray explains that her Georgia homeland "is about as ugly as a place gets," but that "[i]t wasn't always that way." With Ray's descriptions of the now disappearing longleaf pines in mind, write a eulogy for a vanished environment in which you use thoughtful plotting and vivid description to bring to life a place that was important to you in some way. For example, you could write a eulogy for local farmland that has been developed, for a tree that's been knocked over in a storm, or for the lake house where you vacationed with your parents. The idea is to remember and mourn a place that no longer exists for you. This "vanishing" can be tangible (like a once pristine beach that has been lost to erosion) or it can be emotional (like your childhood home, which, though still standing, is no longer the place it was to you then).

■ WHO CARES?

4. Why do you think people like to read memoirs and memoir essays? Explain your response.

Activists Derrick Jensen and Stephanie McMillan teamed to produce the graphic novel As the World Burns: 50 Simple Things You Can Do to Stay in Denial *in 2007. Jensen has written several books and in 2008 was named one of Utne Reader's "50 Visionaries Who Are Changing Your World." McMillan began syndicating her political cartoons in 1999, and a book based on her comic strip "Minimum Security" was published in 2005. Seven Stories Press, which published* As the World Burns, *offers this description of the book on its website: "Two of America's most talented activists team up to deliver a bold and hilarious satire of modern environmental policy in this fully illustrated graphic novel. The U.S. government gives robot machines from space permission to eat the earth in exchange for bricks of gold. A one-eyed bunny rescues his friends from a corporate animal-testing laboratory. And two little girls figure out the secret to saving the world from both of its enemies (and it isn't by using energy-efficient light bulbs or biodiesel fuel).* As the World Burns *will inspire you to do whatever it takes to stop ecocide before it's too late."*

BEFORE YOU READ————————————————————————

Research the critical reception that As the World Burns *has received. What have critics said about the book? What about readers?*

excerpt from
AS THE WORLD BURNS: 50 SIMPLE THINGS YOU CAN DO TO STAY IN DENIAL
Derrick Jensen and Stephanie McMillan

We see this so often.

50 SIMPLE THINGS YOU CAN DO TO SAVE THE EARTH!

CAN STREAMING VIDEO STOP GLOBAL WARMING?

LET TIKI THE PENGUIN GUIDE YOU! FIND OUT HOW KIDS CAN STOP GLOBAL WARMING!

YAHOO CELEBRATES 35 YEARS OF EARTH DAY WITH "10 SIMPLE WAYS YOU CAN SAVE THE WORLD IN A DAY!"

GREEN YOUR EVERYDAY ONLINE SHOPPING AND STOP GLOBAL WARMING!

Wouldn't it be wonderful if life were this simple, the problems we face so easily solvable? Every cell in my body wants for recycling to save the day, wants for shorter showers to save enough water for the rivers to run free.

But they won't. You know that. Fish and turtles and beavers and frogs and bears know that. Everybody knows that.

Sometimes we forget.

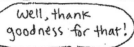

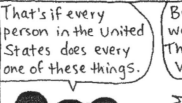

■ WHAT?

1. Look closely at the hand-drawn images in *As the World Burns.* What do you notice about the style of the drawings? How are the humans characterized? The animals? How does the artist represent big corporations? What messages about human impact on the environment (and about environmentalism itself) do these images convey?
2. Do you think the graphic novel is an effective genre for argumentation? Explain your response.

■ WHAT ELSE? WHAT'S NEXT?

3. Using your library's resources or the web, research the definitional criteria for satire. (What is a satire? What are the essential criteria of the genre?) Based on these criteria, do you think this excerpt from *As the World Burns* qualifies as a satire? Why or why not? Do you think the text is effective as a satire?

■ WHO CARES?

4. Any author engaged in public writing must try to connect with their audience or risk being ignored. How is this process of appealing to an audience different in graphic novels? What are the authors and illustrators of graphic novels able to do that other authors are not? What risks are involved when images and words come together to try to make a point?

Anne Marie Todd is an associate professor of communication studies at San Jose State University. Her essay "Prime Time Subversion" was published in the 2002 collection Enviropop: Studies in Environmental Rhetoric and Popular Culture.

BEFORE YOU READ—————————————————————————————————
Find another text—a news article or opinion piece, an essay, a video—that addresses the topic of environmentalism and The Simpsons. *Summarize the text that you find and be prepared to compare it with the "Prime-Time Subversion."*

PRIME-TIME SUBVERSION: THE ENVIRONMENTAL RHETORIC OF THE SIMPSONS Anne Marie Todd

On April 19, 1987, America was introduced to the Simpsons, the title family of the first animated prime-time television series since the 1960s. Described by its creator and executive producer Matt Groening as "a celebration of the American family at its wildest" (Steiger, 1999, p. 1), *The Simpsons* offered a critical view of mainstream social and cultural norms. In a television world dominated by upper-middle-class storybook families like the Huxtables of *The Cosby Show*, *The Simpsons* presented a satirical documentary of a more complex family whose characters and plots related more directly to the familial experience of America's television audience. In fact, *The Simpsons* first aired on prime-time television opposite *The Cosby Show*, assuming a revolutionary position toward mainstream television and the network establishment. The series exhibited a realism that appealed to a widely diverse audience and established *The Simpsons* as a fixture of American prime-time. When the show debuted, it quickly became the FOX Network's highest rated program (Korte, 1997, p.1). The success of *The Simpsons* is evident in the show's impressive popularity with a heterogeneous audience that spans generations. The program has also won critical acclaim, and has received numerous awards, including the Peabody Award (1997), the People's Choice Award (1990-1991) and several Emmies (Steiger, 1999, p.2). As Steiger argued, *The Simpsons'* "vicious social satire" and subtle profound "pop-culture allusions" had a "considerable impact on the television landscape of the nation" (p. 2).

Multiple layers of profound social and cultural commentary distinguish *The Simpsons* from conventional television programs. "The critical humor, self-reflexiveness, intertextuality and form" of *The Simpsons* solidify the literary significance of the series' postmodern commentary (Korte, 1997, p. 3). Such rhetorical elements help establish the Simpson family as an icon of American popular culture. In 1998, *Time* magazine listed Bart Simpson on behalf of the entire series as one of the key cultural and most influential figures of the twentieth century (Steiger, 1999, p.2). The realism of the characters and plot lines of

The Simpsons give the series a dramatic quality; the Simpsons' family adventures expose the nuances of American family life while simultaneously informing the social and cultural experience of the television audience.

Critical and popular acclaim for *The Simpsons* distinguishes the series as a rich multi-dimensional text for rhetorical analysis. In countless interviews, Matt Groening has described *The Simpsons* as a show that rewards its audience for paying attention (Korte, 1997, p. 9). As the most counter-cultural cartoon to hit prime-time, the series is ripe for rhetorical inquiry into its potential as a vehicle for critical political and social commentary. *The Simpsons* contributes significantly to critical analysis of popular culture, particularly in the study of television media, because the show is more literary and complex than regular television programming (Korte, 1997, p. 7). In a decade, *The Simpsons* has secured immense popularity, and its established prime-time slot confirms the magnitude of the show's viewing audience. With its copious literary and cinematic references and interminable political commentary, *The Simpsons* is indisputably embedded in American culture, and thus offers a lens into the rhetorical dimensions of human experience. Rhetorical analysis of popular culture is indispensable in the exposition of the social, cultural, and political motivations of human action. Our understanding of meaning and our comprehension of rhetorical symbols are best achieved through the explication of human motives. Rhetorical analysis of popular culture discloses how communication of symbols in the interpretation of personal experience promotes a persuasive rhetoric that engenders critical commentary regarding the social and cultural dimensions of human experience.

This chapter explicates the meaning and significance of *The Simpsons'* social commentary through two mediums of rhetorical criticism. The first method of analysis utilizes Kenneth Burke's (1959) comic frame to determine the meaning of the show's multi-textual rhetoric. Analysis of televisual communication requires an enhanced application of the comic form through a second mode of inquiry, the explication of the symbolism of *The Simpsons'* visual argument. The show presents a unique rhetorical form that exhibits profound pop-cultural influence, and in particular makes a significant impression on American environmental consciousness. This analysis begins with an explication of the utility of the comic frame and visual argument as prolific tools of rhetorical criticism. The synthesis of these two approaches engenders an enriched analysis, which articulates *The Simpsons'* intertextual environmental rhetoric. Next, the convergence of comic and visual critical practices is examined, which illuminates the symbolic elements of the show's environmental rhetoric. The abundance of episodic material, teeming with rich dialogue and resplendent visuals, rendered focusing this analysis an enigmatic task. As a directive for this criticism, two predominant metaphors are explored: Springfield's nuclear power plant as an icon of irresponsible energy use and the figurative role of nonhuman characters in the series. This project's conclusion articulates the coherent ecological message in *The Simpsons'* rhetoric, and thus renders a conclusive evaluation of the show's televisual environmental commentary. Specifically, I propose that the show's rhetoric presents a strong environmental message regarding the relationship between humans and the rest of nature.

This message is most clearly articulated in the show's rhetorical strategies, which reveal a pervasive ecological criticism of human activity, produced through comedy and visual argument—rhetorical tools that successfully engage the audience in *The Simpsons'* critical environmental commentary. This rhetorical criticism examines the first ten seasons of the series in recognition of the rhetorical force with which these animated social texts exhibit the interface of environmental communication and popular culture. The analysis was conducted by viewing various collected videotapes of the series' first ten seasons (4/9/87-5/16/99)—approximately 80 percent of the episodes—and supplemented with data from Matt Groening's two-volume guide to the show. The ten years of episodes in the sample provide hundreds of rhetorical propositions of ecological tone. Conducting a satisfactory analysis of all such references in the confines of this chapter is impossible. Thus, I focused primarily (almost exclusively) on the show's principal environmental symbols and themes. As a result, the discussion focuses on only a few entire episodes, significant plot lines, familiar environmental theses, and explicit recurring rhetorical symbols. By focusing on the dominant characteristics of *The Simpsons'* environmental communication, I endeavored to limit the scope of criticism, and thus foster a more informed evaluation of the overall environmental message of the show. Ultimately, these televised visual and linguistic images disclose the show itself as an expression of environmental activism, and expose the salience of *The Simpsons'* environmental rhetoric.

■ The Comic Frame: Transcending the Social Order through Symbolic Action

In *A Rhetoric of Motives* (1950), Kenneth Burke describes the study of rhetoric as the understanding of human motives, and his theory of symbolic action provides the basis for innumerable conceptions of the study of rhetoric. Contextualizing the comic frame within a theory of rhetoric as symbolic action, Arne Madsen cites Burke's definition of humans as symbol-using creatures that construct responses to everyday experiences. That is, human action involves using and manipulating symbols to respond to interpretations of experience (Madsen, 1993, p. 166). In this way, rhetorical criticism relies on the explication of symbols to understand human responses to experience. The rhetorical critic must analyze such behavior in order to understand human motives and to comprehend how the manipulation of symbols influences human behavior. Burke expounds on this concept of symbolic rhetoric as an explanation for human motivation in *Language as Symbolic Action* (1966). He argues that human communication involves the expression of symbolic meaning in order to directly influence the behavior and conduct of one's audience (Burke, 1966, p. 28). That is, we use symbols to construct arguments, and conceptually plan courses of action based on our interpretation of our experience.

This discussion of the symbolic expression of motives provides a context for Burke's presentation of the comic frame in *Attitudes Toward History* (1959). He introduces the comic frame as a means to enhance scholars' understanding of human motivations and foster better evaluation of the social and cultural meaning of symbolic action. The comic frame enables individuals to "be observers of themselves, while acting [to create] maximum consciousness. One would 'transcend himself by noting his own foibles'" (Burke, 1959, p.

171). Burke envisioned that applying the comic frame would create social consciousness to expose the impotence of the status quo—the existing social order—and create public awareness to address the failings of the social system. The comic frame fosters more than an ironic self-awareness, but also constructs a position of semi-detachment, where one is able to reflect and comment on human foibles without guilt, shame, or other negative emotion, or without undue involvement in the human comedy. Toward this end, Burke established the utility of frames as tools for rhetorical criticism; he described frames as the perspectives that direct all interpretations of human experience. That is, frames provide symbolic structure that enables human beings to impose order upon their personal and social experiences. Rhetorical criticism involves the dual-purposed application of frames to episodes of human experience—frames function as blueprints for actions that fix social attitudes according to a particular perspective. Frames also embody attitudes and motives, empowering scholars to determine various social and cultural forms of symbolic action (Burke, 1959, p. 20). In this way, the comic frame enriches rhetorical criticism by revealing the flaws of the present system, enabling alternative discourse to gain public recognition.

Comedy provides the means to criticize one's own complicity in the dominant social order. By acknowledging the failings of the bureaucratic system, humans create discursive space for self-analysis. Such personal criticism involves a discourse that promotes historically marginalized opinions within the public sphere. Thus, the comic frame is rhetorically powerful on two levels: through recognition of human error as the cause of social ills, and through the spiritual and moral identification with humanity. By creating social distance between reformers and the clown as a scapegoat, the comic frame also conveys a preference for a social upbraiding, rather than malicious immolation, to promote the rapprochement engendered by comic consciousness. *The Simpsons* utilizes the comic frame to identify the incongruity of human action and the symbolic interpretation of the ecological context of our experience.

■ Popular Culture Imagery As Social Commentary: the Rhetoric of Visual Argument

The coherence of the environmental message of *The Simpsons* is enriched by the show's televisual rhetorical form. The series' animated realism informs traditional methods of rhetorical criticism by illuminating tactics of visual argument. Contemporary rhetorical theory, guided by Susanne Langer, Kenneth Burke, Ernest Bormann and others, emphasizes the symbolic form of rhetorical discourse (Klumpp & Hollihan, 1989, p. 88). Accordingly, the persuasive force of rhetoric is rooted in the motivational power of symbol, located in the relationship between rhetoric and the reality of the social order. The rhetorical critic's objective is to illuminate and evaluate persuasive messages (Andrews, 1990, p. 14) and thus determine the ways in which rhetorical discourse functions as symbolic action in response to different rhetorical situations. Rhetorical criticism is concerned with the persuasiveness of discourse through the "creation of social forms in human symbolic behavior" (Klumpp & Hollihan, 1989, p. 88). That is, the salience of rhetorical propositions is largely based on the correspondence of the symbolic value of a discourse with the established meaning of the existing social order. Stating the case for visual communication, Blair (1996) argues that "the concept of visual argument is an extension of rhetoric's paradigm into a new domain...[R]hetoric in a broader sense is the use of symbols to communicate...[A]ny form of persuasion, including visual persuasion, belongs within rhetoric's province" (p. 37). With the emergence of visual communication as an acknowledged persuasive force, rhetorical critics must identify ways to evaluate the meaning of visual arguments.

Contemporary analysis of the social and cultural context of human communication must account for the increased mediation of rhetorical messages. Analysis of televised communication acts requires amplified discursive frames to evaluate the complex argumentation strategies fostered by expanded media formats. Television media enjoy a substantially larger audience than traditional rhetorical settings, and thus must account for the diverse experiences of television viewers. In addition, televised messages are informed by the broader context of rhetorical symbols and are thus enabled to offer critical commentary on the social, cultural, and political experience of the American viewing public. Gronbeck (1995) offers a defense of visual argument, and argues that rhetorical meaning requires interpretation to decode the symbols of a message. He posits that symbolic meaning is not exclusively linguistic, and visual, aural, and other symbolic systems can offer propositions that affirm or deny social and cultural experience (p. 539).

Visual media are capable of symbolic expression because they are rooted in a particularly rich context of social, cultural and political influences. The complexities of the existing social order are manifest in the stream of televised visual images—elemental, socio-cultural interpretations of human experience. Effective visual communication exhibits rich and visual symbolism that incorporates signs and symbols of conventionalized images (Blair, 1996, p. 25). The symbolic form of visual argument is deeply rooted in the context of pop culture, a rubric for the innumerable vernacular of consumer cultural images. For this reason, visual arguments enjoy an appeal that eludes verbal communication: ocular recognition of pictorial images evokes meaning that is rooted in the memory of personal experience. Visual messages persuade because they provoke "unconscious identification," which are not possible with the linguistic basis of verbal images (Blair, 1996, p. 34). Thus, visual images persuade because they give meaning to personal experience by connecting thematic elements of shared social experience (whether televised experience or actual, real experience) to individual perception. Audience members incorporate the symbolic meaning of the visual image(s) into their personal value system, affecting their individual and social worldviews (Blair, 1996, p. 34). The symbolism of visual images remains ambiguous without a stabilizing linguistic text. Thus, the rhetorical force of one visual image appeals to a heterogeneous audience because pictorial symbols adapt to individualized experience, and encompass many meanings.

Visual argument is gaining particular ascendance as a rhetorical device with the technological improvement of visual communication, notably the advent of digital technology and the remarkable realism of computer animation. A rhetoric of visual discourse employs aesthetic symbols to inform social action. Visual tactics of communication rely on personal allegiances and affinities, which evoke dramatic reactions based on the rhetorical force of the visual image. Individual interpretation entails the personal association of familiar visual images within a normalizing social context. Such personal interpretation makes individual actions meaningful because the actions are grounded in a social context, and the social context in turn guides individual behavior according to established social and cultural norms. Visual argument facilitates social change by compelling individuals to modify their behavior to accommodate the symbolic norms of visual discourse. Visual images resonate with personal experience, facilitating the production of social meaning. Furthermore, visual argument enjoys an element of realism that makes its interpretation of human experience uniquely persuasive to individuals who can understand the context of the rhetorical message.

The Simpsons is an animated cartoon rather than a show filmed with real actors in an actual physical setting. The animation creates an air of detachment from real life, in addition to the detachment created by the comic frame. Animation is a particularly salient medium to television viewers who can suspend belief for plot development (which they would not be able to do with real characters). At the same time, the show establishes a personal connection with viewers because the characters are believable.

Television programming is provocative because it engages the audience through the mediation of social situations, which imparts socially constructed norms under the guise of actual experiential knowledge. Television, particularly animation, misrepresents reality, masquerading as lived experience, in order to manipulate social contexts that provide meaning for personal experience, and guide individual action.

■ The Environmental Politics of the Springfield Nuclear Power Plant

"Both overshadowing and enlightening" (Steiger, 1999, p. 4), Springfield's nuclear power plant is owned and operated by the miserly Montgomery Burns, the town's wealthiest citizen. Homer is an employee of the plant, and holds the title of safety inspector despite his egregious lack of training. A Springfield institution, the plant is prominently featured in the show as a visual scenic element or as a comedic factor in plot development. The plant's prominence as a visual symbol of the show's environmental message is exhibited in the longer version of the show's opening sequence. The camera moves in over a hillside for a view of the picturesque town, marred only by the centrally positioned image of the plant's twin smokestacks, which billow thick clouds of dark gray smoke. The rampant pollution billowing from the smokestacks juxtaposed to the unsullied town landscape is a disturbing image. This disturbing introduction exemplifies the show's dark humor, and the potent combination of visual argument and comic frame. The negative symbolic image of the plant's egregious emissions, the dark gray billowing smoke, is reinforced by its contrast with the depiction of the town, which is animated in unrealistically bright colors. The plant symbolizes the show's environmental commentary by exhibiting a wide range of ecological implications of nuclear power, in general, and of specific conditions in the building itself.

The power plant's interior affords a setting for further visual commentary regarding the pervasive negligence that characterizes company standards for disposing of nuclear waste. A recurring joke in interior scenes is the visual image of open barrels leaking bright green radioactive waste. The plant's inner recesses are overrun with barrels strewn about the halls and open areas of the plant. Painfully bright green waste, a caricature of radioactive refuse, leaks out of the barrels and even out of the trash can in the plant's coffee room (Gewirtz, 1991). The confluence of visual argument with the comic frame establishes the symbolic meaning of the leaking waste as an animated eyesore. The pervasive images of waste enhance the visual argument symbolized in the barrels. The images position the environmental rhetoric within a burlesque comic frame, which reveals the absurdity of the publicly ignored biohazard. That is, the conspicuous barrels reveal the neglect exhibited by their inadequate disposal of the barrels, and the obvious environmental hazard that they pose. The entire scene indicates the derelict administration of safety concerns.

The plant's employees remain oblivious to the adverse situation. Their blasé attitudes enhance the situation's comedic appeal. The more egregious methods of waste disposal demonstrate the comedic effect of the employees' general apathy. Lenny and Karl, Homer's coworkers, push wheelbarrows of nuclear waste down the hallways. As Lenny and Karl discuss proper locations and methods for disposal, one of the wheelbarrows crashes into a cement column and overturns. Lenny and Karl look at each other, shrug their shoulders, and continue down the hall. The waste from the overturned container spreads ominously through the passage, while the workers resume their labor, apparently unaware of the toxic spill. That the employees rarely notice the plant's production of waste adds humorous appeal to this visual image, and contributes to the show's rhetorical condemnation of unsound disposal practices. *The Simpsons* mocks the nuclear safety precautions typified in the overwhelming lack of concern for the hazards of radioactive waste. Leaking radioactive waste is a visual symbol intended to evoke criticism of the pervasive human disregard for the environment.

This social criticism is made more explicit within a burlesque comedic frame, in a parody of safety videos on nuclear energy. *The Simpsons* relies on the burlesque comic frame to render its explicit criticism of current standard practices of nuclear waste disposal. In Springfield's caricature of pro-nukes propaganda, Smilin' Joe Fission describes the preferred method of disposal for nuclear waste: "I'll just put it where nobody'll find it for a million years" (Kogen & Wolodarsky, 1990). This parody represents the typical "out of sight, out of mind" strategy for waste disposal, and attacks the general disregard for the environmental consequences of nuclear waste disposal. The show uses humor to reveal the ridiculousness of such careless disposal strategies—clarifying the obvious problems with improper disposal, and subsequent disregard for the possible environmental consequences. *The Simpsons* employs a comic frame to expose the failings of the social order, and to criticize the audiences' complicity in the normalization of such environmentally unsafe methods. By making light of the impact of nuclear accidents and contamination of the environment, the show forces the audience to adopt a critical eye regarding real social practices that mirror the environmental negligence of the citizens of Springfield. In this way, the show's writers comment on the general human view of the environment and the anthropocentric methods that govern the power plant's safety code.

Through the comic frame, *The Simpsons* carefully balances harsh criticism of American bureaucratic institutions and sardonic commentary of individual consumptive habits. "The comic frame inherently bypasses the extremes of the bureaucratic mindset... Further, the comic frame allows observation of oneself, recognizing one's own failures and limitations" (Madesen, 1993, p. 171). Members of the audience recognize themselves in the show's characters, gaining perspective on the limits and failures of their own actions. Through this self-observation, the comic frame engenders enlightened criticism of the symbolic relationships that ground social action. The comic frame enables *The Simpsons* to rhetorically connect the economic motivations for environmental exploitation with the normalizing power of profit-driven bureaucratic social institutions that foster individual anthropocentric practices. The nuclear plant symbolizes tension between economic and environmental concerns. The plant represents the exploitation of environmental resources for wealth and power. Mr. Burns' priorities, exhibited in his operation of the plant, exemplify the attitude of economic elites and resource barons toward environmental concerns. Burns' methods of operation reveal the assumptions of characters represented by his prototype that environmental concerns are irreconcilable with economic interests. Furthermore, Burns uses his money and power to manipulate the image of his plant in order to make the environmental pollution more salient to the public.

At times *The Simpsons* abandons this charitable attitude in favor of a rhetoric well beyond the boundaries of Burke's comic frame, adopting a satiric or even burlesque style. *The Simpsons'* successful use of the burlesque comic frame is nowhere more evident than in the second season when Bart and Lisa catch a three-eyed fish while fishing near the Springfield Nuclear Reactor (Simon & Swartzwelder, 1990). When the event becomes public, a federal safety inspection team investigates the plant's emissions. In proper burlesque form, the episode chronicles the ludicrous findings of the inspection team: gum used to seal a crack in the coolant tower, a plutonium rod used as a paper-weight, monitoring stations unattended, and nuclear waste shin-deep in the hallways. The Feds threaten to shut down the power plant unless Burns makes significant improvements. Rather than bring his plant up to standard, Burns runs for governor, intending to use his elected power to keep the plant open. Inevitably confronted with Blinky, the three-eyed fish—a travesty of the ecological impacts of nuclear pollution, Burns hires spin doctors to boost his public image. In a brilliant burlesque dialogue, Burns exacerbates Blinky's parodic symbolism with his dramatic interpretation of the fish's mutation as an evolutionary advance, based on the outlandish premise that three eyes are better than two.

Mr. Burns: I'm here to talk to you about my little friend, here. Blinky. Many of you consider him to be a hideous genetic mutation. Well, nothing could be further from the truth. But don't take my word for it, let's ask an actor portraying Charles Darwin what he thinks.

Darwin: Hello, Mr. Burns.

Burns: Oh, hello Charles. Be a good fellow and tell our viewers about your theory of natural selection.

Darwin: Glad to, Mr. Burns. You see, every so often Mother Nature changes her animals, giving them bigger teeth, sharper claws, longer legs, or in this case, a third eye. And if these variations turn out to be an improvement, the new animals thrive and multiply and spread across the face of the earth.

Burns: So you're saying this fish might have an advantage over other fish, that it may in fact be a kind of super-fish.

Darwin: I wouldn't mind having a third eye, would you? (Simon & Swartzwelder, 1990, in Groening, 1997, p. 38).

Mr. Burns' narrative continues the farcical tone of this episode, and performs a lampoon of evolutionary theory. Appealing to the authority of (an actor playing) Charles Darwin, Burns dismisses Blinky's (the so-called super-fish) state as a "hideous" blunder by Mother Nature. He characterizes Blinky's extra eye as an improvement on Mother Nature's original creation, and explains the mutation as the result of the evolutionary process of natural selection that begets superfish like Blinky. This imparts an explicit visual argument in the image of the fish, and articulates a profound contradiction to the verbal text uttered by Mr. Burns. The triply endowed animated fish visually "voices" opposition to Mr. Burns' claims, and through its own vivid image conveys the heinous maltreatment suffered by innumerable other animals in the same predicament in another location. The burlesque form of this episode exposes the outlandish excuses for the plant's pollution, and offers insightful ecological commentary on several levels. Human pollution is characterized as an improvement on nature, and human progress is viewed as an integral part of human evolution. These references articulate specific criticism of current environmental regulations, specifically the lax enforcement of the regulations concerning the dumping, safe storage, and disposal of nuclear waste. Furthermore, this episode condemns the manipulation of political and economic power to disguise ecological accountability and to shift blame for environmental problems. The show comments on the lack of adherence to safety standards for the plant, and criticizes the apathetic acceptance of unenforced environmental inspections. Finally, this episode explicitly criticizes media spin-doctors who distort the impacts of ecological degradation caused by wealthy corporations such as the nuclear power plant. *The Simpsons* artfully employs a burlesque comic frame to condemn the established social order that promotes media distortion of public knowledge, while encouraging self-criticism for viewers to recognize their own fallibility in the show's parody of the disingenuous politics of the resource elites.

As an icon of televised popular culture, *The Simpsons* offers critical social commentary on human experience. The show remarks on the cultural, social, and political ramifications of human activity, in recognizing the limitations of exploitative human existence. "*The Simpsons* works to encourage, critique, demanding that viewers be active in their consumption" (Korte, 1997, p. 3). *The Simpsons* characterizes human activity in an incriminating light, questioning established social institutions and normalized behaviors of the dominant societal frames. The show fosters social change by providing the audience the opportunity to recognize the shortcomings of their own living practices and alter their behavior accordingly. This self-critical observation fosters a charitable attitude toward the motivations of others. The comic frame thus promotes cooperative discussion, rather than tragic blame assignment that offers no possibility for social transcendence. Certainly comic framing exposes the bureaucratic power in everyday life and creates an ironic awareness of hierarchical absurdities, but the comic frame remains charitable rather than tragic, always assuming that negotiation of environmental issues is possible. Some environmental issues, however, inevitably have tragic consequences and may be impossible to reconcile. The comic frame endows us with a sense of social awareness, but it does not necessarily promote social activism. Toward this end, *The Simpsons* offers a critical view of the dominant attitude toward nature and exposes the dangers of human-centered practices. The show's rhetorical message fosters social transformation through comedy—revealing the negative social value of anti-environmentalism in a humorous light, which conveys the potential for positive social change. The comic frame offers a dynamic vision of humanity, and thus precludes the defeatism promoted by a static view of human activity that forecloses the possibility of cooperative action. As a televised communication medium, *The Simpsons* encourages the audience to engage in such dramatistic analysis to infer the implications of the show's humorous message.

■ Springfield's Other Creatures: the Role and Fate of Animals in the Simpsons

Through the comic frame, *The Simpsons* exposes the ecological implications of numerous types of human-animal relationships, and comments on socially accepted practices of animal exploitation. The series offers countless opportunities for rhetorical criticism, but to maintain the close focus of this project, this section analyzes two episodes which provide the richest comedic visual text for an informed rhetorical analysis: the show's portrayal of eating and wearing animals.

In perhaps its most vivid expression of ecological commentary, *The Simpsons* chronicles Lisa's social transformation to a vegetarian lifestyle after she correlates the cute baby lamb she met at the petting zoo with the lamb chop on her dinner plate (Cohen, 1995). When her new lifestyle becomes public, Lisa is constantly under attack, most notably at school, where she is shown an outdated film encouraging the consumption of meat. A production of the beef industry, the film presents a comical depiction of the production of meat that scorns children who do not abide by the dominant social norms that compel consumption of animals. While the film offers a humorous view of dietary norms, it has a dark humor appeal because the film parody exhibits strident similarities with the meat industry's propaganda in the real world. Lisa is further ridiculed at Homer's barbecue where she is scorned for serving gazpacho, a vegetarian soup. The barbecue scene should resonate with vegetarian viewers as a depiction of the ubiquitous resistance to the provision of a vegetarian-friendly menu that offers meatless options in widely diverse social situations. At the barbecue, Lisa endures ridicule from her family as well as the guests, and she retaliates by attempting to vandalize the pig roasting on the rotisserie grill. Lisa's efforts to plunder the barbecue are themselves botched, propelling the entire barbecue—pig, pit, and all—on an airborne trajectory, ruining the year's most momentous social event, in Homer's estimation. The slapstick humor of the barbecue scene employs Burke's comedic frame, and facilitates the self-observation of the audience, questioning socially constructed dietary norms. Through humor, the cookout scene reveals the calamity of intolerance of diverse lifestyles; both Lisa and Homer—representing opposite extremes of the dietary conflict—exhibited a remarkable lack of tolerance for the eating preferences of their counterparts. This egotistic clash destroyed the carnivorous and vegetarian options, demonstrating the need for socially accommodating conditions to facilitate mutual satisfaction.

As the episode continues, Lisa endures an inner conflict about whether she should pursue her individual preferences or admit defeat in a culture inundated with propaganda pushing consumption of meat. Succumbing to this social pressure to eat flesh, Lisa eats a hot dog at the Kwik-E-Mart, but is informed it is a tofu hot dog, so she has not yet compromised her personal environmental code. She then meets Paul and Linda McCartney, who school Lisa in the etiquette of good vegetarianism, respecting others' choices, yet remaining vigilant in one's protest of animal consumption. Lisa's earlier inner conflict is resolved as she reconciles her personal convictions with tolerance for the personal decisions of others. Through Lisa's struggle to resist dominant social norms, this episode sheds light on the inherent incongruity between individual experience and socially constructed normative practices. This is an essential use of the comic frame: to divest one's own fallibility and attain an enriched perspective of the established order and its incumbent social and cultural values.

The concurrence of visual argument and the application of the comic frame in *The Simpsons* establish the potency of this program's environmental message. The episodic commentary on Lisa's vegetarianism exemplifies the rich text of the show as a productive multi-dimensional environmental commentary. At a base level, the show critiques social and cultural norms that vigorously condone the rampant consumption of animals. Through the narration of Lisa's struggle for a dietary choice, this episode reveals the marginalized perspective of vegetarians, which is relegated to the periphery of public discourse by the hegemonic culture of consumption. At another level, this narrative employs the comedic frame to humorously interpret the discrimination suffered by vegetarians and other dissidents against animal cruelty, for instance. The show offers a comedic interpretation of the marginalization of individuals who publicly hold counter-cultural ideals and are ridiculed and ostracized for their lifestyles. This episode reveals the personal suffering of marginalized individuals to promote a culture of social tolerance, and also articulates a formative experience that facilitates the social identification of dissident individuals through common experience who persevere in the knowledge that they are not alone. Through this comedic frame, *The Simpsons* presents a critical view of human exploitation of animals, enabling the audience to perceive the excessiveness of common practices. The program enjoys such significant persuasive influence because fundamentally the show is self-critical, exerting subtle rhetorical messages to promote positive social change.

Another preeminent episode critically comments on the subordinate position of nonhuman animals perpetuated by the extermination of animals expressly for the sartorial value of their coats. Mr. Burns represents the socially established and extremely affluent upper class. He demonstrates an unbridled consumptive appetite, and his social practices are marked by exploitative tactics of manipulation that establish his disregard for persons of inferior social status (all of Springfield). Mr. Burns enjoys the privileged position of a resource elite and exhibits his privilege through excessively wasteful habits that neglect ecological conservation. Aside from his customary exploitative disposition, Mr. Burns displays a unique perspective for rhetorical analysis in his flagrant desire to destroy animals for their fur (Scully, 1995). To realize his special penchant for a fur tuxedo, Burns steals the Simpsons' litter of twenty-five puppies. This episode's literary allusion to *101 Dalmatians* is testament to *The Simpsons'* profound pop-cultural allegory, and points to the significance of the synthesis of visual argument and the comic frame in this pop-cultural, televisual text.

The episode's predominant feature is a musical number performed by Mr. Burns extolling the virtue of wearing fur. Lisa and Bart observe Burns' performance from a window where they learn of his plans for their puppies. As external witnesses to Burns' theatrics, Lisa and Bart are a cruelty-conscious counterpoint to Burns' exploitative extravagance. The children possess a contrapuntal function to Burns' gleeful display—that is, they represent a socially conscious stance in disapproval of Burns' plans to exorcise the puppies. Bart and Lisa, who remain mostly silent spectators precluded from occupying space inside Mr. Burns' room, offer a critical perspective to the television audience through visual argument. Viewers identify with the spatial positioning of Bart and Lisa's visual images because Bart and Lisa's positioning as critical observers parallels the audience's relation to the animated reality of Springfield as critical observers. Bart and Lisa, as critical observers of Burns' flaunted excessive consumerism, serve as intermediaries to the contested practice of fur consumption. Through their mediating role and the spatial position of their visual images, the Simpson children perform an argumentative function. Bart and Lisa are positioned in physical opposition to Mr. Burns' stage (his closet), in a visual representation of social criticism against fur. The symbolic force of the children's visual images comes from the rhetorical power of their counterpoint to Burns. In addition, their discursive space on the second stage of the television itself, their spatial position, empowers the television audience to adopt similar roles as critical observers. The rhetorical tactics of the visual argument of this scene should ideally foster critical commentary regarding the ecological implications of killing animals for their pelts, and thus induce environmentally conscious change.

Mr. Burns provides a verbal text to add meaning to the pictorial, spatial arguments of the scene. He offers the perspective of guiltless consumption that is associated with the implications of environmental degradation. Unconcerned with socially responsible behavior, Mr. Burns sings a song that offers a riotous commentary on the fur trade. "See My Vest" is a hysterical musical number in which Mr. Burns models his wardrobe, making the argument for human wearing of animals. The song is a litany of animal skins and appendages including the title item, a vest "made from real gorilla chest." Mr. Burns describes the softness of his sweater made from "authentic Irish Setter," the elegance of his vampire bat evening-wear, and the warmth of his "grizzly bear underwear." He sings of his "albino African endangered rhino" slippers, his poodle beret, his loafers made of gophers, the hat that was his cat, and his plethora of turtlenecks (literally). Mr. Burns ends the song celebrating the magnificence of his "greyhound fur tuxedo," adding two dogs should be saved for "matching clogs" (Scully, 1995, in Groening, 1997, p. 172).

Burns celebrates his successful acquisition of his impressive collection of clothing exclusively tailored from genuine animal pelts. He sings a lyrical commentary on the pleasure of owning such luxurious garments, and emphasizes the authenticity of these literally "wild" fabrics. The application of the comic frame is evident in the witty rhyming scheme coupled with the lyrical revelry of such outlandish social practices. The comic effect of Burns' eccentric performance is enhanced by the conflation of his morbid subject matter and his jubilant attitude. Burns plays the clown in this episode, performing a comic ritual that highlights social discrepancies, which warrant conscious action. The incongruity of the song's textual and musical elements articulates comedy's usefulness to identify the absurdity of normative social practice. Burns' whimsical inflection belies the literal meaning of his words, and exposes the absurdity of his message. In this way, Burns presents a farcical rendition of human consumption that fosters meaningful critical commentary through the composition of Burns' comedic message and the visual argument of Bart and Lisa's spatial position.

The Simpsons' environmental rhetoric demonstrates the power of the comic frame in pop-culture analysis, enabling the audience to see through "the obfuscation of the bureaucratic, while opening space for discourse by the minority and marginalized voices in society" (Madsen, 1993, p. 171). The comic frame exhibits a two-pronged approach for effective rhetorical commentary: exposing social ills while creating a new discursive space to incorporate marginalized opinions into the public sphere. Through comedic expression, *The Simpsons* presents a complicated environmental message. That message presents enlightened criticism of the hegemonic assumptions of the existing social order, while simultaneously maintaining a self-critical attitude that facilitates a re-conceptualization of social and cultural relationships that grounds social action.

■ Nature As Ideology: The Simpsons' Prime-Time Eco-Critique

This detailed investigation into the meaning of *The Simpsons* seeks to identify the show's environmental message. Granted, most viewers might not impart such significance from thirty minutes of their prime-time experience. Determining the audience's understanding of the environmental message is admittedly difficult. Such critical analysis is crucial, however, to increasing public awareness of mediated discourse. Madsen describes the critic's ultimate task to alter social frames, which increases the chance for constructive social change (Madsen, 1993, p. 170). Such endeavors help foster more informed television audience members who recognize their situation as passive subjects to the manipulation of media messages to influence and direct their behavior as consumers. *The Simpsons'* antics "mirror even our culture's most unrecognized aspects in all its tiny facets. So even if the viewer does not manage to grasp all the messages transmitted by the series' characters, he or she is always very likely to at least decode some of them" (Steiger, 1999, p. 13). *The Simpsons'* success results from a combination of rhetorical elements, which projects more than mere entertainment into America's living rooms (Steiger, 1999, p. 3).

In this way, the show educates its audience while maintaining popular appeal through its humorous, animated form. The series has transferred the expression of political opinion from traditional sources such as radio, and newspapers, to television (Steiger, 1999, p. 13).

The powerful symbolic influence of *The Simpsons* is enhanced through its unique synthesis of comedic and visual rhetorical elements. Televisual media enables a critical look at the complexities of human experience through the manipulation of verbal, acoustic and visual dramatic elements. The combination of these different sense experiences creates a powerfully realistic portrayal of familiar human situations. "By animating *The Simpsons*, Groening managed to reach a higher degree of realism, while he is still entertaining and thus appealing to his audience" (Steiger, 1999, p. 4). The complex symbolism of comic and visual media presents a multidimensional perspective of reality that enjoys powerful rhetorical appeal. Televised reality enjoys an attractiveness that enables persuasive arguments against dominant social and cultural norms. The realism of televisual media is particularly persuasive when offering critical commentary against institutions and practices familiar to America's television audience. *The Simpsons* presents an alternative epistemology that critiques the environmental practices sanctioned by dominant social norms. Through the complex manipulation of multidimensional rhetorical elements, the series reveals the ecological impacts of human activity. The subversive symbolism of *The Simpsons'* environmental rhetoric functions as enlightened criticism of cultural norms of consumption, which exonerate society's ecocidal practices.

The Simpsons presents a strong ideological message about nature as a symbol—as an object for human exploitation. The characters of *The Simpsons* display an overall disregard for the environment, are separated from nature, and often oppose nature. The show portrays the mainstream culture in which the environment has a solely utilitarian value and exists exclusively for human purposes. Through humorous exaggeration, *The Simpsons* offers critical commentary on humanity and points out the danger of destroying the environment. The series' message is revolutionary because it portrays the counterculture of environmental activism as an alternative to anthropocentrism. *The Simpsons'* activism is communicated effectively through the juxtaposition of characters that represent the extremes on an ecological spectrum. Homer represents anthropocentrism, the quintessential exploitative human. Homer's character has a powerful dramatic function: increasing viewers' awareness by evoking reactions to his naivete to media influence of popular culture (Steiger, 1999, p. 5).

Lisa counters Homer's egregious anthropocentrism and symbolizes an environmental ethic of caring for nonhuman creatures. Lisa represents a moral center to the show, which enables her to reveal the irony of her father's anthropocentric actions. When Lisa bemoans the crashing of an oil tanker on Baby Seal Beach, Homer comforts her and reveals his anthropocentric perspective: "It'll be okay, honey. There's lots more oil where that came from" (Appel, 1996). Homer, not considering the ecological implications of the oil spill, instead thinks of the effects on human access to resources.

Through humor, each character's commentary functions differently; Lisa presents a moral force that opposes Homer's flagrant anthropocentrism and effectively points out the absurdity of human action. In this way, the show offers the chance for positive social change. The comic frame permits observation of ourselves, while maintaining the possibility for action by increasing societal consciousness (Carlson, 1986, p. 447). *The Simpsons* is a subversive look at the state of human existence, but is effective because of its chosen methods of rhetorical commentary. The visual communication of the show makes its criticism palatable. The show's writers are well aware that the "pastel colors of animation often blind the censors to their biting critiques of the world" (Korte, 1997, p. 7). "Combining entertainment and subversion, *The Simpsons* angers some people as much as it amuses others...Joe Rhodes of *Entertainment Weekly* notes that *'The Simpsons* at its heart... is guerrilla TV, a wicked satire masquerading as a prime-time cartoon'" (Korte, 1997, p. 9). Through its unique rhetorical methods, *The Simpsons* describes the environmental harms of social ills. Through the humorous interpretations of Springfield's environmental hazards and the moral force of Lisa's portrayal of environmental activism, the show offers an alternative solution to exploitative human practices.

The Simpsons functions as a form of environmental activism and thus reveals popular culture's effectiveness as a medium for ecological commentary. The show increases public awareness of environmental issues, and educates the television audience while entertaining them. "Unlike many shows on TV, *The Simpsons* works to encourage critique, demanding that viewers be active in their consumption" (Korte, 1997, p. 3). Through humor, the show reveals the anthropocentrism of human activity in such a way that otherwise harsh criticism is palatable and potentially effects social change. By pointing out the humorous fallacies in human action, the series offers a significant look at the life of the typical American family, and in this way profoundly impacts the attitudes and beliefs of the television audience. The crude animation of *The Simpsons* transcends conventional boundaries of environmental rhetoric. The series embodies a powerful social force by presenting a multidimensional message that critically comments on institutions and practices of the normative social and cultural context, and engages the audience through rhetorical appeals to viewers' personal experiences.

REFERENCES

Andrews, J.R. (1990). *The Practice of Rhetorical Criticism*. White Plains, NY: Longman.

Appel, R. (1996, November 24). Bart after dark (D. Polcino, Director). In J.L. Brooks, M. Groening, & S. Simon (Executive Producers), *The Simpsons*. New York: Twentieth Century Fox Film Corporation.

Blair, J.A. (1996). The possibility and actuality of visual arguments. *Argumentation and Advocacy*. 33, 23-29.

Burke, K. (1950). *A Rhetoric of Motives*. Berkeley: University of California Press.

Burke, K. (1959). *Attitudes Toward History*. Boston: Beacon Press.

Burke, K. (1966). *Language as Symbolic Action: Essays on Life, Literature, and Method*. Berkeley: University of California Press.

Carlson, A.C. (1986). Gandhi and the comic frame: "Ad bellum purificandum". *Quarterly Journal of Speech*, 72, 446-445.

Cohen, D.S. (1995, October 15). Lisa the vegetarian (M. Kirkland, Director). In J.L. Brooks, M. Groening, & S. Simon (Executive Producers), *The Simpsons*. New York: Twentieth Century Fox Film Corporation.

Gewirtz, J. (1991, October 17). Homer defined (M. Kirkland, Director). In J.L. Brooks, M. Groening, S. Simon (Executive Producers), *The Simpsons*. New York: Twentieth Century Fox Film Corporation.

Groening, M. (1997). *The Simpsons: A Complete Guide to our Favorite Family*. R. Richmond & A. Coffman (Eds.), Harper Perennial: New York.

Groening, M. (1999). *The Simpsons Forever: A Complete Guide to our Favorite Family... Continued*. S.M. Gimple (Ed.), Harper Perennial: New York.

Gronbeck, B.E. (1995). Unstated propositions: Relationships among verbal, visual and acoustic languages. In S. Jackson (Ed.), *Argumentation and Values* (pp. 539-542). Annandale, VA: Speech Communication Association.

Klumpp, J.F. & Hollihan, T. (1989). Rhetorical criticism as moral action. *Quarterly Journal of Speech*, 75, 84-97.

Kogen, J. & Wolodarsky, W. (1990, January 21). Homer's odyssey (W. Archer, Director). In J.L. Brooks, M. Groening, & S. Simon (Executive Producers), *The Simpsons*. New York: Twentieth Century Fox Film Corporation.

Korte, D. (1997). *The Simpsons* as quality television. *The Simpsons Archive* [On-line]. Available: http://www.snpp.com/other/papers/dk.paper.html

Madsen, A. (1993). The comic frame as a corrective to bureaucratization: A dramatistic perspective on argumentation. *Argumentation and Advocacy*, 29, 64-177.

Scully, M. (1995, April 9). Two dozen and one greyhounds (B. Anderson, Director). In J.L. Brooks, M. Groening, & S. Simon (Executive Producers), *The Simpsons*. New York: Twentieth Century Fox Film Corporation.

Simon, S. & Swartzwelder, J. (1990, November 1). Two Cars in every Garage and Three Eyes on every Fish (W. Archer, Director). In J.L. Brooks, M. Groening, & S. Simon (Executive Producers), *The Simpsons*. New York: Twentieth Century Fox Film Corporation.

Steiger, G. (1999). *The Simpsons* - just funny or more? *The Simpsons Archive* [On-line]. Available: http://www.snpp.com/other/papers/gs.paper.html

■ WHAT?

1. What is Todd's analytical argument about *The Simpsons*? What support does she marshal to make this case? What details does she use from the episodes themselves? Do you find her analysis persuasive?

■ WHAT ELSE? WHAT'S NEXT?

2. What documentation system does Todd use in her essay (hint: it's not MLA). Briefly explain what the system is and how it is different from the MLA's. Make sure you include your source(s) in your response.

3. Todd argues in part that *The Simpsons* uses humor to offer up a cutting cultural critique of the way we treat the environment. Do some online searching to find another humorous text (this could be a clip from a TV show, a film, or a stand-up act, among other possibilities) that makes a claim about an environmental issue. Bring this text to class and present it to your classmates, explaining the argument you see emerging there.

■ WHO CARES?

4. Todd's essay was originally published in a collection titled *Enviropop: Studies in Environmental Rhetoric and Popular Culture.* Look this book up online (you might try Amazon.com or Google Books) and examine the table of contents and any summaries or descriptions you can find. Based on this research and your reading of Todd's piece, explain who you think Todd's target audience is.

Kevin Bullis is the energy editor for the journal Technology Review, *where this article was published in early 2010. In it, Bullis explains the controversial topic of geoengineering, the use of risky technologies to try to undue some of the damage we have caused the planet.*

BEFORE YOU READ

Research the geoengineering movement and find three geoengineering projects that are under way. Be prepared to explain your findings—and the process you used to search for and select this information—in class.

THE GEOENGINEERING GAMBIT Kevin Bullis

Rivers fed by melting snow and glaciers supply water to over one-sixth of the world's population—well over a billion people. But these sources of water are quickly disappearing: the Himalayan glaciers that feed rivers in India, China, and other Asian countries could be gone in 25 years. Such effects of climate change no longer surprise scientists. But the speed at which they're happening does. "The earth appears to be changing faster than the climate models predicted," says Daniel Schrag, a professor of earth and planetary sciences at Harvard University, who advises President Obama on climate issues.

Atmospheric levels of carbon dioxide have already climbed to 385 parts per million, well over the 350 parts per million that many scientists say is the upper limit for a relatively stable climate. And despite government-led efforts to limit carbon emissions in many countries, annual emissions from fossil-fuel combustion are going up, not down: over the last two decades, they have increased 41 percent. In the last 10 years, the concentration of carbon dioxide in the atmosphere has increased by nearly two parts per million every year. At this rate, they'll be twice preindustrial levels by the end of the century. Meanwhile, researchers are growing convinced that the climate might be more sensitive to greenhouse gases at this level than once thought. "The likelihood that we're going to avoid serious damage seems quite low," says Schrag. "The best we're going to do is probably not going to be good enough."

This shocking realization has caused many influential scientists, including Obama advisors like Schrag, to fundamentally change their thinking about how to respond to climate change. They have begun calling for the government to start funding research into geoengineering—large-scale schemes for rapidly cooling the earth.

Strategies for geoengineering vary widely, from launching trillions of sun shields into space to triggering vast algae blooms in oceans. The one that has gained the most attention in recent years involves injecting millions of tons of sulfur dioxide high into the atmosphere to form microscopic particles that would shade the planet. Many geoengineering proposals date back decades, but until just a few years ago, most climate scientists considered them something between high-tech hubris and science fiction. Indeed, the subject was "forbidden territory," says Ronald Prinn, a professor of atmospheric sciences at MIT. Not only is it unclear how such engineering feats would be accomplished and whether they would, in fact, moderate the climate, but most scientists worry that they could have disastrous unintended consequences. What's more, relying on geoengineering to cool the earth, rather than cutting greenhouse-gas emissions, would commit future generations to maintaining these schemes indefinitely. For these reasons, mere discussion of geoengineering was considered a dangerous distraction for policy makers considering how to deal with global warming. Prinn says that until a few years ago, he thought its advocates were "off the deep end."

It's not just a fringe idea anymore. The United Kingdom's Royal Society issued a report on geoengineering in September that outlined the research and policy challenges ahead. The National Academies in the United States are working on a similar study. And John Holdren, the director of the White House Office of Science and Technology Policy, broached the idea soon after he was appointed. "Climate change is happening faster than anyone previously predicted," he said during one talk. "If we get sufficiently desperate, we may try to engage in geoengineering to try to create cooling effects." To prepare ourselves, he said, we need to understand the possibilities and the possible side effects. Even the U.S. Congress has now taken an interest, holding its first hearings on geoengineering in November.

Geoengineering might be "a terrible idea," but it might be better than doing nothing, says Schrag. Unlike many past advocates, he doesn't think it's an alternative to reducing greenhouse-gas emissions. "It's not a techno-fix. It's not a Band-Aid. It's a tourniquet," he says. "There are potential side effects, yes. But it may be better than the alternative, which is bleeding to death."

■ Sunday Storms

The idea of geoengineering has a long history. In the 1830s, James Espy, the first federally funded meteorologist in the United States, wanted to burn large swaths of Appalachian forest every Sunday afternoon, supposing that heat from the fires would induce regular rainstorms. More than a century later, meteorologists and physicists in the United States and the Soviet Union separately considered a range of schemes for changing the climate, often with the goal of warming up northern latitudes to extend growing seasons and clear shipping lanes through the Arctic. In 1974 a Soviet scientist, Mikhail Budyko, first suggested what is today probably the leading plan for cooling down the earth: injecting gases into the upper reaches of the atmosphere, where they would form microscopic particles to block sunlight. The idea is based on a natural phenomenon. Every few decades a volcano erupts so violently that it sends several millions of tons of sulfur—in the form of sulfur dioxide—more than 10 kilometers into the upper reaches of the atmosphere, a region called the stratosphere. The resulting sulfate particles spread out quickly and stay suspended for years. They reflect and diffuse sunlight, creating a haze that whitens blue skies and causes dramatic sunsets. By decreasing the amount of sunlight that reaches the surface, the haze also lowers its temperature. This is what happened after the 1991 eruption of Mount Pinatubo in the Philippines, which released about 15 million tons of sulfur dioxide into the stratosphere. Over the next 15 months, average temperatures dropped by half a degree Celsius. (Within a few years, the sulfates settled out of the stratosphere, and the cooling effect was gone.)

Scientists estimate that compensating for the increase in carbon dioxide levels expected over this century would require pumping between one million and five million tons of sulfur into the stratosphere every year. Diverse strategies for getting all that sulfur up there have been proposed. Billionaire investor Nathan Myhrvold, the former chief technology officer at Microsoft and the founder and CEO of Intellectual Ventures, based in Bellevue, Washington, has thought of several, one of which takes advantage of the fact that coal-fired power plants already emit vast amounts of sulfur dioxide. These emissions stay close to the ground, and rain washes them out of the atmosphere within a couple of weeks. But if the pollution could reach the stratosphere, it would circulate for years, vastly multiplying its impact in reflecting sunlight. To get the sulfur into the stratosphere, Myhrvold suggests, why not use a "flexible, inflatable hot-air-balloon smokestack" 25 kilometers tall? The emissions from just two coal-fired plants might solve the problem, he says. He estimates that his solution would cost less than $100 million a year, including the cost of replacing balloons damaged by storms.

Not surprisingly, climate scientists are not ready to sign off on such a scheme. Some problems are obvious. No one has ever tried to build a 25-kilometer smokestack, for one thing. Moreover, scientists don't understand atmospheric chemistry well enough to be sure what would happen; far from alleviating climate change, shooting tons of sulfates into the stratosphere could have disastrous consequences. The chemistry is too complex for us to be certain, and climate models aren't powerful enough to tell the whole story.

"We know Pinatubo cooled the earth, but that's not the question," Schrag says. "Average temperature is not the only issue." You've also got to account for regional variations in temperature and effects on precipitation, he explains—the very things that climate models are notoriously bad at accounting for. Prinn concurs: "If we lower levels of sunlight, we are unsure of the exact response of the climate system to doing that, for the same reason that we don't know exactly how the climate will respond to a particular level of greenhouse gases." He adds, "That's the big issue. How can you engineer a system you don't fully understand?"

The actual effects of Mount Pinatubo were, in fact, complex. Climate models at the time predicted that by decreasing the amount of sunlight hitting the surface of the earth, the haze of sulfates produced in such an eruption would reduce evaporation, which in turn would lower the amount of precipitation worldwide. Rainfall did decrease—but by much more than scientists had expected. "The year following Mount Pinatubo had by far the lowest amount of rainfall on record," says Kevin Trenberth, a senior scientist at the National Center for Atmospheric Research in Boulder, CO. "In fact, it was 50 percent lower than the previous low of any year." The effects, however, weren't uniform; in some places, precipitation actually increased. A human-engineered sulfate haze could have similarly unpredictable results, scientists warn.

Even in a best-case scenario, where side effects are small and manageable, cooling the planet by deflecting sunlight would not reduce the carbon dioxide in the atmosphere, and elevated levels of that gas have consequences beyond raising the temperature. One is that the ocean absorbs more carbon dioxide and becomes more acidic as a result. That harms shellfish and some forms of plankton, a key source of food for fish and whales. The fishing industry could be devastated. What's more, carbon dioxide levels will continue to rise if we don't address them directly, so any sunlight-reducing technology would have to be continually ratcheted up to compensate for their warming effects.

And if the geoengineering had to stop—say, for environmental or economic reasons—the higher levels of greenhouse gases would cause an abrupt warm-up. "Even if the geoengineering worked perfectly," says Raymond Pierrehumbert, a professor of geophysical sciences at the University of Chicago, "you're still in the situation where the whole planet is just one global war or depression away from being hit with maybe a hundred years' worth of global warming in under a decade, which is certainly catastrophic. Geoengineering, if it were carried out, would put the earth in an extremely precarious state."

■ Smarter Sulfates

Figuring out the consequences of various geoengineering plans and developing strategies to make them safer and more effective will take years, or even decades, of research. "For every dollar we spend figuring out how to actually do geoengineering," says Schrag, "we need to be spending 10 dollars learning what the impacts will be."

To begin with, scientists aren't even sure that sulfates delivered over the course of decades, rather than in one short volcanic blast, will work to cool the planet down. One key question is how microscopic particles interact in the stratosphere. It's possible that sulfate particles added repeatedly to the same area over time would clump together. If that happened, the particles could start to interact with longer-wave radiation than just the wavelengths of electromagnetic energy in visible light. This would trap some of the heat that naturally escapes into space, causing a net heating effect rather than a cooling effect. Or the larger particles could fall out of the sky before they had a chance to deflect the sun's heat. To study such phenomena, David Keith, the director of the Energy and Environmental Systems Group at the University of Calgary, envisions experiments in which a plane would spray a gas at low vapor pressure over an area of 100 square kilometers. The gas would condense into particles in the stratosphere, and the plane would fly back through the particle cloud to take measurements. Systematically altering the size of the particles, the quantity of particles in a given area, the timing of their release, and other variables could reveal key details about their microscale interactions.

Yet even if the behavior of sulfate particles can be understood and managed, it's far from clear how injecting them into the stratosphere would affect vast, complex climate systems. So far, most models have been crude; only recently, for example, did they start taking into account the movement of ice and ocean currents. Sulfates would cool the planet during the day, but they'd make no difference when the sun isn't shining. As a result, nights would probably be warmer relative to days, but scientists have done little to model this effect and study how it could affect ecosystems. "Similarly, you could affect the seasons,"

FIVE GEOENGINEERING SCHEMES

Researchers and entrepreneurs have proposed approaches ranging from the relatively cheap and simple to the elaborate. Here are the ones that have received the most attention so far.

SULFATE INJECTION

Aircraft, or a hose suspended by hundreds of wing-shaped balloons, could inject aerosols into the upper atmosphere. The particles would reflect light and shade the earth.
Pros: It could be cheap and fast-acting, cooling the earth in months.
Cons: It could cause droughts. Injections might need to continue for hundreds of years.

CLOUD BRIGHTENING

Tiny droplets made by spraying an extremely fine mist of seawater into low-lying clouds could make them reflect more sunlight than ordinary clouds.
Pros: Shading could be targeted—to stop the melting of Arctic Sea ice, for example.
Cons: Scientists don't know how it would affect precipitation and temperatures over land, where it would matter most.

OCEAN FERTILIZATION

Adding iron or other nutrients to the ocean could promote algae blooms, which would capture carbon dioxide and store some of it deep in the ocean.

Pros: It would directly address the root of climate change: carbon dioxide in the atmosphere.
Cons: At best, it could offset an eighth of the greenhouse-gas emissions attributed to humans, and it could harm ecosystems.

SPACE SHADES

Trillions of disks launched into space could reflect incoming sunlight.
Pros: Space-based systems don't pollute the atmosphere. Once in place, they would cool the earth quickly.
Cons: The technology could take decades to develop. And launching trillions of disks is fantastically expensive.

ARTIFICIAL TREES

Various chemical reactions can be used to capture carbon dioxide from the atmosphere for permanent storage.
Pros: In the long run, this could reduce atmospheric concentrations of carbon dioxide. There is no obvious limit to how much of the greenhouse gas could be stored.
Cons: It could be very expensive and energy intensive, and it would take a long time to reduce temperatures.

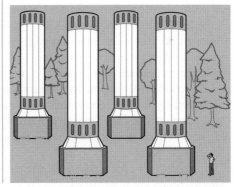

Schrag says: the sulfates would lower temperatures less during the winter (when there's less daylight) and more during the summer. And scientists have done little to understand how stratospheric circulation patterns would change with the addition of sulfates, or precisely how any of these things could affect where and when we might experience droughts, floods, and other disasters.

If scientists could learn more about the effects of sulfates in the stratosphere, it could raise the intriguing possibility of "smart" geoengineering, Schrag says. Volcanic eruptions are crude tools, releasing a lot of sulfur in the course of a few days, and all from one location. But geoengineers could choose exactly where to send sulfates into the stratosphere, as well as when and how fast.

"So far we're thinking about a very simplistic thing," Schrag says. "We're talking about injecting stuff in the stratosphere in a uniform way." The effects that have been predicted so far, however, aren't evenly distributed. Changes in evaporation, for example, could be devastating if they caused droughts on land, but if less rain falls over the ocean, it's not such a big deal. By taking advantage of stratospheric circulation patterns and seasonal variations in weather, it might be possible to limit the most damaging consequences. "You can pulse injections," he says. "You could build smart systems that might cancel out some of those negative effects."

Rather than intentionally polluting the stratosphere, a different and potentially less risky approach to geoengineering is to pull carbon dioxide out of the air. But the necessary technology would be challenging to develop and put in place on large scale.

In his 10th-floor lab in the Manhattan neighborhood of Morningside Heights, Klaus Lackner, a professor of geophysics in the Department of Earth and Environmental Engineering at Columbia University, is experimenting with a material that chemically binds to carbon dioxide in the air and then, when doused in water, releases the gas in a concentrated form that can easily be captured. The work is at an early stage. Lackner's carbon-capture devices look like misshapen test-tube brushes; they have to be hand dipped in water, and it's hard to quickly seal them into the improvised chamber used to measure the carbon dioxide they release. But he envisions automated systems—millions of them, each the size of a small cabin—scattered over the countryside near geologic reservoirs that could store the gases they capture. A system based on this material, he calculates, could remove carbon dioxide from the air a thousand times as fast as trees do now. Others at Columbia are working on ways to exploit the fact that peridotite rock reacts with carbon dioxide to form magnesium carbonate and other minerals, removing the greenhouse gas from the atmosphere. The researchers hope to speed up these natural reactions.

It's far from clear that these ideas for capturing carbon will be practical. Some may even require so much energy that they create a net increase in carbon dioxide. "But even if it takes us a hundred years to learn how to do it," Pierrehumbert says, "it's still useful, because CO_2 naturally takes a thousand years to get out of the atmosphere."

■ The Seeds of War

Several existing geoengineering schemes, though, could be attempted relatively cheaply and easily. And even if no one knows whether they would be safe or effective, that doesn't mean they won't be tried.

David Victor, the director of the Laboratory on International Law and Regulation at the University of California, San Diego, sees two scenarios in which it might happen. First, "the desperate Hail Mary pass:" "A country quite vulnerable to changing climate is desperate to alter outcomes and sees that efforts to cut emissions are not bearing fruit. Crude geoengineering schemes could be very inexpensive, and thus this option might even be available to a Trinidad or Bangladesh—the former rich in gas exports and quite vulnerable, and the latter poor but large enough that it might do something seen as essential for survival." And second, "the Soviet-style arrogant engineering scenario:" "A country run by engineers and not overly exposed to public opinion or to dissenting voices undertakes geoengineering as a national mission—much like massive building of poorly designed nuclear reactors, river diversion projects, resettlement of populations, and other national missions that are hard to pursue when the public is informed, responsive, and in power." In either case, a single country acting alone could influence the climate of the entire world.

How would the world react? In extreme cases, Victor says, it could lead to war. Some countries might object to cooling the earth, especially if higher temperatures have brought them advantages such as longer growing seasons and milder winters. And if geoengineering decreases rainfall, countries that have experienced droughts due to global warming could suffer even more.

No current international laws or agreements would clearly prevent a country from unilaterally starting a geoengineering project. And too little is known now for a governing body such as the United Nations to establish sound regulations—regulations that might in any case be ignored by a country set on trying to save itself from a climate disaster. Victor says the best hope is for leading scientists around the world to collaborate on establishing as clearly as possible what dangers could be involved in geoengineering and how, if at all, it might be used. Through open international research, he says, we can "increase the odds—not to 100 percent—that responsible norms would emerge."

■ Ready or Not

In 2006, Paul Crutzen, the Dutch scientist who won the Nobel Prize in chemistry for his discoveries about the depletion of the stratospheric ozone layer, wrote an essay in the journal *Climatic Change* in which he declared that efforts to reduce greenhouse-gas emissions "have been grossly unsuccessful." He called for increased research into the "feasibility and environmental consequences of climate engineering," even though he acknowledged that injecting sulfates into the stratosphere could damage the ozone layer and cause large, unpredictable side effects. Despite these dangers, he said, climatic engineering could ultimately be "the only option available to rapidly reduce temperature rises."

At the time, Crutzen's essay was controversial, and many scientists called it irresponsible. But since then it has served to bring geoengineering into the open, says David Keith, who started studying the subject in 1989. After a scientist of Crutzen's credentials, who understood the stratosphere as well as anyone, came out in favor of studying sulfate injection as a way to cool the earth, many other scientists were willing to start talking about it.

Among the most recent converts is David Battisti, a professor of atmospheric sciences at the University of Washington. One problem in particular worries him. Studies of heat waves show that crop yields drop off sharply when temperatures rise 3 °C to 4 °C above normal—the temperatures that MIT's Prinn predicts we might reach even with strict emissions controls. Speaking at a geoengineering symposium at MIT this fall, Battisti said, "By the end of the century, just due to temperature alone, we're looking at a 30 to 40 percent reduction in [crop] yields, while in the next 50 years demand for food is expected to more than double."

Battisti is well aware of the uncertainties that surround geoengineering. According to research he's conducted recently, the first computer models that tried to show how shading the earth would affect climate were off by 2 °C to 3 °C in predictions of regional temperature change and by as much as 40 percent in predictions of regional rainfall. But with a billion people already malnourished, and billions more who could go hungry if global warming disrupts agriculture, Battisti has reluctantly conceded that we may need to consider "a climate-engineering patch." Better data and better models will help clarify the effects of geoengineering. "Give us 30 or 40 years and we'll be there," he said at the MIT symposium. "But in 30 to 40 years, at the level we're increasing CO_2, we're going to need this, whether we're ready or not."

■ WHAT?

1. What, according to this piece, is geoengineering? Why is geoengineering a controversial subject?

2. Bullis writes, "Many geoengineering proposals date back decades, but until just a few years ago, most climate scientists considered them something between high-tech hubris and science fiction." Why, according to Bullis, have these proposals been pushed to the fringes for so long? What has changed in recent years to bring geoengineering into more acceptable scientific and political discussions? What do you think the future holds for these approaches to dealing with climate change?

3. Among journalists, scientists, and policymakers, the critical question surrounding geoengineering is not, "How we would do it?" but rather, "Should we do it?" Briefly describe the ethical dilemmas attached to geoengineering and then write your own response to these dilemmas. If we had the technology to cool the planet through geoengineering, should we do it? Why or why not?

■ WHAT ELSE? WHAT'S NEXT?

4. If you haven't already, read Edward O. Wilson's "For the Love of Life," which opens this chapter. Based on that essay, how do you think Wilson

might respond to the concept of geoengineering? Would he consider it a good idea? Explain your response.

5. Research the following question, and summarize your findings in a brief report, complete with a bibliography of the sources you consulted: Are any geoengineering projects considered unqualified successes?

■ WHAT?

6. If you had to write an explanatory essay about geoengineering for an audience drawn from the population of Columbia, S.C., how would you go about making your readers care about the issue and help them understand the need for immediate attention and action?

IMAGE 4.2
"Technology can be good for the environment," Stewart Brand writes in "Reframing the Problems." Based on your reading of Brand's piece and "The Geoengineering Gambit" by Kevin Bullis, how might this be the case? Why might some environmentalists be wary of such a statement?

In the fall of 1968, Stewart Brand founded, edited, and published the Whole Earth Catalog, *a pioneering resource that changed the way many people thought about the environment (parts of the catalog are available online at http://www.wholeearth.com/index.php). "Reframing the Problems" is an excerpt from Brand's 2000 book* The Clock of the Long Now: Time and Responsibility, *which "challenges readers to get outside themselves and combat the short-term irresponsible thinking that has led to environmental destruction and social chaos," according to a* Publisher's Weekly *review.*

BEFORE YOU READ————————————————————————
Browse the original Whole Earth Catalog *(it is available online at http://www. wholeearth.com/index.php) and choose one article or advertisement dealing with the environment that you find interesting. Be prepared to share your choice with your classmates.*

REFRAMING THE PROBLEMS   Stewart Brand

In 1996, a suddenly growing multibillion-dollar California foundation asked me and others to write a short paper on the question, "What are the most serious environmental problems confronting humankind at the beginning of the twenty-first century?" Figuring I would have nothing original to add to that list, I decided to write the piece from the perspective of the Clock of the Long Now. *Looking from outside the present time gave a sideways rather than end-on view of the current environmental problems and invited rethinking them in terms of eventual practical solutions rather than only how great a threat they pose. I think the paper fits in at this point in the discussion, where the uses and advantages of long-view thinking are explored. The foundation (now the third-largest in America) is endowed with the wealth of David Packard, cofounder of Hewlett-Packard, the brilliantly successful electronics firm based in Palo Alto, California.*

To the David and Lucile Packard Foundation:
My contribution may be to bend your question a little. Environmental problems these days come in a pretty familiar litany of pretty familiar names. The World Population problem. Climate Change problem. Loss of Biodiversity. Ocean Fisheries. Freshwater Aquifers. North/South Economic Disparity. Rain Forests. Agricultural and Industrial Pollution. Identifying these issues and making them everyone's concern has been a major triumph of environmental science and activism in the late twentieth century.

I propose that the Packard Foundation could make a contribution beyond even the splendid effect of its funding by helping to rethink—reframe—the very structure of how environmental problems are stated. This is a common practice among inventive engineers such as the late Mr. Packard. When a design problem resists solution, reframe the problem in such a way that it invites solution.

An example of spontaneous reframing occurred in 1969, when the Apollo program began returning color photographs of the Earth from space. Everyone saw the photographs and saw that we occupied a planet that was beautiful, all one, very finite, and possibly fragile. The environmental movement took off from that moment—the first Earth Day was in 1970. That effect of the American space program was never intended or anticipated. Indeed, nearly all environmentalists in the sixties (except Jacques Cousteau) actively fought against the space program, saying that we had to solve Earth's problems before exploring space.

What might be some further helpful reframings?

(1) *Civilization's shortening attention span is mismatched with the pace of environmental problems.*

What with accelerating technology and the short-horizon perspective that goes with burgeoning market economics (next quarter) and the spread of democracy (next election), we have a situation where steady but gradual environmental degradation escapes our notice. The slow, inexorable pace of ecological and climatic cycles and lag times bear no relation to the hasty cycles and lag times of human attention, decision, and action. We can't slow down all of human behavior, and shouldn't, but we might slow down parts.

Now is the period in which people feel they live and act and have responsibility. For most of us *now* is about a week, sometimes a year. For some traditional tribes in the American northeast and Australia *now* is seven generations back and forward (175 years each direction). Just as the Earth photographs gave us a sense of *the big here*, we need things that give people a sense of *the long now*.

Candidate now-lengtheners might include: abiding charismatic artifacts; extreme longitudinal scientific studies; very large, slow, ambitious projects; human life extension (with delayable childbearing); some highly durable institutions; reward systems for slow responsible behavior; honoring patience and sometimes disdaining rush; widespread personal feeling for the span of history; planning practices that preserve options for the future.

In a sense, the task here is to make the world safe for hurry by slowing some parts way down.

(2) *Natural systems can be thought of pragmatically as "natural infrastructure."*

One area in which governments and other institutions seem comfortable thinking in the long term is the realm of infrastructure, even though there is no formal economics of infrastructure benefits and costs. (There should be and could be.) We feel good about investing huge amounts in transportation systems, utility grids, and buildings.

Infrastructure thinking is directly transferable to natural systems. Lucky for us, we don't have to build the atmosphere that sustains us, the soils, the aquifers, the wild fisheries, the forests, the rich biological complexity that keeps the whole thing resilient. All we have to do is defend these systems—from ourselves. It doesn't take much money. It doesn't even take much knowledge, though knowledge certainly helps.

A bracing way to think about this matter would be to seriously take on the project of terraforming Mars—making it comfortable for life. Then think about reterraforming Earth if we lose the natural systems that previously built themselves here. The fact is that humans are now so powerful that we are in effect terraforming Earth. Rather poorly so far. We can't undo our power; it will only increase. We can terraform more intelligently—with a light, slow hand, and with the joy and pride that goes with huge infrastructure projects. Current efforts by the Army Corps of Engineers to restore the Florida Everglades, for example, have this quality.

(3) *Technology can be good for the environment.*

My old biology teacher, Paul Ehrlich, has a formula declaring that environmental degradation is proportional to "population times affluence times technology." It now appears that the coming of information technology is reversing that formula, so that better technology and more affluence leads to less environmental harm—*if* that is one of the goals of the society.

"Doing more with less"—Buckminister Fuller's "ephemeralization"—is creating vastly more efficient industrial and agricultural processes, with proportionately less impact on natural systems. It is also moving ever more of human activity into an *infosphere* less harmfully entwined with the biosphere.

Given its roots, the Packard Foundation is particularly well suited to evaluate and foster what a Buddhist engineer might call *right technology*. It would be helpful to assemble a roster of existing environmentally benign technologies. Satellites for communication and remote sensing come to mind. So does Jim Levelock's gas chromatograph (which detected atmospheric chlorofluorocarbons)—invented for Hewlett-Packard, as I recall.

The foundation might support activities such as Eric Drexler's Foresight Institute, which is aiming to shape nanotechnology (molecular engineering) toward cultural and environmental responsibility. It might support services on the Internet that distribute information and discussion about the environmental impacts of new and anticipated technologies and their interactions. Good effects should be investigated as well as ill effects.

(4) *Feedback is the primary tool for tuning systems, especially at the natural/artificial interface.*

German military officers are required to eat what their troops eat and after they eat. That single tradition assures that everyone's meals are excellent and timely, and it enhances unit morals, and respect for the officers. The feedback cycle is local and immediate, not routed through bureaucratic specialists or levels of hierarchy.

In similar fashion, factories, farms, and cities that pollute rivers and water tables could be required to release their outflows upstream of their own water intake rather than downstream.

The much-lamented "tragedy of the commons" is a classic case of pathological feedback—where each individual player is rewarded rather than punished for wasting the common resource. In fact, healthy self-governing commons systems are frequent in the world and in history, as examined in Elinor Ostrum's *Governing the Commons*. The commons she dissects include communally held mountain meadows and forests in Switzerland, irrigation cooperatives in Japan and Spain, and jointly managed fisheries in Turkey, Sri Lanka, and Nova Scotia. The successful ones are maintained (and maintainable) neither by the state nor the market but by a local set of community feedbacks adroitly tuned to ensure the system's long-term health and prosperity. Ostrum detects eight design principles that keep a wide variety of common systems self-balancing. They are: clear boundaries; locally appropriate rules; collective agreement; monitoring; graduated sanctions; conflict-resolution mechanisms; rights to organize; nested enterprises.

The Packard Foundation could encourage feedback analysis of environmental problems and help devise local-feedback solutions.

(5) *Environmental health requires peace, prosperity, and continuity.*

War, especially civil war, destroys the environment and displaces caring for the environment for generations. Widespread poverty destroys the environment and undermines all ability to think and act for the long term.

Environmental activists and peace activists are still catching on that they are natural partners, and both remain averse to business boosters who might aid prosperity. Peacekeeping soldiers are not in the mix at all. But for a culture and its environment to come into abiding equanimity you need all four—eco-activists, peace activists, marketeers, and honest cops—each of them with a light touch, comfort with collaboration, and eagerness to replace themselves with local talent. An example of productive joining of regional business and environmental goals is the Ecotrust project at Willapa Bay, Washington.

By its funding choices and guidelines, Packard Foundation could foster "jointness" in world-saving endeavors. In support of the long now, it could promote people, ideas, and organizations that are in for the long haul.

■ WHAT?

1. In his letter to the Packard Foundation, Brand calls for a reframing "of the very structure of how environmental problems are stated." What does he mean by this? How does he say this "reframing" will help? What examples does he give to support his position?
2. Brand argues for, among other things, "what a Buddhist engineer might call right technology." How does Brand define this? After you've established his definition, read "The Geoengineering Gambit" by Jeff Bullis. Do you think the technologies Bullis describes there fit the definition advocated by Brand?

■ WHAT ELSE? WHAT'S NEXT?

3. Brand suggests that the first color photographs of the Earth from space, taken by Apollo 11 in 1969, sparked the environmental movement. This effect, he says, was an unintended benefit of the U.S. space program. Go online to find those first images of Earth (search for "NASA photo ID AS11-44-6552" and "NASA photo ID AS11-36-5355" to find the most famous of these pictures). Spend some time looking at what you find. What details do you notice? How are the photographs composed? Why do you think these images motivated people to action? What might have been so compelling or persuasive about them four decades ago?
4. In an interview with *Seed* magazine titled "A Manifesto for the Planet," Brand makes a distinction between environmentalists he calls "Greens" and "Turquoises." What is the difference between the two? Using resources from the web and from your library, distinguish one environmental movement from the other. Based on what you've discovered, which approach seems the most useful or perhaps the most necessary to you?

■ WHO CARES?

5. Brand's piece is a letter, which he later included in a book. What rhetorical effects can an author achieve by taking a letter written to a specific reader and sharing it with a much broader audience? What does such an action do for the author's ethos? How might it make the larger audience feel? Do you see any pitfalls in such an action?

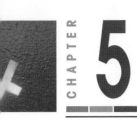

Reading Eating

IMAGE 5.1 shows one of the families featured in *Hungry Planet: What the World Eats* by Peter Menzel and Faith D'Aluisio. This 2005 book presents a photographic study of families from around the world, revealing what people eat during the course of one week. The Aboubakar family, pictured here, of the Breidjing Camp in Chad spent 685 CFA Francs, or $1.23, for a week's worth of food. Think about the rhetorical effects of this photograph. How does it make you feel? What does it make you think? What arguments does it make? Compare this image with those on pages 296 and 363.

While it may be true that we are *what* we eat, the writers in this chapter present compelling evidence that we are *how* we eat, too. These academics, poets, journalists, and activists argue that the food choices we make—individually, as communities, and as a nation— can affect everything from our health to the health of the planet, from the livelihood and culture of billions of people to economic and political stability around the world. Chew on that for a while.

Elisabeth Townsend writes about food, wine, and travel for The Boston Globe and other newspapers and magazines. She conducted the following interview with primatologist Richard Wrangham in 2005 for Gastronomica: The Journal of Food and Culture. Wrangham's book Catching Fire: How Cooking Made Us Human—The Cooking Ape was a working title—was published in 2009.

BEFORE YOU READ

Write a paragraph or two in which you explain what "food literacy" means to you.

excerpts from
THE COOKING APE   Elisabeth Townsend

Primatologist Richard Wrangham might be best known for the 1996 book he coauthored with writer Dale Peterson, *Demonic Males: Apes and the Origins of Human Violence,* where he used his research on intergroup aggression in chimpanzees to reflect on combative male behavior. Wrangham's twenty-five years of research have always been based on a deep interest in human evolution and behavior, and recently he's shifted his focus to the evolution of cooking in humans.

An anthropology professor at Harvard University, Wrangham, fifty-six, was first mesmerized by Africa when he spent a year working in Kafue National Park in western Zambia before going to college. There, he assisted a research biologist in studying the behavior and ecology of the waterbuck, falling "in love with the excitement of finding out about African habitats and species." He's been back to Africa every year since then, with only one exception—the year his first son was born.

Though Wrangham has made his reputation explaining the similarities and differences across species in primate social organizations, he expects that his work on cooking will have the broadest impact because cooking affects many human behaviors—such as those associated with food choice, familial relationships, and food production that can satisfy a huge world population. His favorite part of the day is when he can steal an hour from teaching to

Richard Wrangham
Photo by Jim Harrison

analyze chimp data or to work on his new book, *The Cooking Ape*. But Wrangham is happiest at his Ugandan research site, enjoying those quiet moments alone with the chimps, watching their relationships and catching up on the social gossip. He hasn't eaten a mammal since 1976 because of his profound empathy for the ones he has enjoyed and spent so much time with in the wild. Occasionally, his vegetarianism makes life a bit harder, as when a host offers him meat, but he'll never turn down seconds on a chocolate roulade. Wrangham spoke from his home in Weston, Massachusettes.

ET: *What prompted your research into how cooking affected human evolution?*

RW: As a Primatologist, I am often asked to think about human evolution. I sat one evening in my living room preparing a lecture for the next day, thinking about the standard story that involved hunting being important around two million years ago. As I was staring at the fire, I had an almost ghostly experience where I just allowed my eyes to be drawn deep into the fire. I could feel around me the presence of hominids, from up to one million years ago, sitting in the African bush.

I started thinking about the fact that fire is something that has been on the Earth ever since there's been plant vegetation and how when I'm in the bush there is no way that I'm going to spend a night without sitting next to a fire. I was thinking about the impact of fire on the "cookability" of food.

Then I thought, "Well, would there really have been a fire for our early ancestors—a million years ago, say?"

I realized I didn't know the answer to the question. But I also realized that it was extremely difficult to imagine that they did not have cooking, because even as long as 1,500,000 years ago humans looked incredibly similar from the neck down to humans living today. Even our heads are very similar—though we have larger brains and we don't have quite as big a mouth or teeth as they did. So surely, if those million-year-old ancestors were generally like us in the size and shape of their bodies, they should have been eating cooked food. After all, cooking has this huge impact. It changes so much about how we relate to the natural environment: it changes the ease with which we digest the food; it changes the availability of calories; and it changes the distribution of food.

If cooking has such a big evolutionary impact, in other words, and we haven't changed much, then there are only two possibilities. Either we somehow managed to adopt cooking without it affecting us very much, which would be very mysterious, or it happened so early that cooking had already been adopted by a million years ago.

ET: *What's an example of how changes in the food supply affected primates and how that led you to think cooking had a significant impact on humans?*

RW: If you compare chimpanzees to gorillas, they eat very similar things. They both like to eat fruits when fruits are available. They both eat more leaves and stems when there aren't many fruits available. But there's one relatively small difference when there's a shortage of fruit, gorillas will switch entirely to eating leaves and stems, whereas chimpanzees absolutely insist on finding their daily ration of fruits before they go bulk up on leaves and stems. That's why gorillas can live entirely without fruit—in the mountains of Uganda, for instance—whereas we don't know of any place where chimpanzees can live entirely without access to fruit.

The small difference in food supply between chimps and gorillas can account for the fact that the gorillas are three to four times the body size of chimpanzees and that they live in more-stable groups. Therefore, gorillas have an entirely different set of sexual relationships, with males being enormously bigger than females, and so on. This is just one example where a relatively small difference in the food supply creates a big difference in the way that two species look and behave. And to shift from eating raw food to eating cooked food is a much bigger change!

ET: *How did cooking change calorie intake and thus the human species?*
RW: Amazingly, we still don't have a good picture of the most important ways in which cooking changes food. There are different effects on plant foods and meat, though. One impact on plant foods is probably to increase digestibility. That means that our food has a relatively low proportion of indigestible materials; in modern surveys you see the 10 percent or less of what we eat is indigestible plant material (fiber, in other words). Whereas in chimpanzees, for instance, fiber is over 30 percent, which therefore seems a reasonable guess for what it might have been like in our raw-food-eating ancestors. Well, if we ate 30 percent fiber, compared with 10 percent now, that 20 percent of the food our ancestors were eating was just bulk material passing through the gut. So, they simply absorbed less energy.

That 20 percent figure is a lot. When we compare the actual rate of energy expenditure in human foragers, which is between 1.5 and 2.2 times the basal metabolic rate, as compared with 1.4 times for chimpanzees, we're getting a lot of extra energy from somewhere compared to the chimpanzees. Where are we getting it from? I think it's because the food that humans are eating is more digestible. Instead of spending all day with our guts holding a high proportion of indigestible material, we're able to have a higher continuous stream of calories going through our guts.

What's the result? Maybe, it explains why humans used so much energy, starting around 1.9 million years ago. First, that's when we got our bigger body, made by the greater amount of energy. Second, it means that we can have a relatively large proportion of expensive organs, such as brains (they're expensive in the sense of using calories at a particularly high rate). For a long time people have been interested in the notion that, since the brain is unusually expensive, our ancestors needed to have some way of getting more energy in order to afford having a bigger brain. At 1.9 million years ago, you have arguably the largest increase in brain size in evolution. Third, there's the opportunity for longer travel distance per day because you just got more energy to put into traveling. Chimpanzees are quite long-distance travelers at 2.5, 3, 4.5 kilometers a day, but humans, males in particular, are traveling 9, 10, 15, 20 kilometers a day—a lot more than chimps.

This extra energy probably comes from the fact that, as a result of cooking, we're able to eat a relatively compact food that is full of calories. And then at the same time, of course, the food has become softer, and that enables us to have smaller teeth and smaller jaws, a flatter face, and less prognathous jaws. At the same time we, in fact, have smaller guts and a shift in the arrangement of our guts that reflects the fact that we're eating food that is relatively highly digestible. So we have long small intestines, the part of the gut that absorbs the products of digestion, and we have short large intestines where fermentation goes on when you retain food that takes twenty-four hours or more to be fermented under the action of bacteria. We have relatively little food that comes in that needs to be fermented. All of these changes are easily explained by the adoption of cooking.

ET: *How much did our brains and bodies change as a result of eating cooked food?*
RW: The standard estimate is that female bodies increased in weight by about 60 percent around the 1.9-million-year mark. So, if you compare the body size of about 125 pounds for an average woman with the average range of 70 to 80 pounds for a chimp, it's really quite a big increase. And the brain size is going up…it might be 60 percent.

ET: *You've said that cooking and meat eating are the only two proposals for what transformed the ape into a human. Why couldn't the changes just be from eating more raw meat rather than cooking?*
RW: We don't know too much about what it's like to chew raw meat because people don't do it. But chimpanzees are a good model because they have teeth that are just about the same size in relation to their bodies as those of our early ancestors 1.9 million years ago. When we look at chimpanzees eating raw meat, it turns out that they're eating it so slowly that it would just take a tremendous amount of time to rely on eating nothing but raw meat. And that would be a problem.

Think about how many calories our early ancestors would have needed at that stage, estimated at somewhere in the low 2000s. This would take five to six hours a day of simply chewing *without* going out and finding more meat, cutting it up, and looking after your babies and so on. And they would have had to develop some kind of tooth arrangement that was sharp and enabled them to chop it up quickly and swallow it in the manner of a carnivore.

It just seems very unlikely that, at any time since 1.9 million years ago, our ancestors were chewing for half the day, because animals that chew a lot have got deep jaws and robust bones in the mouth to accommodate the stresses of the chewing. That's not what you see—our ancestors' jaws have been built relatively lightly ever since 1.9 million years ago. So, it's not that I think that meat is unimportant; it probably was eaten a lot. It's just that to become important it had to be tenderized to allow it to be eaten easily. The tenderizing could have begun in a physical way by hammering it with stones, maybe, but cooking would have solved the problem much more efficiently.

ET: *When did humans learn how to master fire and then use it for cooking?*
RW: No one knows for sure. But there is such good evidence from caves in southern Europe that humans controlled fire by 400,000 years ago that essentially everyone accepts that fire was controlled by then. So the conservative view is that we started our control of fire then. The 800,000-year date recently published by Goren-Inbar and colleagues in *Science* (April, 2004) is perhaps the best evidence yet for an earlier date for fire. It's particularly nice support for the notion that control of fire must have started before we can see it, because around 800,000 years ago even less happened in human evolution than at 500,000 years ago. People rarely lived in caves before 400,000 years ago, so the remains of earlier campfires can't easily be found. But the more radical view, which seems right to

me, is that bits and pieces of archaeological evidence for control of fire at earlier dates, all the way back to 1.9 million years ago, are right. In other words, I believe our species started to control fire at 1.9 million years ago.

Then, the question is, what's the relationship between control of fire and cooking? Some people imagine a period when our ancestors had fire but ate raw food. But, once we had control of fire, I think that we would have started cooking very soon, maybe within a week, maybe within ten generations—but waiting 1,000 or 10,000 or 100,000 years? It's unthinkable. Modern primates, such as monkeys in captivity, allow foods to cook in fires before they take them out. It's obviously just not a big cognitive step from controlling fire to cooking.

So, if humans were cooking by 800,000 years ago, it seems likely that they had been cooking since 1.9 million years ago, because that's when our modern frame evolved. Basically nothing happened in human evolution between 1.9 million years and 800,000 years ago to suggest any improvement in the diet—certainly nothing as radical as being able to shift from raw to cooked food.

ET: *Who was the first cook?*
RW: It was not fully human. It was one of these prehuman hominids around the 2-million-years-ago mark, living somewhere in Africa, perhaps an australopithecine or a species like Homo ergaster [an early form of Homo erectus].

Whenever cooking evolved, we've got this problem of how on earth did the first cook manage to solve the problem of getting to use fire and controlling it rather than running away from it.

One fantasy that I enjoy is the notion that there was something like the chimera that we now see in western Turkey. In western Turkey you've got a mountain, Mount Olympus, where there were several holes in the ground, quite small, just a foot or two across, with fire coming out of them. This fire has been going for at least 2,700 years, judging by the fact that Homer recorded its presence.

To call it permanent fire is too exaggerated, perhaps, but it's said that an earthquake was a cause of some release of gas that's been seeping out ever since then and which has been burning all that time. There are several places around the world where you get little patches of permanent fire burning like this. So it doesn't seem unreasonable to imagine that there was some permanent fire in Africa somewhere.

We know that chimpanzees can learn to be happy with fire. Kanzi is a captive Bonobo (pygmy chimpanzee) who goes for walks with Sue Savage-Rumbaugh in the forests of Georgia (United States). When she asks him to go get firewood and to use matches to light a fire and then to cook up some sausages, he does so. These things are not that difficult for a species as big-brained as a chimpanzee.

So, it's relatively easy to imagine an australopithecine who keeps coming back, sees these flames roaring out of the ground, and starts playing with them. Then it wouldn't be long before they see what happens to one of the roots they have been eating when it is heated by the fire. That may not be the way it happened, but at least it gives a sense of the possibility of the transition. You don't have to be fully human, I think, to imagine that you could tame fire. So, if indeed you were prehuman and started being able to use fire, then

Photo courtesy of shutterstock

that knowledge could be passed on from generation to generation in the many, many years before these species would have actually been able to make fire.

ET: *How do you imagine they were cooking?*
RW: The cooking would have been very, very simple. Once you've got a campfire, then it's the way that people cook nowadays. In the bush the main plant food would be roots—African versions of carrots or potatoes often dug from the edge of swamps or lakes. Many would be tough and leathery, pretty nasty in the best of times, but improved enormously by being heated. You'd just rest these on the coals next to the dying flames. After twenty minutes and occasionally turning them, the roots change from something that is extremely fibrous into something that is a lot softer and easier to eat.

Very often the way that people eat meat is they throw a small animal on the flames and that singes the hair off. Then they cut it up. We know that at 1.9 million years they were capable of cutting meat up because there are cut marks [made by stone knives] on fossil animal bones that go back 2.5 million years. So they could have laid strips of meat onto sticks above the fire. Well, maybe it would have taken a little time before that happened. But it doesn't seem very difficult if they had already been cutting up meat for 500,000 years to imagine that they could put small chunks on the embers next to the fire or next to the flames themselves. And all you need to do is heat meat to 170° Fahrenheit, and it reduces enormously the problems that make meat so difficult to eat when it's raw, which is the toughness. Heat coagulates the collagen fibers that make meat tough and turns them brittle. Suddenly, you've got something that you can eat pretty quickly.

ET: *How did humans make the transition from cooking over an outdoor fire to hearths and then to earth ovens?*

RW: No one knows. I imagine that the way things started is that the first kind of controlled fire would be simply sticks on the flat earth. Then at some point you'd start digging a little pit and you might surround it with some stones that would protect it against the wind a little bit further, and maybe other ways I don't know about making the fire more efficient.

An earth oven is a little hole that has been dug in the ground. Hot stones are put into the hole, and the food that you want to cook is put in with those hot stones. Then you stop the hole with earth, and the heat from the stones combined with the moisture of the earth leads to a sort of steaming effect, and you get a rather nice, gentle, slow cooking. That's practiced nowadays in various parts of the world, such as New Guinea and India.

There are other complicated kinds of hearth arrangements in sites in southern Europe, for instance in France in Pech de l'Azé II, that go back 250,000 to 300,000 years. At the entrance you have one kind of hearth arrangement, rings of stones where probably there was some kind of lighting arrangement to scare off predators from coming into the cave. And then inside the cave, in addition to something like an earth oven, there was apparently a cooking area more than a yard across, indicated by flat stones whose red and black colors indicate repeated burning.

But to assume that earth ovens start very quickly seems to me to be an unnecessarily optimistic assumption. Earth ovens look like a pretty complicated kind of technical achievement. I had assumed that this was just a signal that cooking had been going on so long at the point that they had been able to devise various rather ingenious ways of making cooked food even nicer.

ET: *How did cooking affect the social structure?*
RW: I think the social structure is a really interesting question because this is in many ways the biggest gap in the way anybody has thought about cooking so far. Everyone's aware that cooking would have improved the quality of food, so it's not that big a deal to think about it affecting our energy and our teeth and so on. But there's been amazingly little thought given to this question of what cooking did to social structure.

My colleagues and I made the following argument in a paper that we wrote in 1999 that cooking lay at the base of human evolution: The huge problem that cooking presents is that it changes a species from feeding as it picks the food to forcing a species to keep its food for some time, which will be at least twenty minutes to probably several hours during the period when it is gathering it and going to cook it. That means for a period of time there is individual ownership, and once you have ownership, then there is the possibility of competition over those owned goods.

In other words, just as with any other animal where somebody gets a piece of food that is relatively valuable, others will try to pinch it. Female lions bring down the antelope; the male lion comes and takes it away. The low-ranking male chimp kills a monkey; the high-ranking chimp comes and takes it away. The female baboon digs for some roots; the male baboon watches, and just as she reaches to get the results of her labor, he says, "I'll take over, thank you." And in a similar way it seems impossible to imagine that when our ancestors first started cooking there wasn't pressure by which the hungry high-ranking individuals would not have taken advantage of the low-ranking individuals who had done all the hard work to get some meat or dig up the roots and get it cooked. And that problem seems to me to be really severe. We need to think about how we solved it.

ET: *How do you suppose humans solved this problem?*

RW: The human species is the only one, in all of the animals we know, in which there is a thing we call "sexual division of labor." I think it is a slight misnomer because it underestimates the extent to which there is a bias in favor of the male. It implies that the male and female are equal, doing equally well under the sexual division of labor. But women are always the ones that get to do the least favorite tasks, and women are the ones who predictably have to take responsibility for producing a meal in the evening.

Men are free to do what they want. A man can go off every day and hunt for three weeks and never get anything, and still he's going to get food, given to him by his wife in the form of a cooked meal when he returns in the evening. But if a woman goes off and tries to dig for food and never gets anything, she's in big trouble. A man knows that he can rely on a woman to produce food for him; a woman has nobody to rely on, she has to do it for herself.

So a woman is more like a chimpanzee, as it were: she is producing for herself, and then she has the problem of somebody who's taking some food away from her. A man is an entirely new species of animal, because a man is relying on others to feed him every evening. Now it's true that he will often produce foods that he will give to his wife, and the relationship can be beneficial. But some men don't. Some men are lousy producers, and they are still able to take advantage of the system. The problem is not so much why did men and women divide and then cooperate. We should be asking this question instead: "Why it is that men are able to get away without having to be responsible for their own food supply?"

ET: *Why aren't men responsible for their own food supply?*

RW: I put these two observations together: On the one hand, there's the fact that you know that there's going to be pressure to steal the food of low-ranking individuals. On the other hand, there's the fact that only in our species is there a sex that doesn't have to collect their own food every day. Among hunters and gatherers, men are able to get away with not feeding themselves. The solution is that males have developed a relationship with females in which they protect a female's food supply from everybody else in the community. And in exchange, she feeds him.

The way I imagine it working in the past was something like this. Around the ancient campfire you have females getting their own food. Then you find males who are coming back in the evening, having been unsuccessful in hunting or getting any other food. Maybe they were off chasing other women instead of trying to find honey. So now they've got nothing to eat, and they bully a female into giving them some of her food.

And that kind of social pressure creates a situation in which it pays every female to develop a friendly relationship with a male who will protect her from being bullied by a whole herd of males. Better to have one male to protect your food supply and predictably feed him, if he can keep everybody else off, than be a lone female who is exposed to the possibility of theft from many other individuals. The male is an effective protector of her food supply because he's part of a system of respect among males. In a sense, he pays other males to stay away because he's part of a food-getting system in which whenever he does get food, he shares it on a predictably culturally agreed equal basis with other males. So, all the males are in an arrangement whereby they agree not to interfere with each other, and the female is in a relationship with the male whereby he agrees to keep all the other males off. It seems to make sense.

ET: *How has cooking affected human life history—how fast we grow, for instance?*
RW: These are areas that still haven't been well explored. But of course one of the most dramatic things about human life history is the fact that we have children that are dependent. This is different from chimpanzees, for instance, where the infants are weaned at about the three- to five-year stage and then they're independent. The only way chimpanzees feed each other is through nursing.

Whereas with humans, the child is being fed until it's an early adolescent. Children make some contribution to the domestic work and food gathering and so on, but nevertheless, the net flow of energy is definitely from the parent to the child, not just until weaning but all the time until at least 10 to 12 years old. So, childhood (a period of economic dependency beyond weaning) is normally regarded as a special human feature.

And childhood is made possible by cooking, because a species that cooks can easily overproduce. A chimpanzee that spends six hours collecting and chewing her own food doesn't have time to collect extra food to give to her children. But a foraging woman can collect and cook enough food to feed her family. Instead of spending six hours a day eating, she spends only about one hour eating. That leaves enough time to gather and cook for others.

Then, earlier in the life span, for at least 20,000 years, babies have been given cooked mush so they can abandon nursing very early. The result is that the mother has less energetic strain on her body, so she's able to have a relatively quick interbirth interval of three to four years, whereas in chimpanzees it's more like five to six years. That is presumably because even though the women still have children with them, they're able to feed them by cooking and still get enough food themselves to return to a high rate of ovulation.

So, cooking gives us big families—dependent children, produced relatively quickly.

ET: *What effect does cooking have on the human mortality rate?*
RW: Well, it's very interesting that humans have a very low rate of mortality. If you compare humans and chimps, at every age humans are dying more slowly than chimpanzees. This is not because of predation, because most of the chimp populations have not been subject to predation. It's just something inherent about their bodies. The implication is that the immune system or other systems of defense are less effective in chimps than they are in humans. I don't want to suggest that this is well known, but I think it's an interesting speculation. Part of what's happening as humans are able to acquire more energy as a result of cooking and eating superior food may be that they're able to divert a proportion of that energy into the kinds of defenses that enable us to live a long time.

ET: *Are there problems with humans today eating too much or only meat?*
RW: Nowadays, people can eat a tremendous amount of meat because there's a lot of fat to go with it. But if you're eating meat from the wild, which has very little fat and is mostly protein, then there is a problem with getting rid of the urea that is produced by digestion of excess protein. Urea poisoning can result. So too much meat can definitely be bad for you.

Of course, people in rich countries eat too much of everything. Indeed, the irony is that although cooked food has been so important for human evolution, raw food might be one of the healthiest diets for today. A raw-food diet is possible in rich countries today because of our low level of physical activity, the high agricultural quality of foods that go into a modern raw-food diet, and the extensive processing that makes raw foods palatable and easily digested. Even so, it takes a tremendous amount of determination to stick to a raw-food diet, because you'll feel hungry so much of the time. If you can do it, however, you'll bring your caloric intake nicely down, and maybe you'll have the philosophical satisfaction of imagining what the lives of our prehuman ancestors were like in those distant days before cooking was invented.

■ WHAT?

1. Summarize the causal links that Wrangham lays out in his argument that mastering fire and using it to cook are what made humans who we are.
2. Wrangham uses a range of evidence—primary and secondary studies, empirical analysis, deductive and inductive reasoning—to convince his audiences of the radical change in the human species with the advent of cooking. Find examples of the different kinds of evidence Wrangham presents to support his claims and evaluate the strengths and weaknesses of his case.

■ WHAT ELSE? WHAT'S NEXT?

3. In his interview, Wrangham locates our evolution from ape to human in cooking and meat eating. Search online—either the Internet or the databases available through the library—for responses to Wrangham's ideas and to his book *Catching Fire: How Cooking Made Us Human.* What kind of reaction has Wrangham's book generated? Do any readers find his claims controversial? Explain your response.

■ WHO CARES?

4. Find the website for *Gastronomica,* the journal that published this interview with Wrangham. Study the site, thinking specifically about audience. Then, find a different publication—print or electronic— that you think would also be an appropriate fit for the Wrangham interview. Write a brief description of the publication you choose and an explanation of your reasoning.

Poet, novelist, and essayist Wendell Berry has spent much of his life thinking, writing, and teaching about American life in general and agricultural life in particular. Berry wrote the following essay in 1989, and as it makes clear, he is an eloquent and determined critic of farm and food policies that continue to move Americans further away from the land—literally and figuratively.

BEFORE YOU READ

Write a 250-word biography of Wendell Berry that you think will help you better understand the points he makes in this essay. Make sure you document the sources you use.

THE PLEASURES OF EATING Wendell Berry

Many times, after I have finished a lecture on the decline of American farm life, someone in the audience has asked, "What can city people do?"

"Eat responsibly," I have usually answered. Of course, I have tried to mean by that, but afterwards I have invariably felt there was more to be said able to say. Now I would like to attempt a better explanation.

I begin with the proposition that eating is an agricultural act. Eating drama of the food economy that begins with planting and birth. Most eaters no longer aware that this is true. They think of food as an agricultural product, perhaps, but they do not think of themselves as participants in agriculture. They think of themselves as "consumers." If they think beyond that, they recognize that they are passive consumers. They buy what they want—or what they have been persuaded to want—within the limits of what they can get. They pay, mostly without protest, what they are charged. And they mostly ignore certain critical questions about the quality and the cost of what they are sold: How fresh is it? How pure or clean is it, how free of dangerous chemicals? How far was it transported, and what did transportation add to the cost? How much did manufacturing or packaging or advertising add to the cost? When the food product has been manufactured or "processed" or "precooked," how has that affected its quality or price or nutritional value?

Most urban shoppers would tell you that food is produced on farms. But most of them do not know what farms, or what kinds of farms, or where the farms are, or what knowledge of skills are involved in farming. They apparently have little doubt that farms will continue to produce, but they do not know how or over what obstacles. For them, then, food is pretty much an abstract idea—something they do not know or imagine—until it appears on the grocery shelf or on the table.

The specialization of production induces specialization of consumption. Patrons of the entertainment industry, for example, entertain themselves less and less and have become more and more passively dependent on commercial suppliers. This is certainly true also of patrons of the food industry, who have tended more and more to be mere consumers—passive, uncritical, and dependent. Indeed, this sort of consumption may be said to be one of the chief goals of industrial production. The food industrialists have by now persuaded millions of consumers to prefer food that is already prepared. They will grow, deliver, and cook your food for you and (just like your mother) beg you to eat it. That they do not yet offer to insert it, prechewed, into our mouth is only because they have found no profitable way to do so. We may rest assured that they would be glad to find such a way. The ideal industrial food consumer would be strapped to a table with a tube running from the food factory directly into his or her stomach.

Perhaps I exaggerate, but not by much. The industrial eater is, in fact, one who does not know that eating is an agricultural act, who no longer knows or imagines the connections between eating and the land, and who is therefore necessarily passive and uncritical—in short, a victim. When food, in the minds of eaters, is no longer associated with farming and with the land, then the eaters are suffering a kind of cultural amnesia that is misleading and dangerous. The current version of the "dream home" of the future involves "effortless" shopping from a list of available goods on a television monitor and heating precooked food by remote control. Of course, this implies and depends on, a perfect ignorance of the history of the food that is consumed. It requires that the citizenry should give up their hereditary and sensible aversion to buying a pig in a poke. It wishes to make the selling of pigs in pokes an honorable and glamorous activity. The dreams in this dream home will perforce know nothing about the kind or quality of this food, or where it came from, or how it was produced and prepared, or what ingredients, additives, and residues it contains—unless, that is, the dreamer undertakes a close and constant study of the food industry, in which case he or she might as well wake up and play an active an responsible part in the economy of food.

There is, then, a politics of food that, like any politics, involves our freedom. We still (sometimes) remember that we cannot be free if our minds and voices are controlled by someone else. But we have neglected to understand that we cannot be free if our food and its sources are controlled by someone else. The condition of the passive consumer of food is not a democratic condition. One reason to eat responsibly is to live free.

But if there is a food politics, there are also a food esthetics and a food ethics, neither of which is dissociated from politics. Like industrial sex, industrial eating has become a degraded, poor, and paltry thing. Our kitchens and other eating places more and more resemble filling stations, as our homes more and more resemble motels. "Life is not very interesting," we seem to have decided. "Let its satisfactions be minimal, perfunctory, and fast." We hurry through our meals to go to work and hurry through our work in order to "recreate" ourselves in the evenings and on weekends and vacations. And then we hurry, with the greatest possible speed and noise and violence, through our recreation—for what? To eat the billionth hamburger at some fast-food joint hellbent on increasing the "quality" of our life? And all this is carried out in a remarkable obliviousness to the causes and effects, the possibilities and the purposes, of the life of the body in this world.

One will find this obliviousness represented in virgin purity in the advertisements of the food industry, in which food wears as much makeup as the actors. If one gained one's whole knowledge of food from these advertisements (as some presumably do), one would not know that the various edibles were ever living creatures, or that they all come from the soil, or that they were produced by work. The passive American consumer, sitting down to a meal of pre-prepared or fast food, confronts a platter covered with inert, anonymous substances that have been processed, dyed, breaded, sauced, gravied, ground, pulped, strained, blended, prettified, and sanitized beyond resemblance to any part of any creature that ever lived. The products of nature and agriculture have been made, to all appearances, the products of industry. Both eater and eaten are thus in exile from biological reality. And the result is a kind of solitude, unprecedented in human experience, in which the eater may think of eating as, first, a purely commercial transaction between him and a supplier and then as a purely appetitive transaction between him and his food.

And this peculiar specialization of the act of eating is, again, of obvious benefit to the food industry, which has good reasons to obscure the connection between food and farming. It would not do for the consumer to know that the hamburger she is eating came from a steer who spent much of his life standing deep in his own excrement in a feedlot, helping to pollute the local streams, or that the calf that yielded the veal cutlet on her plate spent its life in a box in which it did not have room to turn around. And, though her sympathy for the slaw might be less tender, she should not be encouraged to meditate on the hygienic and biological implications of mile-square fields of cabbage, for vegetables grown in huge monocultures are dependent on toxic chemicals—just as animals in close confinements are dependent on antibiotics and other drugs.

The consumer, that is to say, must be kept from discovering that, in the food industry—as in any other industry—the overriding concerns are not quality and health, but volume and price. For decades now the entire industrial food economy, from the large farms and feedlots to the chains of supermarkets and fast-food restaurants has been obsessed with volume. It has relentlessly increased scale in order to increase volume in order (probably) to reduce costs. But as scale increases, diversity declines; as diversity declines, so does health; as health declines, the dependence on drugs and chemicals necessarily increases. As capital replaces labor, it does so by substituting machines, drugs, and chemicals for human workers and for the natural health and fertility of the soil. The food is produced by any means or any shortcuts that will increase profits. And the business of the cosmeticians of advertising is to persuade the consumer that food so produced is good, tasty, healthful, and a guarantee of marital fidelity and long life.

It is possible, then, to be liberated from the husbandry and wifery of the old household food economy. But one can be thus liberated only by entering a trap (unless one sees ignorance and helplessness as the signs of privilege, as many people apparently do). The trap is the ideal of industrialism: a walled city surrounded by valves that let merchandise in but no consciousness out. How does one escape this trap? Only voluntarily, the same way that one went in: by restoring one's consciousness of what is involved in eating; by reclaiming responsibility for one's own part in the food economy. One might begin with the illuminating principle of Sir Albert Howard's *The Soil and Health*, that we should understand "the whole problem of health in soil, plant, animal, and man as one great subject." Eaters, that is, must understand that eating takes place inescapably in the world, that it is inescapably an agricultural act, and how we eat determines, to a considerable extent, how the world is used. This is a simple way of describing a relationship that is inexpressibly complex. To eat responsibly is to understand and enact, so far as we can, this complex relationship. What can one do? Here is a list, probably not definitive:

1. Participate in food production to the extent that you can. If you have a yard or even just a porch box or a pot in a sunny window, grow something to eat in it. Make a little compost of your kitchen scraps and use it for fertilizer. Only by growing some food for yourself can you become acquainted with the beautiful energy cycle that revolves from soil to seed to flower to fruit to food to offal to decay, and around again. You will be fully responsible for any food that you grow for yourself, and you will know all about it. You will appreciate it fully, having known it all its life.
2. Prepare your own food. This means reviving in your own mind and life the arts of kitchen and household. This should enable you to eat more cheaply, and it will give you a measure of "quality control": you will have some reliable knowledge of what has been added to the food you eat.
3. Learn the origins of the food you buy, and buy the food that is produced closest to your home. The idea that every locality should be, as much as possible, the source of its own food makes several kinds of sense. The locally produced food supply is the most secure, freshest, and the easiest for local consumers to know about and to influence.
4. Whenever possible, deal directly with a local farmer, gardener, or orchardist. All the reasons listed for the previous suggestion apply here. In addition, by such dealing you eliminate the whole pack of merchants, transporters, processors, packagers, and advertisers who thrive at the expense of both producers and consumers.
5. Learn, in self-defense, as much as you can of the economy and technology of industrial food production. What is added to the food that is not food, and what do you pay for those additions?
6. Learn what is involved in the best farming and gardening.
7. Learn as much as you can, by direct observation and experience if possible, of the life histories of the food species.

The last suggestion seems particularly important to me. Many people are now as much estranged from the lives of domestic plants and animals (except for flowers and dogs and cats) as they are from the lives of the wild ones. This is regrettable, for these domestic creatures are in diverse ways attractive; there is such pleasure in knowing them. And farming, animal husbandry, horticulture, and gardening, at their best, are complex and comely arts; there is much pleasure in knowing them, too.

It follows that there is great displeasure in knowing about a food economy that degrades and abuses those arts and those plants and animals and the soil from which they come. For anyone who does know something of the modern history of food, eating away from home can be a chore. My own inclination is to eat seafood instead of red meat or poultry when I am traveling. Though I am by no means a vegetarian, I dislike the thought that some animal has been made miserable in order to feed me. If I am going to eat meat, I want it to be from an animal that has lived a pleasant, uncrowded life outdoors, on bountiful pasture, with good water nearby and trees for shade. And I am getting almost as fussy about food plants. I like to eat vegetables and fruits that I know have lived happily and healthily in good soil, not the products of the huge, bechemicaled factory-fields that I have seen, for example, in the Central Valley of California. The industrial farm is said to have been patterned on the factory production line. In practice, it looks more like a concentration camp.

The pleasure of eating should be an extensive pleasure, not that of the mere gourmet. People who know the garden in which their vegetables have grown and know that the garden is healthy and remember the beauty of the growing plants, perhaps in the dewy first light of morning when gardens are at their best. Such a memory involves itself with the food and is one of the pleasures of eating. The knowledge of the good health of the garden relieves and frees and comforts the eater. The same goes for eating meat. The thought of the good pasture and of the calf contentedly grazing flavors the steak. Some, I know, will think of it as bloodthirsty or worse to eat a fellow creature you have known all its life. On the contrary, I think it means that you eat with understanding and with gratitude. A significant part of the pleasure of eating is in one's accurate consciousness of the lives and the world from which food comes. The pleasure of eating, then, may be the best available standard of our health. And this pleasure, I think, is pretty fully available to the urban consumer who will make the necessary effort.

I mentioned earlier the politics, esthetics, and ethics of food. But to speak of the pleasure of eating is to go beyond those categories. Eating with the fullest pleasure—pleasure, that is, that does not depend on ignorance—is perhaps the profoundest enactment of our connection with the world. In this pleasure we experience and celebrate our dependence and our gratitude, for we are living from mystery, from creatures we did not make and powers we cannot comprehend. When I think of the meaning of food, I always remember these lines by the poet William Carlos Williams, which seem to me merely honest:

> There is nothing to eat,
> seek it where you will,
> but the body of the Lord.
> The blessed plants
> and the sea, yield it
> to the imagination
> intact.

■ WHAT?

1. What does Berry mean when he encourages people to "eat responsibly"?
2. Berry's famous line "eating is an agricultural act" has become a battle cry for farmers and food activists around the world. How do you define "eating"? How else might the term be defined to reflect the politics of food?

■ WHAT ELSE? WHAT'S NEXT?

3. Working with a group of classmates, investigate and catalog the sources of the food served on the University of South Carolina campus—from dining halls to fast-food outlets. Some questions to keep in mind as you conduct your research: What companies supply the meals that are offered on campus? Where do they get the food to produce these meals? Does any of the food come from local resources (farms, ranches, or farmer's markets)? If not, why not? With your group, use your research findings to compose a report on the state of USC's food supply.
4. Berry describes "patrons of the food industry" as "passive, uncritical, and dependent" for their lack of active questioning and involvement in food production. Do you know where your food comes from? Interview one of your food providers—your school's food contractor, the manager or chef at a restaurant that you frequently visit, your grocery's produce or meat manager, or a farmer at a farmers' market—and trace the steps a particular food item goes through to make it to you. Where was the item grown, processed, handled? How was it grown? By whom? How and how far was it transported? What route did your food travel to get to you? When necessary, conduct online research to fill in any gaps.

■ WHO CARES?

5. Berry concludes his piece with a list of seven concrete actions readers can take to become more responsible eaters. Revise this list to target a dorm-dwelling, college-aged audience. Think about, for instance, how you might make these suggestions more realistic for a person living in a dorm with little to no kitchen or garden spaces.

© Peter Menzel / menzelphoto.com

IMAGE 5.2 shows the Revis family of North Carolina, one of many families featured in *Hungry Planet: What the World Eats* by Peter Menzel and Faith D'Aluisio, a 2005 book that presents a photographic study of what people around the world eat during the course of one week. The Revises spent $341.98 on their week's worth of food, compared with the $1.23 spent by the Aboubakar family of the Breidjing Camp in Chad (see page 279) and the $68.53 spent by the Ahmed family of Cairo, Egypt (see page 363). What are the rhetorical effects of viewing these images as a group? What arguments might the authors have been trying to make by collecting photographs like these from around the world?

Jessica B. Harris, a professor at the City University of New York, is the author
of 10 cookbooks that document the culture and food of the African diaspora.
This memoir was published in Gastropolis: Food and New York City, a 2009
collection about New Yorkers' relationships with food.

BEFORE YOU READ
*Many of the essays in this chapter speak, in one way or another, of the need for
Americans to return to the kitchen, to learn how to cook meals from scratch. Research
this issue to find out if there are any organized movements—in schools, churches, or
communities, for example—whose goal it is to teach Americans, especially children,
to cook. Be prepared to share your findings with the class.*

THE CULINARY SEASONS OF MY CHILDHOOD Jessica B. Harris

Few culinary traditions are as undocumented as those of middle-class African Americans.
Scroll back to the 1950s, when segregation was still rampant in the South, and the foodways
are even less well known. Although they are briefly mentioned in a few autobiographical
narratives and in some fiction, the concern of most African Americans was more than
throwing off the shackles of southern segregations that our forebears had come north to
escape. This is reflected in our life tales more than in our recollections of meals eaten and
foods purchased. The result is that most outsiders believe that ham hocks and hard times
are the only remnants of our culinary past. Certainly there were plenty of ham hocks and
no shortage of hard times. In fact, my New Jersey-born and-raised mother always claimed
that that state could best Mississippi in the racist sweepstakes and that she had the stories to
prove it! In North and South alike, middle-class African Americans ate the same cornbread
and fried chicken and chitterlings and foods from the traditions of the African diaspora
as did our less well-off counterparts, but we also ate differently, foods that expressed our
middle classness and reflected our social and political aspirations.

Even though chitterlings might be on the menu, they could equally likely be
accompanied by a mason jar of corn liquor or a crystal goblet of champagne. Southern
specialties like fried porgies and collard greens show up for dinner, but they might be
served along with dishes becoming common in an increasingly omnivorous United States
that was just beginning its love affair with food. Nowhere is this more evident than in my
own life and in the culinary season of my childhood.

A descendant of the enslaved and free Africans who made their way north in the Great
Migration, I grew up in a transplanted southern culture that still remains a vibrant region
of the African American culinary world. My family, like many others long separated from
the South, raised me in ways that continued their eating traditions, so now I can head south
and sop biscuits in gravy, suck chewy bits of fat from a pig's foot spattered with hot sauce,
and yes'm and no'm with the best of 'em.

But that's not all of me. I also am a postwar baby who was the only child of striving middle-class parents who were old enough to have been young African American adults in the poverty of the Great Depression. They showered me with love and childhood coddling that makes my childhood seem like an African American version of *The Little Princess*. I also am a child at the confluence of two major African American culinary traditions. My mother's family could claim a smidge of black southern aristocracy, as they were descended from free people of color who migrated to Roanoke, Virginia. My father's family was from Tennessee and had upcountry Georgia roots that extended down the Natchez Trace. Both families showed their backgrounds at the table.

My maternal grandmother, Bertha Philpot Jones, was the quintessential African American matriarch presiding over a groaning board filled with savory goods. The role has become a visual cliché in movies like *The Nutty Professor Part II: The Klumps, Soul Food*, and *Dear Departed*, which revel in the dysfunction of African American life. No such dysfunction, however, was tolerated at Grandma Jones's table; she would not allow it. She was the matriarch and absolute sovereign of the Jones family; she ruled with a delicate but steel-boned hand, and the family marched to her tune. Watermelon-rind pickles spiced with fragrant cinnamon and whole cloves and the reassuring warmth of a full oven wafting smells of roasted joints and freshly baked bread are the aromas I most associate with her. She was a Baptist minister's wife and could put a hurtin' on some food. She had to, for as the minister's wife, she had not only her own brood of twelve children plus husband to feed, but the church folks who dropped in to take care of as well. She pickled fruits like Seckel pears, which had a curiously tart-sweet taste that comes back to me even today. The smell of Parker House rolls, the warmth of the kitchen, and the closeness of a large family all were part of the thrill of Grandma Jones's house. I didn't see her often—only on holidays and special occasions when we'd take the Holland Tunnel to head off to Plainfield, New Jersey, to visit and sit around the table.

Ida Irene Harris, my paternal grandmother, was at the other end of the culinary spectrum. I saw her much more often, at least once a week. When I travel in the South, folks are astounded to hear that as a child I had no southern roots, no grandmother to visit by segregated train or bus under the tutelage of kindly porters and with a tag pinned to my coat. Instead, my South was in the North, for Grandma Harris, in her day-to-day existence, re-created the preserved-in-amber South of her nineteenth-century rural youth in the precincts of her small apartment in the South Jamaica projects. I remember her apartment well, particularly the kitchen, with the four-burner stove on which she made lye soap, the refrigerator that always contained a pitcher of grape Kool-Aid with lemons cut up in it, and the sink in which she washed clothes, punching them with a broomstick to make sure they would get clean. Most of all, I remember the taste of the collard greens that she prepared: verdant, lush with just enough smoked pig tarts and fat for seasoning; they were the culinary embodiment of her love and, along with her silky beaten biscuits, one of the few dishes that she made well.

Grandma Harris lived in a self-created southern world. For years, she maintained a small garden plot at the back of the South Jamaica projects. This was just after the victory gardens of World War II when tenants could plant a small plot of land if they wished. Grandma Harris grew southern staples: collard and mustard greens, peanuts, snap beans, and more. I remember her weeding the peanuts and breaking off a leaf of the greens to test for ripening as the Long Island Rail Road train roared by on the tracks above. She taught me to love the slip of boiled peanuts, to sop biscuits in Alaga syrup with butter cut up in it, and to savor the tart sourness of buttermilk long before there was any romance to things southern.

I didn't understand the education she'd given me until years later, in Senegal's Theatre Daniel Sorano, I heard a griot sing. It was as though Grandma Harris had leaned down from the clouds and touched me. The timbre, the tone, the almost keening wail of the Mandinka singer captured the tuneless songs that Grandma sang as she went about her daily tasks, as much as the tastes of the Senegalese food recalled flavors from my childhood. It was then that I realized that unknown to both of us, Grandma Harris had taught me the ways of the past in her demeanor, her stalwartness, her faith, and her food. Those ways would help me survive. She also taught me to behave. I will never forget the summer day when she administered the only childhood whipping I can recall.

"Whipping" was not a word that was used in my house as I was growing up. I was a Dr. Spock baby through and through, and discipline was more about firm conversation than about Daddy's belt. At Grandma Harris's apartment, though, the rules changed and that one time, I knew I was going to get a whipping for sure.

Grandma Harris was another kind of old-line southern matriarch. It didn't matter that she lived on the third floor of the South Jamaica projects in Queens; her world was deeply rooted in the traditions of her South. She would brook no contradiction about manners. In her home, New Year's was celebrated with a mix of collard, mustard, and turnip greens that she had stewed down to a low gravy to accompany the obligatory hoppin' John and chitterlings. I always passed on the chitterlings and ate the hoppin' John, but the greens were my favorite. I had even more respect for them after they caused my downfall and earned me my only childhood whipping.

It happened on a summer's day when I was about six or seven. My mother worked, so I was sent to Grandma's apartment to spend the day in the traditional, extended-family day-care arrangement. I spent most of those urban summer days of my early childhood in her small one-bedroom apartment reading in a chair and staying out from under her feet in order to avoid going outside to play with the other kids, who invariably made fun of my private-school vowels and bookish ways. She, on the other side, spent her days insisting that I go out and play with the "nice children" who all called her Mother Harris.

On the day in question, when I had managed to avoid the dreaded piss-smelling barrels and rough boys and girls of the playground, she looked up from her sewing and said, "Jessica, come here." I was in for it. I was pleasantly surprised when, instead of ordering me downstairs, she instead went for her purse and gave me some money wrapped in a hankie with instructions to go to Miranda's, the Italian-owned corner market, and get a piece of "streak-a-lean-streak-a-fat" for the greens that she was going to cook.

Thrilled at being sent on an errand and overjoyed at escaping the barrel torture, I headed off. The walk was short, only a scant block through the maze of red-brick buildings that had not yet deteriorated into the breeding ground of hopelessness they were to become. A few small trees were in leaf, and the sounds of other children playing reminded me how grown up I was. I was on an errand. Arriving at Miranda's, I went directly to the meat counter, where, as in most African American neighborhoods, there was a vast array of pig parts both identifiable and unknown. Having not a clue about streak-a-lean-streak-a-fat but feeling exceptionally sophisticated in my seven-year-old head, I pointed to the slab bacon that my mother used to season things and asked for the requisite amount. It was brought out for my examination, and I grandly pronounced it fine. Cut off to the desired thickness and wrapped in slick brown paper, it was presented to me with solemnity. I tucked it into the net shopping bag that Grandma had provided and headed back home, proud and pleased.

I pushed open the heavy downstairs door and ran up the concrete steps, heels clanking on the metal treads that lined them. When I got to 3B, I pushed through the door that Grandma always kept open in those kinder times and headed in to present my parcel. To my amazement, when she opened it, she began to mutter and ask me what I had gotten.

"Steak-a-lean-streak-a-fat," I replied.

"Did you ask for it?" she questioned.

"No, I pointed it out to the man," I ventured with increasing timidity.

"Well, this isn't it! I wanted what I asked for, streak-a-lean-streak-a-fat," she countered. "This is slab bacon!"

"It's the same thing, isn't it?" I queried.

"NO! Now you march right back there and get me what I asked for, streak-a-lean-streak-a-fat. Take this back!"

"But?"

"No Buts!" Just march back there, young lady! Right Now!"

I trudged back to Miranda's, each step made heavier with the thought of having to tell the butcher that I'd made an error and hoping that he'd take back the offending bacon. The joy of escape of the prior hour had soured into a longing for the nasty boys and the stinky barrels. Luckily, the man took pity on bourgie old me and took back the bacon, replacing it with a fattier piece of streaky pork that was a fraction of the price.

When I got back to the building, Grandma was sitting on the benches out front and waiting for me. She uttered the five words that I'd never heard her say: "Go cut me a switch."

Terrified, I set off and hunted for the smallest branch that I could find in this virtually treeless urban landscape, knowing what was coming next. I returned with a smallish green switch that I had unearthed lord knows where. She took a few halfhearted passes at my legs, solemnly repeating with each one, "Don't think you're smarter than your elders." Tears flowed on both sides: mine because I'd certainly learned my lesson through the humiliation of returning the bacon followed by the public whipping, Grandma's because she adored me and wanted a respectful granddaughter. Despite that childhood trauma, I still love collard greens and never eat my New Year's mess of them without remembering Grandma Harris. I always season them with what I have come to think of as streak-a-lean-streak-a-fat-cut-me-a-switch; savor their smoky, oily splendor; and think of the southern lessons she taught me with every bite.

The other days of my early summers were spent with my working parents. We left New York City for family vacations, and I can remember the ice man delivering big blocks of ice wrapped in burlap to chill the icebox of the small cabin that we rented on Three Mile Harbor Road in East Hampton long before the area attained its current vogue. The year after my whipping, when I was eight, we visited Oak Bluffs, Massachusetts, the African American summer community on Martha's Vineyard that has become much touted these days. It was love at first sight, and my parents bought a summer house there that winter.

From the time I was nine until the present, this house has been a part of every summer. Then we made long trips on the Boston Post Road and the Merritt Parkway up to the Wood's Hole ferry dock. Old habits die hard, and my parents in the 1950s would no more think of hitting the road without a shoebox full of fried chicken, deviled eggs, pound cake, oranges, and raisins and a thermos full of lemonade or some other cool drink that they would leave home without maps and a tank full of gas.

Oak Bluffs was just beginning to grow in popularity among New Yorkers; Bostonians knew about its glories long before we did. Middle-class African Americans from New York and New Jersey summered in Sag Harbor near the Hamptons, but my prescient father did not want to be so close to the city that friends could drop in unannounced on the weekends, so it was Martha's Vineyard for us. We joked that if we lost our way to the Vineyard, we could simply follow the trail of chicken bones left by fellow black New Yorkers and find the ferry pier with no problem. Like us, they were marked by segregated back doors and the lack of on-the-road facilities and also stuck to the old ways. We brought our chicken along for years until the Connecticut Turnpike was completed, and then we gradually left the chicken and deviled eggs at home and settled for the mediocre fare of the rest stops. I was thrilled several years ago when a friend, Alexander Smalls, opened a restaurant in Grand Central Terminal celebrating our traveling ways; it was called the Shoebox Café. While the menu was his own inventive interpretation of the black food of the South, I knew he was also honoring the past that many black Americans share.

My Vineyard summers were where I caught my first fish, a porgy of respectable size, and learned to strip the skin off an eel and find out just how delicious the sweet meat was, once you got over the snake look, and to pick mussels off the docks at Menemsha. The days were punctuated by sharing meals with family and friends, waiting for my father to appear on the Friday night "daddy boat" to spend the weekends, and savoring rainy days because my mother treated us with one of her fantastic blueberry cobblers prepared with berries we had picked before the storm came, from the bushes that grew wild along the roadside. July folded into August marked by county fairs, cotton candy, Illumination Night, Darling's molasses puff, swordfish at Giordano's restaurant, and movies at the Strand or Islander movie houses, accompanied by hot buttered popcorn served from a copper kettle. Soon it was time to pack the car again and head back to our house in Queens. I never really minded because autumn brought the return to school, and my world expanded one hundredfold. My school saw to that.

The United Nations International School was and is a special place. As the first non-UN-connected child to attend the school and one of very few Americans enrolled in the early years, my playmates were the world. UNIS, as the school is called by the cognoscenti, was small, then so small that it added a grade each year until it finally stretched from prekindergarten through high school. Inside Queens's Parkway Village apartments that had been transformed into classrooms, I made lifelong friends and learned how to function in a world that extended to the globe's four corners. A trip to Vasu's or Shikha's house brought smells of the Indian subcontinent, and on occasions when I was fortunate enough to be invited to birthday parties, there were tastes of rich spices and heady unknown flavors that would never have turned up on the table of my garlic-free household. The rich stews of central Europe were featured at Danuta's, and steak and kidney pie might turn up on the table at Eluned's. I can still feel the rasp of the embossed silver spoon-backs that were used on the table at Jennifer and Susan's house in Great Neck and remember their mother's wonderful way with shortbread with nostalgia that can still make my mouth water more than forty-five years later. The annual round of birthday parties was interrupted by school events like international potluck suppers. Parents brought dishes from around the globe, and students began culinary competitions like eating spaghetti with chopsticks in the days before Asian noodle bowls and the vast array of Italian pastas became common culinary currency.

As more Americans joined the school community, even they displayed amazing culinary inventiveness, and I remember being invited to a formal Coke-tail party at Anne's house, where we were served all manner of multihued nonalcoholic cocktails in delicate stemmed glassware complete with swizzle sticks, umbrella garnishes, and lots of maraschino cherries at a birthday fete that was every young girl's dream. All the class events seemed to center on international households of like-acting folk who proved to me at an early age that no matter what turned up on the table, it was to be savored and eaten with gusto.

During the twelve or so years that I attended UNIS, I grew to understand something about the world's food. My core group of friends spent many of those years together, and we became familiar with one another's households and foods and, with that growing knowledge, came to realize that the table was not only where we held our parties and our class fetes but also where we worked out our problems and got answers to questions about one another. With hindsight, I now realize that we achieved at our birthday tables and communal suppers the same détente and understanding that the parents of many of my friends worked so hard to attain at the tables at which they tried to bring peace to the world.

If my grandmothers' tables gave me a grounding in the African American past that is so much the bedrock of all that I do, and UNIS gave me an understanding of the food of the world, a palate that is open to tasting just about anything, and the knowledge that more friends are made around the table than just about anywhere else, my parents and our daily life completed the picture with the finishing touches.

I have saved my household for last, for it, more than any of the other outside influences, marked the season of my childhood eating. While I grew up at the confluence of two African American culinary traditions and lived in an international world at school, at home on Anderson Road in St. Albans, Queens, my surroundings were a wondrous combination of my parents' dueling culinary wills.

Very few African Americans are to the manor born; most of us have a past of want or need, if not for love, than for cash and the opportunities it can bring. My father, Jesse Brown Harris, was such a person. He was a black man and a striking one at that, aubergine-hued with the carriage of an emperor of Songhai. Early photos show him tall and slender, looking very proprietary about his little family of three. Daddy was not a numbers runner. Daddy was not a welfare ducker or an absentee father. Daddy was just Daddy, and the constancy of that statement and my lack of awareness that this was not the norm for all black children made me different.

As a teenager, Daddy had lived over the stables and worked as a Shabbas goy in Williamsburg, Brooklyn. Until the day he died, he was marked by a childhood of grinding poverty during which he had worn flour-bag suits to school and church, cadged coal at the railroad yard for heat, and picked dandelion leaves on the Fisk College campus for dinner. He was torn between the desire to overcome his past and provide differently for his family and the need to remember it with honor.

My father ate southern food whenever he could cajole my mother into preparing the hog maws or chitterlings that he adored. We even put a stove into the basement of our house so that the smell would not taint our living quarters. He would occasionally bring home cartons of buttermilk, which he would savor with squares of the flaky and hot cornbread that my mother baked at the drop of a hat. Sunday breakfast was his special time, and he would proudly sit at the head of the table and sop up his preferred mix of Karo dark with butter cut up in it with the hoecake that was off-limits to anyone else in the household.

He was the only one in his family of man children who did not and could not cook. My Uncle Bill, his older brother, gave me my first taste of rabbit stew, and my Uncle

Jim's spaghetti sauce was the stuff of family legend. Actually, my father cared little for food, but he loved restaurants and, with his increasing affluence, dined out with the best of them. In the early years, dining out meant heading to the local silver bullet diner near our house for specials like mashed potatoes with gravy and Salisbury steak or sauerbraten (the neighborhood was German before we moved in). The bakery on Linden Boulevard, the main shopping street, sold flaky butter cookies and gingerbread at Christmas. Later, when St. Albans became blacker, we would head to Sister's Southern Diner after church on Sundays, still dressed in our Sabbath finery, for down-home feasts of smothered pork chops and greens or stewed okra and fried fish in an orgy of southern feasting that Mommy did not have to cook. In later years, restaurants like the Brasserie, La Fonda del Sol, and the Four Seasons were where we celebrated birthdays and anniversaries. There, my father's duality surfaced, and he would order wine for the bucket or "spittoon," as we had baptized it in our family jargon, and crepes suzette or Caesar salad for the flamboyant tableside service, but we three secretly knew that all the while what he really wanted was a ham hock and some butterbeans to satisfy the tastes of his youth.

My mother, though, truly loved food and had amazing taste buds that could analyze the components of a dish with startling accuracy. She would then reproduce her version of it at home, to the delight of all. Trained as a dietician, my mother reveled in entertaining and entranced her friends with her culinary inventiveness. Decades later, she revealed that at school, she had been required to sit through classes on how to keep black people out of restaurants and was discouraged from doing anything with food demonstrations that would put her in public view. After a brief stint as a dietitian at Bennett College in North Carolina and an even briefer stay in domestic service as a private dietitian, she found that she did not enjoy the field. Instead, she put her talents to use at the supper table, and I grew up eating homemade applesauce and tea sandwiches of olives and cream cheese when my friends were chowing down Gerber's finest and processed cheese spread. Weeknights featured balanced meals like breaded veal cutlets with carrots and peas and a salad, alternating with sublime fried chicken and mashed potatoes or rice and always a green vegetable and salad, or string beans, potatoes, and ham ends slow cooked into what we called a New England boiled dinner.

Parties were the occasion for pulling out all the stops. My mother would prepare ribbon and pinwheel sandwiches from whole wheat bread, cream cheese, white bread, and strips of red and green bell pepper, long before the spectrum opened up to admit such hues as orange, purple, white, and even yellow! She created cabarets in the basement—persuading her friends to come as babies or in nightclothes, hiring calypso singers, serving drinks with small umbrellas, and devising smoking centerpieces with dry ice and punch bowls—and, each Sunday, presided over table overflowing with roasts and a multiplicity of vegetables.

My mother created magic in the kitchen and made cooking exciting and fun, with a trick for every dish and a sense of adventure at the stove. As her only child, I got the benefit of this knowledge and accompanied her in the kitchen almost from my birth. In later years, she began to tire of the kitchen, but eventually, she renewed her interest in things culinary and discovered the wonder of ingredients like confit of duck, fresh garlic, pimentos, and arugula. Ever curious, her life was a constant adventure. I did not learn to cook; I simply absorbed it in her kitchen, moving from high chair to small tasks to whole dishes and entire meals.

I am very much the product of all of this, and these seasons of my personal and yet very New York childhood gave me the foods of the world on my plate. For the first years of my life, my fork ranged throughout the world from the simple country food of Grandma Harris to the more elegant Virginia repasts of Grandma Jones and the dishes of the 1950s and 1960s that were, for me, the tastes of home. I also sampled fare from the globe's four corners at the homes of my international classmates and learned that no matter where our origins or our regionalisms, when we eat together and share the commensalisms of the table, we make ourselves and our worlds better. It has been said that we are what we eat. I certainly am, and in the many seasons of my New York youth, that included an amazing amount of mighty good food.

■ WHAT?

1. Though Harris has written a memoir essay, she does present an implicit argument about food. What is her claim? What kinds of support does she provide to persuade her audience to consider her way of thinking about food?

2. How does Harris use her family history to reject and correct common stereotypes about foods that African Americans eat? How does she use food to weave together the various threads of her family background?

3. Compare Harris's essay with one of the more explicit arguments in this chapter (Bittman's, for example, or Berry's or Salatin's). Which do you think is more effective as an argument? Why?

■ WHAT ELSE? WHAT'S NEXT?

4. Late in her essay, Harris writes: "My core group of friends … became familiar with one another's households and foods and, with that growing knowledge, came to realize that the table was not only where we held our parties and our class fetes but also where we worked out our problems and got answers to questions about one another." Research how others have written about the experience of preparing and sharing a meal with others. Find at least two sources that you like, summarize them, and explain why you think they are worth sharing with others.

■ WHO CARES?

5. What does Harris do, specifically, to connect with her readers and to make her own experiences relevant to others? Point to specific strategies and passages in the essay in your response.

Alice Waters, owner and founder of Chez Panisse Restaurant and Foundation in Berkeley, California, has championed local, organic food for more than thirty-eight years. She is introducing her ideas into public schools through Edible Education, a model garden and kitchen program. This essay was first published in the September 21, 2009 edition of The Nation.

BEFORE YOU READ

Use the "News" function on Google—or some other news-oriented search engine—to find out what Alice Waters has been up to lately. How does she show up in the news? What are others saying about her?

A HEALTHY CONSTITUTION Alice Waters

I was moved by the way Morgan Spurlock framed a narrow long-distance shot down the corridor of a Beckley, West Virginia, middle school in his outstanding 2004 film, *Super Size Me.* The film is about the toll that fast and processed food takes on all of us. Clearly visible in the background of this particular shot were dozens of students, many of whom were overweight.

Perhaps it should come as no surprise that Beckley's cafeteria offers only processed food, which is high in fat, sodium and sugar and of very little nutritional value.

Contrast this with the Central Alternative High School in Appleton, Wisconsin. The school serves troubled youth, but teachers, parents and administrators found a way to turn things around; and when they did, discipline problems dropped sharply. Their secret? Instead of the usual processed meals, the school cafeteria offers fresh, locally grown, low-fat, low-sugar alternatives. The healthier meals are delicious. The students love them. They perform better in class and don't get sick as often.

We are learning that when schools serve healthier meals, they solve serious educational and health-related problems. But what's missing from the national conversation about school lunch reform is the opportunity to use food to teach values that are central to democracy. Better food isn't just about test scores, health and discipline. It is about preparing students for the responsibilities of citizenship.

That's why we need to talk about edible education, not just school lunch reform. Edible education is a radical yet common-sense approach to teaching that integrates classroom instruction, school lunch, cooking and gardening into the studies of math, science, history and reading.

Edible education involves not only teaching children about where food comes from and how it is produced but giving them responsibilities in the school garden and kitchen. Students literally enjoy the fruits of their labor when the food they grow is served in healthy, delicious lunches that they can help prepare.

I learned this firsthand through the Chez Panisse Foundation—the organization I helped create to inspire a network of food activists around the world with edible education programs in their own communities. Here in Berkeley, I see children in our edible education program learn about responsibility, sharing and stewardship and become more connected to themselves and their peers. In the process, they come to embody the most important values of citizenship.

Listen to what one student named Charlotte has to say: "Next we went from the blue corn to the sweet corn and each picked an ear to grill. I must say it tasted really good, even without butter." Or Mati: "I think cleaning up is as important as eating. Cleaning up is sort of fun. And we can't just leave it for the teachers, because we made the mess." Or Jose: "I remember the first time I came to the kitchen. I was afraid to do anything. But then I realized, this is my kitchen. So then I started to enjoy it."

Charlotte, Mati and Jose are learning about so much more than lunch. They're learning that farmers depend on the land; we depend on farmers; and our nation depends on all of us. That cooperation with one another is necessary to nurture the community. And that, by setting the table for one another, we also take care of ourselves. School should be the place where we build democracy, not just by teaching about the Constitution but by becoming connected to our communities and the land in more meaningful ways.

In 1785, Thomas Jefferson declared that "Cultivators of the earth are the most valuable citizens. They are the most vigorous, the most independent, the most virtuous, and they are tied to their country and wedded to its liberty and interests by the most lasting bonds."

I believe he was right. The school cafeteria, kitchen and garden, like the town square, can and should be the place where we plant and nourish the values that guide our democracy. We need to join a delicious revolution that can reconnect our children to the table and to what it means to be a steward. This is the picture of a caring society, and this is the promise of edible education.

■ WHAT?

1. How, according to Waters, can food be used "to teach values that are central to democracy"? Why isn't this happening now?
2. Explain the link that Waters makes between healthy meals and learning. What kind of evidence does she offer to support these links? Do you think more evidence would have strengthened her argument?

■ WHAT ELSE? WHAT'S NEXT?

3. Are any schools in South Carolina serving what Waters would call "fresh, locally grown, low-fat, low-sugar" meals? Are any schools in the state involved in anything like the "edible education" program she describes?

■ WHO CARES?

4. Summarize Waters' argument for an audience of elementary school students in Richland School District 1 (in Columbia).

ANGELICA KITCHEN MENU

Many of the essays in this chapter—from "The Cooking Ape," to "The Culinary Seasons of My Childhood," to "Declare Your Independence"—are, in one way or another, about *dining in.* That is, they focus on the ways that food deeply connects with family, home, and individual identity.

Over the next few pages, you'll find a menu, from Angelica Kitchen, a restaurant in the East Village of New York City, that works to establish on a different kind of identity—one based on *dining out.* As you read the menu, think of it as more than just a list of food items from which to choose when you're hungry for lunch. Think of it instead as the textual representation of the restaurant itself.

A complete and effective menu is a sophisticated rhetorical document. It articulates the relationship the restaurant wants to establish with its guests, and it creates an ethos for the restaurant and the people who work there. As you read Angelica Kitchen's menu, consider what it says about the restaurant, its identity, its politics, and the experience it promises its guests. After the menu, you'll find research, invention, and writing prompts to help you accomplish this.

BEFORE YOU READ———————————————————————
Visit the restaurant's website, and spend some time examining the various links and other information.

Soups Starters & Sides

Miso Soup with wakame and tofu   cup 3.50 bowl 3.75

☼ Soup of the day   cup 3.50 bowl 4.25

Kombu Vegetable Bouillon   1.75
A warm invigorating cup of broth, rich in minerals, delicately
seasoned with ginger, sage & thyme

Soba Sensation   6.50
Rich, velvety sesame sauce ladled over soba noodles, topped
with pickled red cabbage garnish.

Curried Cashew Spread   4.75
An intriguing live blend of raw cashews, sprouted chickpeas,
freshly ground curry powder & unpasteurized miso.
Accompanied by crisp crudités.

Thai Mee Up   7.25
All Raw – delicate strands of daikon radish, zucchini
& carrot dressed with Thai tahini sauce, garnished with
garlic-lemon marinated kale.

Hummus   6.50
Served with baked zahtar pita wedges and crisp crudités.

☼ Norimaki   8.00
Six pieces of rolled vegetable sushi, served with wasabi,
pickled ginger & lemon-shoyu dipping sauce.
(ingredients vary daily)

Angelica Pickle Plate   4.25
Garlic pickled shiitakes, assorted seasonal pickled vegetables
& marinated beets.

Kimchee   3.25
Homemade, mild style, tangy fermented cabbage
with carrot, daikon & jalapeno pepper.

Ruby Kraut   2.75
Homemade red cabbage sauerkraut.

Walnut-Lentil Pâté   6.75
Topped with tofu sour cream, served with baked rice crackers
and crisp crudités.

Mashed Yukon Gold Potatoes   4.75
Served with brown rice gravy

Special Appetizer **Agrarian Salgado**   8.00
Baked rounds of mashed Yukon Gold potatoes and herbed seitan,
with a basil-walnut pesto center; topped with dill-tofu sour cream
& garnished with piquant marinated kale.

*Brazil's mass social movements are mobilizing forces to end hunger.
A portion of the proceeds from this appetizer goes to* FRIENDS OF THE
BRAZILIAN LANDLESS WORKERS MOVEMENT (MST) *to support their
implementation of agrarian reform and widespread development of
sustainable agriculture. Learn more by visiting* www.mstbrazil.org

---

Union Square farmer's market

FB

Beverages

Juices – Made to Order	
Carrot	5.00
Carrot/apple	5.00
Carrot/mixed vegetable	6.50
added fresh ginger	.35

Lemonade – Vibrant!   2.75
Hibiscus Cooler   2.75
   – Chilled hibiscus flower served with lime
Apple Cider – Chilled   2.75
Grain Coffee with Rice Dream   2.50
   grain coffee refill   1.25

Chai – Black tea, chai spices & soymilk;   2.75
sweetened with agave nectar
   chai tea refill   1.50

Green Tea   1.75
Kukicha Tea   Hot/Chilled   1.25/1.50
Mu 16 Tea   1.50
   first tea refill free

☼ See the Special Today page for today's selections

Angelica Kitchen

Entrees

☀ Daily Seasonal Specials
Descriptions of today's selections listed on overleaf.
À la carte 15.25   With choice of two Basics or cup of soup   17.50

Dashi and Noodles
Bowl of traditional Japanese broth made with shiitake mushrooms, kombu, fresh ginger & shoyu; served warm or cool over soba noodles. Adorned with chef's select garnishes.   small   8.50
large   10.50

Three Bean Chili
Piquant chili made with homemade seitan, kidney and pinto beans & lentils; slowly simmered with sun-dried tomatoes and a blend of chiles; topped with lime-jalapeño tofu sour cream. Served with fluffy Southern style cornbread & cucumber-red onion salsa.
wee   9.00
grand   11.50

Olé Man Seitan
Homemade seitan & roasted vegetable mix folded into a warm whole wheat tortilla; dressed with spicy traditional mole sauce (peanuts & chocolate), & lime-jalapeño tofu sour cream; garnished with pimento.   14.50

Thai Mee Up
An All Raw Entree - delicate strands of daikon radish, zucchini & carrot, on a bed of garlic-lemon marinated kale, dressed with Thai tahini sauce.   11.25

☀ Norimaki
Nine pieces of rolled vegetable sushi, served with wasabi, pickled ginger & lemon-shoyu dipping sauce *(ingredients vary daily)*   11.50

Sandwiches

Wrapsody
Seasonal selection of roasted vegetables, balsamic marinated beets, creamy hummus, dill pickles, sunflower sprouts & arugula, folded & wrapped in a soft whole wheat tortilla.   10.50

Sam or I Sandwich
Herbed baked tofu layered with marinated hiziki & arame, crisp grated daikon, ruby kraut, a smear of mellow sesame spread & lettuce. Served on choice of mixed grain or spelt bread.   8.75
Half a sandwich with simple salad or cup of soup & kukicha tea.   9.50

Marinated Tofu Sandwich
Lemon herbed baked tofu layered with roasted vegetables, a smear of basil-walnut pesto & lettuce. Served on choice of mixed grain or spelt bread.   8.75
Half a sandwich with simple salad or cup of soup & kukicha tea.   9.50

☀ See the Special Today page for today's selections

Salads

House
Assorted lettuces; sunflower sprouts; grated red & green cabbage, daikon, carrots and beets; topped with clover sprouts; served with your choice of dressing.   7.50

Roasted Vegetable Salad
A seasonal selection of roasted vegetables tossed with arugula in a balsamic vinaigrette. Garnished with garlic crostini spread with creamy hummus, & cherry tomatoes.   12.75

Sea Caesar
Crisp romaine lettuce tossed with creamy garlic dressing. Topped with seasoned sourdough croutons, a sprinkle of smoked dulse & nori strips.   8.75

Orchard
Mesclun lettuces, apple, toasted pecans, dried bing cherries & sourdough croutons; tossed in a rosemary vinaigrette.   9.25

Mixed Sprout
A refreshing toss of snow pea shoots, sunflower sprouts & seeds, and mint; mixed with cabbage, daikon & carrots in a cool mint vinaigrette. Adorned with toasted peanuts, onion sprouts & watercress.   8.75

Si Se Puede
Balsamic roasted cherry tomatoes & basil-olive marinated chickpeas, over local greens tossed with extra virgin olive oil, fresh squeezed lemon juice & coarse sea salt. Accompanied by garlic crostini topped with tofu ricotta & chives.   10.00

Well Cultured
Mélange of seasonal greens & watercress tossed with homemade kimchee, nori strips, toasted sesame seeds & extra virgin olive oil; garnish of radish slices.   8.75

Tempeh Reuben Sandwich (served warm)
Our version of this classic features baked marinated tempeh, seasoned with caraway & cumin, tofu Russian dressing, sauerkraut & lettuce. Served on choice of mixed grain or spelt bread.   8.75
Half a sandwich with simple salad or cup of soup & kukicha tea.   9.50

Hot Open Face Tempeh Sandwich
Slices of sourdough baguette topped with lightly marinated & baked tempeh, napped with savory mushroom gravy. Served on a bed of raw spinach, garnished with ruby kraut.   10.50
With a scoop of mashed potatoes   11.50

Angelica Kitchen

Dragon Bowls

Part of the Angelica Kitchen menu since day one, this special combination of Basics is named for the Chinese bowl in which it was originally served.
(one substitution only)

Dragon Bowl	13.00

Rice, beans, tofu, sea vegetables & steamed vegetables; served with your choice of dressing.

Dragon Bargain	18.00

A Dragon Bowl served with cup of soup and bread with spread.

Wee Dragon	9.00

A Dragon Bowl in half portion.

Wee Dragon Bargain	14.00

A half Dragon served with cup of soup and bread with spread.

Combo Bowls

Any combination of the Basics at right served with your choice of dressing

	choice of 2	7.25
	choice of 3	9.50
	choice of 4	11.00

Dressings & Sauces

House – Puree of tahini, scallions & parsley

Tangy Basil – Sweet & sour, oil free

Black Sesame – with wasabi, garlic & toasted sesame oil

Balsamic Vinaigrette – Balsamic vinegar, olive oil & mustard

Creamy Carrot – with ginger & dill

Brown Rice Gravy – Brown rice flour roux with a savory blend of herbs, spices & tamari

Refills are .95 on all dressings above

Soba Sensation Sauce – Rich, velvety sesame sauce	1.90
Sea Caesar Dressing – Creamy garlic dressing	1.90

Angelica Kitchen Organic Brittle

Ingredients: pumpkin seeds, sunflower seeds, sesame seeds, pecans, rice syrup, maple sugar, vanilla, sea salt.

Packaged To Go.

small 1.1 oz	2.75
large 3.2 oz	6.75

☀ See the Special Today page for today's selections

Picnic Plate

Select menu items, served cool, to mix & match.
*starred items available in larger à la carte portions elsewhere on menu.

3 items	7.75
4 items	9.50
5 items	11.50

Assorted Seasonal Pickled Vegetables* Baked Marinated Tofu
Walnut-Lentil Pâté* Today's Special Vegetable
Norimaki* *(two pieces)* Marinated Hiziki & Arame Salad
Simple Salad* Baked Marinated Tempeh
Hummus* Today's Salad Special*
Ruby Kraut* Live Curried Cashew Spread*
Kimchee* Garlic Lemon Marinated Kale

Basics

Served with your choice of dressing

Tofu	3.75
Tempeh	4.25
Beans	3.00
Sea Vegetables	4.25
Steamed Vegetables	4.00
Simple Salad	5.50
Soba Noodles	3.75
Rice	2.75
Millet	3.50
3 Grain Mix	3.75
(quinoa, teff & amaranth)	

Breads & Spreads

Angelica Cornbread	
Rustic, whole grain slice (wheat free)	2.00
Sourdough Bread	
Authentic tangy whole wheat slice	1.75
Southern Style Cornbread	
Generous square, light & fluffy (wheat)	3.25
Small Angelica Cornbread Loaf	7.50
Miso-Tahini Spread	
Rich & smooth	2.00
Ginger-Carrot Spread	
Light & bright	1.75
Onion Spread	
Sweet & savory	1.75

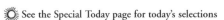

Angelica Kitchen

glossary

Agar
Marine algae used as a vegetarian gelling agent.

Amaranth
Tiny golden seeds, extraordinarily nutritious, amaranth was once the sacred food of the Aztecs. Cooked as a grain, it has the aroma of fresh corn & the crunch & appearance of blonde caviar. Higher than milk in protein & calcium.

Arame *(AHR-ah-may)*
Dark brown sea vegetable, thin & thread-like, with a mild, sweet taste; rich in iron, calcium & iodine.

Burdock
A slender root vegetable with a sweet, earthy flavor & a tender crisp texture. Acts as a blood purifier & is an excellent source of potassium

Daikon *(DI-kon)*
Large white radish; mild, pungent & crisp with remarkable medicinal qualities.

Dulse
Reddish purple sea vegetable, often an immediate favorite of those first tasting seaweed. High in iron & protein, our dulse is harvested from the coast of Maine.

Gomasio
A low sodium table condiment consisting of dry roasted, crushed sesame seeds & sea salt

Grain Coffee
Caffeine free beverage made from roasted barley, rye, chicory & roots

Hiziki *(hijiki)*
A dark brown sea vegetable with a strong flavor of the ocean. Resembling thin black spaghetti, hiziki is the most mineral rich of all foods & is considered by the Japanese as "esteemed beauty food"

Kamut *(Kah-MOOT)*
Heirloom durum wheat, plump, golden & high in protein & minerals. Many people allergic to common wheat find kamut easier to digest.

Kanten
Light, soothing gelled dessert made with apple cider, agar & fruit

Kombu
Wide, thick, dark green sea vegetable, very high in vitamins A & C as well as potassium & calcium. Useful as a natural flavor & health enhancer.

Kukicha Tea
A satisfying cup with body & deep flavor, made from the roasted twigs of the tea plant. A digestive aid, "twig tea" has less than one quarter of the caffeine content of black tea.

Millet
A gluten-free small yellow grain with a nutty flavor, easy to digest & having a rich amino acid profile, millet is among the earliest cultivated grains.

Mirin
Ambrosial cooking wine, naturally brewed & fermented from sweet brown rice.

Miso
A protein-rich fermented paste made from soybeans, sea salt, koji & a grain; sweet & light to deep & hearty in taste depending on the grain used & the aging time. An invaluable digestive aid, miso is also known for reducing the effects of environmental pollution.

Mu 16 Tea
A distinctive combination of 16 plants & herbs with a natural sweetness from licorice root. Delicate, full-bodied & caffeine free, Mu tea is good for relieving tiredness.

Nori
Thin black or dark green crisp sheets of dried sea vegetable, with a delicate nutlike flavor & a fresh sea essence. Remarkably, nori contains more vitamin A than carrots & is 35.6% protein.

Quinoa *(KEEN-wha)*
A staple of the ancient Incas, who called it the Mother Grain, quinoa is light & fluffy & the highest source of protein of any grain.

Sea Palm
Domestic brown sea vegetable, mildly sweet with a pleasing al dente texture. Helps reduce cholesterol & supports normal thyroid function.

Seitan *(SAY-tan)*
Made from whole wheat flour, seitan is concentrated wheat protein. Succulent & chewy, it takes on the flavor of other ingredients with which it is cooked. At Angelica's, we make our own here, fresh on the premises.

Shoyu
Fermented nutritious flavor enhancer made from whole soybeans, salt, water & wheat koji. Shoyu provides richer seasoning with less salt, containing 1/7 the amount of sodium as plain salt.

Soba
Tan Japanese noodles made of buckwheat or a blend of buckwheat & whole wheat.

Spelt
An ancient red wheat. People with sensitivities to wheat often have a better tolerance for spelt because it contains a unique form of gluten that is easier to digest.

Tahini
Smooth, creamy high-protein paste made from hulled ground sesame seeds.

Teff
Tiny grain with giant nutritional superiority. Having a pleasing nutty flavor, teff boasts 12% protein & is especially high in calcium & iron.

Tempeh
A traditional Indonesian soy food, exceptionally high in protein; made into a firm cake from soybeans, water & special culture. One of the plant kingdom's richest sources of vitamin B12.

Tofu
Soybean curd made from fresh soymilk, then pressed into blocks. Fresh Tofu in Pennsylvania produces Angelica's tofu from non-hybridized New York State organically grown soybeans.

Udon
A light flat Japanese wheat noodle.

Umeboshi *(Ume)*
Salty, refreshingly sour, pickled plums that stimulate the appetite & enhance digestion.

Wakame
Long thin green sea vegetable with sweet taste & delicate texture. High in calcium & rich in iodine.

Rebecca Wood's The New Whole Foods Encyclopedia has been a great resource in compiling this glossary.

We Happily Accept only cash

The Angelica Home Kitchen cookbook is available for purchase.

Gift Certificates Available

Gratuities will be added to parties of 6 or more.

www.angelicakitchen.com

*Illustration at left by Tom Donald   Inside illustrations by Flavia Bacarella
Cover photograph by John Bigelow Taylor*

Angelica Kitchen

WHAT ELSE? WHAT'S NEXT?

1. Working with a group of classmates, develop a new menu item for Angelica Kitchen. The item you propose should fit with the restaurant's overall image and food philosophy. (For example, it wouldn't make any sense to propose a rare fillet of beef, would it?) After you've decided on your dish, write an appropriate name and menu description, and think about how you would propose this to the restaurant's owner for inclusion on the menu. You might need to consult some cookbooks or websites to come up with your dish, but have some fun and be creative. Take this chance to fill a gap in a menu or to propose something you'd really like to eat.

2. Using Angelica Kitchen's home page, as well as other publications that have written about the restaurant (you can find these online), gather some background about the business. Use the information you've found to write a brief profile of the restaurant, remembering to properly cite your sources. As you conduct your research, consider the following questions:

   ■ How long has the restaurant been in business?

   ■ What kind of business model does the restaurant have?

   ■ What is the restaurant's mission?

   ■ What kinds of advertising does the restaurant use? What kinds of affiliated merchandise does it sell?

   ■ Who is the target demographic for the restaurant?

   ■ What kinds of notices has the restaurant received?

   ■ How does the restaurant seem to interact with its surrounding community?

3. Write a descriptive analysis of Angelica Kitchen's food and eating philosophy as it emerges from the menu's words, images, and document design. To generate ideas for your analysis, consider the following questions:

■ How would you describe the menu as a visual document? Think, for example, about typography, including font selection; the kind, use and placement of images; and the use of space. Consider how each of these elements works separately and how they come together as a whole to produce a rhetorical effect.

■ How is the menu organized? What kind of food narrative does it create?

■ How does the menu try to connect with its customers? Think about the level of formality, about diction—including the names given to items on the menu—and about appeals to the customers' emotions and intellect.

■ Based on reading the menu, what kind of dining experience would you expect if you went to this restaurant?

■ What is the restaurant's ethos? In other words, how does the restaurant want to be perceived by its customers? And what does the menu do to convey this business persona?

■ What is the restaurant's food philosophy or mission? Think about the actual food items the restaurant prepares and sells and about how the menu names and describes these items.

Robert Paarlberg is B.F. Johnson professor of political science at Wellesley College, an associate at Harvard University's Weatherhead Center for International Affairs, and author of Food Politics: What Everyone Needs to Know. *He wrote this essay for the May/June 2010 edition of* Foreign Policy *magazine.*

BEFORE YOU READ————————————————————————
Research how other writers and/or organizations define and enact "food politics." What does the term mean to you?

ATTENTION WHOLE FOOD SHOPPERS
Robert Paarlberg

From Whole Foods recyclable cloth bags to Michelle Obama's organic White House garden, modern eco-foodies are full of good intentions. We want to save the planet. Help local farmers. Fight climate change—and childhood obesity, too. But though it's certainly a good thing to be thinking about global welfare while chopping our certified organic onions, the hope that we can help others by changing our shopping and eating habits is being wildly oversold to Western consumers. Food has become an elite preoccupation in the West, ironically, just as the most effective ways to address hunger in poor countries have fallen out of fashion.

Helping the world's poor feed themselves is no longer the rallying cry it once was. Food may be today's cause célèbre, but in the pampered West, that means trendy causes like making food "sustainable"—in other words, organic, local, and slow. Appealing as that might sound, it is the wrong recipe for helping those who need it the most. Even our understanding of the global food problem is wrong these days, driven too much by the single issue of international prices. In April 2008, when the cost of rice for export had tripled in just six months and wheat reached its highest price in 28 years, a *New York Times* editorial branded this a "World Food Crisis." World Bank President Robert Zoellick warned that high food prices would be particularly damaging in poor countries, where "there is no margin for survival." Now that international rice prices are down 40 percent from their peak and wheat prices have fallen by more than half, we too quickly conclude that the crisis is over. Yet 850 million people in poor countries were chronically undernourished before the 2008 price spike, and the number is even larger now, thanks in part to last year's global recession. This is the real food crisis we face.

It turns out that food prices on the world market tell us very little about global hunger. International markets for food, like most other international markets, are used most heavily by the well-to-do, who are far from hungry. The majority of truly undernourished people—62 percent, according to the U.N. Food and Agriculture Organization—live in either Africa or South Asia, and most are small farmers or rural landless laborers living in the countryside of Africa and South Asia. They are significantly shielded from global price fluctuations both by the trade policies of their own governments and by poor roads and infrastructure. In Africa, more than 70 percent of rural households are cut off from the closest urban markets because, for instance, they live more than a 30-minute walk from the nearest all-weather road.

Poverty—caused by the low income productivity of farmers' labor—is the primary source of hunger in Africa, and the problem is only getting worse. The number of "food insecure" people in Africa (those consuming less than 2,100 calories a day) will increase 30 percent over the next decade without significant reforms, to 645 million, the U.S. Agriculture Department projects.

What's so tragic about this is that we know from experience how to fix the problem. Wherever the rural poor have gained access to improved roads, modern seeds, less expensive fertilizer, electrical power, and better schools and clinics, their productivity and their income have increased. But recent efforts to deliver such essentials have been undercut by deeply misguided (if sometimes well-meaning) advocacy against agricultural modernization and foreign aid.

In Europe and the United States, a new line of thinking has emerged in elite circles that opposes bringing improved seeds and fertilizers to traditional farmers and opposes linking those farmers more closely to international markets. Influential food writers, advocates, and celebrity restaurant owners are repeating the mantra that "sustainable food" in the future must be organic, local, and slow. But guess what: rural Africa already has such a system, and it doesn't work. Few smallholder farmers in Africa use any synthetic chemicals, so their food is *de facto* organic. High transportation costs force them to purchase and sell almost all of their food locally. And food preparation is painfully slow. The result is nothing to celebrate: average income levels of only $1 a day and a one-in-three chance of being malnourished.

If we are going to get serious about solving global hunger, we need to de-romanticize our view of pre-industrial food and farming. And that means learning to appreciate the modern, science-intensive, and highly capitalized agricultural system we've developed in the West. Without it, our food would be more expensive and less safe. In other words, a lot like the hunger-plagued rest of the world.

■ Original Sins

Thirty years ago, had someone asserted in a prominent journal or newspaper that the Green Revolution was a failure, he or she would have been quickly dismissed. Today the charge is surprisingly common. Celebrity author and eco-activist Vandana Shiva claims the Green Revolution has brought nothing to India except "indebted and discontented farmers." A 2002 meeting in Rome of 500 prominent international NGOs, including Friends of the Earth and Greenpeace, even blamed the Green Revolution for the rise in world hunger. Let's set the record straight.

The development and introduction of high-yielding wheat and rice seeds into poor countries, led by American scientist Norman Borlaug and others in the 1960s and '70s, paid huge dividends. In Asia these new seeds lifted tens of millions of small farmers out of desperate poverty and finally ended the threat of periodic famine. India, for instance, doubled its wheat production between 1964 and 1970 and was able to terminate all dependence on international food aid by 1975. As for indebted and discontented farmers, India's rural poverty rate fell from 60 percent to just 27 percent today. Dismissing these great achievements as a "myth" (the official view of Food First, a California-based organization that campaigns globally against agricultural modernization) is just silly.

It's true that the story of the Green Revolution is not everywhere a happy one. When powerful new farming technologies are introduced into deeply unjust rural social systems, the poor tend to lose out. In Latin America, where access to good agricultural land and credit has been narrowly controlled by traditional elites, the improved seeds made available by the Green Revolution increased income gaps. Absentee landlords in Central America, who previously allowed peasants to plant subsistence crops on underutilized land, pushed them off to sell or rent the land to commercial growers who could turn a profit using the new seeds. Many of the displaced rural poor became slum dwellers. Yet even in Latin America, the prevalence of hunger declined more than 50 percent between 1980 and 2005.

In Asia, the Green Revolution seeds performed just as well on small non-mechanized farms as on larger farms. Wherever small farmers had sufficient access to credit, they took up the new technology just as quickly as big farmers, which led to dramatic income gains and no increase in inequality or social friction. Even poor landless laborers gained, because more abundant crops meant more work at harvest time, increasing rural wages. In Asia, the Green Revolution was good for both agriculture and social justice.

And Africa? Africa has a relatively equitable and secure distribution of land, making it more like Asia than Latin America and increasing the chances that improvements in farm technology will help the poor. If Africa were to put greater resources into farm technology, irrigation, and rural roads, small farmers would benefit.

■ Organic Myths

There are other common objections to doing what is necessary to solve the real hunger crisis. Most revolve around caveats that purist critics raise regarding food systems in the United States and Western Europe. Yet such concerns, though well-intentioned, are often misinformed and counterproductive—especially when applied to the developing world.

Take industrial food systems, the current bugaboo of American food writers. Yes, they have many unappealing aspects, but without them food would be not only less abundant but also less safe. Traditional food systems lacking in reliable refrigeration and sanitary packaging are dangerous vectors for diseases. Surveys over the past several decades by the Centers for Disease Control and Prevention have found that the U.S. food supply became steadily safer over time, thanks in part to the introduction of industrial-scale technical improvements. Since 2000, the incidence of E. coli contamination in beef has fallen 45 percent. Today in the United States, most hospitalizations and fatalities from unsafe food come not from sales of contaminated products at supermarkets, but from the mishandling or improper preparation of food inside the home. Illness outbreaks from contaminated foods sold in stores still occur, but the fatalities are typically quite limited. A nationwide scare over unsafe spinach in 2006 triggered the virtual suspension of all fresh and bagged spinach sales, but only three known deaths were recorded. Incidents such as these command attention in part because they are now so rare. Food Inc. should be criticized for filling our plates with too many foods that are unhealthy, but not foods that are unsafe.

Where industrial-scale food technologies have not yet reached into the developing world, contaminated food remains a major risk. In Africa, where many foods are still purchased in open-air markets (often uninspected, unpackaged, unlabeled, unrefrigerated, unpasteurized, and unwashed), an estimated 700,000 people die every year from food- and water-borne diseases, compared with an estimated 5,000 in the United States.

Food grown organically—that is, without any synthetic nitrogen fertilizers or pesticides—is not an answer to the health and safety issues. *The American Journal of Clinical Nutrition* last year published a study of 162 scientific papers from the past 50 years on the health benefits of organically grown foods and found no nutritional advantage over conventionally grown foods. According to the Mayo Clinic, "No conclusive evidence shows that organic food is more nutritious than is conventionally grown food."

Health professionals also reject the claim that organic food is safer to eat due to lower pesticide residues. Food and Drug Administration surveys have revealed that the highest dietary exposures to pesticide residues on foods in the United States are so trivial (less than one one-thousandth of a level that would cause toxicity) that the safety gains from buying organic are insignificant. Pesticide exposures remain a serious problem in the developing world, where farm chemical use is not as well regulated, yet even there they are more an occupational risk for unprotected farmworkers than a residue risk for food consumers.

When it comes to protecting the environment, assessments of organic farming become more complex. Excess nitrogen fertilizer use on conventional farms in the United States has polluted rivers and created a "dead zone" in the Gulf of Mexico, but halting synthetic nitrogen fertilizer use entirely (as farmers must do in the United States to get organic certification from the Agriculture Department) would cause environmental problems far worse.

Here's why: Less than 1 percent of American cropland is under certified organic production. If the other 99 percent were to switch to organic and had to fertilize crops without any synthetic nitrogen fertilizer, that would require a lot more composted animal manure. To supply enough organic fertilizer, the U.S. cattle population would have to increase roughly fivefold. And because those animals would have to be raised organically on forage crops, much of the land in the lower 48 states would need to be converted to pasture. Organic field crops also have lower yields per hectare. If Europe tried to feed itself organically, it would need an additional 28 million hectares of cropland, equal to all of the remaining forest cover in France, Germany, Britain, and Denmark combined.

Mass deforestation probably isn't what organic advocates intend. The smart way to protect against nitrogen runoff is to reduce synthetic fertilizer applications with taxes, regulations, and cuts in farm subsidies, but not try to go all the way to zero as required by the official organic standard. Scaling up registered organic farming would be on balance harmful, not helpful, to the natural environment.

Not only is organic farming less friendly to the environment than assumed, but modern conventional farming is becoming significantly more sustainable. High-tech farming in rich countries today is far safer for the environment, per bushel of production, than it was in the 1960s, when Rachel Carson criticized the indiscriminate farm use of DDT in her environmental classic, *Silent Spring*. Thanks in part to Carson's devastating critique, that era's most damaging insecticides were banned and replaced by chemicals that could be applied in lower volume and were less persistent in the environment. Chemical use in American agriculture peaked soon thereafter, in 1973. This was a major victory for environmental advocacy.

And it was just the beginning of what has continued as a significant greening of modern farming in the United States. Soil erosion on farms dropped sharply in the 1970s with the introduction of "no-till" seed planting, an innovation that also reduced dependence on diesel fuel because fields no longer had to be plowed every spring. Farmers then began conserving water by moving to drip irrigation and by leveling their fields with lasers to minimize wasteful runoff. In the 1990s, GPS equipment was added to tractors, autosteering the machines in straighter paths and telling farmers exactly where they were in the field to within one square meter, allowing precise adjustments in chemical use. Infrared sensors were brought in to detect the greenness of the crop, telling a farmer exactly how much more (or less) nitrogen might be needed as the growing season went forward. To reduce wasteful nitrogen use, equipment was developed that can insert fertilizers into the ground at exactly the depth needed and in perfect rows, only where it will be taken up by the plant roots.

These "precision farming" techniques have significantly reduced the environmental footprint of modern agriculture relative to the quantity of food being produced. In 2008, the Organization for Economic Cooperation and Development published a review of the "environmental performance of agriculture" in the world's 30 most advanced industrial countries—those with the most highly capitalized and science-intensive farming systems. The results showed that between 1990 and 2004, food production in these countries continued to increase (by 5 percent in volume), yet adverse environmental impacts were reduced in every category. The land area taken up by farming declined 4 percent, soil erosion from both wind and water fell, gross greenhouse gas emissions from farming declined 3 percent, and excessive nitrogen fertilizer use fell 17 percent. Biodiversity also improved, as increased numbers of crop varieties and livestock breeds came into use.

■ Seeding the Future

Africa faces a food crisis, but it's not because the continent's population is growing faster than its potential to produce food, as vintage Malthusians such as environmental advocate Lester Brown and advocacy organizations such as Population Action International would have it. Food production in Africa is vastly less than the region's known potential, and that is why so many millions are going hungry there. African farmers still use almost no fertilizer; only 4 percent of cropland has been improved with irrigation; and most of the continent's cropped area is not planted with seeds improved through scientific plant breeding, so cereal yields are only a fraction of what they could be. Africa is failing to keep up with population growth not because it has exhausted its potential, but instead because too little has been invested in reaching that potential.

One reason for this failure has been sharply diminished assistance from international donors. When agricultural modernization went out of fashion among elites in the developed world beginning in the 1980s, development assistance to farming in poor countries collapsed. Per capita food production in Africa was declining during the 1980s and 1990s and the number of hungry people on the continent was doubling, but the U.S. response was to withdraw development assistance and simply ship more food aid to Africa. Food aid doesn't help farmers become more productive—and it can create long-term dependency. But in recent years, the dollar value of U.S. food aid to Africa has reached 20 times the dollar value of agricultural development assistance.

The alternative is right in front of us. Foreign assistance to support agricultural improvements has a strong record of success, when undertaken with purpose. In the 1960s, international assistance from the Rockefeller Foundation, the Ford Foundation, and donor governments led by the United States made Asia's original Green Revolution possible. U.S. assistance to India provided critical help in improving agricultural education, launching a successful agricultural extension service, and funding advanced degrees for Indian agricultural specialists at universities in the United States. The U.S. Agency for International Development, with the World Bank, helped finance fertilizer plants and infrastructure projects, including rural roads and irrigation. India could not have done this on its own—the country was on the brink of famine at the time and dangerously dependent on food aid. But instead of suffering a famine in 1975, as some naysayers had predicted, India that year celebrated a final and permanent end to its need for food aid.

Foreign assistance to farming has been a high-payoff investment everywhere, including Africa. The World Bank has documented average rates of return on investments in agricultural research in Africa of 35 percent a year, accompanied by significant reductions in poverty. Some research investments in African agriculture have brought rates of return estimated at 68 percent. Blind to these realities, the United States cut its assistance to agricultural research in Africa 77 percent between 1980 and 2006.

When it comes to Africa's growing hunger, governments in rich countries face a stark choice: They can decide to support a steady new infusion of financial and technical assistance to help local governments and farmers become more productive, or they can take a "worry later" approach and be forced to address hunger problems with increasingly expensive shipments of food aid. Development skeptics and farm modernization critics keep pushing us toward this unappealing second path. It's time for leaders with vision and political courage to push back.

■ WHAT?

1. Summarize Paarlberg's argument in 100 words.
2. What, according to Paarlberg, is the world's "real hunger crisis"? How can it be solved?
3. Read "Declare Your Independence" by Joel Salatin (it's the last essay in this chapter). After considering the arguments Paarlberg and Salatin make, develop a list of points that each author might use to respond to the other's central claim. Whose piece do you find the more persuasive? Why?

■ WHAT ELSE? WHAT'S NEXT?

4. Paarlberg throws his support behind industrial food production: "If we are going to get serious about solving global hunger, we need to de-romanticize our view of preindustrial food and farming." Find at least two other sources that embrace industrial food production and that offer what you think are sound reasons for their positions. Summarize these, and explain why you find them to be reliable sources.
5. Locate images from the book *Hungry Planet: What the World Eats* (you can find many of them online). Of these families pictured, who do you think eats local? Who eats organic? Which of the diets do you think is most nutritious? Which is the most environmentally sustainable? How do these images affect your reading of Paarlberg's essay?

■ WHO CARES?

6. Why do you think Paarlberg mentions Whole Foods in the title and first paragraph so prominently even though his piece isn't about the grocery chain? What might this rhetorical choice say about his intended audience?

Matthew Scully served as special assistant and deputy director of speechwriting to President George W. Bush and also wrote for vice presidents Dick Cheney and Dan Quayle. The author of Dominion: The Power of Man, the Suffering of Animals, and the Call to Mercy, *Scully wrote this essay for the May 23, 2005, issue of* The American Conservative *magazine.*

BEFORE YOU READ

Visit the website for The American Conservative *and, based on what you find there, characterize the audience that might have read Scully's essay.*

FEAR FACTORIES: THE CASE FOR COMPASSIONATE CONSERVATISM— FOR ANIMALS Matthew Scully

A few years ago I began a book about cruelty to animals and about factory farming in particular, problems that had been in the back of my mind for a long while. At the time I viewed factory farming as one of the lesser problems facing humanity—a small wrong on the grand scale of good and evil but too casually overlooked and too glibly excused.

This view changed as I acquainted myself with the details and saw a few typical farms up close. By the time I finished the book, I had come to view the abuses of industrial farming as a serious moral problem, a truly rotten business for good reason passed over in polite conversation. Little wrongs, when left unattended, can grow and spread to become grave wrongs, and precisely this had happened on our factory farms.

The result of these ruminations was *Dominion: The Power of Man, the Suffering of Animals, and the Call to Mercy.* And though my tome never quite hit the bestseller lists, there ought to be some special literary prize for a work highly recommended in both the *Wall Street Journal* and *Vegetarian Teen.* When you enjoy the accolades of PETA and *Policy Review,* Deepak Chopra and Gordon Liddy, Peter Singer and Charles Colson, you can at least take comfort in the diversity of your readership.

The book also provided an occasion for fellow conservatives to get beyond their dislike for particular animal-rights groups and to examine cruelty issues on the merits. Conservatives have a way of dismissing the subject, as if where animals are concerned nothing very serious could ever be at stake. And though it is not exactly true that liberals care more about these issues—you are no more likely to find reflections or exposés concerning cruelty in *The Nation* or *The New Republic* than in any journal of the Right— it is assumed that animal-protection causes are a project of the Left, and that the proper conservative position is to stand warily and firmly against them.

I had a hunch that the problem was largely one of presentation and that by applying their own principles to animal-welfare issues conservatives would find plenty of reasons to be appalled. More to the point, having acknowledged the problems of cruelty, we could then support reasonable remedies. Conservatives, after all, aren't shy about discoursing on moral standards or reluctant to translate the most basic of those standards into law. Setting aside the distracting rhetoric of animal rights, that's usually what these questions come down to: what moral standards should guide us in our treatment of animals, and when must those standards be applied in law?

Industrial livestock farming is among a whole range of animal-welfare concerns that extends from canned trophy-hunting to whaling to product testing on animals to all sorts of more obscure enterprises like the exotic-animal trade and the factory farming of bears in China for bile believed to hold medicinal and aphrodisiac powers. Surveying the various uses to which animals are put, some might be defensible, others abusive and unwarranted, and it's the job of any conservative who attends to the subject to figure out which are which. We don't need novel theories of rights to do this. The usual distinctions that conservatives draw between moderation and excess, freedom and license, moral goods and material goods, rightful power and the abuse of power, will all do just fine.

As it is, the subject hardly comes up at all among conservatives, and what commentary we do hear usually takes the form of ridicule directed at animal-rights groups. Often conservatives side instinctively with any animal-related industry and those involved, as if a thing is right just because someone can make money off it or as if our sympathies belong always with the men just because they are men.

I had an exchange once with an eminent conservative columnist on this subject. Conversation turned to my book and to factory farming. Holding his hands out in the "stop" gesture, he said, "I don't want to know." Granted, life on the factory farm is no one's favorite subject, but conservative writers often have to think about things that are disturbing or sad. In this case, we have an intellectually formidable fellow known to millions for his stern judgments on every matter of private morality and public policy. Yet nowhere in all his writings do I find any treatment of any cruelty issue, never mind that if you asked him he would surely agree that cruelty to animals is a cowardly and disgraceful sin.

And when the subject is cruelty to farmed animals—the moral standards being applied in a fundamental human enterprise—suddenly we're in forbidden territory and "I don't want to know" is the best he can do. But don't we have a responsibility to know? Maybe the whole subject could use his fine mind and his good heart.

As for the rights of animals, rights in general are best viewed in tangible terms, with a view to actual events and consequences. Take the case of a hunter in Texas named John Lockwood, who has just pioneered the online safari. At his canned-hunting ranch outside San Antonio, he's got a rifle attached to a camera and the camera wired up to the Internet, so that sportsmen going to Live-shot.com will actually be able to fire at baited animals by remote control from their computers. "If the customer were to wound the animal," explains the *San Antonio Express-News*, "a staff person on site could finish it off." The "trophy mounts" taken in these heroics will then be prepared and shipped to the client's door, and if it catches on Lockwood will be a rich man.

Very much like animal farming today, the hunting "industry" has seen a collapse in ethical standards, and only in such an atmosphere could Lockwood have found inspiration for this latest innovation—denying wild animals the last shred of respect. Under the laws of Texas and other states, Lockwood and others in his business use all sorts of methods once viewed as shameful: baits, blinds, fences to trap hunted animals in ranches that advertise a "100-percent-guaranteed kill." Affluent hunters like to unwind by shooting cage-reared pheasants, ducks, and other birds, firing away as the fowl of the air are released before them like skeet, with no limit on the day's kill. Hunting supply stores are filled with lures, infrared lights, high-tech scopes, and other gadgetry to make every man a marksman.

Lockwood doesn't hear anyone protesting those methods, except for a few of those nutty activist types. Why shouldn't he be able to offer paying customers this new hunting experience as well? It is like asking a smut-peddler to please have the decency to keep children out of it. Lockwood is just one step ahead of the rest, and there is no standard of honor left to stop him.

First impressions are usually correct in questions of cruelty to animals, and here most of us would agree that Live-shot.com does not show our fellow man at his best. We would say that the whole thing is a little tawdry and even depraved, that the creatures Lockwood has "in stock" are not just commodities. We would say that these animals deserve better than the fate he has in store for them.

As is invariably the case in animal-rights issues, what we're really looking for are safeguards against cruel and presumptuous people. We are trying to hold people to their obligations, people who could spare us the trouble if only they would recognize a few limits on their own conduct.

Conservatives like the sound of "obligation" here, and those who reviewed *Dominion* were relieved to find me arguing more from this angle than from any notion of rights. "What the PETA crowd doesn't understand," Jonah Goldberg wrote, "or what it deliberately confuses, is that human compassion toward animals is an obligation of humans, not an entitlement for animals." Another commentator put the point in religious terms: "[W]e have a moral duty to respect the animal world as God's handiwork, treating animals with 'the mercy of our Maker' ... But mercy and respect for animals are completely different from rights for animals—and we should never confuse the two." Both writers confessed they were troubled by factory farming and concluded with the uplifting thought that we could all profit from further reflection on our obligation of kindness to farm animals.

The only problem with this insistence on obligation is that after a while it begins to sounds like a hedge against actually being held to that obligation. It leaves us with a high-minded attitude but no accountability, free to act on our obligations or to ignore them without consequences, personally opposed to cruelty but unwilling to impose that view on others.

Treating animals decently is like most obligations we face, somewhere between the most and the least important, a modest but essential requirement to living with integrity. And it's not a good sign when arguments are constantly turned to precisely how much is mandatory and how much, therefore, we can manage to avoid.

If one is using the word "obligation" seriously, moreover, then there is no practical difference between an obligation on our end not to mistreat animals and an entitlement on their end not to be mistreated by us. Either way, we are required to do and not do the same things. And either way, somewhere down the logical line, the entitlement would have to arise from a recognition of the inherent dignity of a living creature. The moral standing of our fellow creatures may be humble, but it is absolute and not something within our power to confer or withhold. All creatures sing their Creator's praises, as this truth is variously expressed in the Bible, and are dear to Him for their own sakes.

A certain moral relativism runs through the arguments of those hostile or indifferent to animal welfare—as if animals can be of value only for our sake, as utility or preference decrees. In practice, this outlook leaves each person to decide for himself when animals rate moral concern. It even allows us to accept or reject such knowable facts about animals as their cognitive and emotional capacities, their conscious experience of pain and happiness.

Elsewhere in contemporary debates, conservatives meet the foe of moral relativism by pointing out that, like it or not, we are all dealing with the same set of physiological realities and moral truths. We don't each get to decide the facts of science on a situational basis. We do not each go about bestowing moral value upon things as it pleases us at the moment. Of course, we do not decide moral truth at all: we discern it. Human beings in their moral progress learn to appraise things correctly, using reasoned moral judgment to perceive a prior order not of our devising.

C.S. Lewis in *The Abolition of Man* calls this "the doctrine of objective value, the belief that certain attitudes are really true, and others really false, to the kind of thing the universe is and the kind of things we are." Such words as honor, piety, esteem, and empathy do not merely describe subjective states of mind, Lewis reminds us, but speak to objective qualities in the world beyond that merit those attitudes in us. "[T]o call children delightful or old men venerable," he writes, "is not simply to record a psychological fact about our own parental or filial emotions at the moment, but to recognize a quality which demands a certain response from us whether we make it or not."

This applies to questions of cruelty as well. A kindly attitude toward animals is not a subjective sentiment; it is the correct moral response to the objective value of a fellow creature. Here, too, rational and virtuous conduct consists in giving things their due and in doing so consistently. If one animal's pain—say, that of one's pet—is real and deserving of sympathy, then the pain of essentially identical animals is also meaningful, no matter what conventional distinctions we have made to narrow the scope of our sympathy. If it is wrong to whip a dog or starve a horse or bait bears for sport or grossly abuse farm animals, it is wrong for all people in every place.

The problem with moral relativism is that it leads to capriciousness and the despotic use of power. And the critical distinction here is not between human obligations and animal rights, but rather between obligations of charity and obligations of justice.

Active kindness to animals falls into the former category. If you take in strays or help injured wildlife or donate to animal charities, those are fine things to do, but no one says you should be compelled to do them. Refraining from cruelty to animals is a different matter, an obligation of justice not for us each to weigh for ourselves. It is not simply unkind behavior, it is unjust behavior, and the prohibition against it is non-negotiable. Proverbs reminds us of this—"a righteous man regardeth the life of his beast, but the tender mercies of the wicked are cruel"—and the laws of America and of every other advanced nation now recognize the wrongfulness of such conduct with our cruelty statutes. Often applying felony-level penalties to protect certain domestic animals, these state and federal statutes declare that even though your animal may elsewhere in the law be defined as your property, there are certain things you may not do to that creature, and if you are found harming or neglecting the animal, you will answer for your conduct in a court of justice.

There are various reasons the state has an interest in forbidding cruelty, one of which is that cruelty is degrading to human beings. The problem is that many thinkers on this subject have strained to find indirect reasons to explain why cruelty is wrong and thereby to force animal cruelty into the category of the victimless crime. The most common of these explanations asks us to believe that acts of cruelty matter only because the cruel person does moral injury to himself or sullies his character—as if the man is our sole concern and the cruelly treated animal is entirely incidental.

Once again, the best test of theory is a real-life example. In 2002, Judge Alan Glenn of Tennessee's Court of Criminal Appeals heard the case of a married couple named Johnson, who had been found guilty of cruelty to 350 dogs lying sick, starving, or dead in their puppy-mill kennel—a scene videotaped by police. Here is Judge Glenn's response to their supplications for mercy:

> The victims of this crime were animals that could not speak up to the unbelievable conduct of Judy Fay Johnson and Stanley Paul Johnson that they suffered. Several of the dogs have died and most had physical problems such as intestinal worms, mange, eye problems, dental problems and emotional problems and socialization problems ... . Watching this video of the conditions that these dogs were subjected to was one of the most deplorable things this Court has observed. ...
>
> [T]his Court finds that probation would not serve the ends of justice, nor be in the best interest of the public, nor would this have a deterrent effect for such gross behavior. ... The victims were particularly vulnerable. You treated the victims with exceptional cruelty. ...
>
> There are those who would argue that you should be confined in a house trailer with no ventilation or in a cell three-by-seven with eight or ten other inmates with no plumbing, no exercise and no opportunity to feel the sun or smell fresh air. However, the courts of this land have held that such treatment is cruel and inhuman, and it is. You will not be treated in the same way that you treated these helpless animals that you abused to make a dollar.

Only in abstract debates of moral or legal theory would anyone quarrel with Judge Glenn's description of the animals as "victims" or deny that they were entitled to be treated better. Whether we call this a "right" matters little, least of all to the dogs, since the only right that any animal could possibly exercise is the right to be free from human abuse, neglect, or, in a fine old term of law, other "malicious mischief." What matters most is that prohibitions against human cruelty be hard and binding. The sullied souls of the Johnsons are for the Johnsons to worry about. The business of justice is to punish their offense and to protect the creatures from human wrongdoing. And in the end, just as in other matters of morality and justice, the interests of man are served by doing the right thing for its own sake.

There is only one reason for condemning cruelty that doesn't beg the question of exactly why cruelty is a wrong, a vice, or bad for our character: that the act of cruelty is an intrinsic evil. Animals cruelly dealt with are not just things, not just an irrelevant detail in some self-centered moral drama of our own. They matter in their own right, as they matter to their Creator, and the wrongs of cruelty are wrongs done to them. As *The Catholic Encyclopedia* puts this point, there is a "direct and essential sinfulness of cruelty to the animal world, irrespective of the results of such conduct on the character of those who practice it."

Our cruelty statutes are a good and natural development in Western law, codifying the claims of animals against human wrongdoing, and, with the wisdom of men like Judge Glenn, asserting those claims on their behalf. Such statutes, however, address mostly random or wanton acts of cruelty. And the persistent animal-welfare questions of our day center on institutional cruelties—on the vast and systematic mistreatment of animals that most of us never see.

Having conceded the crucial point that some animals rate our moral concern and legal protection, informed conscience turns naturally to other animals—creatures entirely comparable in their awareness, feeling, and capacity for suffering. A dog is not the moral equal of a human being, but a dog is definitely the moral equal of a pig, and it's only human caprice and economic convenience that say otherwise. We have the problem that these essentially similar creatures are treated in dramatically different ways, unjustified even by the very different purposes we have assigned to them. Our pets are accorded certain protections from cruelty, while the nameless creatures in our factory farms are hardly treated like animals at all. The challenge is one of consistency, of treating moral equals equally, and living according to fair and rational standards of conduct.

Whatever terminology we settle on, after all the finer philosophical points have been hashed over, the aim of the exercise is to prohibit wrongdoing. All rights, in practice, are protections against human wrongdoing, and here too the point is to arrive at clear and consistent legal boundaries on the things that one may or may not do to animals, so that every man is not left to be the judge in his own case.

More than obligation, moderation, ordered liberty, or any of the other lofty ideals we hold, what should attune conservatives to all the problems of animal cruelty—and especially to the modern factory farm—is our worldly side. The great virtue of conservatism is that it begins with a realistic assessment of human motivations. We know man as he is, not only the rational creature but also, as Socrates told us, the rationalizing creature, with a knack for finding an angle, an excuse, and a euphemism. Whether it's the pornographer who thinks himself a free-speech champion or the abortionist who looks in the mirror and sees a reproductive health-care services provider, conservatives are familiar with the type.

So we should not be all that surprised when told that these very same capacities are often at work in the things that people do to animals—and all the more so in our $125 billion a year livestock industry. The human mind, especially when there is money to be had, can manufacture grand excuses for the exploitation of other human beings. How much easier it is for people to excuse the wrongs done to lowly animals.

Where animals are concerned, there is no practice or industry so low that someone, somewhere, cannot produce a high-sounding reason for it. The sorriest little miscreant who shoots an elephant, lying in wait by the water hole in some canned-hunting operation, is just "harvesting resources," doing his bit for "conservation." The swarms of government-subsidized Canadian seal hunters slaughtering tens of thousands of newborn pups—hacking to death these unoffending creatures, even in sight of their mothers—offer themselves as the brave and independent bearers of tradition. With the same sanctimony and deep dishonesty, factory-farm corporations like Smithfield Foods, ConAgra, and Tyson Foods still cling to countrified brand names for their labels—Clear Run Farms, Murphy Family

Farms, Happy Valley—to convince us and no doubt themselves, too, that they are engaged in something essential, wholesome, and honorable.

Yet when corporate farmers need barbed wire around their Family Farms and Happy Valleys and laws to prohibit outsiders from taking photographs (as is the case in two states) and still other laws to exempt farm animals from the definition of "animals" as covered in federal and state cruelty statutes, something is amiss. And if conservatives do nothing else about any other animal issue, we should attend at least to the factory farms, where the suffering is immense and we are all asked to be complicit.

If we are going to have our meats and other animal products, there are natural costs to obtaining them, defined by the duties of animal husbandry and of veterinary ethics. Factory farming came about when resourceful men figured out ways of getting around those natural costs, applying new technologies to raise animals in conditions that would otherwise kill them by deprivation and disease. With no laws to stop it, moral concern surrendered entirely to economic calculation, leaving no limit to the punishments that factory farmers could inflict to keep costs down and profits up. Corporate farmers hardly speak anymore of "raising" animals, with the modicum of personal care that word implies. Animals are "grown" now, like so many crops. Barns somewhere along the way became "intensive confinement facilities" and the inhabitants mere "production units."

The result is a world in which billions of birds, cows, pigs, and other creatures are locked away, enduring miseries they do not deserve, for our convenience and pleasure. We belittle the activists with their radical agenda, scarcely noticing the radical cruelty they seek to redress.

At the Smithfield mass-confinement hog farms I toured in North Carolina, the visitor is greeted by a bedlam of squealing, chain rattling, and horrible roaring. To maximize the use of space and minimize the need for care, the creatures are encased row after row, 400 to 500 pound mammals trapped without relief inside iron crates seven feet long and 22 inches wide. They chew maniacally on bars and chains, as foraging animals will do when denied straw, or engage in stereotypical nest-building with the straw that isn't there, or else just lie there like broken beings. The spirit of the place would be familiar to police who raided that Tennessee puppy-mill run by Stanley and Judy Johnson, only instead of 350 tortured animals, millions—and the law prohibits none of it.

Efforts to outlaw the gestation crate have been dismissed by various conservative critics as "silly," "comical," "ridiculous." It doesn't seem that way up close. The smallest scraps of human charity—a bit of maternal care, room to roam outdoors, straw to lie on—have long since been taken away as costly luxuries, and so the pigs know the feel only of concrete and metal. They lie covered in their own urine and excrement, with broken legs from trying to escape or just to turn, covered with festering sores, tumors, ulcers, lesions, or what my guide shrugged off as the routine "pus pockets."

C.S. Lewis's description of animal pain—"begun by Satan's malice and perpetrated by man's desertion of his post"—has literal truth in our factory farms because they basically run themselves through the wonders of automation, and the owners are off in spacious corporate offices reviewing their spreadsheets. Rarely are the creatures' afflictions examined by a vet or even noticed by the migrant laborers charged with their care, unless of course some ailment threatens production—meaning who cares about a lousy ulcer or broken leg, as long as we're still getting the piglets?

Kept alive in these conditions only by antibiotics, hormones, laxatives, and other additives mixed into their machine-fed swill, the sows leave their crates only to be driven or dragged into other crates, just as small, to bring forth their piglets. Then it's back to the gestation crate for another four months, and so on back and forth until after seven or eight pregnancies they finally expire from the punishment of it or else are culled with a club or bolt-gun.

As you can see at www.factoryfarming.com/gallery.htm, industrial livestock farming operates on an economy of scale, presupposing a steady attrition rate. The usual comforting rejoinder we hear—that it's in the interest of farmers to take good care of their animals—is false. Each day, in every confinement farm in America, you will find cull pens littered with dead or dying creatures discarded like trash.

For the piglets, it's a regimen of teeth cutting, tail docking (performed with pliers, to heighten the pain of tail chewing and so deter this natural response to mass confinement), and other mutilations. After five or six months trapped in one of the grim warehouses that now pass for barns, they're trucked off, 355,000 pigs every day in the life of America, for processing at a furious pace of thousands per hour by migrants who use earplugs to muffle the screams. All of these creatures, and billions more across the earth, go to their deaths knowing nothing of life, and nothing of man, except the foul, tortured existence of the factory farm, having never even been outdoors.

But not to worry, as a Smithfield Foods executive assured me, "They love it." It's all "for their own good." It is a voice conservatives should instantly recognize, as we do when it tells us that the fetus feels nothing. Everything about the picture shows bad faith, moral sloth, and endless excuse-making, all readily answered by conservative arguments.

We are told "they're just pigs" or cows or chickens or whatever and that only urbanites worry about such things, estranged as they are from the realities of rural life. Actually, all of factory farming proceeds by a massive denial of reality—the reality that pigs and other animals are not just production units to be endlessly exploited but living creatures with natures and needs. The very modesty of those needs—their humble desires for straw, soil, sunshine—is the gravest indictment of the men who deny them.

Conservatives are supposed to revere tradition. Factory farming has no traditions, no rules, no codes of honor, no little decencies to spare for a fellow creature. The whole thing is an abandonment of rural values and a betrayal of honorable animal husbandry—to say nothing of veterinary medicine, with its sworn oath to "protect animal health" and to "relieve animal suffering."

Likewise, we are told to look away and think about more serious things. Human beings simply have far bigger problems to worry about than the well being of farm animals, and surely all of this zeal would be better directed at causes of human welfare.

You wouldn't think that men who are unwilling to grant even a few extra inches in cage space, so that a pig can turn around, would be in any position to fault others for pettiness. Why are small acts of kindness beneath us, but not small acts of cruelty? The larger problem with this appeal to moral priority, however, is that we are dealing with suffering that occurs through human agency. Whether it's miserliness here, carelessness there, or greed throughout, the result is rank cruelty for which particular people must answer.

Since refraining from cruelty is an obligation of justice, moreover, there is no avoiding the implications. All the goods invoked in defense of factory farming, from the efficiency and higher profits of the system to the lower costs of the products, are false goods unjustly derived. No matter what right and praiseworthy things we are doing elsewhere in life, when we live off a cruel and disgraceful thing like factory farming, we are to that extent living unjustly, and that is hardly a trivial problem.

For the religious-minded, and Catholics in particular, no less an authority than Pope Benedict XVI has explained the spiritual stakes. Asked recently to weigh in on these very questions, Cardinal Ratzinger told German journalist Peter Seewald that animals must be respected as our "companions in creation." While it is licit to use them for food, "we cannot just do whatever we want with them. ... Certainly, a sort of industrial use of creatures, so that geese are fed in such a way as to produce as large a liver as possible, or hens live so packed together that they become just caricatures of birds, this degrading of living creatures to a commodity seems to me in fact to contradict the relationship of mutuality that comes across in the Bible."

Factory farmers also assure us that all of this is an inevitable stage of industrial efficiency. Leave aside the obvious reply that we could all do a lot of things in life more efficiently if we didn't have to trouble ourselves with ethical restraints. Leave aside, too, the tens of billions of dollars in annual federal subsidies that have helped megafarms undermine small family farms and the decent communities that once surrounded them and to give us the illusion of cheap products. And never mind the collateral damage to land, water, and air that factory farms cause and the more billions of dollars it costs taxpayers to clean up after them. Factory farming is a predatory enterprise, absorbing profit and externalizing costs, unnaturally propped up by political influence and government subsidies much as factory-farmed animals are unnaturally sustained by hormones and antibiotics.

Even if all the economic arguments were correct, conservatives usually aren't impressed by breathless talk of inevitable progress. I am asked sometimes how a conservative could possibly care about animal suffering in factory farms, but the question is premised on a liberal caricature of conservatism—the assumption that, for all of our fine talk about moral values, "compassionate conservatism" and the like, everything we really care about can be counted in dollars. In the case of factory farming, and the conservative's blithe tolerance of it, the caricature is too close to the truth.

Exactly how far are we all prepared to follow these industrial and technological advances before pausing to take stock of where things stand and where it is all tending? Very soon companies like Smithfield plan to have tens of millions of cloned animals in their factory farms. Other companies are at work genetically engineering chickens without feathers so that one day all poultry farmers might be spared the toil and cost of de-feathering their birds. For years, the many shills for our livestock industry employed in the "Animal Science" and "Meat Science" departments of rural universities (we used to call them Animal Husbandry departments) have been tampering with the genes of pigs and other animals to locate and expunge that part of their genetic makeup that makes them stressed in factory farm conditions—taking away the desire to protect themselves and to live. Instead of redesigning the factory farm to suit the animals, they are redesigning the animals to suit the factory farm.

Are there no boundaries of nature and elementary ethics that the conservative should be the first to see? The hubris of such projects is beyond belief, only more because of the foolish and frivolous goods to be gained—blood-free meats and the perfect pork chop.

No one who does not profit from them can look at our modern factory farms or frenzied slaughter plants or agricultural laboratories with their featherless chickens and fear-free pigs and think, "Yes, this is humanity at our finest—exactly as things should be." Devils charged with designing a farm could hardly have made it more severe. Least of all should we look for sanction in Judeo-Christian morality, whose whole logic is one of gracious condescension, of the proud learning to be humble, the higher serving the lower, and the strong protecting the weak.

Those religious conservatives who, in every debate over animal welfare, rush to remind us that the animals themselves are secondary and man must come first are exactly right—only they don't follow their own thought to its moral conclusion. Somehow, in their pious notions of stewardship and dominion, we always seem to end up with singular moral dignity but no singular moral accountability to go with it.

Lofty talk about humanity's special status among creatures only invites such questions as: what would the Good Shepherd make of our factory farms? Where does the creature of conscience get off lording it over these poor creatures so mercilessly? "How is it possible," as Malcolm Muggeridge asked in the years when factory farming began to spread, "to look for God and sing his praises while insulting and degrading his creatures? If, as I had thought, all lambs are the Agnus Dei, then to deprive them of light and the field and their joyous frisking and the sky is the worst kind of blasphemy."

The writer B.R. Meyers remarked in *The Atlantic*, "research could prove that cows love Jesus, and the line at the McDonald's drive-through wouldn't be one sagging carload shorter the next day …. Has any generation in history ever been so ready to cause so much suffering for such a trivial advantage? We deaden our consciences to enjoy—for a few minutes a day—the taste of blood, the feel of our teeth meeting through muscle."

That is a cynical but serious indictment, and we must never let it be true of us in the choices we each make or urge upon others. If reason and morality are what set human beings apart from animals, then reason and morality must always guide us in how we treat them, or else it's all just caprice, unbridled appetite with the pretense of piety. When people say that they like their pork chops, veal, or foie gras just too much ever to give them up, reason hears in that the voice of gluttony, willfulness, or at best moral complaisance. What makes a human being human is precisely the ability to understand that the suffering of an animal is more important than the taste of a treat.

Of the many conservatives who reviewed *Dominion*, every last one conceded that factory farming is a wretched business and a betrayal of human responsibility. So it should be a short step to agreement that it also constitutes a serious issue of law and public policy. Having granted that certain practices are abusive, cruel, and wrong, we must be prepared actually to do something about them.

Among animal activists, of course, there are some who go too far—there are in the best of causes. But fairness requires that we judge a cause by its best advocates instead of making straw men of the worst. There isn't much money in championing the cause of animals, so we're dealing with some pretty altruistic people who on that account alone deserve the benefit of the doubt.

If we're looking for fitting targets for inquiry and scorn, for people with an angle and a truly pernicious influence, better to start with groups like Smithfield Foods (my candidate for the worst corporation in America in its ruthlessness to people and animals alike), the National Pork Producers Council (a reliable Republican contributor), or the various think tanks in Washington subsidized by animal-use industries for intellectual cover.

After the last election, the National Pork Producers Council rejoiced, "President Bush's victory ensures that the U.S. pork industry will be very well positioned for the next four years politically, and pork producers will benefit from the long-term results of a livestock agriculture-friendly agenda." But this is no tribute. And millions of good people who live in what's left of America's small family-farm communities would themselves rejoice if the president were to announce that he is prepared to sign a bipartisan bill making some basic reforms in livestock agriculture.

Bush's new agriculture secretary, former Nebraska Gov. Mike Johanns, has shown a sympathy for animal welfare. He and the president might both be surprised at the number and variety of supporters such reforms would find in the Congress, from Republicans like Chris Smith and Elton Gallegly in the House to John Ensign and Rick Santorum in the Senate, along with Democrats such as Robert Byrd, Barbara Boxer, or the North Carolina congressman who called me in to say that he, too, was disgusted and saddened by hog farming in his state.

If such matters were ever brought to President Bush's attention in a serious way, he would find in the details of factory farming many things abhorrent to the Christian heart and to his own kindly instincts. Even if he were to drop into relevant speeches a few of the prohibited words in modern industrial agriculture (cruel, humane, compassionate), instead of endlessly flattering corporate farmers for virtues they lack, that alone would help to set reforms in motion.

We need our conservative values voters to get behind a Humane Farming Act so that we can all quit averting our eyes. This reform, a set of explicit federal cruelty statutes with enforcement funding to back it up, would leave us with farms we could imagine without wincing, photograph without prosecution, and explain without excuses.

The law would uphold not only the elementary standards of animal husbandry but also of veterinary ethics, following no more complicated a principle than that pigs and cows should be able to walk and turn around, fowl to move about and spread their wings, and all creatures to know the feel of soil and grass and the warmth of the sun. No need for labels saying "free-range" or "humanely raised." They will all be raised that way. They all get to be treated like animals and not as unfeeling machines.

On a date certain, mass confinement, sow gestation crates, veal crates, battery cages, and all such innovations would be prohibited. This will end livestock agriculture's moral race to the bottom and turn the ingenuity of its scientists toward compassionate solutions. It will remove the federal support that unnaturally serves agribusiness at the expense of small farms. And it will shift economies of scale, turning the balance in favor of humane farmers—as those who run companies like Wal-Mart could do right now by taking their business away from factory farms.

In all cases, the law would apply to corporate farmers a few simple rules that better men would have been observing all along: we cannot just take from these creatures, we must give them something in return. We owe them a merciful death, and we owe them a merciful life. And when human beings cannot do something humanely, without degrading both the creatures and ourselves, then we should not do it at all.

■ WHAT?

1. How does Scully build and support his case that cruelty to animals, especially in the factory farming system, should be a conservative cause?
2. In his essay, Scully writes: "If reason and morality are what set human beings apart from animals, then reason and morality must always guide us in how we treat them, or else it's all just caprice, unbridled appetite with the pretense of piety." What do you think Scully means by this? Do you agree with him? Explain your response.
3. Where does Scully stand on the "rights" of animals? Point to specific passages from his essay to support your response.

■ WHAT ELSE? WHAT'S NEXT?

4. What do other conservative writers and commentators have to say about the issue of animal rights? Find at least three sources that address the issue from a conservative point of view but that offer different perspectives otherwise. Compile these into an annotated bibliography, following MLA guidelines.

■ WHO CARES?

5. Read through the essay and identify the sources that Scully uses to support his argument. Why do you think he chose these particular people and publications? How do these sources help him reach his intended audience?

Molly J. Dahm and Amy R. Shows are on the faculty of the Department of Family and Consumer Sciences at Lamar University in Beaumont, Texas. Aurelia V. Samonte works with Buckner Children and Family Services in Beaumont. They wrote this article for the Journal of American College Health *in 2009.*

BEFORE YOU READ

Find out some basic information about the "organic" label. What does it mean when a food product is labeled "organic"? Who sets the standards? Is there disagreement over how such food is labeled?

ORGANIC FOODS: DO ECO-FRIENDLY ATTITUDES PREDICT ECO-FRIENDLY BEHAVIORS?

Molly J. Dahm, Aurelia V. Samonte, and Amy R. Shows

■ Consumption of Organic Foods

New research and mounting public interest have increased global awareness of organic food products. The primary consumers of organic food are women aged 30 to 45 who have children in the household and who are environmentally conscious.[1,2] However, interest in organic foods along with a sense of responsibility for the environment is growing among younger people, specifically college students, who are likely to identify issues that will influence their attitudes and activities in the future. Purchase and consumption of organic foods is another positive socially conscious behavior.[3]

One way universities in the United States have responded to students' increased interest in the environment is by adding organic foods to their menus. In fact, the presence of organic foods may ultimately factor into a student's choice of school.[4] Purchase and consumption of organic foods is one way students can practice eco-friendly behaviors. Eco-friendly behaviors might also be referred to as environmentally conscious behaviors, or "green consumption," e.g., legitimate means of exhibiting environmentally safe and responsible behaviors.[1] Other eco-friendly practices include recycling, energy conservation, water conservation, driving hybrid cars or carpooling, and ozone protection.

In this study, we examined the awareness (knowledge), attitudes, and behaviors of university students towards organic foods. We also attempted to determine if positive attitudes about organic foods and other environmental issues would predict consumption of organic foods and other healthy and eco-friendly practices.

■ Federal Standards for Organic Foods

The United States Department of Agriculture (USDA) informs consumers that the terms natural and organic are not interchangeable.[5] "Natural" refers to products without artificial flavorings, colorings, or chemical preservatives and minimal processing.[5] The USDA defines "organic foods" as products grown without the use of pesticides, synthetic fertilizers, sewage sludge, genetically modified organisms, or ionizing radiation.[5] The agency also requires that organic meat, poultry, eggs, and dairy products be produced from animals free of antibiotics or growth hormones.[6] The term "organic" is increasingly recognized as a trusted symbol of eco-friendly products.[7] Companies that handle or process organic foods for public consumption must be certified by the USDA.[5] The USDA Organic Seal (Figure 1) exhibits evidence of this certification.

Consumers who want to buy organic products should be able to correctly identify them. The USDA's label standards for organic products include 100% Organic (made with 100% organic ingredients); the word organic or the organic seal (95% organic); made with organic ingredients (minimum of 70% organic ingredients); and organic ingredients listed on the side panel (less than 70% organic ingredients).[5,6]

Other certification programs, such as Oregon's eco-labeling program and the system of integrated management (SIM) in Greece, promote eco-friendly products to consumers.[7] Loureiro et al.[8] studied consumers' level of awareness of certified products using eco-labeled apples and found that although general level of awareness about organic products was high (86%), awareness of the label meaning was limited.

■ Consumer Attitudes and Behaviors

Much of the current research about consumer attitudes and behaviors regarding organic foods has been conducted outside the United States, where scholars have noted consumer trust in organic products. In a Swedish study, attitudes towards and purchase of organic foods were strongly related to the perceived human health benefits of those foods.[2] Researchers in the United Kingdom found the term "organic" had emotional resonance for consumers in terms of personal well-being, health, benefits to the environment, and a healthy diet.[9,10]

FIGURE 1. USDA Organic Seal

As attitudes towards organic products evolve, values play an important but mixed role in how organic products are perceived.[11,12] Dreezens et al.[12] indicated that organic foods were viewed positively and associated with the values of welfare for all people and protection of nature. By contrast, Chryssohoidis and Krystallis[11] found that external values such as belonging to society were less important to consumers who purchased organic foods than internal values such as self-respect and enjoyment of life.

Consumer perception of appearance, taste, and texture of organic foods varies. In Northern Ireland, a focus group found organic products bland and lacking in color, yet stated that some organic foods, especially mixed vegetables, had desirable texture and flavor.[13] Researchers in the United Kingdom and Australia concluded that the taste of organic food was better than conventionally grown products[10] and that organic food had sensual qualities.[1]

As consumers develop more positive attitudes towards organic food, they are faced with purchase decisions. Studies have examined decision-making factors. Padel and Foster[9] concluded that the process is complex, and that motives and barriers may vary with product categories. Researchers have found a widespread perception of organic foods as expensive[10] and that the primary barrier to purchasing organic food was the consumer's level of personal disposable income.[14] Lockie et al.[1] suggested that increased education and household income is positively associated with the likelihood that an individual has consumed organic foods. However, other scholars have found that the main factor that hinders the purchase of organic food is limited availability of such foods.[11,15]

Consumer purchases of organic foods have increased. In 1994, Tregear et al.[18] found that 29% of the general public occasionally bought organic foods. A later study found that almost half of respondents purchased organic food on a regular basis.[13] Fruits and vegetables tend to be the first, and often the only, organic products that consumers buy.[9] Nonetheless, few consumers follow a diet that is mainly organic.[1]

■ Other Eco-Friendly Behaviors

There is some disagreement about whether there is an association between consumption of organic foods and other environmentally friendly behaviors. Davies et al.[14] found that consumers of organic foods were not necessarily concerned about the environment. However, two more recent studies found a significant relationship between environmentally friendly behaviors and organic food consumption.[1,2] In Oregon, the likelihood that a consumer will pay a premium for eco-labeled apples was positively associated with being environmentally conscious.[7] In Greece, willingness to pay for organic products was higher among consumers who placed importance on health.[8]

■ Attitudes and Behaviors of Young People

In a study of 651 high school students in a major metropolitan area, Bissonnette and Contento[3] found that American adolescents had positive attitudes about organic foods.

Students believed organic foods were healthier, tasted better, and were better for the environment. Yet their beliefs were not strong enough to urge them to act.[3]

Interest in organic foods or alternative food sources is evident in college age individuals who show an increasing enthusiasm for a healthy lifestyle and a sense of environmental responsibility.[4] Over the past 10 years, universities across the United States have introduced organic food options in response to student demand. For example, in 2000 the University of Wisconsin at Madison became the first major American public university to consistently place foods grown on local farms on the regular menu.[16]

In April 2006, the University of California-Berkeley received the nation's first organic certification on a college campus.[17] Menlo College uses nearly 100% organic foods and beverages on campus.[18] Also in 2006, Colorado State University and the University of Pennsylvania, in 2003, introduced student food venues that sell locally grown food. Oral Roberts University introduced its Green Cuisine brand in 2006, which includes organic salads, sandwiches, and packaged goods made from local food.[18,19] Thus, universities have responded to student demands for organic foods.

Because the literature is unclear whether consumer purchases follow upon knowledge and attitudes, the links between knowledge, attitudes, and behaviors with regard to organic foods (and other eco-friendly behaviors) should be explored to better understand and respond to consumer needs on college campuses.

METHOD

■ Population and Sample

The population for this study was students at a mid-size university in the southeastern United States. The sample included 443 students who were enrolled in one of the mandated entry-level political science classes. Thus, the sampling method ensured a representative sample of the student body.

■ Instrumentation

The instrument, designed by the researchers, was 4 pages long and consisted of 28 items. Consent information was included on the first page of the instrument. Completion of the survey constituted consent to participate in the study. Study protocol was approved by the university's Institutional Review Board.

The first 5 questions requested demographic information: gender, race, age, student classification, place of residence, and income level. Four questions evaluated the subjects' awareness/knowledge of organic foods and 5 questions addressed the subjects' attitudes toward organic foods. In the fnal section, 12 questions sought information about student eating behaviors in relation to organic foods and healthy lifestyle practices, and 2 multipart questions examined attitudes and behaviors regarding other eco-friendly practices (recycling, energy conservation, water conservation, driving hybrid cars or carpooling).

■ Procedures

After departmental approval was granted, researchers obtained permission from individual professors to administer the survey in each class. The average class size was 50 students. The survey was administered over a 2-week period to students present on the day of the survey. Several classes were not surveyed due to scheduling conflicts. A research assistant read procedures from a script before the surveys were distributed. Students were informed that the survey was voluntary and anonymous.

■ Statistical Analysis

Data analysis was conducted using SPSS Version 14.0 and Jump Version 5.0. Descriptive statistics described the sample and displayed frequencies of responses to survey items. Chi-square analysis was conducted to determine associations between categorical variables of interest. Linear regression tested whether student awareness/knowledge of organic foods predicted attitude about organic foods. Multiple correlation was used to examine the relationship between attitudes about organic foods and the purchase and consumption of those foods in different contexts. Linear regression and path analysis determined whether attitudes about organic foods might predict organic food purchase and consumption and healthy lifestyle practices. Finally, multiple correlation tested whether attitudes about other eco-friendly practices might predict corresponding behaviors.

RESULTS

The sample ($N = 443$) was 44.2% male and 55.8% female. The mean age of the group was 21.6 (SD ±5.01) years, with a range of 16 to 48 years. The racial/ethnic background of students was 54.6% White/Non-Hispanic, 30.6% African American, 7.0% Hispanic, 3.9% Asian, and 3.7% Other. The majority (59.5%) of the students were classified as sophomores. Approximately one third (27.4%) of the students lived on campus; the remaining students (72.6%) were commuters. Household annual income for 32.6% of the respondents was less than $20,000. Twenty-seven percent reported an annual household income of $20,001 to $50,000. The remainder (40.2%) reported annual income above $50,001.

When asked to identify the definition of the term "organic," 214 respondents (49.0%) selected the correct definition. Meanwhile, 138 (31.7%) recognized the USDA-approved organic seal. Knowledge of the correct definition of organic and recognition of the seal were significantly associated ($r_s = .161$, $p < .001$). Younger students (<21.6 years) were more likely to know the definition of organic and recognize the organic seal.

A majority of students knew that organic foods were available for purchase in grocery stores and in health food stores (72.2% and 79.0%, respectively). Few (9.7%) believed organic foods were available in restaurants. When asked in what form organic foods could be purchased (subjects could indicate all that applied), responses were as follows: produce

(87.1%), grains (72.2%), dairy (53.5%), snacks (31.4%), meat (29.3%), beverages (28.2%), and candy (7.7%).

Most students (56.4%) were neutral in their opinion about organic foods, but 41.3% either "accept organic foods" or "only eat organic foods." Students ranked taste as the factor that influenced them most when selecting organic foods, followed by price, appearance, availability, and package information (Table 1). Approximately one third (31.1%) of respondents believed organic foods tasted the same as conventionally grown products, whereas 15.8% felt organic foods tasted better, and 12.3% felt organic foods tasted worse.

Only 20.7% of respondents reported they could purchase organic foods on campus, and few consumed more than 50% organic diets, no matter where they purchased foods. However, between 33.2% and 45.5% reported they purchased and consumed some organic foods on campus, in restaurants, or at home. The highest number (45.5%) purchased for consumption at home. When asked where they purchased organic foods 47.4% indicated the grocery store and 13.5% indicated a health food store. The frequencies of types of organic foods purchased were as follows: produce (40.4%), grains (28.2%), dairy (22.8%), drinks/beverages (20.8%), snacks (16.3%), and meat (13.8%). Interestingly, 50.5% of the students indicated they would support the use of organic foods on campus, and 64.0% reported they would buy organic foods if offered on campus.

There were significant positive relationships between knowledge of the definition of the term organic and opinion about organic foods (attitude) ($r_s = .103, p < .05$) and between recognition of the organic seal (knowledge) and opinion about organic foods (attitude) ($r_s = .197, p < .01$). Thus, awareness and attitude about organic foods were associated. Linear regression was used to test if the two knowledge variables predicted attitude. Results were significant ($R^2 = .04, F(2, 422) = 9.73, p < .000$). Recognition of the seal was the strongest of the 2 predictors.

There was also a significant positive relationship between recognition of the organic seal and opinion about the taste of organic foods as compared to conventionally grown products ($r_s = .298, p < .01$). The relationship between the other knowledge variable

TABLE 1   FREQUENCY RANKINGS OF FACTORS AFFECTING PURCHASE OR CONSUMPTION OF ORGANIC FOODS

Factors	Rankings	
	Frequency	Percentage (%)
Price	193	46.5
Taste	247	59.7
Appearance	120	29.0
Package Information	46	11.2
Other	12	5.6

(definition of organic) and attitude was not significant. Linear regression tested recognition of the organic seal as a predictor of attitude and was found to be significant ($R^2 = .08$, $F(2, 418) = 20.09$, $p < .000$). When knowledge of the definition of organic was added as a predictor and tested in a second linear regression, model fit did not change significantly, corroborating the previous conclusion that the stronger predictor of attitude was recognition of the seal.

Multiple correlation was used to examine the relationship between attitudes about organic foods and subject responses about the support and purchase of organic foods (behavior) in different contexts (Table 2). Attitude towards organic foods was found to be significantly related to (1) purchase and consumption of organic foods on campus, (2) purchase and consumption of organic foods (usually in restaurants), and (3) purchase for consumption of foods at home.

Given the significant findings of the correlational analysis and linear regression, we conducted a path analysis (Figure 2) to determine whether attitudes toward organic foods would predict the three sets of purchase and consumption behaviors. Attitude was found to be a significant predictor ($p < .01$) of all 3 behaviors. Path analysis can be used to determine the significance and magnitude of the direct effect of predictor variables on response variables. It is an empirical tool to test cause-and-effect relationships.[20]

Attitude towards organic foods was found to be significantly related to student perceptions of whether or not they lead healthy lifestyles ($r_s = .160$, $p < .01$). A second path analysis was conducted to determine the direct effect of attitude towards organic foods on other healthy lifestyle practices. Significant path coefficients were calculated for relationships between positive attitudes towards organic foods and healthy diet ($p = .22$, $R^2 = 5.1\%$), regular exercise ($p = .14$, $R^2 = 2.1\%$), and consumption of organic foods ($p = .12$, $R^2 = 1.2\%$) only.

TABLE 2   CORRELATION BETWEEN ATTITUDE TOWARDS AND CONSUMPTION OF ORGANIC FOOD

	Attitude towards organic foods	Purchase and consumption of organic foods		
		On campus	Off campus (restaurant)	Home
Attitude towards organic foods	—	.284**	.309**	.298**
Purchase/consumption of organic foods				
On campus		—	.670**	.524**
Off campus (restaurant)			—	.641**
Home				—

Note. **$p < .01$.

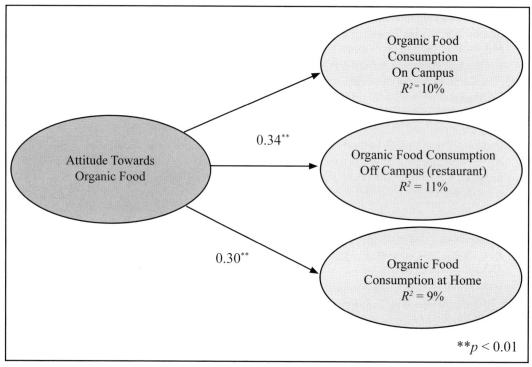

FIGURE 2. Path analysis: Direct effect of student's overall attitude towards organic foods on their food choices on-campus, off-campus, and at home.

A final analysis examined the relationship between attitudes about other eco-friendly behaviors and the actual behaviors. Multiple correlation determined that most of the attitudes expressed about such behaviors were related to the practice of the behaviors. Further, in many instances, the respondents' attitudes about an eco-friendly behavior such as recycling and energy conservation were significantly related to supportive behaviors such as recycling, energy conservation, driving hybrid cars or carpooling, and ozone protection.

COMMENT

We found that students are relatively knowledgeable about organic food products and believe that organic foods are beneficial and necessary. Many expressed an interest in having more organic foods available on campus and indicated they would be willing to purchase organic foods if made available on campus. Contrary to the literature, we found that students were more likely to act upon the beliefs they expressed about both organic foods and eco-friendly behaviors.

Equal numbers of males and females knew the correct definition of the term organic, recognized the federal organic seal, and expressed a positive attitude towards organic foods. This finding varies somewhat from the literature, which identifies females as being more aware and having stronger attitudes about organic foods. Perhaps students, as a group, are simply more informed consumers. In future research, student responses could be compared to other types of consumers. When examining the relationship between awareness (knowledge) and attitude, we concluded that although many students selected the incorrect definition of the term organic, even these students had positive opinions in support of organic foods and other eco-friendly practices.

Most of the students in this study clustered in household income levels of under $20,000 or above $50,000. More than 30% of respondents from the upper household income levels reported that they "accept organic foods." Similar findings in the literature indicate higher levels of awareness and support for organic foods among individuals with higher incomes.[1] Future research should explore the degree to which parental/family household income affects student consumer choices. More students under the mean age of 21.6 years knew the correct definition of the term organic and recognized the organic seal. Further, twice as many younger respondents expressed positive attitudes toward organic foods as those over the mean age. This suggests that younger people may seek out organic foods in various food environments or at least feel strongly about having them available. In that case, it makes sense that university food services should integrate more organic food options into their on-campus menus.

When subjects ranked factors that influenced their buying decisions, taste was reported to be most important, followed in order by price, appearance, availability, and package information. Consumers tend to associate health benefits with organic foods. Perhaps a younger, health-minded generation of educated consumers places more emphasis on quality (taste) and value (price). Such a conclusion might also support the fact that students knew of the availability of many forms of organic foods. A future study might include a tasting panel in which student consumers identify how various factors interact to influence the buying decision.

Students indicated that they purchased organic foods for consumption at home rather than on- or off-campus. This reinforces the finding that these foods were primarily purchased at grocery stores and health food stores. Produce, grains, and dairy products were the most often purchased organic foods. We agree with the literature that health educators need to work with food service operators to develop informational materials such as table tents and posters to help students learn about other organic food options.[9]

Few students followed an all-organic diet. Most purchased and consumed "50% or less" organic foods. However, more than half reported they would support the integration of organic foods into campus menus, and even more said they would buy organic foods if offered on campus. Such findings reinforce the current move on university campuses to provide more organic food options.

Students who were able to identify the correct definition of the term organic and who recognized the USDA organic seal were more likely to have positive opinions supporting organic foods. Recognition of the organic seal was a significant predictor of the perception that organic foods tasted as good as or better than their conventionally grown counterparts.

An extension of this study might involve a taste panel in which a perceptions and preferences are tested with respect to awareness and attitudes about organic foods.

The primary purpose of this study was to determine if student attitudes actually predicted corresponding behaviors with regard to organic foods. We concluded that they did. Tracking responses over time might determine if increased exposure to/availability of organic food products influences students who currently have no opinion about organic foods. We also found that students who had positive opinions about organic foods purchased and consumed such foods in different venues, most often for consumption at home. Therefore, attitude predicted behavior.

Botonaki et al.[7] suggested that consumers of organic foods are likely to engage in other healthy lifestyle practices. In our study, a positive attitude towards organic foods was significantly associated with consuming a healthy diet and exercising regularly. Health educators should further examine differences in student perceptions about healthy lifestyle practices.

Lockie et al.[1] and Magnusson et al.[2] found the consumption of organic foods and other environmentally conscious behaviors to be significantly related. In the present study, when students were asked about eco-friendly practices, there was a significant relationship between a positive attitude about these practices and the corresponding behavior. Clearly, students in this study not only felt strongly about environmental issues, but they also felt compelled towards eco-friendly practices.

CONCLUSION

In a classroom administration format or as with any self-report instrument, there is always the concern that subjects respond truthfully to the instrument items. In addition, the population characteristics of this university may be different. Thus, our findings that attitudes generally predicted behaviors must be interpreted with caution. Future studies should focus on other types of universities and track student behaviors to determine through observation whether a significant link with attitudes actually exists.

Some instrument items were forced choice, with an option to write in additional information. Forced-choice items do not accommodate the full range of possible responses even with the write-in option. For example, students with food allergies or concerns about chemical preservatives might opt for an organic diet. We may not have identified all opinions and factors relevant to the purchase and consumption of organic foods, healthy lifestyle or eco-friendly practices.

This study sampled students (young adults) from an American university, which helps to fill certain gaps in the literature. Additional research in the United States about the attitudes towards purchase and consumption of organic foods is needed.

A principle finding in this study was that students are knowledgeable about organic foods and that they support the integration of organic foods into their menu choices and diets. Although less than half of the students indicated they purchased and consumed organic products in various environments, more than half of study respondents reported they would support the use of organic products on campus and would actually purchase organic foods on campus.

This sentiment is an important indicator for college and universities. There is already a demand for healthy food options on university campuses.[4,18] It seems that campus food services should evaluate not only their menu offerings, but even what they term healthy choices, in terms of organic food standards. It would be interesting to sample a portion of the respondents in this study in a year or so to determine if their attitudes have changed with regard to organic food purchase or consumption.

Our study focused on students as primary consumers; however, campuses also accommodate faculty and staff, many of whom may have opinions similar to those expressed by the students in this study. A future study might examine not only the opinions of other students on other campuses as well as other groups on campuses.

This study found that students who felt positively about organic foods were also inclined to behave accordingly. In other words, they were more likely to act on their opinions and choose to purchase and consume organic foods. Such a finding has implications for market food producers in general, in that college students are both consumers today as well as primary consumers of the future. It will be important to address this growing demand in more venues than college campuses.

REFERENCES

1. Lockie S, Lyons K, Lawrence G, Grice J. "Choosing organics: a path analysis of factors underlying the selection of organic food among Australian consumers." *Appetite.* 2004;43:135-146.
2. Magnusson M, Arvola A, Hursti U, Aberg L, Sjoden P. "Choice of organic foods is related to perceived consequences for human health and to environmentally friendly behaviour." *Appetite.* 2003;40:109-117.
3. Bissonnette M, Contento I. "Adolescents' perspectives and food choice behaviors in terms of the environmental impacts of food production practices: application of a psychosocial model." *J Nutr Educ.* 2001;33:72-82.
4. Horovitz B. "More university students call for organic, 'sustainable' food." *USAToday. com*, September 26, 2006:A.
5. "The National Organic Program." *Organic Food Standards and labels: The Facts.* Agricultural Marketing Service at United States Department of Agriculture Web site. http://www.ams.usda.gov/nop/Consumers/brochure.html. Accessed March 8, 2007.
6. "Organic faq." Organic.org Web site. http://www.organic.org/home/faq. Accessed October 17, 2006.
7. Botonaki A, Polymeros K, Tsakindou E, Mattas K. "The role of food quality certification on consumers' food choices." *Br Food J.* 2006;108:77-91.
8. Loureiro M, McCluskey J, Mittelhammer R. "Will consumers pay a premium for eco-labeled apples?" *J Consumer Affairs.* 2002;36:203-219.
9. Padel S, Foster C. "Exploring the gap between attitudes and behaviour: understanding why consumers buy or do not buy organic food." *Br Food J.* 2005;107:606-625.
10. Tregear A, Dent J, McGregor M. "The demand for organically-grown produce." *Br Food J.* 1994;96:21-26.

11 Chryssohoidis G, Krystallis, A. "Organic consumers' personal values research: testing and validating the list of values (LOV) scale and implementing a value-based segmentation task." *Food Qual Prefer.* 2005;16:585-599.

12. Dreezens E, Martijn C, Tenbult P, Kok G, de Vries N. "Food and values: an examination of values underlying attitudes toward genetically modified—and organically grown food products." *Appetite.* 2005;44:115-122.

13. Connor R, Douglas L. "Consumer attitudes to organic foods." *Nutr Food Sci.* 2001;31:254-258.

14. Davies A, Titterington A, Cochrane C. "Who buys organic food? A profile of the purchasers of organic food in Northern Ireland." *Br Food J.* 1995;97:17-24.

15. Fotopoulos, G. "Factors affecting the decision to purchase organic food." *J Eur-Marketing.* 2000;9:45-66.

16. "University of Wisconsin goes organic." *Organic Consumer Association Web site. 2006.* http://www.orgaanicconsumers.org/organic/uofw101903.cfm. Accessed October 17, 2006.

17. *Organic certification.* University of California-Berkeley Web site. http://caldining.berkeley.edu/environment.organic.cert.html. Accessed October 17, 2006.

18. Horovitz B. "Organic food spreads across campuses." *USAToday*, September 27, 2006:B2.

19. Oral Roberts Fall 2007 "Student Catalogue." *Oral Roberts University* Web site. http://www.oru.edu/catalog/ORU.hb0203.pdf. Accessed March 12, 2008.

20. Williams W, Jones M, Demment M. "A concise table for path analysis statistics." *Agron J.* 1990;82:1022-1024.

■ WHAT?

1. Do the conclusions presented by Dahm, Samonte, and Shows reflect your experiences with organic food? Explain your response.

2. Evaluate Dahm, Samonte, and Shows' findings. Did you find the survey questions appropriate? Were there any questions that you think should have been added? Were the charts useful in explaining the researchers' results? Do you find this type of article more or less convincing than personal narratives such as "The Pleasures of Eating" or "The Culinary Seasons of My Childhood"? Why?

■ WHAT ELSE? WHAT'S NEXT?

3. Research USC's organic food offerings. What are they? Were you aware of these offerings (or lack thereof) before your research? If organic options are available, do you regularly take advantage of them? Next, find other schools that stock local or organic food for students. What different levels of commitment to organic food in higher education do you find in your research?

■ WHO CARES?

4. Dahm, Samonte, and Shows wrote their article for the *Journal of American College Health.* Look online for more information about this journal and its primary audience. How are the journal's mission and audience reflected in the content and style of this article?

> *"I'm not a chef," Mark Bittman writes on his website (markbittman.com). "I've never had formal training, and I've never worked in a restaurant. None of which has gotten in the way of my mission to get people cooking simply, comfortably, and well." As part of this mission, Bittman regularly writes about food for the opinion section of* The New York Times, *where this column was published in 2011.*

BEFORE YOU READ—————————————————————————————————
Try keeping a food diary for a day or so. Write down everything that you consume— and be honest!

BAD FOOD? TAX IT Mark Bittman

What will it take to get Americans to change our eating habits? The need is indisputable, since heart disease, diabetes and cancer are all in large part caused by the Standard American Diet. (Yes, it's SAD.)

Though experts increasingly recommend a diet high in plants and low in animal products and processed foods, ours is quite the opposite, and there's little disagreement that changing it could improve our health and save tens of millions of lives. And—not inconsequential during the current struggle over deficits and spending—a sane diet could save tens if not hundreds of billions of dollars in health care costs.

Yet the food industry appears incapable of marketing healthier foods. And whether its leaders are confused or just stalling doesn't matter, because the fixes are not really their problem. Their mission is not public health but profit, so they'll continue to sell the health-damaging food that's most profitable, until the market or another force skews things otherwise. That "other force" should be the federal government, fulfilling its role as an agent of the public good and establishing a bold national fix.

Rather than subsidizing the production of unhealthful foods, we should turn the tables and tax things like soda, French fries, doughnuts and hyperprocessed snacks. The resulting income should be earmarked for a program that encourages a sound diet for Americans by making healthy food more affordable and widely available.

The average American consumes 44.7 gallons of soft drinks annually. (Although that includes diet sodas, it does not include noncarbonated sweetened beverages, which add up to at least 17 gallons a person per year.) Sweetened drinks could be taxed at 2 cents per ounce, so a six-pack of Pepsi would cost $1.44 more than it does now. An equivalent tax on fries might be 50 cents per serving; a quarter extra for a doughnut. (We have experts who can figure out how "bad" a food should be to qualify, and what the rate should be; right now they're busy calculating ethanol subsidies. Diet sodas would not be taxed.)

Simply put: taxes would reduce consumption of unhealthful foods and generate billions of dollars annually. That money could be used to subsidize the purchase of staple foods like seasonal greens, vegetables, whole grains, dried legumes and fruit. We could sell those staples cheap—let's say for 50 cents a pound—and almost everywhere: drugstores, street corners, convenience stores, bodegas, supermarkets, liquor stores, even schools, libraries and other community centers.

This program would, of course, upset the processed food industry. Oh well. It would also bug those who might resent paying more for soda and chips and argue that their right to eat whatever they wanted was being breached. But public health is the role of the government, and our diet is right up there with any other public responsibility you can name, from water treatment to mass transit.

Some advocates for the poor say taxes like these are unfair because low-income people pay a higher percentage of their income for food and would find it more difficult to buy soda or junk. But since poor people suffer disproportionately from the cost of high-quality, fresh foods, subsidizing those foods would be particularly beneficial to them.

Right now it's harder for many people to buy fruit than Froot Loops; chips and Coke are a common breakfast. And since the rate of diabetes continues to soar—one-third of all Americans either have diabetes or are pre-diabetic, most with Type 2 diabetes, the kind associated with bad eating habits—and because our health care bills are on the verge of becoming truly insurmountable, this is urgent for economic sanity as well as national health.

■ Justifying a Tax

At least 30 cities and states have considered taxes on soda or all sugar-sweetened beverages, and they're a logical target: of the 278 additional calories Americans on average consumed per day between 1977 and 2001, more than 40 percent came from soda, "fruit" drinks, mixes like Kool-Aid and Crystal Light, and beverages like Red Bull, Gatorade and dubious offerings like Vitamin Water, which contains half as much sugar as Coke.

Some states already have taxes on soda—mostly low, ineffective sales taxes paid at the register. The current talk is of excise taxes, levied before purchase.

"Excise taxes have the benefit of being incorporated into the shelf price, and that's where consumers make their purchasing decisions," says Lisa Powell, a senior research scientist at the Institute for Health Research and Policy at the University of Illinois at Chicago. "And, as per-unit taxes, they avoid volume discounts and are ultimately more effective in raising prices, so they have greater impact."

Much of the research on beverage taxes comes from the Rudd Center for Food Policy and Obesity at Yale. Its projections indicate that taxes become significant at the equivalent of about a penny an ounce, a level at which three very good things should begin to happen: the consumption of sugar-sweetened beverages should decrease, as should the incidence of disease and therefore public health costs; and money could be raised for other uses.

Even in the current antitax climate, we'll probably see new, significant soda taxes soon, somewhere; Philadelphia, New York (city and state) and San Francisco all considered them last year, and the scenario for such a tax spreading could be similar to that of legalized gambling: once the income stream becomes apparent, it will seem irresistible to cash-strapped governments.

Currently, instead of taxing sodas and other unhealthful food, we subsidize them (with, I might note, tax dollars!). Direct subsidies to farmers for crops like corn (used, for example, to make now-ubiquitous high-fructose corn syrup) and soybeans (vegetable oil) keep the prices of many unhealthful foods and beverages artificially low. There are indirect subsidies as well, because prices of junk foods don't reflect the costs of repairing our health and the environment.

Other countries are considering or have already started programs to tax foods with negative effects on health. Denmark's saturated-fat tax is going into effect Oct. 1, and Romania passed (and then un-passed) something similar; earlier this month, a French minister raised the idea of tripling the value added tax on soda. Meanwhile, Hungary is proposing a new tax on foods with "too much" sugar, salt or fat, while increasing taxes on liquor and soft drinks, all to pay for state-financed health care; and Brazil's Fome Zero (Zero Hunger) program features subsidized produce markets and state-sponsored low-cost restaurants.

Putting all of those elements together could create a national program that would make progress on a half-dozen problems at once—disease, budget, health care, environment, food access and more—while paying for itself. The benefits are staggering, and though it would take a level of political will that's rarely seen, it's hardly a moonshot.

The need is dire: efforts to shift the national diet have failed, because education alone is no match for marketing dollars that push the very foods that are the worst for us. (The fast-food industry alone spent more than $4 billion on marketing in 2009; the Department of Agriculture's Center for Nutrition Policy and Promotion is asking for about a third of a percent of that in 2012: $13 million.) As a result, the percentage of obese adults has more than doubled over the last 30 years; the percentage of obese children has tripled. We eat nearly 10 percent more animal products than we did a generation or two ago, and though there may be value in eating at least some animal products, we could perhaps live with reduced consumption of triple bacon cheeseburgers.

■ Government and Public Health

Health-related obesity costs are projected to reach $344 billion by 2018—with roughly 60 percent of that cost borne by the federal government. For a precedent in attacking this problem, look at the action government took in the case of tobacco.

The historic 1998 tobacco settlement, in which the states settled health-related lawsuits against tobacco companies, and the companies agreed to curtail marketing and finance antismoking efforts, was far from perfect, but consider the results. More than half of all Americans who once smoked have quit and smoking rates are about half of what they were in the 1960s.

It's true that you don't need to smoke and you do need to eat. But you don't need sugary beverages (or the associated fries), which have been linked not only to Type 2 diabetes and increased obesity but also to cardiovascular diseases and decreased intake of valuable nutrients like calcium. It also appears that liquid calories provide less feeling of fullness; in other words, when you drink a soda it's probably in addition to your other calorie intake, not instead of it.

To counter arguments about their nutritional worthlessness, expect to see "fortified" sodas—à la Red Bull, whose vitamins allegedly "support mental and physical performance"—and "improved" junk foods (Less Sugar! Higher Fiber!). Indeed, there may be reasons to make nutritionally worthless foods less so, but it's better to decrease their consumption.

Forcing sales of junk food down through taxes isn't ideal. First off, we'll have to listen to nanny-state arguments, which can be countered by the acceptance of the anti-tobacco movement as well as a dozen other successful public health measures. Then there are the predictions of job loss at soda distributorships, but the same predictions were made about the tobacco industry, and those were wrong. (For that matter, the same predictions were made around the nickel deposit on bottles, which most shoppers don't even notice.) Ultimately, however, both consumers and government will be more than reimbursed in the form of cheaper healthy staples, lowered health care costs and better health. And that's a big deal.

■ The Resulting Benefits

A study by Y. Claire Wang, an assistant professor at Columbia's Mailman School of Public Health, predicted that a penny tax per ounce on sugar-sweetened beverages in New York State would save $3 billion in health care costs over the course of a decade, prevent something like 37,000 cases of diabetes and bring in $1 billion annually. Another study shows that a two-cent tax per ounce in Illinois would reduce obesity in youth by 18 percent, save nearly $350 million and bring in over $800 million taxes annually.

Scaled nationally, as it should be, the projected benefits are even more impressive; one study suggests that a national penny-per-ounce tax on sugar-sweetened beverages would generate at least $13 billion a year in income while cutting consumption by 24 percent. And those numbers would swell dramatically if the tax were extended to more kinds of junk or doubled to two cents an ounce. (The Rudd Center has a nifty revenue calculator online that lets you play with the numbers yourself.)

A 20 percent increase in the price of sugary drinks nationally could result in about a 20 percent decrease in consumption, which in the next decade could prevent 1.5 million Americans from becoming obese and 400,000 cases of diabetes, saving about $30 billion.

It's fun—inspiring, even—to think about implementing a program like this. First off, though the reduced costs of healthy foods obviously benefit the poor most, lower prices across the board keep things simpler and all of us, especially children whose habits are just developing, could use help in eating differently. The program would also bring much needed encouragement to farmers, including subsidies, if necessary, to grow staples instead of commodity crops.

Other ideas: We could convert refrigerated soda machines to vending machines that dispense grapes and carrots, as has already been done in Japan and Iowa. We could provide recipes, cooking lessons, even cookware for those who can't afford it. Television public-service announcements could promote healthier eating. (Currently, 86 percent of food ads now seen by children are for foods high in sugar, fat or sodium.)

Money could be returned to communities for local spending on gyms, pools, jogging and bike trails; and for other activities at food distribution centers; for Meals on Wheels in those towns with a large elderly population, or for Head Start for those with more children; for supermarkets and farmers' markets where needed. And more.

By profiting as a society from the foods that are making us sick and using those funds to make us healthy, the United States would gain the same kind of prestige that we did by attacking smoking. We could institute a national, comprehensive program that would make us a world leader in preventing chronic or "lifestyle" diseases, which for the first time in history kill more people than communicable ones. By doing so, we'd not only repair some of the damage we have caused by first inventing and then exporting the Standard American Diet, we'd also set a new standard for the rest of the world to follow.

■ WHAT?

1. Bittman has written a policy argument: He identifies a problem and then makes a case for a specific course of action to address that problem. What is the problem that Bittman identifies? What kinds of evidence does he present to help his readers see that there really is a problem that needs to be addressed? What is the course of action that he proposes? How does he try to persuade his readers to buy into his argument?

2. After you have compiled your food diary entries (as described at the start of this essay), examine the list and determine how much of what you ate might be subject to the kinds of "bad food" taxes that Bittman describes. Do you think higher prices would discourage your consumption of unhealthy foods? Would lower prices and increased availability cause you to eat healthier foods? Explain your responses.

■ WHAT ELSE? WHAT'S NEXT?

3. In making his argument, Bittman mentions a handful of cities, states, and nations that are considering or are already imposing taxes on certain foods as a way to discourage poor eating habits and to reduce obesity and its companion health problems. Choose one of these locations (or find another place that taxes "bad food") and research how the issue is playing out. As you conduct your research, consider the following questions:

■ Who initiated the tax in question? What foods are specifically targeted?

■ Where does the issue stand now? (Is there a tax in place? Or has one simply been proposed?)

■ Who has lined up to support the tax? What reasons do they give for their support? Who, on the other hand, opposes the tax? Why?

■ If the tax is in place, how is it being enforced? (If the tax is still under consideration, how do supporters say it will be enforced?)

■ How do citizens of the locale feel about the tax? How about restaurant owners and others in food-related businesses?

■ If the tax is in place, what have been the effects?

Use the information you find through your research to prepare a brief report about the location you have selected and where the food-tax issue stands there. Make sure you document any sources that you use.

■ WHO CARES?

4. What—if anything—does Bittman do in his essay to specifically address those who might object to his proposal? Do you think he does enough to try to persuade people who don't already agree with him? Explain your response.

Joel Salatin is a third-generation alternative farmer at Polyface Farm in Virginia's Shenandoah Valley. He and his farm have been featured in several national publications, in Michael Pollan's book The Omnivore's Dilemma, *and in the documentary film* Food, Inc. *Salatin wrote this essay for* Food, Inc.: How Industrial Food Is Making Us Sicker, Fatter, and Poorer—and What You Can Do about It, *the companion book to that film.*

BEFORE YOU READ——————————————————
Visit the website for Food, Inc. *(http://www.takepart.com/foodinc) and watch the trailer for the movie (click on the tab labeled "The Film"). What does the trailer—and Joel Salatin's inclusion in it (he's the farmer in the white hat near the end)—tell you about Salatin's food politics?*

DECLARE YOUR INDEPENDENCE   Joel Salatin

Perhaps the most empowering concept in any paradigm-challenging movement is simply opting out. The opt-out strategy can humble the mightiest forces because it declares to one and all, "You do not control me."

The time has come for people who are ready to challenge the paradigm of factory-produced food and to return to a more natural, wholesome, and sustainable way of eating (and living) to make that declaration to the powers that be, in business and government, that established the existing system and continue to prop it up. It's time to opt out and simply start eating better—right here, right now.

Impractical? Idealistic? Utopian? Not really. As I'll explain, it's actually the most realistic and effective approach to transforming a system that is slowly but surely killing us.

What Happened to Food?

First, why am I taking a position that many well-intentioned people might consider alarmist or extreme? Let me explain.

At the risk of stating the obvious, the unprecedented variety of bar-coded packages in today's supermarket really does not mean that out generation enjoys better food options than our predecessors. These packages, by and large, having passed through the food inspection fraternity, the industrial food fraternity, and the lethargic cheap-food-purchasing consumer fraternity, represent an incredibly narrow choice. If you took away everything with an ingredient foreign to our three trillion intestinal microflora, the shelves would be bare indeed. (I'm talking here about the incredible variety of microorganisms that live in our digestive tracts and perform an array of useful functions, including training our immune systems and producing vitamins like biotin and vitamin K.) In fact, if you just eliminated every product that would have been unavailable in 1900, almost everything would be gone, including staples that had been chemically fertilized, sprayed with pesticides, or ripened with gas.

Rather than representing newfound abundance, these packages wending their way to store shelves after spending a month in the belly of Chinese merchant marines are actually the meager offerings of a tyrannical food system. Strong words? Try buying real milk—as in raw. See if you can find meat processed in the clean open air under sterilizing sunshine. Look for pot pies made with local produce and meat. How about good old unpasteurized apple cider? Fresh cheese? Unpasteurized almonds? All these staples that our great-grandparents relished and grew healthy on have been banished from today's supermarket.

They've been replaced by an array of pseudo-foods that did not exist a mere century ago. The food additives, preservatives, colorings, emulsifiers, corn syrups, and unpronounceable ingredients listed on the colorful packages bespeak a centralized control mindset that actually reduces the options available to fill Americans' dinner plates. Whether by intentional design or benign ignorance, the result has been the same—the criminalization and/or demonization of heritage foods.

The mindset behind this radical transformation of American eating habits expresses itself in at least a couple of ways.

One is the completely absurd argument that without industrial food, the world would starve. "How can you feed the world?" is the most common question people ask me when they tour Polyface Farm. Actually, when you consider the fact that millions of people, including many vast cities, were fed and sustained using traditional farming methods until just a few decades ago, the answer is obvious. America has traded seventy-five million buffalo, which required no tillage, petroleum, or chemicals, for a mere forty-two million head of cattle. Even with all the current chemical inputs, our production is a shadow of what it was 500 years ago. Clearly, if we returned to herbivorous principles five centuries old, we could double our meat supply. The potential for similar increases exists for other food items.

The second argument is about food safety. "How can we be sure that food produced on local farms without centralized inspection and processing is really safe to eat?" Here, too, the facts are opposite to what many people assume. The notion that indigenous food is unsafe simply has no scientific backing. Milk-borne pathogens, for example, became a significant health problem only during a narrow time period between 1900 and 1930, before refrigeration but after unprecedented urban expansion. Breweries needed to be located near metropolitan centers, and adjacent dairies fed herbivore-unfriendly brewery waste to cows. The combination created real problems that do not exist in grass-based dairies practicing good sanitation under refrigeration conditions.

Lest you think the pressure to maintain the industrialized food system is all really about food safety, consider that all the natural-food items I listed above can be given away, and the donors are considered pillars of community benevolence. But as soon as money changes hands, all these wonderful choices become "hazardous substances," guaranteed to send our neighbors to the hospital with food poisoning. Maybe it's not human health but corporate profits that are really being protected.

Furthermore, realize that many of the same power brokers (politicians and the like) encourage citizens to go out into the woods on a 70-degree fall day; gun-shoot a deer with possible variant Creutzfeld-Jacob's disease (like mad cow for deer); drag the carcass a mile through squirrel dung, sticks, and rocks; then drive parade-like through town in the blazing afternoon sun with the carcass prominently displayed on the hood of the Blazer. The hunter takes the carcass home, strings it up in the backyard tree under roosting birds for a week, then skins it out and feeds the meat to his children. This is all considered noble and wonderful, even patriotic. Safety? It's not an issue.

The question is, who decides what food is safe? In our society, the decisions are made by the same type of people who decided in the Dred Scott ruling that slaves were not human beings. Just because well-educated, credentialed experts say something does not make it true. History abounds with expert opinion that turned out to be dead wrong. Ultimately, food safety is a personal matter of choice, of conscience. In fact, if high-fructose corn syrup is hazardous to health—and certainly we could argue that it is—then half of the government-sanctioned food in supermarkets is unsafe. Mainline soft drinks would carry a warning label. Clearly, safety is a subjective matter.

◼ RECLAIMING FOOD FREEDOM

Once we realize that safety is a matter of personal choice, individual freedom suddenly— and appropriately—takes center stage. What could be a more basic freedom than the freedom to choose what to feed my three-trillion-member internal community?

In America I have the freedom to own guns, speak, and assemble. But what good are those freedoms if I can't choose to eat what my body wants in order to have the energy to shoot, preach, and worship? The only reason the framers of the American Constitution and Bill of Rights did not guarantee freedom of food choice was that they couldn't envision a day when neighbor-to-neighbor commerce would be criminalized…when the bureaucratic-industrial food fraternity would subsidize corn syrup and create a nation of diabetes sufferers, but deny my neighbor a pound of sausage from my Thanksgiving hog killin'.

People tend to have short memories. We all assume that whatever is must be normal. Industrial food is not normal. Nothing about it is normal. In the continuum of human history, what western civilization has done to its food in the last century represents a mere blip. It is a grand experiment on an ever-widening global scale. We have not been here before. The three trillion members of our intestinal community have not been here before. If we ate like humans have eaten for as long as anyone has kept historical records, almost nothing in the supermarket would be on the table.

A reasonable person, looking at the lack of choice we now suffer, would ask for a Food Emancipation Proclamation. Food has been enslaved by so-called inspectors that deem the most local, indigenous, heritage-based, and traditional foods unsafe and make them illegal. It has been enslaved by a host-consuming agricultural parasite called "government farm subsidies." It has been enslaved by corporate-subsidized research that declared for four decades that feeding dead cows to cows was sound science—until mad cows came to dinner.

The same criminalization is occurring on the production side. The province of Quebec has virtually outlawed outdoor poultry. Ponds, which stabilize hydrologic cycles and have forever been considered natural assets, are now considered liabilities because they encourage wild birds, which could bring avian influenza. And with the specter of a National Animal Identification System being rammed down farmers' throats, small flocks and herds are being economized right out of existence.

On our Polyface Farm nestled in Virginia's Shenandoah Valley, we have consciously opted out of the industrial production and marketing paradigms. Meat chickens move every day in floorless, portable shelters across the pasture, enjoying bugs, forage, and local grain (grown free of genetically modified organisms). Tyson-style, inhumane, fecal factory chicken houses have no place here.

The magical land-healing process we use, with cattle using mob-stocking, herbivorous, solar conversion, lignified carbon sequestration fertilization, runs opposite the grain-based feedlot system practiced by mainline industrial cattle production. We move the cows every day from paddock to paddock, allowing the forage to regenerate completely through its growth curve, metabolizing solar energy into biomass.

Our pigs aerate anaerobic, fermented bedding in the hay feeding shed, where manure, carbon, and corn create a pig delight. We actually believe that honoring and respecting the "pigness" of the pig is the first step in an ethical, moral cultural code. By contrast, today's industrial food system views pigs as merely inanimate piles of protoplasmic molecular structure to be manipulated with whatever cleverness the egocentric human mind can conceive. A society that views its plants and animals from that manipulative, egocentric, mechanistic mindset will soon come to view its citizens in the same way. How we respect and honor the least of these is how we respect and honor the greatest of these.

The industrial pig growers are even trying to find the stress gene so it can be taken out of the pig's DNA. That way the pigs can be abused but won't be stressed about it. Then they can be crammed in even tighter quarters without cannibalizing and getting sick. In the name of all that's decent, what kind of ethics encourages such notions?

In just the last couple of decades, Americans have learned a new lexicon of squiggly Latin words: camphylobacter, lysteria, E. coli, salmonella, bovine spongiform encephalopathy, avian influenza. Whence these strange words? Nature is speaking a protest, screaming to our generation: "Enough!" The assault on biological dignity has pushed nature to the limit. Begging for mercy, its pleas go largely unheeded on Wall Street, where Conquistadors subjugating weaker species think they can forever tyrannize without an eventual payback. But the rapist will pay—eventually. You and I must bring a nurturing mentality to the table to balance the industrial food mindset.

Here at Polyface, eggmobiles follow the cows through the grazing cycle. These portable laying hen trailers allow the birds to scratch through the cows' dung and harvest newly uncovered crickets and grasshoppers, acting like a biological pasture sanitizer. This biomimicry stands in stark contrast to chickens housed beak by wattle in egg factories, never allowed to see sunshine or chase a grasshopper.

We have done all of this without money or encouragement from those who hold the reins of food power, government or private. We haven't asked for grants. We haven't asked for permission. In fact, to the shock and amazement of our urban friends, our farm is considered a Typhoid Mary by our industrial farm neighbors. Why? Because we don't medicate, vaccinate, genetically adulterate, irradiate, or exudate like they do.

They fear our methods because they've been conditioned by the powers that be to fear our methods.

The point of all this is that if anyone waits for credentialed industrial experts, whether government or nongovernment, to create ecologically, nutritionally, and emotionally friendly food, they might as well get ready for a long, long wait. For example, just imagine what a grass-finished herbivore paradigm would do to the financial and power structure of America. Today, roughly seventy percent of all grains go through herbivores, which aren't supposed to eat them and, in nature, never do. If the land devoted to that production were converted to perennial prairie polycultures under indigenous biomimicry management, it would topple the grain cartel and reduce petroleum usage, chemical usage, machinery manufacture, and bovine pharmaceuticals.

Think about it. That's a lot of economic inertia resisting change. Now do you see why the Farm Bill that controls government input into our agricultural system never changes by more than about two percent every few years? Even so-called conservation measures usually end up serving the power brokers when all is said and done.

◾ Opting Out

If things are going to change, it is up to you and me to make the change. But what is the most efficacious way to make the change? Is it through legislation? Is it by picketing the World Trade Organization talks? Is it by dumping cow manure on the parking lot at McDonald's? Is it by demanding regulatory restraint over the aesthetically and aromatically repulsive industrial food system?

At the risk of being labeled simplistic, I suggest that the most efficacious way to change things is simply to declare our independence from the figurative kings in the industrial system. To make the point clear, here are the hallmarks of the industrial food system:

- Centralized production

- Mono-speciation

- Genetic manipulation

- Centralized processing

- Confined animal feeding operations

- Things that end in "cide" (Latin for death)

- Ready-to-Eat food

- Long-distance transportation

- Externalized costs—economy, society, ecology

- Pharmaceuticals

- Opaqueness

- Unpronounceable ingredients

- Supermarkets

- Fancy packaging

- High fructose corn syrup

- High liability insurance

- "No Trespassing" signs

Reviewing this list shows the magnitude and far-reaching power of the industrial food system. I contend that it will not move. Entrenched paradigms never move…until outside forces move them. And those forces always come from the bottom up. The people who sit on the throne tend to like things the way they are. They have no reason to change until they are forced to do so.

The most powerful force you and I can exert on the system is to opt out. Just declare that we will not participate. Resistance movements from the antislavery movement to women's suffrage to sustainable agriculture always have and always will begin with opt-out resistance to the status quo. And seldom does an issue present itself with such a daily— in fact, thrice daily—opportunity to opt out.

Perhaps the best analogy in recent history is the home-school movement. In the late 1970s, as more families began opting out of institutional educational settings, credentialed educational experts warned us about the jails and mental asylums we'd have to build to handle the educationally and socially deprived children that home-schooling would produce. Many parents went to jail for violating school truancy laws. A quarter-century later, of course, the paranoid predictions are universally recognized as wrong. Not everyone opts for home-schooling, but the option must be available for those who want it. In the same way, an opt-out food movement will eventually show the Henny Penny food police just how wrong they are.

■ Learn to Cook Again

I think the opt-out strategy involves at least four basic ideas.

First, we must rediscover our kitchens. Never has a culture spent more to remodel and techno-glitz its kitchens, but at the same time been more lost as to where the kitchen is and what it's for. As a culture, we don't cook any more. Americans consume nearly a quarter of all their food in their cars, for crying out loud. Americans graze through the kitchen, popping precooked, heat-and-eat, bar-coded packages into the microwave for eating-on-the-run.

That treatment doesn't work with real food. Real heritage food needs to be sliced, peeled, sautéed, marinated, pureed, and a host of other things that require true culinary skills. Back in the early 1980s when our farm began selling pastured poultry, nobody even asked for boneless, skinless breast. To be perfectly sexist, every mom knew how to cut up a chicken. That was generic cultural mom information. Today, half of the moms don't know that a chicken even has bones.

I was delivering to one of our buying club drops a couple of months ago, and one of the ladies discreetly pulled me aside and asked: "How do you make a hamburger?" I thought I'd misunderstood, and asked her to repeat the question. I bent my ear down close to hear her sheepishly repeat the same question. I looked at her incredulously and asked: "Are you kidding?"

"My husband and I have been vegetarians. But now that we realize we can save the world by eating grass-based livestock, we're eating meat, and he wants a hamburger. But I don't know how to make it." This was an upper-middle-income, college-educated, bright, intelligent woman.

The indigenous knowledge base surrounding food is largely gone. When "scratch" cooking means actually opening a can, and when church and family reunion potlucks include buckets of Kentucky Fried Chicken, you know our culture has suffered a culinary information implosion. Big time. Indeed, according to marketing surveys roughly seventy percent of Americans have no idea what they are having for supper at 4:00 pm. That's scary.

Whatever happened to planning the week's menus? We still do that at our house. In the summer, our Polyface interns and apprentices enjoy creating a potluck for all of us Salatins every Saturday evening. All week they connive to plan the meal. It develops throughout the week, morphs into what is available locally and seasonally, and always culminates in a fellowship feast.

As a culture, if all we did was rediscover our kitchens and quit buying prepared foods, it would fundamentally change the industrial food system. The reason I'm leading this discussion with the option is because too often the foodies and greenies seem to put the onus for change on the backs of farmers. But this is a team effort, and since farmers do not even merit Census Bureau recognition, non-farmers must ante up to the responsibility for the change. And both moms and dads need to reclaim the basic food preparation knowledge that was once the natural inheritance of every human being.

■ Buy Local

After rediscovering your kitchen, the next opt-out strategy is to purchase as directly as possible from your local farmer. If the money pouring into industrial food dried up tomorrow, that system would cease to exist. Sounds easy, doesn't it? Actually, it is. It doesn't take any legislation, regulation, taxes, agencies, or programs. As the money flows to local producers, more producers will join them. The only reason the local food system is still minuscule is because few people patronize it.

Even organics have been largely co-opted by industrial systems. Go to a food co-op drop, and you'll find that more than half the dollars are being spent for organic corn chips, treats, and snacks. From far away.

Just for fun, close your eyes and imagine walking down the aisle of your nearby Wal-Mart or Whole Foods. Make a note of each item as you walk by and think about what could be grown within one hundred miles of that venue. I recommend this exercise when speaking at conferences all over the world, and it's astounding the effect it has on people. As humans, we tend to get mired in the sheer monstrosity of it all. But if we break it down into little bits, suddenly the job seems doable. Can milk be produced within one hundred miles of you? Eggs? Tomatoes? Why not?

Not everything can be grown locally, but the lion's share of what you eat certainly can. I was recently in the San Joaquin Valley looking at almonds—square miles of almonds. Some eighty-five percent of all the world's almonds are grown in that area. Why not grow a variety of things for the people of Los Angeles instead? My goodness, if you're going to irrigate anyway, why not grow things that will be eaten locally rather than things that will be shipped to some far corner of the world. Why indeed? Because most people aren't asking for local. Los Angeles is buying peas from China so almonds can be shipped to China.

Plenty of venues exist for close exchange to happen. Farmers' markets are a big and growing part of this movement. They provide a social atmosphere and a wide variety of fare. Too often, however, their politics and regulations stifle vendors. And they aren't open every day for the convenience of shoppers.

Community-supported agriculture (CSA) is a shared-risk investment that answers some of the tax and liability issues surrounding food commerce. Patrons invest in a portion of the farm's products and receive a share every week during the season. The drawback is the paperwork and lack of patron choice.

Food boutiques or niche retail facades are gradually filling a necessary role because most farmers' markets are not open daily. The price markup may be more, but the convenience is real. These allow farmers to drop off products quickly and go back to farming or other errands. Probably the biggest challenge with these venues is their overhead relative to scale.

Farmgate sales, especially near cities, are wonderful retail opportunities. Obviously, traveling to the farm has its drawbacks, but actually visiting the farm creates an accountability and transparency that are hard to achieve in any other venue. To acquire food on the farmer's own turf creates a connection, relationship, and memory that heighten the intimate dining experience. The biggest hurdle is zoning laws that often do not allow neighbors to collaboratively sell. (My book *Everything I Want to Do Is Illegal* details the local food hurdles in greater detail.)

Metropolitan buying clubs (MBCs) are developing rapidly as a new local marketing and distribution venue. Using the Internet as a farmer-to-patron real-time communication avenue, this scheme offers scheduled drops in urban areas. Patrons order via the Internet from an inventory supplied by one or more farms. Drop points in their neighborhoods offer easy access. Farmers do not have farmers' market politics or regulations to deal with, or sales commissions to pay. This transaction is highly efficient because it is nonspeculative— everything that goes on the delivery vehicle is preordered, and nothing comes back to the farm. Customizing each delivery's inventory for seasonal availability offers flexibility and an info-dense menu.

Many people ask, "Where do I find local food, or a farmer?" My answer: "They are all around. If you will put as much time into sourcing your local food as many people put into picketing and political posturing, you will discover a whole world that Wall Street doesn't know exists." I am a firm believer in the Chinese proverb: "When the student is ready, the teacher will appear." This nonindustrial food system lurks below the radar in every locality. If you seek, you will find.

Buy What's in Season

After discovering your kitchen and finding your farmer, the third opt-out procedure is to eat seasonally. This includes "laying by" for the off season. Eating seasonally does not mean denying yourself tomatoes in January if you live in New Hampshire. It means procuring the mountains of late-season tomatoes thrown away each year and canning, freezing, or dehydrating them for winter use.

In our basement, hundreds of quarts of canned summer produce line the pantry shelves. Green beans, yellow squash, applesauce, pickled beets, pickles, relish, and a host of other delicacies await off-season menus. I realize this takes time, but it's the way for all of us to share bioregional rhythms. To refuse to join this natural food ebb and flow is to deny connectedness. And this indifference to life around us creates a jaundiced view of our ecological nest and our responsibilities within it.

For the first time in human history, a person can move into a community, build a house out of outsourced material, heat it with outsourced energy, hook up to water from an unknown source, send waste out a pipe somewhere else, and eat food from an unknown source. In other words, in modern America we can live without any regard to the ecological life raft that undergirds us. Perhaps that is why many of us have become indifferent to nature's cry.

The most unnatural characteristic of the industrial food system is the notion that the same food items should be available everywhere at once at all times. To have empty grocery shelves during inventory downtime is unthinkable in the supermarket world. When we refuse to participate in the nonseasonal game, it strikes a heavy blow to the infrastructure, pipeline, distribution system, and ecological assault that upholds industrial food.

Plant a Garden

My final recommendation for declaring your food independence is to grow some of your own. I am constantly amazed at the creativity shown by urban-dwellers who physically embody their opt-out decision by growing something themselves. For some, it may be a community garden where neighbors work together to grow tomatoes, beans, and squash. For others, it may be three or four laying hens in an apartment. Shocking? Why? As a culture, we think nothing of having exotic tropical birds in city apartments. Why not use that space for something productive, like egg layers? Feed them kitchen scraps and gather fresh eggs every day.

Did someone mention something about ordinances? Forget them. Do it anyway. Defy. Don't comply. People who think nothing of driving around Washington, D.C., at eighty miles an hour in a fifty-five speed limit zone often go apoplectic at the thought of defying a zoning- or building-code ordinance. The secret reality is that the government is out of money and can't hire enough bureaucrats to check up on everybody anyway. So we all need to just begin opting out and it will be like five lanes of speeders on the beltway—who do you stop?

Have you ever wanted to have a cottage business producing that wonderful soup, pot pie, or baked item your grandmother used to make? Well, go ahead and make it, sell it to your neighbors and friends at church or garden club. Food safety laws? Forget them. People getting sick from food aren't getting it from their neighbors; they are getting it from USDA-approved, industrially produced, irradiated, amalgamated, adulterated, reconstituted, extruded, pseudo-food laced with preservatives, dyes, and high fructose corn syrup.

If you live in a condominium complex, approach the landlord about taking over a patch for a garden. Plant edible landscaping. If all the campuses in Silicon Valley would plant edible varieties instead of high maintenance ornamentals, their irrigation water would actually be put to ecological use instead of just feeding hedge clippers and lawn mower engines. Urban garden projects are taking over abandoned lots, and that is a good thing. We need to see more of that. Schools can produce their own food. Instead of hiring Chemlawn, how about running pastured poultry across the yard? Students can butcher the chickens and learn about the death-life-death-life cycle.

Clearly, so much can be done right here, right now, with what you and I have. The question is not, "What can I force someone else to do?" The question is "What am I doing today to opt out of the industrial food system?" For some, it may be having one family sit-down, locally-sourced meal a week. That's fine. We haven't gotten where we've gotten overnight, and we certainly won't extract ourselves from where we are overnight.

But we must stop feeling like victims and adopt a proactive stance. The power of many individual right actions will then compound to create a different culture. Our children deserve it. And the earthworms will love us—along with the rest of the planet.

■ WHAT?

1. If the industrial food system is going to change, Salatin writes, "it is up to you and me to make the change." And the best way to do this, he says, is to "declare your independence" from the status quo. How can we do this, according to Salatin? What specifically does he mean by "opting out"?

2. How does Salatin address the two major concerns he mentions about his proposal—that the world will not be able to feed itself without industrial food and that locally grown food is not always safe? Do you think his handling of these concerns is sufficient?

3. Write a formal letter to Salatin in which you raise any questions you have about his proposal—about its feasibility, for example, or its effectiveness.

■ WHAT ELSE?

4. Reread the section titled "Learn to Cook Again" in Joel Salatin's essay. With the principles Salatin states in mind, plan a meal you could cook using your own kitchen (or whatever available means you have to cook). Start by seeking out recipes and local ingredients (you might interview family members for the former and visit a local farmer's market for the latter). Then, plan your meal and prepare a menu and explanation of how the meal fits Salatin's ideas about leaving the industrial food system behind.

■ WHO CARES?

5. How would you characterize the tone of Salatin's essay? Point to passages in the text that Salatin uses to establish this tone. Do you find the tone compelling? What effect do you think it has on readers? Explain your response.

© Peter Menzel / menzelphoto.com

IMAGE 5.3, like those on pages 279 and 296, is from the book *Hungry Planet: What the World Eats* by Peter Menzel and Faith D'Aluisio. Here, the Ahmed family of Cairo, Egypt, poses with a week's supply of food, which cost them 387.85 Egyptian Pounds, or $68.53. If you look closely, you can see some packaged and apparently processed foods mixed in with the fresh produce. Several of the readings in this chapter mention the worldwide reach of America's industrial food system, but none fully explores the issue. Using library and internet resources, research the following question: How does the U.S. industrial food system—including factory farms—affect the availability, quality, and cost of food in other parts of the world? Use your research to compile an annotated bibliography of at least six informative and reliable sources that you can use in a later writing project.

Credits

Introduction

Obama, Barack. "National Information Literacy Awareness Month Proclamation." The White House, Office of the Press Secretary, Oct. 1, 2009. Web.

Gleick, James. "Drowning, Surfing and Surviving." New Scientist 210.2806 (April 2, 2011): 30-31. Print.

Chapter One

Plato. "The Allegory of the Cave." The Dialogues of Plato. Trans. Benjamin Jowett. New York: Random House. 773-780. Print. (Copyright © 2001 Random House.)

Dillard, Annie. "The Wreck of Time: Taking Our Century's Measure." Harper's Magazine 296.1772 (Jan. 1998): 51-56. Print.

Winterson, Jeanette. "Imagination and Reality." Art Objects: Essays on Ecstasy and Effrontery. Copyright © 1997.

Appiah, Kwame Anthony. "What Will Future Generations Condemn Us For?" The Washington Post 26 Sept. 2010: B01. Print.

Warner, Joel. "One Professor's Attempt to Explain Every Joke Ever." Wired 19.5 (May 2011). Print.

Oswald, Patton. "Wake Up Geek Culture. It's Time to Die." Wired 19.1 (Jan. 2011). Print.

Slouka, Mark. "Dehumanized: When Math and Science Rule the School." Harper's Magazine (Sept. 2009): 32-40. Print.

Leonhardt, David. "Even for Cashiers, College Pays Off." The New York Times 26 June 2011. Print.

Chapter Two

Wiesel, Elie, and Richard D. Heffner. "Am I My Brother's Keeper." *Conservations with Elie Wiesel.* New York: Random House, 2001. 3-15. Print. (Copyright © 2001 by Random House.)

Olds, Jacqueline and Richard S. Schwartz. "The Lonely American." Utne Reader (March-April 2009). Web.

Martin, Courtney. Do It Anyway: The New Generation of Activists. Massachusetts: Beacon Press, 2010. xi-xxiv. Print.

Lichtenberg, Judith. "Is Pure Altruism Possible?" *The New York Times* 9 Oct. 2010: n. pag. Web. 10 Oct. 2010.

Horton, Guy. "Why He's Putting Your Face All Over the World." GOOD 4 March 2011. Web.

Valenti, Jessica. "Slutwalks and the Future of Feminism." Washington Post 5 June 2011: B01. Print.

Lakshmi, Rama. "Indian Women Alter Slutwalk." Washington Post 24 July 2011: A16. Print.

Aafjes, Astrid. "Sports: A Powerful Strategy to Advance Women's Rights." The Fletcher Forum on World Affairs 35.2 (Summer 2011): 53-63. Print.

Wolff, Alexander. "Sports Saves the World." Sports Illustrated 26 Sept. 2011: 62-74. Print.

Potts, Monica. "How Much Are We Willing to Share?" The American Prospect 22.8 (Oct. 2011). Print.

Chapter Three

Blackmore, Susan. "The Third Replicator." The New York Times 22 Aug. 2010. Web.

Lanier, Jaron. "Trolls." You Are Not a Gadget: A Manifesto. New York: Alfred A. Knopf, 2010. 60-72. Print.

Neyfakh, Leon. "What If Privacy Is Keeping Us from Reaping the Real Benefits of the Infosphere?" Boston Globe 22 May 2011. Web.

Richtel, Matt. "Hooked on Technology, and Paying a Price." The New York Times 7 June 2010. Web.

Carr, Nicholas. "Is Google Making Us Stupid." The Atlantic Monthly 302.1 (July/August 2008): 56-63. Print. (Copyright © 2008 by Nicholas Carr. Reprinted with permission of the author.)

Cascio, Jamais. "Get Smarter." The Atlantic Monthly 304.1 (July/August 2009): 94-100. Print.

The Onion. "Nation Shudders at Large Block of Uninterrupted Text." The Onion 9 March 2010. Web.

Saval, Nikil. "Wall of Sound." N+1 (Spring 2011). Print.

Franzen, Jonathan. "Liking Is for Cowards. Go for What Hurts." The New York Times 29 May 2011: WK10. Print.

Dewey, Caitlin. "Even in Real Life, There Were Screens Between Us." The New York Times 1 May 2011: ST6. Print.

Chapter Four

Wilson, Edward O. "For the Love of Life." The Future of Life. New York: Knopf Doubleday, 2002. 129-140. Print.

Montenegro, Maywa, and Terry Glavin. "In Defense of Difference." Seed magazine 9 July 2010: n pag. Web. 20 Oct. 2010.

Muir, John. "The American Forests." The Atlantic Monthly 80 (Aug. 1897): n. pag. Web. 10 Oct. 2010. (The Atlantic Monthly Group, www.theatlantic.com.)

Ray, Janisse. Ecology of a Cracker Childhood. Minneapolis: Milkweed Editions, 1999. 5-12 and 123-127. Print.

Jensen, Derrick and McMillan, Stephanie. As the World Burns: 50 Simple Things You Can Do to Stay in Denial. New York: Seven Stories Press, 2007. 1-10. Print.

Todd, Anne Marie. "Prime-Time Subversion: The Environmental Rhetoric of The Simpsons" Enviropop: Studies in Environmental Rhetoric and Popular Culture. Ed. Mark Meister and Phyllis M. Japp. Westport, CT: Praeger Publishers, 2002. 63-80. Print.

Bullis, Kevin. "The Geoengineering Gambit." Technology Review 113.1 (Jan./Feb. 2010): 50-56. Print. (MIT Technology Review Press).

Brand, Stewart. "Reframing the Problems." The Clock of the Long Now: Time and Responsibility. New York: Basic Books, 2000. 131-136. Print.

Chapter Five

Townsend, Elisabeth. "The Cooking Ape: An Interview with Richard Wrangham." Gastronomica: The Journal of Food and Culture 5.1 (Winter 2005): 29-37. Web.

Berry, Wendell. "The Pleasures of Eating." What Are People For? New York: North Point Press, 2000. 145-152. Print.

Harris, Jessica B. "The Culinary Seasons of My Childhood." Gastropolis: Food and New York City. Ed. Annie Hauck-Lawson and Jonathan Deutsch. New York: Columbia UP, 2009. 108-115. Print. (Copyright © 2009 Columbia University Press. Reprinted with permission.)

Waters, Alice. "A Healthy Constitution." The Nation 289.8 (Sept. 21, 2009): 11-15. Print.

Paarlberg, Robert. "Attention Whole Food Shoppers." Foreign Policy May/June 2010.Web.

Scully, Matthew. "Fear Factories: The Case for Compassionate Conservatism—for Animals." The American Conservative May 23, 2005. Web. (Copyright © 2005 The American Conservative. Reprinted with permission.)

Dahm, Molly J., Aurelia V. Samonte, and Amy R. Shows. "Organic Foods: Do Eco-Friendly Attitudes Predict Eco-Friendly Behaviors?" Journal of American College Health 58.3 (2009): 195-202. Print.

Bittman, Mark. "Bad Food? Tax It." The New York Times 24 July 2011: SR1. Print.

Salatin, Joel. "Declare Your Independence." Food, Inc. Ed. Karl Weber. New York: Perseus Books, 2009. 183-196. Print. (Copyright © 2009 Perseus Books Group.)

NOTES

NOTES

NOTES